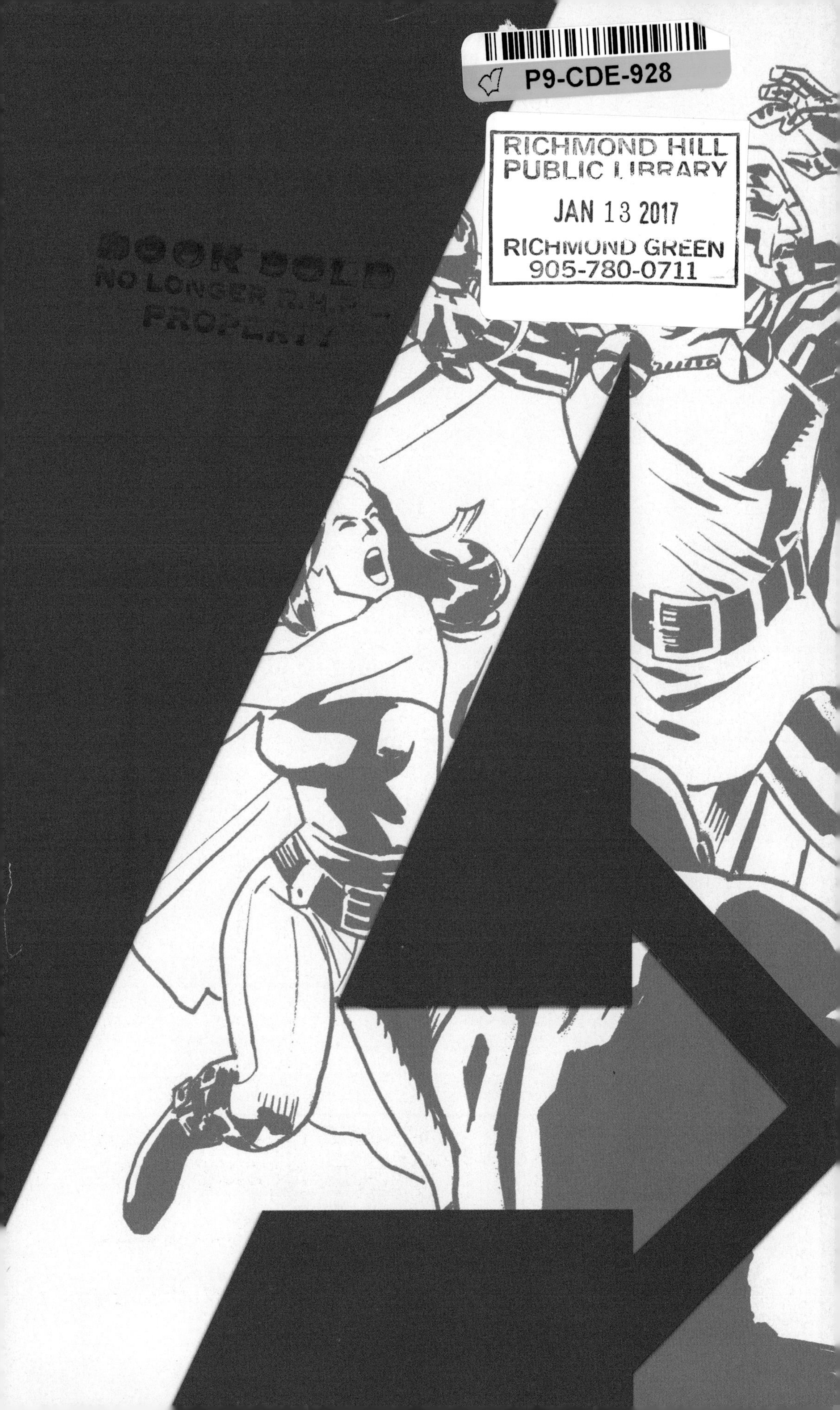

JESSICA JONES:

BRIAN MICHAEL BENDIS
WRITER

NEW AVENGERS (2004) #38

MICHAEL GAYDOS
ARTIST

JOSÉ VILLARRUBIA
COLOR ARTIST

RS & COMICRAFT's ALBERT DESCHESNE
LETTERER

MARKO DJURDJEVIĆ
COVER ART

MOLLY LAZER
ASSOCIATE EDITOR

TOM BREVOORT
EDITOR

NEW AVENGERS ANNUAL (2006) #3

MIKE MAYHEW
ARTIST

ANDY TROY
COLOR ARTIST

RS & COMICRAFT's ALBERT DESCHESNE
LETTERER

MIKE MAYHEW
COVER ART

LAUREN SANKOVITCH
ASSOCIATE EDITOR

TOM BREVOORT
EDITOR

NEW AVENGERS (2004) #47

BILLY TAN & MICHAEL GAYDOS
PENCILERS

MATT BANNING & MICHAEL GAYDOS
INKERS

JUSTIN PONSOR
COLORIST

RS & COMICRAFT's ALBERT DESCHESNE
LETTERER

ALEKSI BRICLOT
COVER ART

JEANINE SCHAEFER
ASSOCIATE EDITOR

TOM BREVOORT
EDITOR

NEW AVENGERS (2010) #8

DANIEL ACUÑA
ARTIST/COLORS

VC's JOE CARAMAGNA
LETTERER

MIKE DEODATO & RAIN BEREDO
COVER ART

LAUREN SANKOVITCH
ASSOCIATE EDITOR

TOM BREVOORT
EDITOR

"THE BEST VERSION OF MYSELF" FROM AMAZING SPIDER-MAN (1999) #601

JOE QUESADA
ARTIST

MORRY HOLLOWELL
COLOR ARTIST

VC's CHRIS ELIOPOULOS
LETTERER

J. SCOTT CAMPBELL
COVER ART

TOM BRENNAN
ASSOCIATE EDITOR

STEPHEN WACKER
EDITOR

NEW AVENGERS (2010) #31

MICHAEL GAYDOS
ARTIST

RAIN BEREDO
COLOR ARTIST

VC's JOE CARAMAGNA
LETTERER

BRANDON PETERSON
COVER ART

JAKE THOMAS
ASSOCIATE EDITOR

TOM BREVOORT WITH LAUREN SANKOVITCH
EDITORS

AVENGER

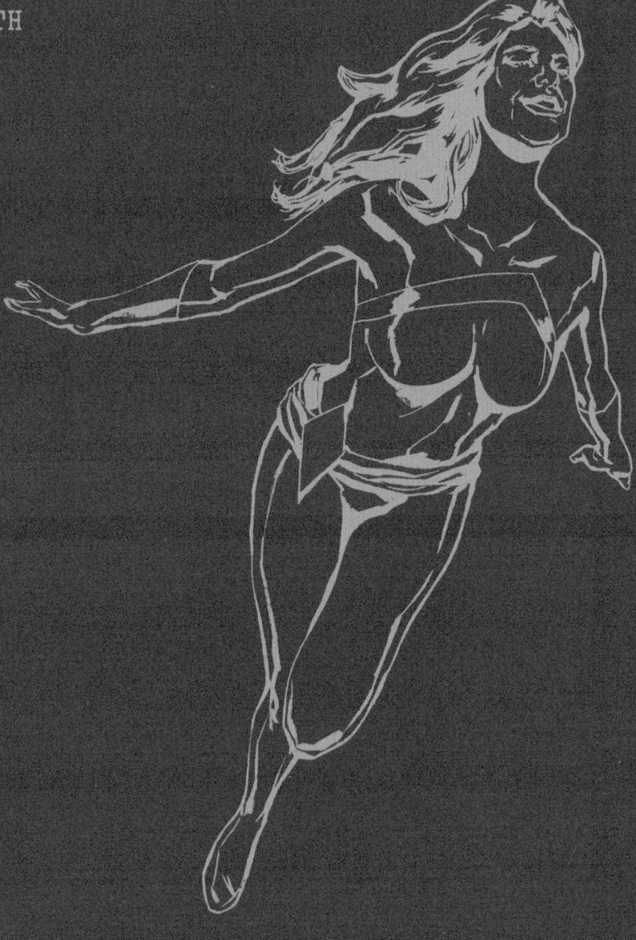

"ALIAS" FROM MARVEL 75TH ANNIVERSARY CELEBRATION #1

MICHAEL GAYDOS
ARTIST

MATT HOLLINGSWORTH
COLOR ARTIST

VC's CORY PETIT
LETTERER

PAOLO RIVERA
COVER ART

JAKE THOMAS
ASSOCIATE EDITOR

TOM BREVOORT WITH WIL MOSS
EDITORS

WHAT IF JESSICA JONES HAD JOINED THE AVENGERS? #1

MICHAEL GAYDOS
ARTIST

JOSE VILLARRUBIA
COLOR ARTIST

VC's CORY PETIT
LETTERER

STEVE McNIVEN, MARK MORALES & MORRY HOLLOWELL
COVER ART

JOHN BARBER
ASSOCIATE EDITOR

C.B. CEBULSKI
EDITOR

JESSICA JONES #1

MICHAEL GAYDOS
ARTIST

RICO RENZI
COLOR ARTIST

VC's JOE SABINO
LETTERER

DAVID MACK
COVER ART

MARK BASSO
PROJECT MANAGER/ASSISTANT EDITOR

DARREN SANCHEZ
EDITOR/PROJECT MANAGER

JENNIFER GRÜNWALD
COLLECTION EDITOR

SARAH BRUNSTAD
ASSOCIATE EDITOR

MARK D. BEAZLEY
EDITOR, SPECIAL PROJECTS

JEFF YOUNGQUIST
VP, PRODUCTION & SPECIAL PROJECTS

DAVID GABRIEL
SVP PRINT, SALES & MARKETING

ADAM DEL RE
BOOK DESIGNER

AXEL ALONSO
EDITOR IN CHIEF

JOE QUESADA
CHIEF CREATIVE OFFICER

DAN BUCKLEY
PUBLISHER

ALAN FINE
EXECUTIVE PRODUCER

JESSICA JONES CREATED BY
BRIAN MICHAEL BENDIS & MICHAEL GAYDOS

JESSICA JONES: AVENGER. Contains material originally published in magazine form as NEW AVENGERS (2004) #38 and #47, NEW AVENGERS ANNUAL #3, NEW AVENGERS (2010) #8 and #31, WHAT IF JESSICA JONES HAD JOINED THE AVENGERS?, CUSTOM NETFLIX JESSICA JONES NYCC COMIC, AMAZING SPIDER-MAN #601, and MARVEL 75TH ANNIVERSARY CELEBRATION #1. First printing 2016. ISBN# 978-1-302-90215-5. Published by MARVEL WORLDWIDE, INC., a subsidiary of MARVEL ENTERTAINMENT, LLC. OFFICE OF PUBLICATION: 135 West 50th Street, New York, NY 10020. **Printed in the U.S.A.** ALAN FINE, President, Marvel Entertainment; DAN BUCKLEY, President, TV, Publishing & Brand Management; JOE QUESADA, Chief Creative Officer; TOM BREVOORT, SVP of Publishing; DAVID BOGART, SVP of Business Affairs & Operations, Publishing & Partnership; C.B. CEBULSKI, VP of Brand Management & Development, Asia; DAVID GABRIEL, SVP of Sales & Marketing, Publishing; JEFF YOUNGQUIST, VP of Production & Special Projects; DAN CARR, Executive Director of Publishing Technology; ALEX MORALES, Director of Publishing Operations; SUSAN CRESPI, Production Manager; STAN LEE, Chairman Emeritus. For information regarding advertising in Marvel Comics or on Marvel.com, please contact Vit DeBellis, Integrated Sales Manager, at vdebellis@marvel.com. For Marvel subscription inquiries, please call 888-511-5480. **Manufactured between 7/8/2016 and 8/15/2016 by R.R. DONNELLEY, INC., SALEM, VA, USA.**

10 9 8 7 6 5 4 3 2 1

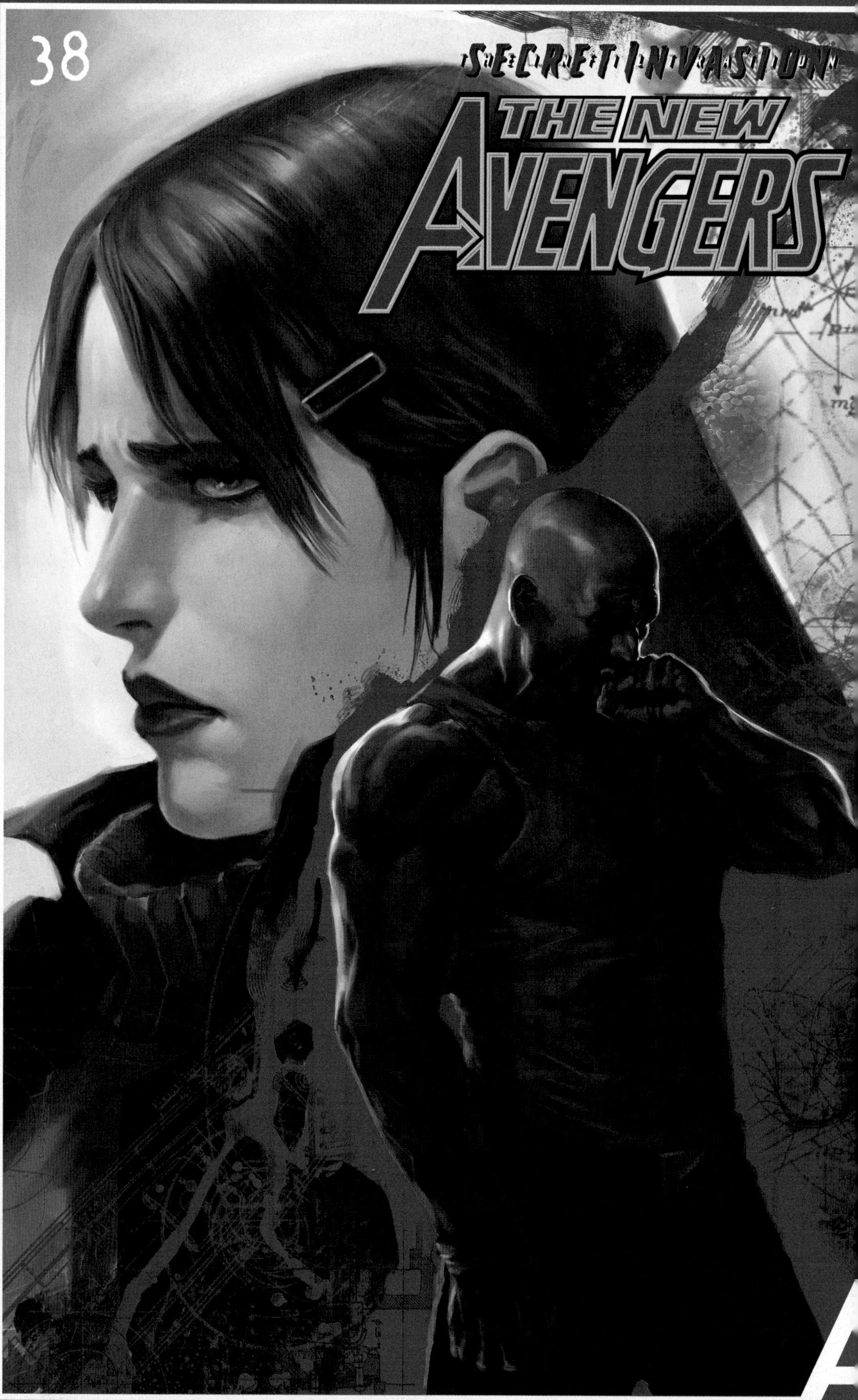
38
SECRET INVASION
THE NEW AVENGERS

THE BREAKUP
PREVIOUSLY...

The New Avengers know that the shape-shifting aliens known as the Skrulls have invaded the Earth. And, since they cannot tell who is really a Skrull, they cannot trust anyone to be who they seem to be, including each other. This has sent the Avengers into a tailspin of mistrust.

Recently, the Avengers stopped the Hood's newly-organized gang of super-villains, but the Hood broke his cohorts out of S.H.I.E.L.D. custody and took them right back to the Avengers. The attack at the Sanctum Sanctorum was fierce, and though the Avengers won the day, they did so at the cost of Doctor Strange, who lost both his mastery of the mystic arts and his home. Luke Cage's wife, Jessica Jones, fled the battle in mortal fear for their child's safety. Jessica has found asylum with the registered Mighty Avengers, even though she betrayed her husband's beliefs by doing so...

Writer	Artist	Color Art	Letterers
Brian Michael Bendis	Michael Gaydos	Jose Villarrubia	RS & Comicraft's Albert Deschesne

Cover Artist	Associate Editor	Editor	Editor in Chief	Publisher
Marko Djurdjevic	Molly Lazer	Tom Brevoort	Joe Quesada	Dan Buckley

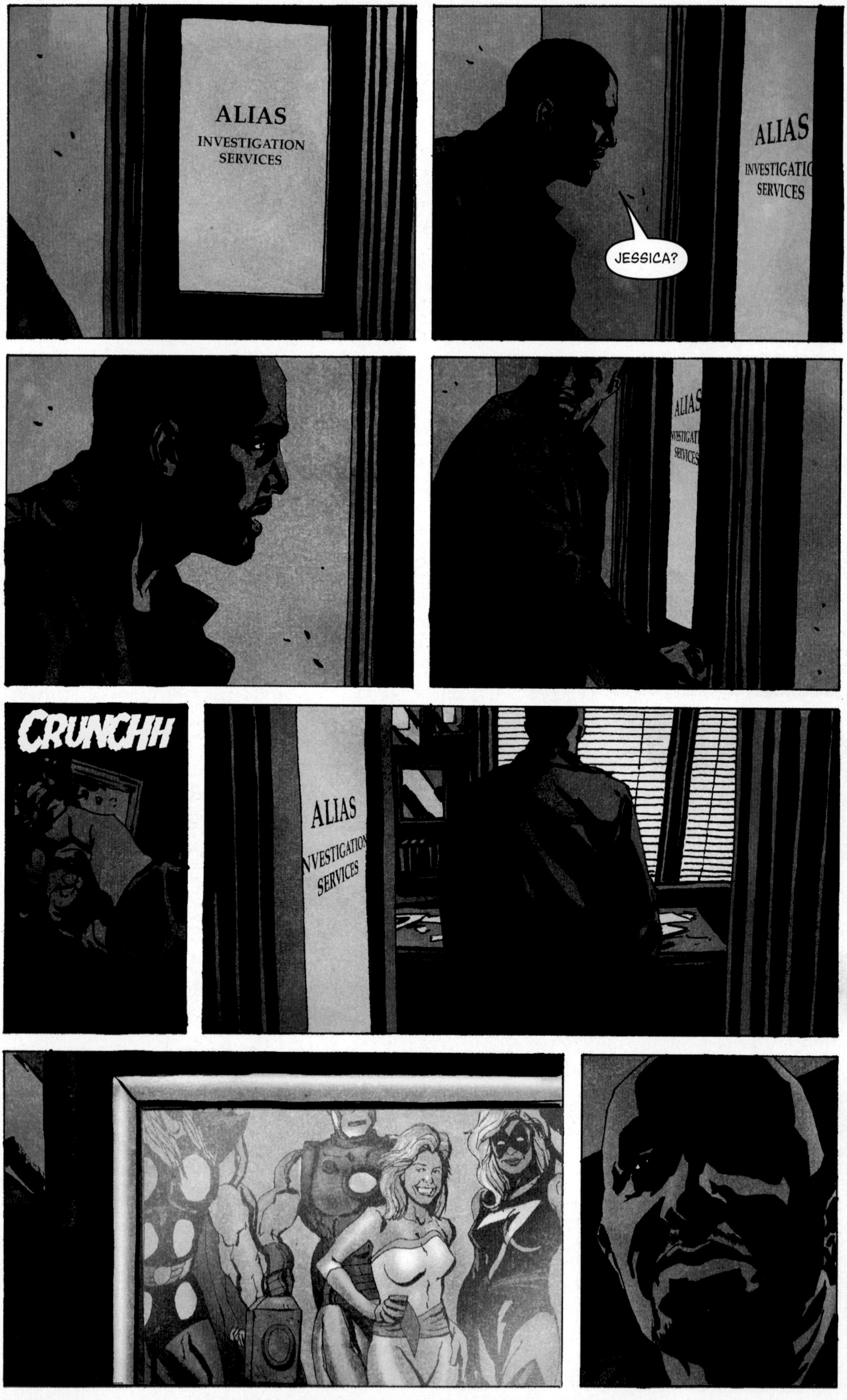
ALIAS
INVESTIGATION
SERVICES
JESSICA?
CRUNCHH

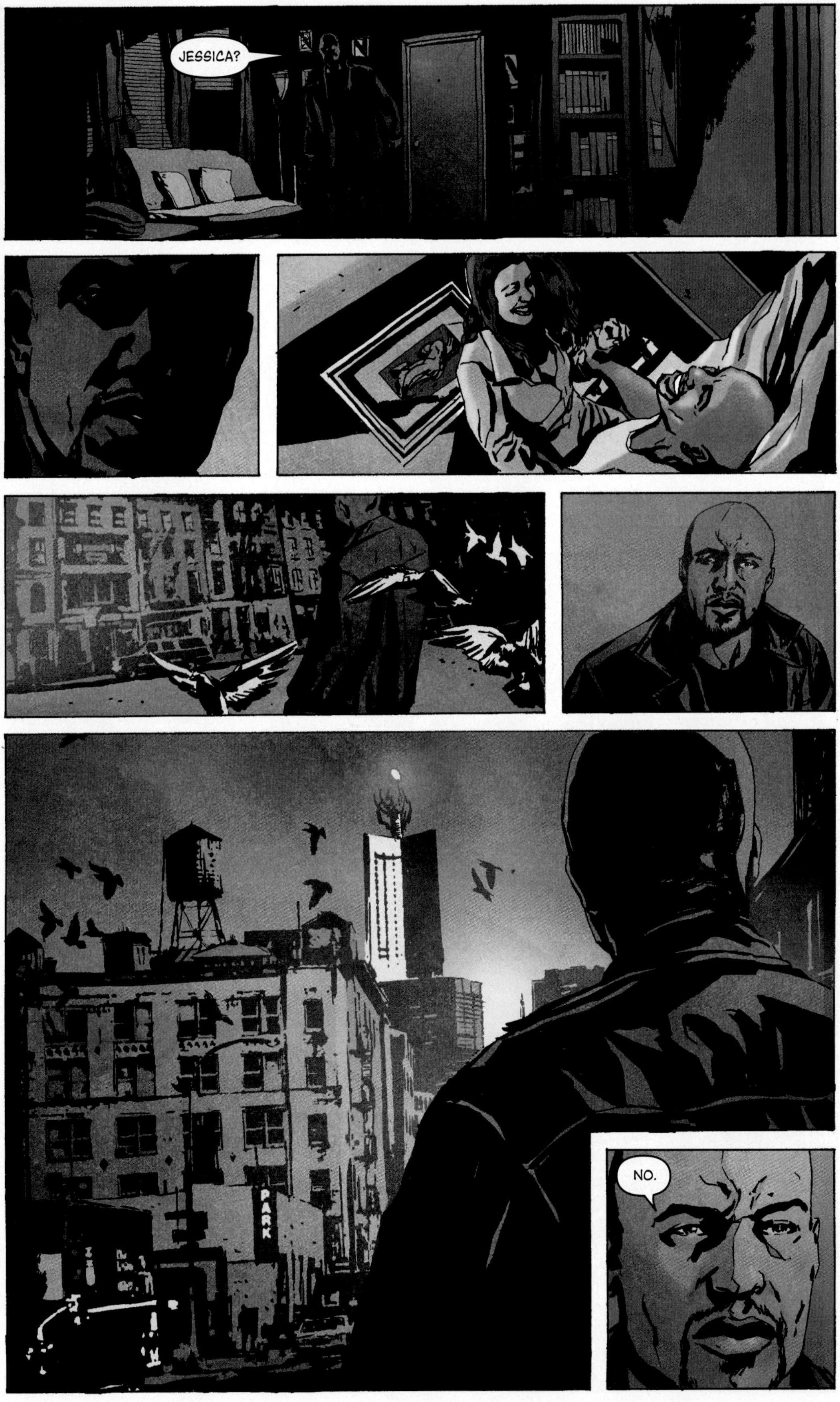
JESSICA?
NO.

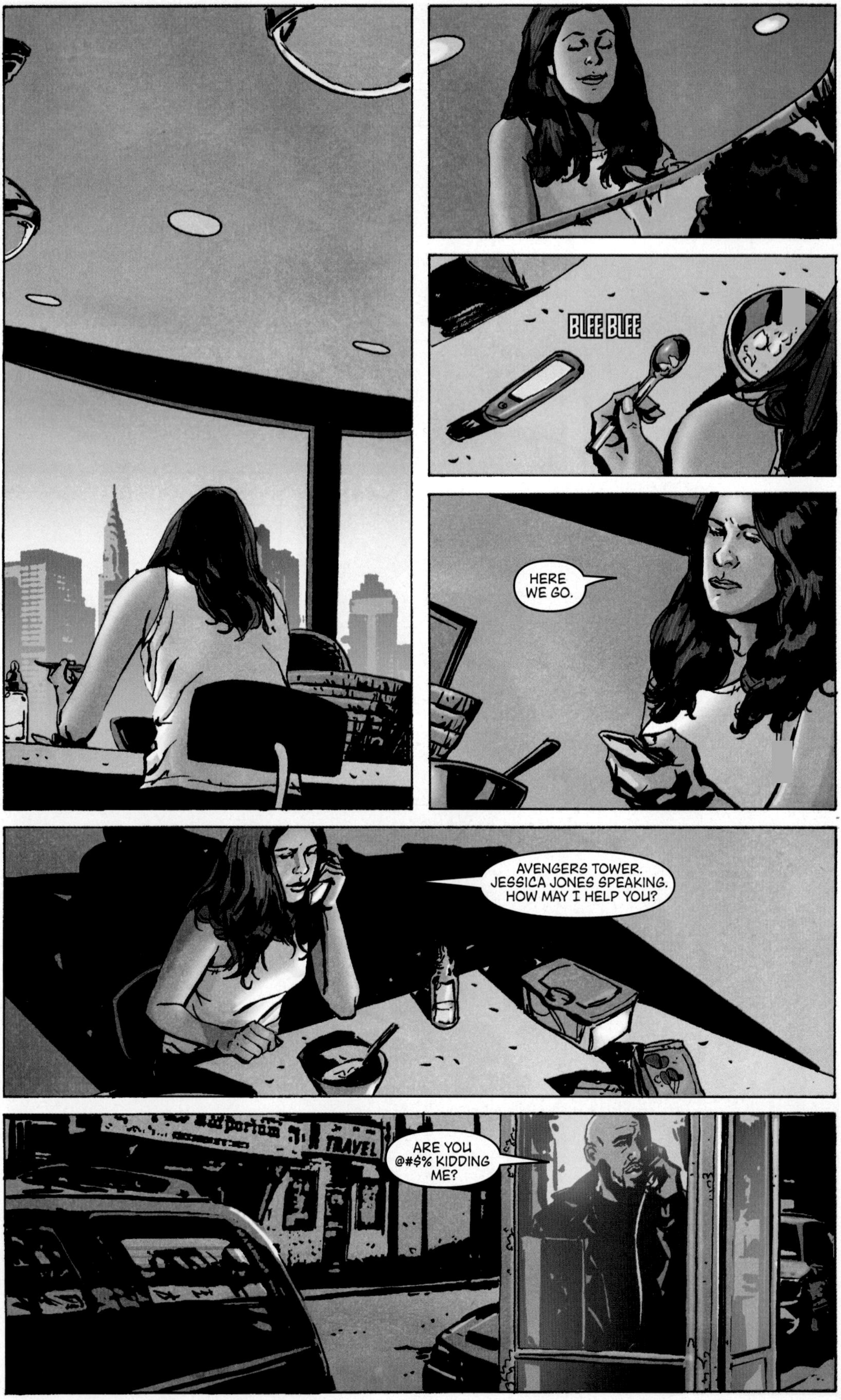
BLEE BLEE
HERE WE GO.
AVENGERS TOWER. JESSICA JONES SPEAKING. HOW MAY I HELP YOU?
TRAVEL
ARE YOU @#$% KIDDING ME?

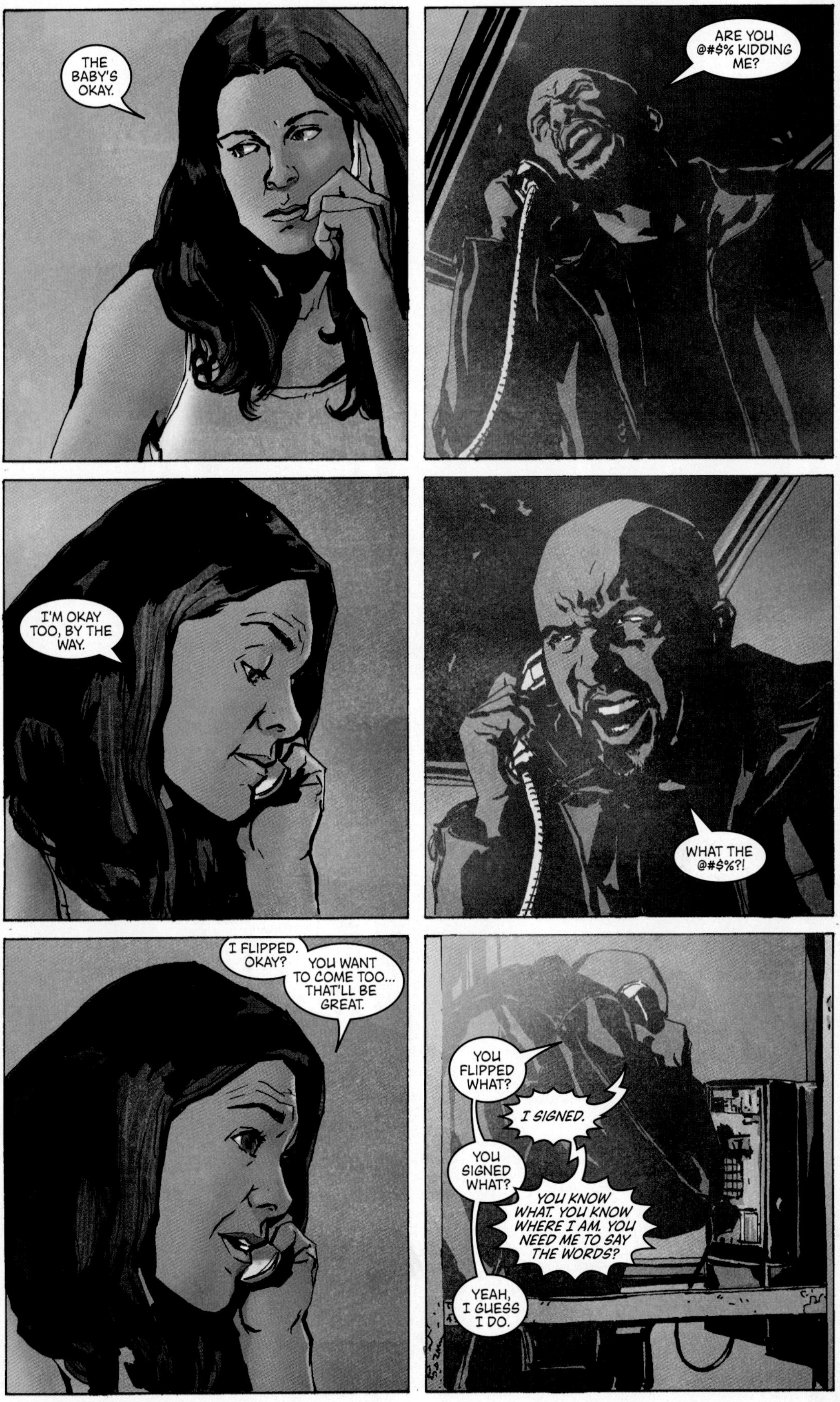
THE BABY'S OKAY.
ARE YOU @#$% KIDDING ME?
I'M OKAY TOO, BY THE WAY.
WHAT THE @#$%?!
I FLIPPED. OKAY?
YOU WANT TO COME TOO... THAT'LL BE GREAT.
YOU FLIPPED WHAT?
I SIGNED.
YOU SIGNED WHAT?
YOU KNOW WHAT. YOU KNOW WHERE I AM. YOU NEED ME TO SAY THE WORDS?
YEAH, I GUESS I DO.

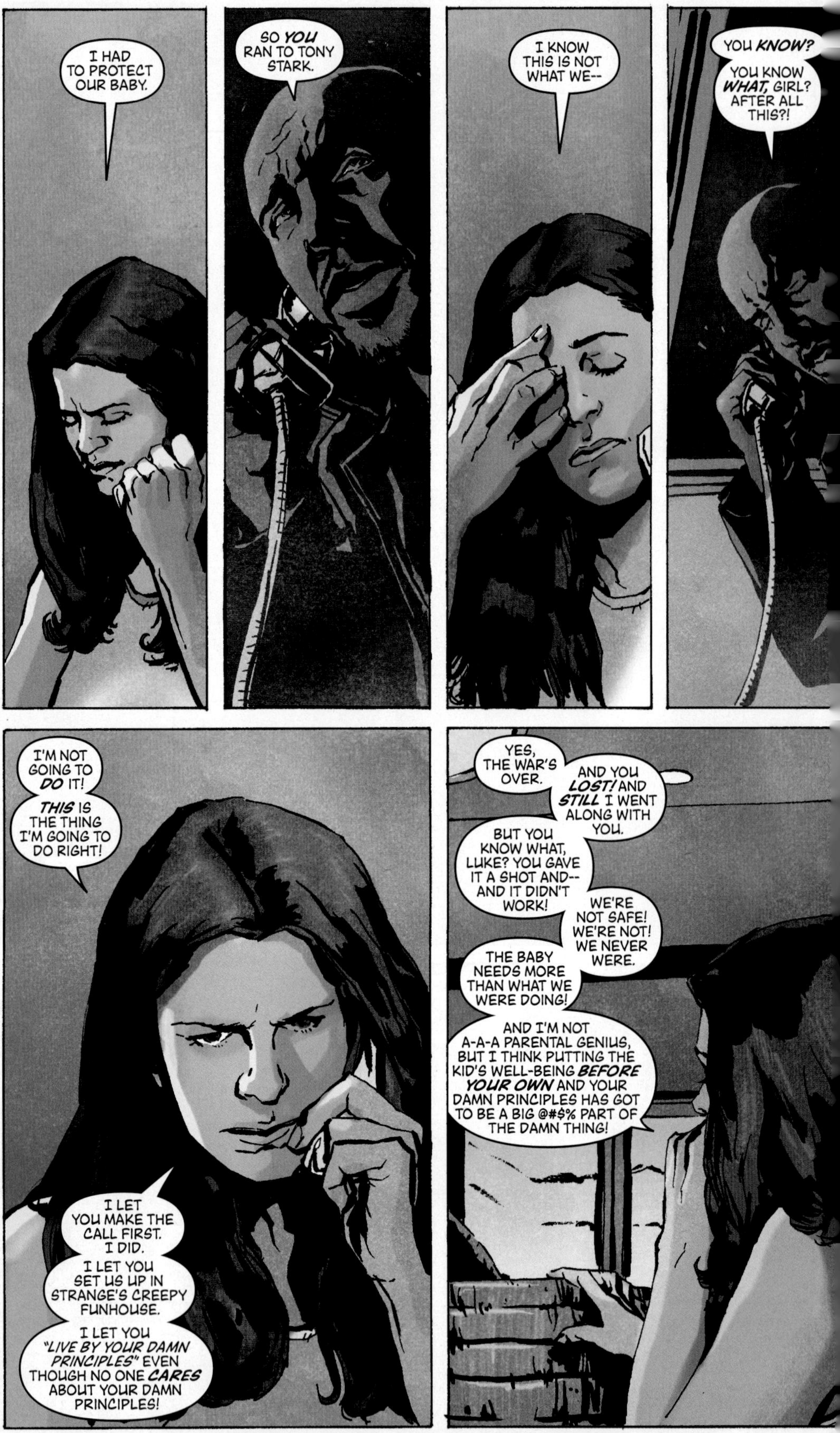

I HAD TO PROTECT OUR BABY.
SO *YOU* RAN TO TONY STARK.
I KNOW THIS IS NOT WHAT WE--
YOU *KNOW?*
YOU KNOW *WHAT,* GIRL? AFTER ALL THIS?!
I'M NOT GOING TO *DO* IT!
THIS IS THE THING I'M GOING TO DO RIGHT!
I LET YOU MAKE THE CALL FIRST. I DID.
I LET YOU SET US UP IN STRANGE'S CREEPY FUNHOUSE.
I LET YOU *"LIVE BY YOUR DAMN PRINCIPLES"* EVEN THOUGH NO ONE *CARES* ABOUT YOUR DAMN PRINCIPLES!
YES, THE WAR'S OVER.
AND YOU *LOST!* AND *STILL* I WENT ALONG WITH YOU.
BUT YOU KNOW WHAT, LUKE? YOU GAVE IT A SHOT AND-- AND IT DIDN'T WORK!
WE'RE NOT SAFE! WE'RE NOT! WE NEVER WERE.
THE BABY NEEDS MORE THAN WHAT WE WERE DOING!
AND I'M NOT A-A-A PARENTAL GENIUS, BUT I THINK PUTTING THE KID'S WELL-BEING *BEFORE YOUR OWN* AND YOUR DAMN PRINCIPLES HAS GOT TO BE A BIG @#$% PART OF THE DAMN THING!

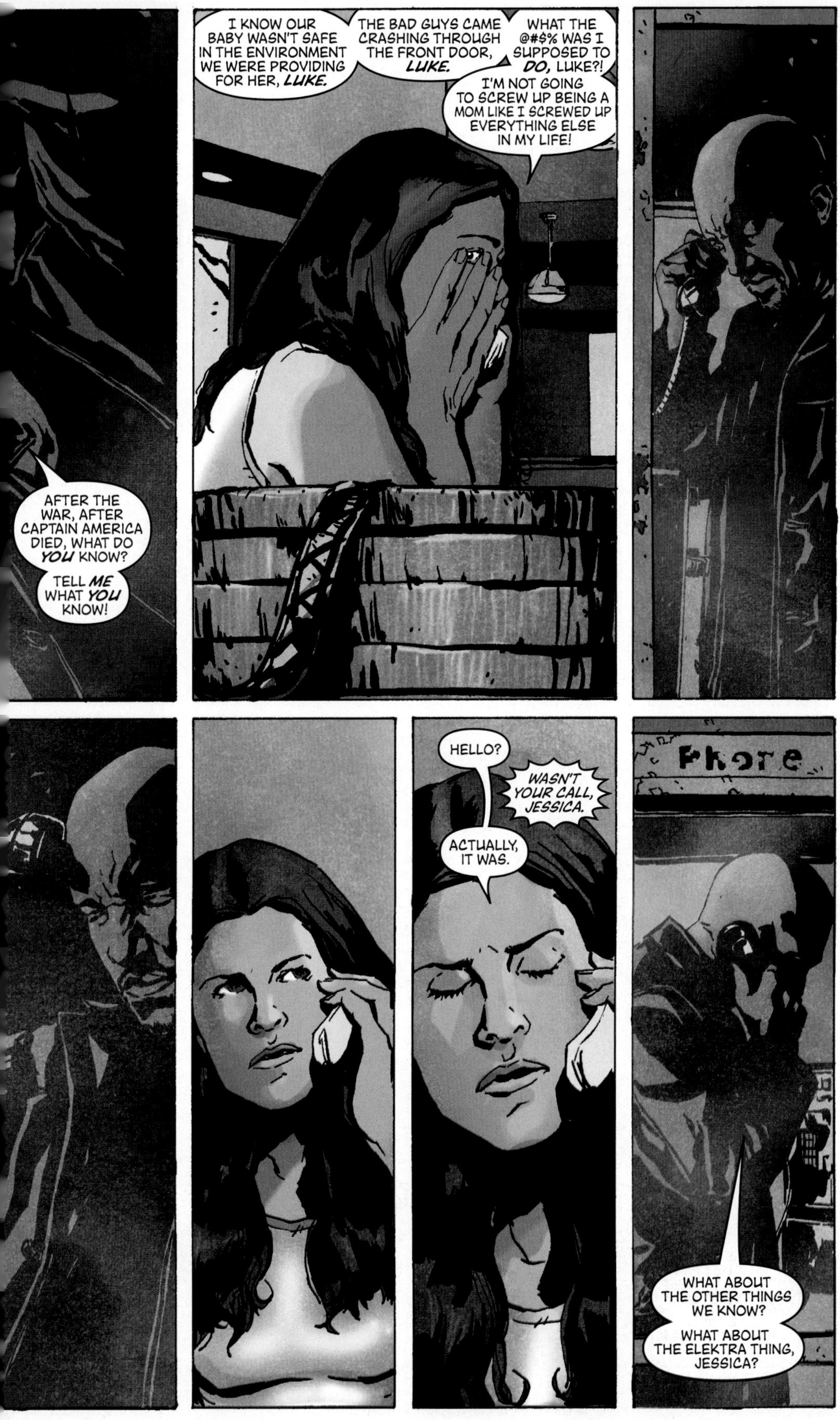

I KNOW OUR BABY WASN'T SAFE IN THE ENVIRONMENT WE WERE PROVIDING FOR HER, LUKE.
THE BAD GUYS CAME CRASHING THROUGH THE FRONT DOOR, LUKE.
WHAT THE @#$% WAS I SUPPOSED TO DO, LUKE?!
I'M NOT GOING TO SCREW UP BEING A MOM LIKE I SCREWED UP EVERYTHING ELSE IN MY LIFE!
AFTER THE WAR, AFTER CAPTAIN AMERICA DIED, WHAT DO YOU KNOW?
TELL ME WHAT YOU KNOW!
HELLO?
WASN'T YOUR CALL, JESSICA.
ACTUALLY, IT WAS.
Phone
WHAT ABOUT THE OTHER THINGS WE KNOW?
WHAT ABOUT THE ELEKTRA THING, JESSICA?

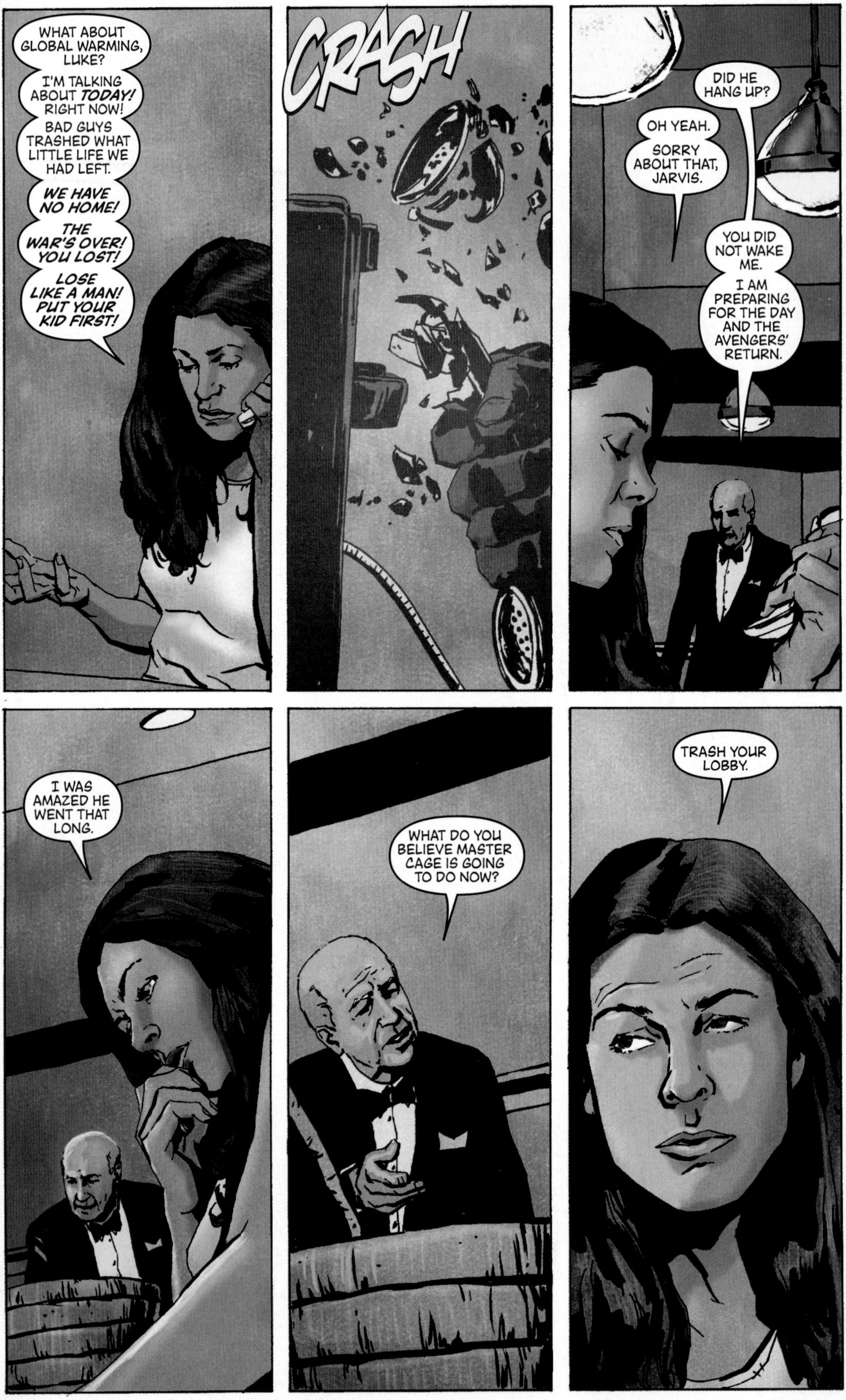
WHAT ABOUT GLOBAL WARMING, LUKE?
I'M TALKING ABOUT TODAY! RIGHT NOW!
BAD GUYS TRASHED WHAT LITTLE LIFE WE HAD LEFT.
WE HAVE NO HOME!
THE WAR'S OVER! YOU LOST!
LOSE LIKE A MAN! PUT YOUR KID FIRST!
CRASH
DID HE HANG UP?
OH YEAH.
SORRY ABOUT THAT, JARVIS.
YOU DID NOT WAKE ME.
I AM PREPARING FOR THE DAY AND THE AVENGERS' RETURN.
I WAS AMAZED HE WENT THAT LONG.
WHAT DO YOU BELIEVE MASTER CAGE IS GOING TO DO NOW?
TRASH YOUR LOBBY.

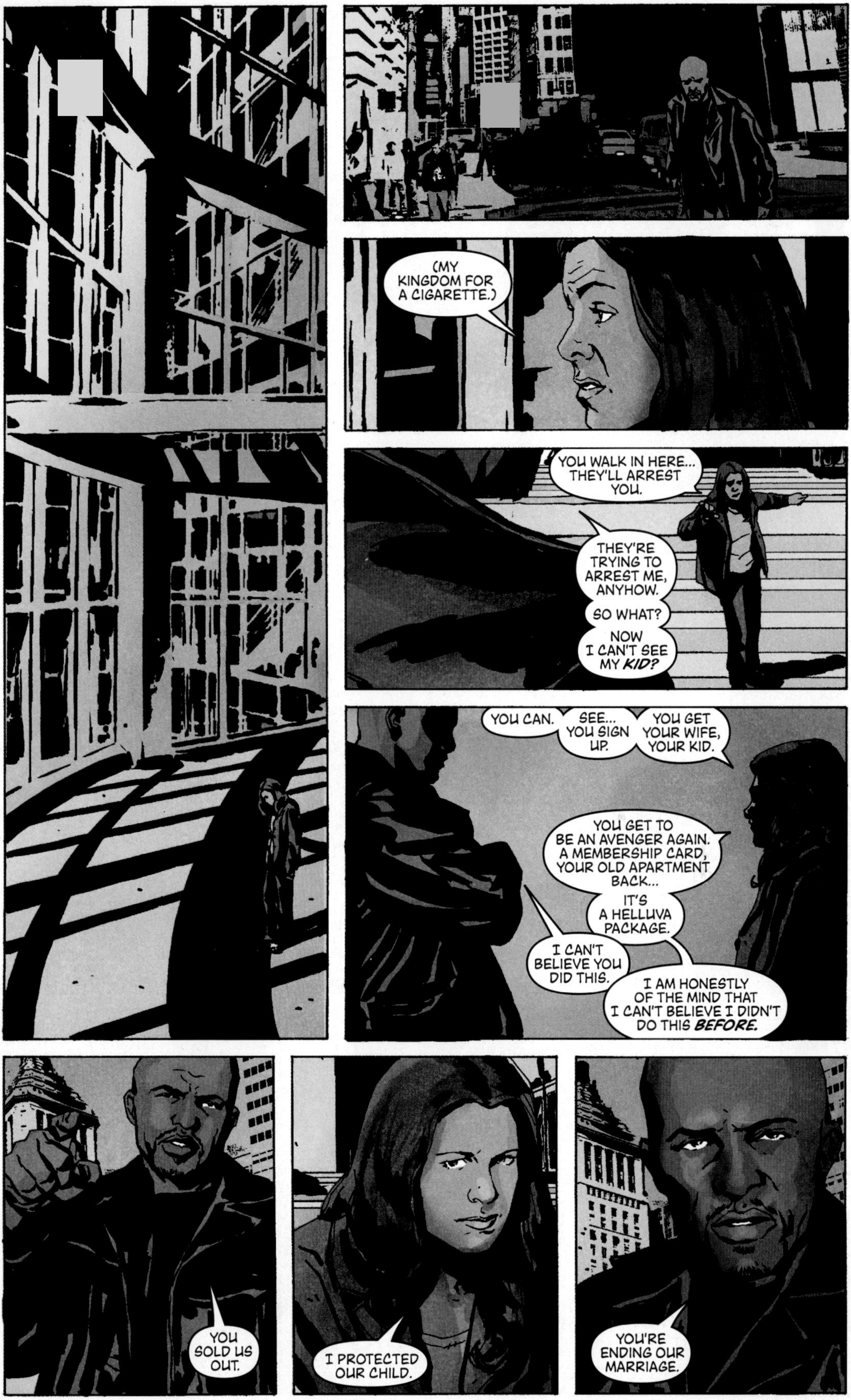
(MY KINGDOM FOR A CIGARETTE.)
YOU WALK IN HERE... THEY'LL ARREST YOU.
THEY'RE TRYING TO ARREST ME, ANYHOW.
SO WHAT?
NOW I CAN'T SEE MY *KID?*
YOU CAN.
SEE... YOU SIGN UP.
YOU GET YOUR WIFE, YOUR KID.
YOU GET TO BE AN AVENGER AGAIN. A MEMBERSHIP CARD, YOUR OLD APARTMENT BACK...
IT'S A HELLUVA PACKAGE.
I CAN'T BELIEVE YOU DID THIS.
I AM HONESTLY OF THE MIND THAT I CAN'T BELIEVE I DIDN'T DO THIS *BEFORE.*
YOU SOLD US OUT.
I PROTECTED OUR CHILD.
YOU'RE ENDING OUR MARRIAGE.

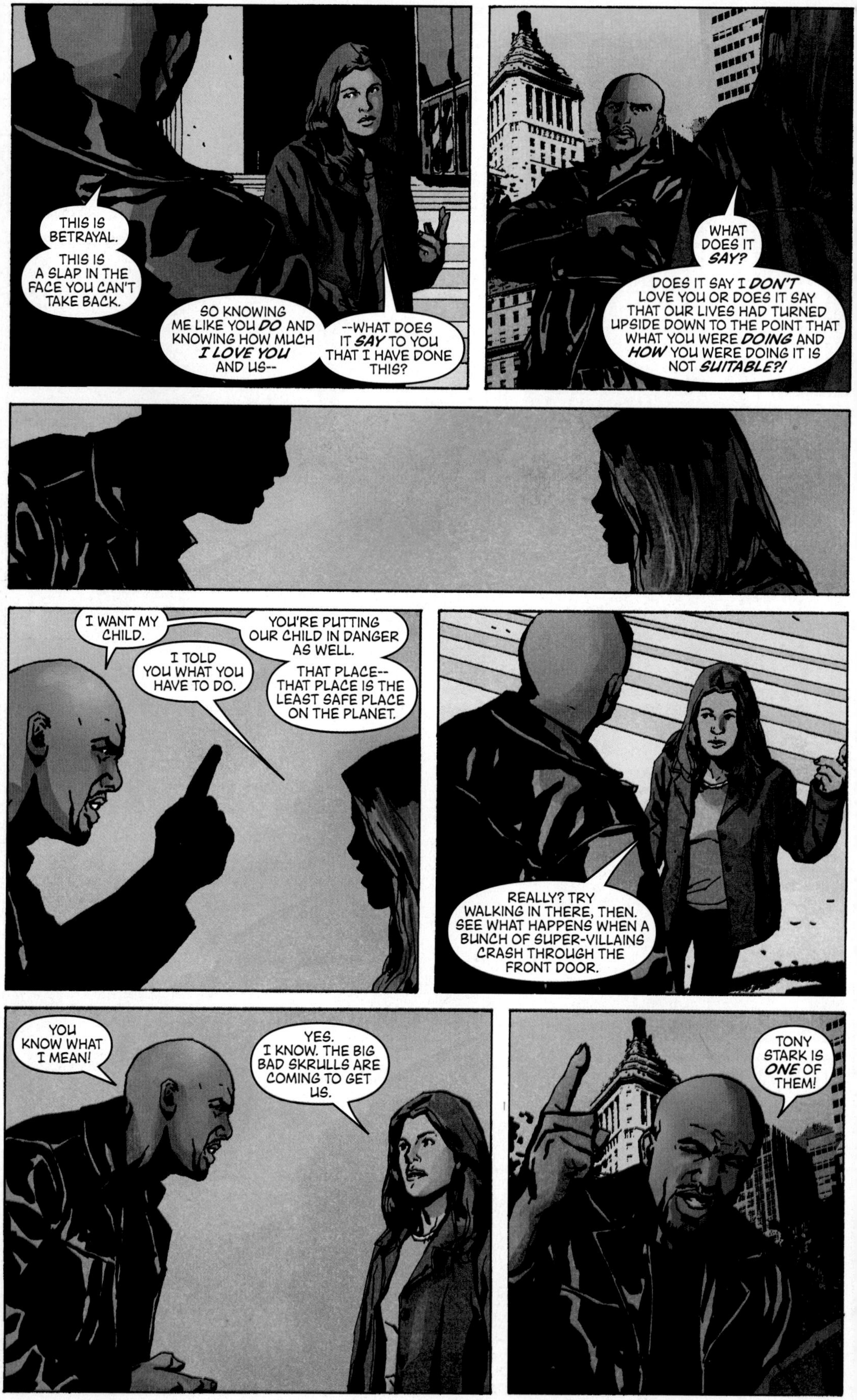

THIS IS BETRAYAL.
THIS IS A SLAP IN THE FACE YOU CAN'T TAKE BACK.
SO KNOWING ME LIKE YOU *DO* AND KNOWING HOW MUCH *I LOVE YOU* AND US--
--WHAT DOES IT *SAY* TO YOU THAT I HAVE DONE THIS?
WHAT DOES IT *SAY?*
DOES IT SAY I *DON'T* LOVE YOU OR DOES IT SAY THAT OUR LIVES HAD TURNED UPSIDE DOWN TO THE POINT THAT WHAT YOU WERE *DOING* AND *HOW* YOU WERE DOING IT IS NOT *SUITABLE?!*
I WANT MY CHILD.
YOU'RE PUTTING OUR CHILD IN DANGER AS WELL.
I TOLD YOU WHAT YOU HAVE TO DO.
THAT PLACE--THAT PLACE IS THE LEAST SAFE PLACE ON THE PLANET.
REALLY? TRY WALKING IN THERE, THEN. SEE WHAT HAPPENS WHEN A BUNCH OF SUPER-VILLAINS CRASH THROUGH THE FRONT DOOR.
YOU KNOW WHAT I MEAN!
YES. I KNOW. THE BIG BAD SKRULLS ARE COMING TO GET US.
TONY STARK IS *ONE* OF THEM!

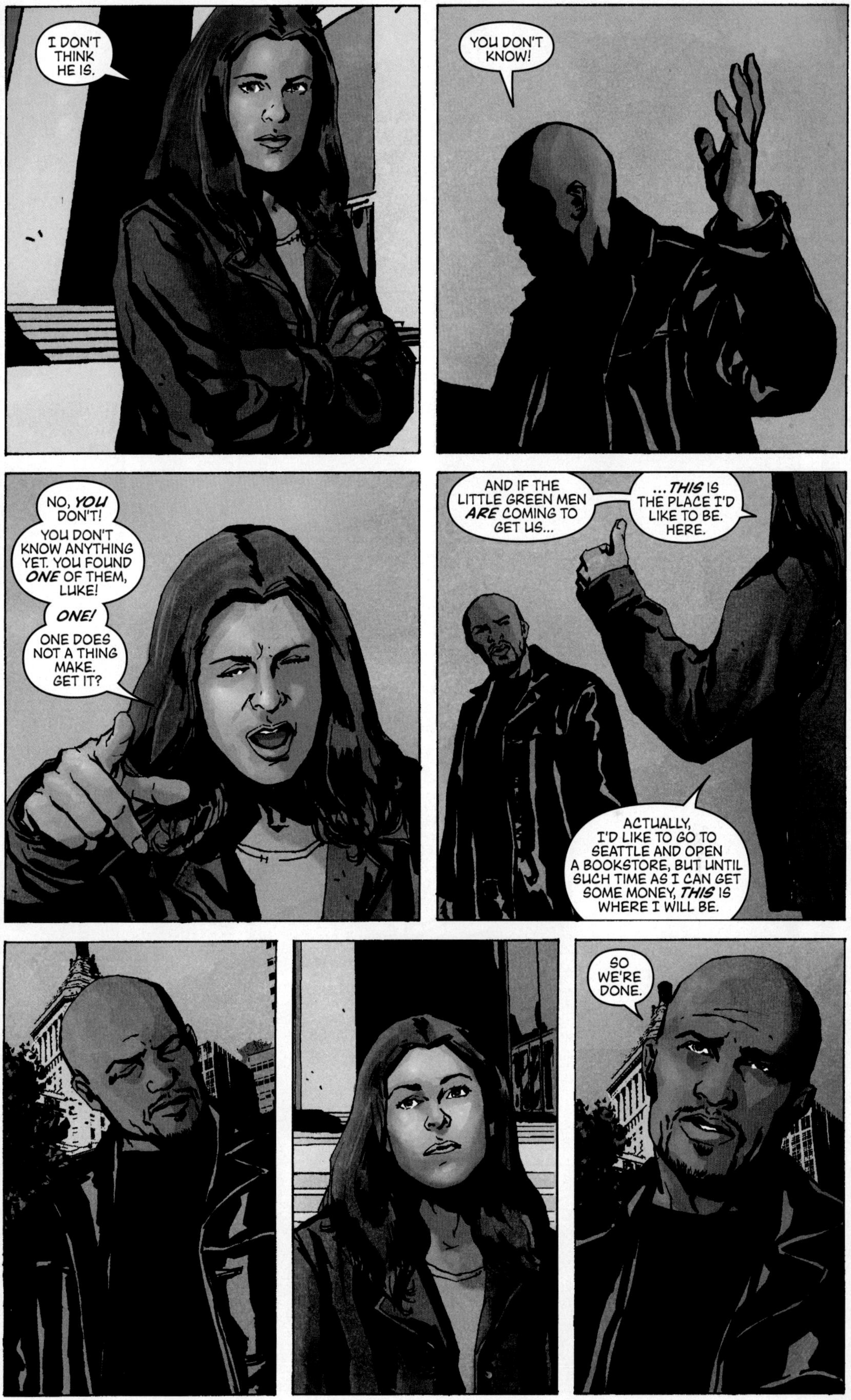
I DON'T THINK HE IS.
YOU DON'T KNOW!
NO, *YOU* DON'T!
YOU DON'T KNOW ANYTHING YET. YOU FOUND *ONE* OF THEM, LUKE!
ONE!
ONE DOES NOT A THING MAKE. GET IT?
AND IF THE LITTLE GREEN MEN *ARE* COMING TO GET US...
...*THIS* IS THE PLACE I'D LIKE TO BE. HERE.
ACTUALLY, I'D LIKE TO GO TO SEATTLE AND OPEN A BOOKSTORE, BUT UNTIL SUCH TIME AS I CAN GET SOME MONEY, *THIS* IS WHERE I WILL BE.
SO WE'RE DONE.

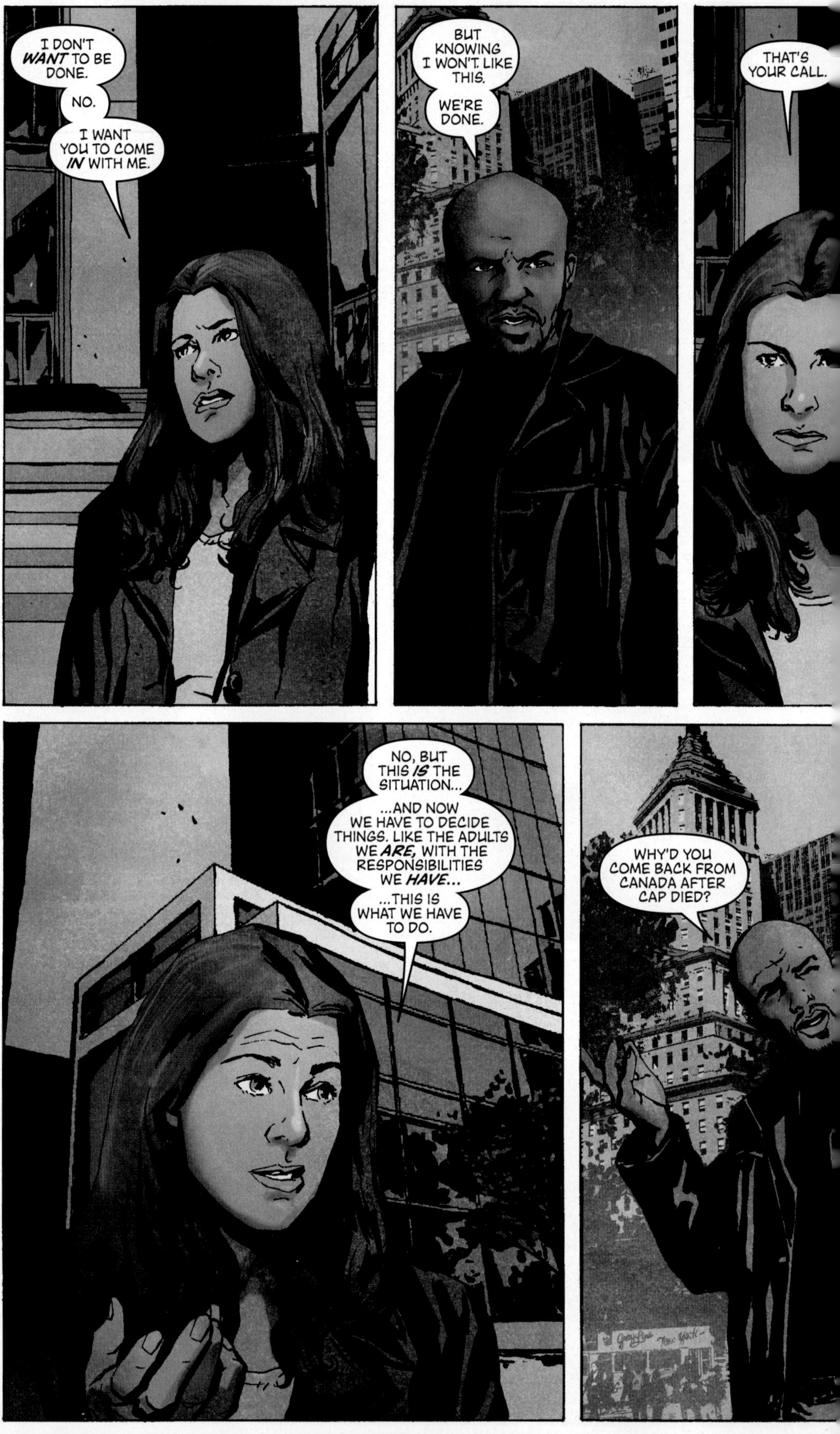
I DON'T *WANT* TO BE DONE.
NO.
I WANT YOU TO COME *IN* WITH ME.
BUT KNOWING I WON'T LIKE THIS.
WE'RE DONE.
THAT'S YOUR CALL.
NO, BUT THIS *IS* THE SITUATION...
...AND NOW WE HAVE TO DECIDE THINGS. LIKE THE ADULTS WE *ARE,* WITH THE RESPONSIBILITIES WE *HAVE*...
...THIS IS WHAT WE HAVE TO DO.
WHY'D YOU COME BACK FROM CANADA AFTER CAP DIED?

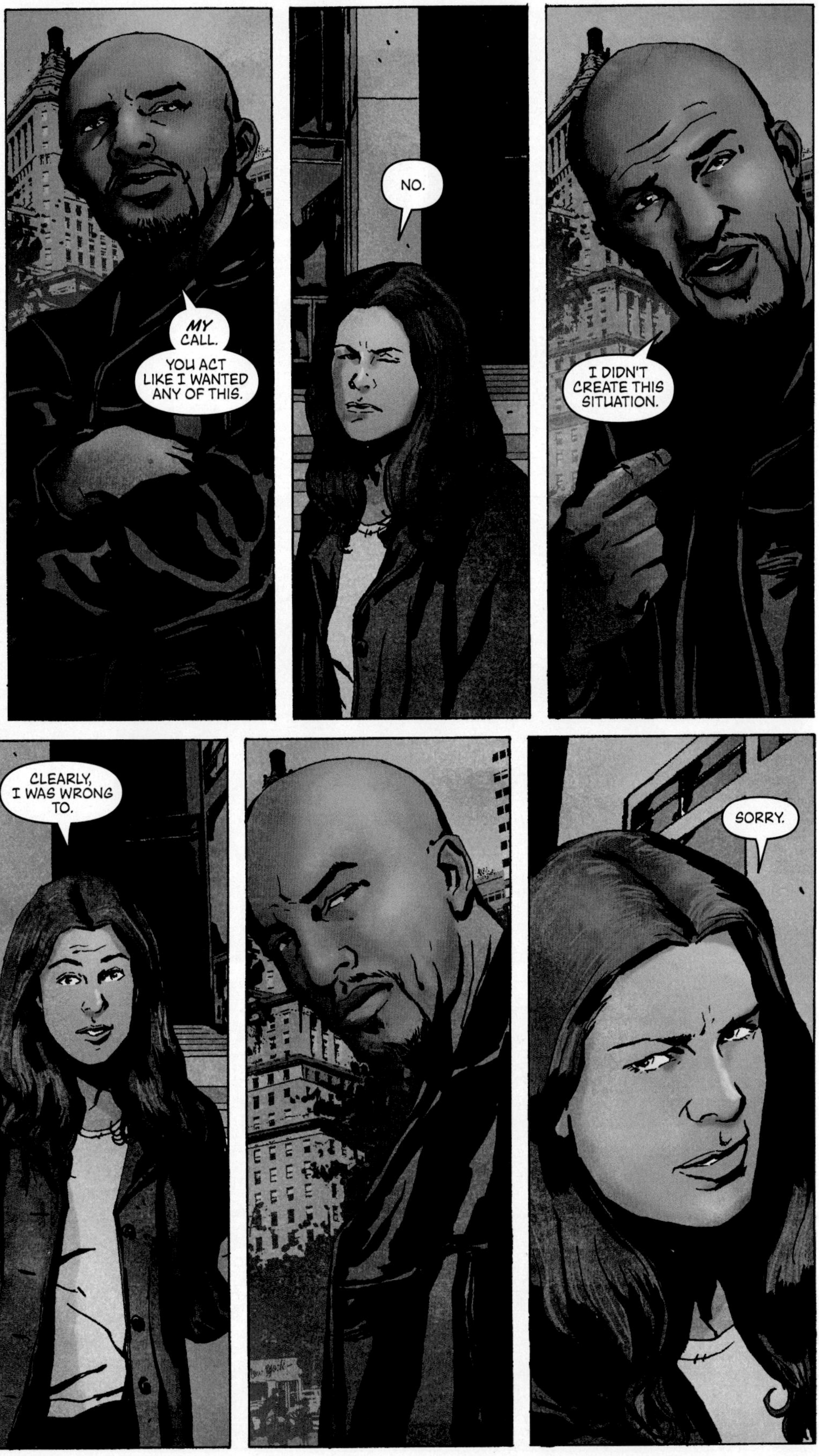
MY CALL.
YOU ACT LIKE I WANTED ANY OF THIS.
NO.
I DIDN'T CREATE THIS SITUATION.
CLEARLY, I WAS WRONG TO.
SORRY.

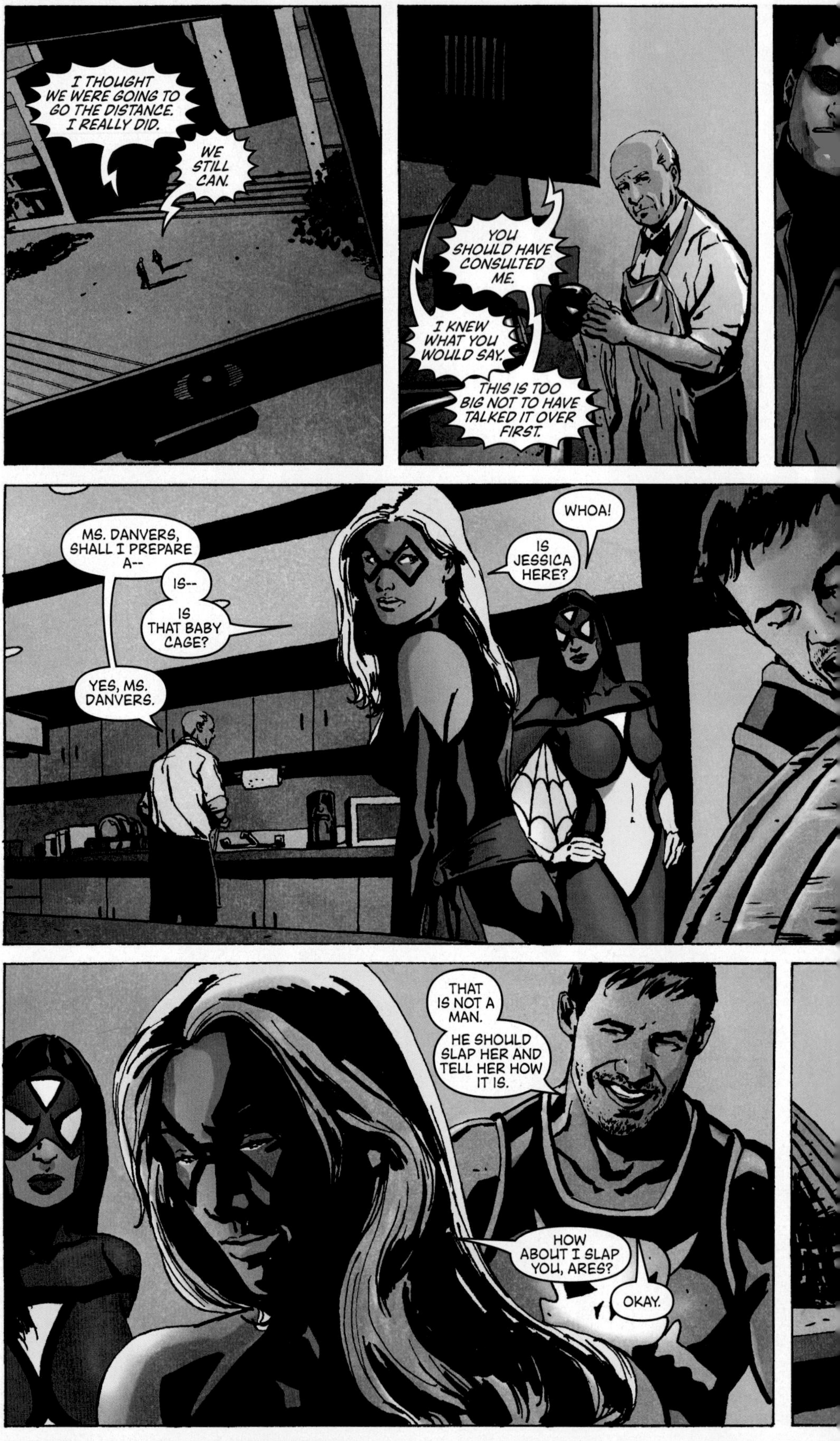
I THOUGHT WE WERE GOING TO GO THE DISTANCE. I REALLY DID.
WE STILL CAN.
YOU SHOULD HAVE CONSULTED ME.
I KNEW WHAT YOU WOULD SAY.
THIS IS TOO BIG NOT TO HAVE TALKED IT OVER FIRST.
MS. DANVERS, SHALL I PREPARE A--
IS--
IS THAT BABY CAGE?
YES, MS. DANVERS.
WHOA!
IS JESSICA HERE?
THAT IS NOT A MAN.
HE SHOULD SLAP HER AND TELL HER HOW IT IS.
HOW ABOUT I SLAP YOU, ARES?
OKAY.

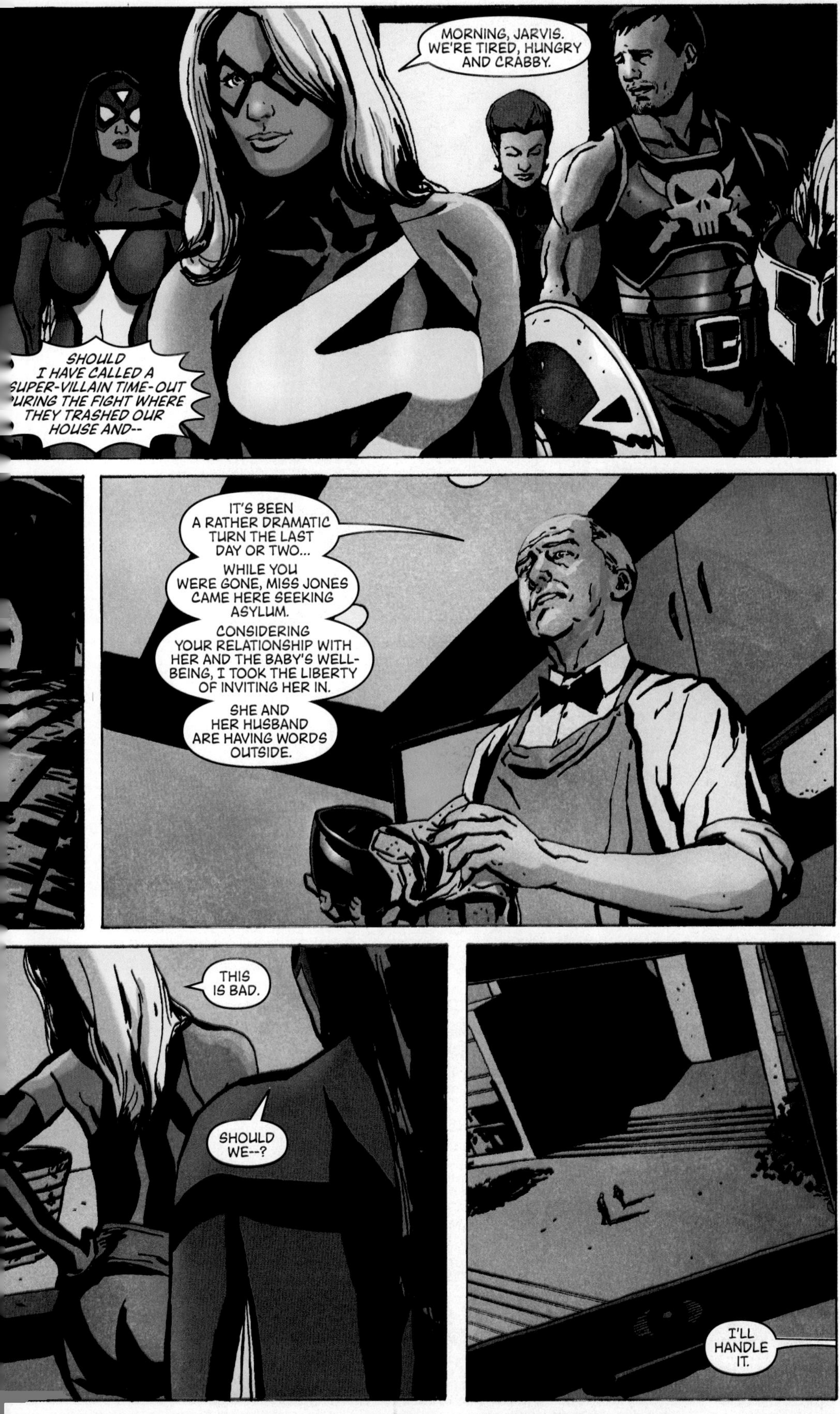
MORNING, JARVIS. WE'RE TIRED, HUNGRY AND CRABBY.
SHOULD I HAVE CALLED A SUPER-VILLAIN TIME-OUT DURING THE FIGHT WHERE THEY TRASHED OUR HOUSE AND--
IT'S BEEN A RATHER DRAMATIC TURN THE LAST DAY OR TWO...
WHILE YOU WERE GONE, MISS JONES CAME HERE SEEKING ASYLUM.
CONSIDERING YOUR RELATIONSHIP WITH HER AND THE BABY'S WELL-BEING, I TOOK THE LIBERTY OF INVITING HER IN.
SHE AND HER HUSBAND ARE HAVING WORDS OUTSIDE.
THIS IS BAD.
SHOULD WE--?
I'LL HANDLE IT.

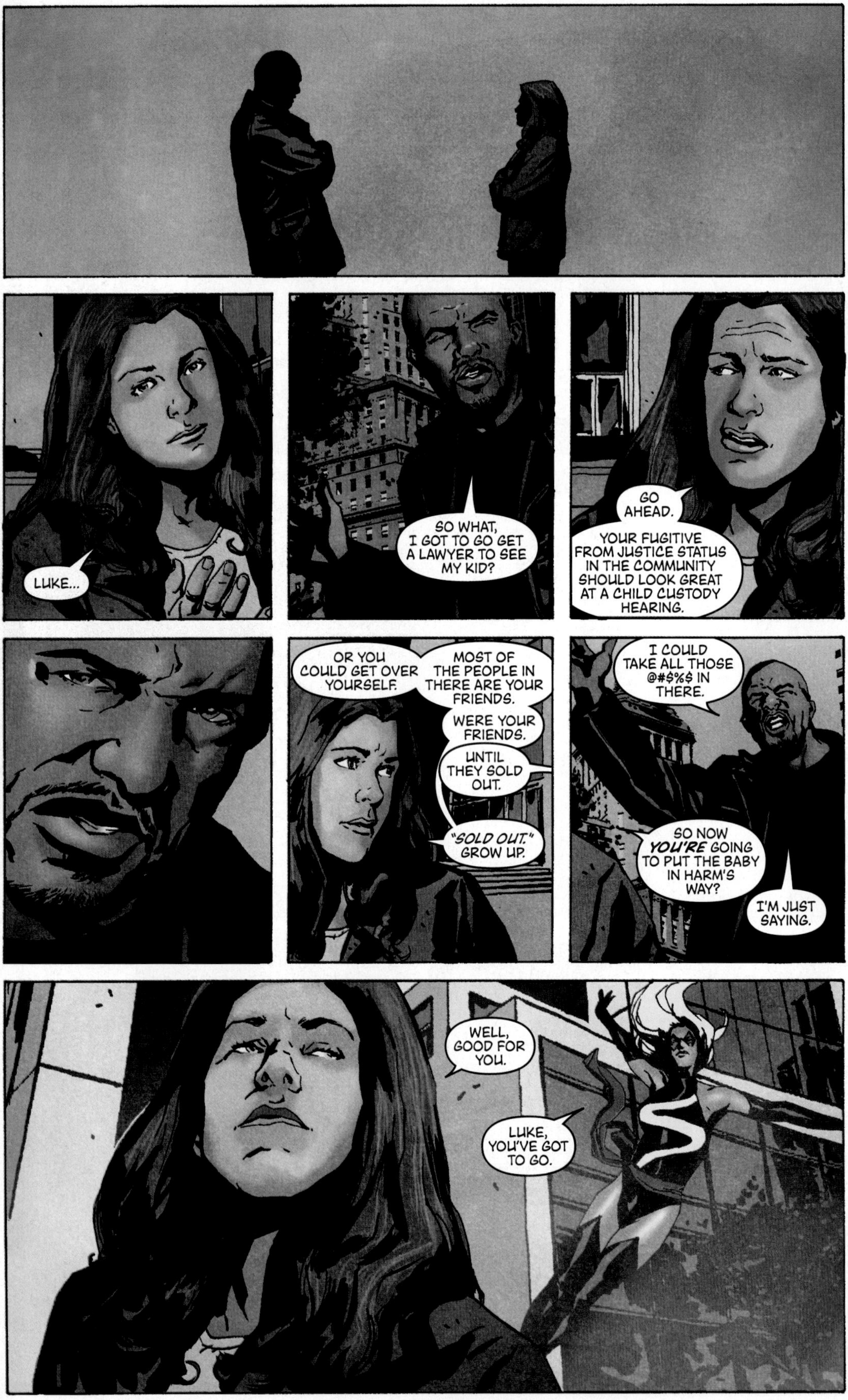
LUKE...
SO WHAT, I GOT TO GO GET A LAWYER TO SEE MY KID?
GO AHEAD.
YOUR FUGITIVE FROM JUSTICE STATUS IN THE COMMUNITY SHOULD LOOK GREAT AT A CHILD CUSTODY HEARING.
OR YOU COULD GET OVER YOURSELF.
MOST OF THE PEOPLE IN THERE ARE YOUR FRIENDS.
WERE YOUR FRIENDS.
UNTIL THEY SOLD OUT.
"SOLD OUT." GROW UP.
I COULD TAKE ALL THOSE @#$%$ IN THERE.
SO NOW YOU'RE GOING TO PUT THE BABY IN HARM'S WAY?
I'M JUST SAYING.
WELL, GOOD FOR YOU.
LUKE, YOU'VE GOT TO GO.

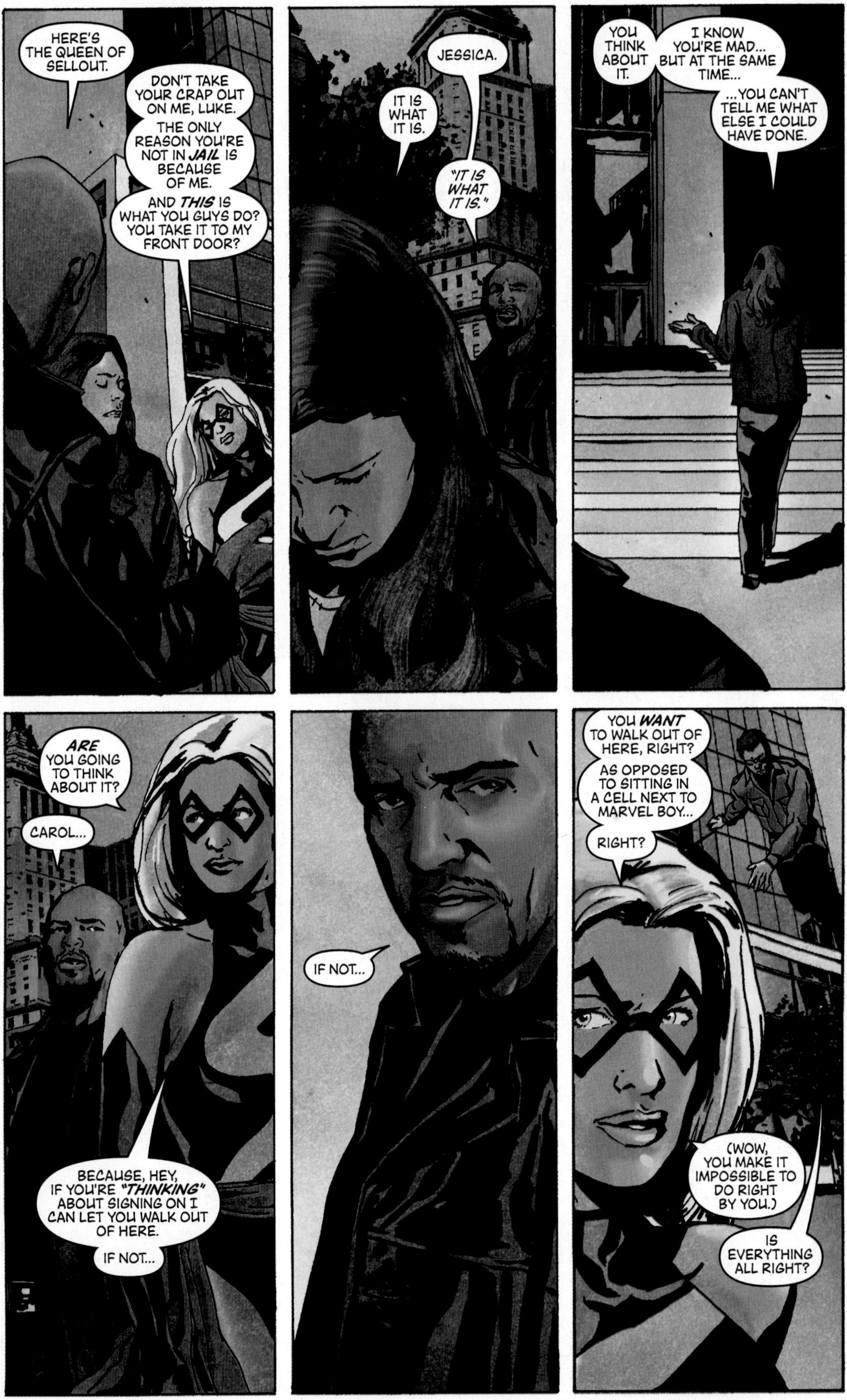
HERE'S THE QUEEN OF SELLOUT.
DON'T TAKE YOUR CRAP OUT ON ME, LUKE.
THE ONLY REASON YOU'RE NOT IN JAIL IS BECAUSE OF ME.
AND THIS IS WHAT YOU GUYS DO? YOU TAKE IT TO MY FRONT DOOR?
JESSICA.
IT IS WHAT IT IS.
"IT IS WHAT IT IS."
YOU THINK ABOUT IT.
I KNOW YOU'RE MAD... BUT AT THE SAME TIME...
...YOU CAN'T TELL ME WHAT ELSE I COULD HAVE DONE.
ARE YOU GOING TO THINK ABOUT IT?
CAROL...
BECAUSE, HEY, IF YOU'RE "THINKING" ABOUT SIGNING ON I CAN LET YOU WALK OUT OF HERE.
IF NOT...
IF NOT...
YOU WANT TO WALK OUT OF HERE, RIGHT?
AS OPPOSED TO SITTING IN A CELL NEXT TO MARVEL BOY...
RIGHT?
(WOW, YOU MAKE IT IMPOSSIBLE TO DO RIGHT BY YOU.)
IS EVERYTHING ALL RIGHT?

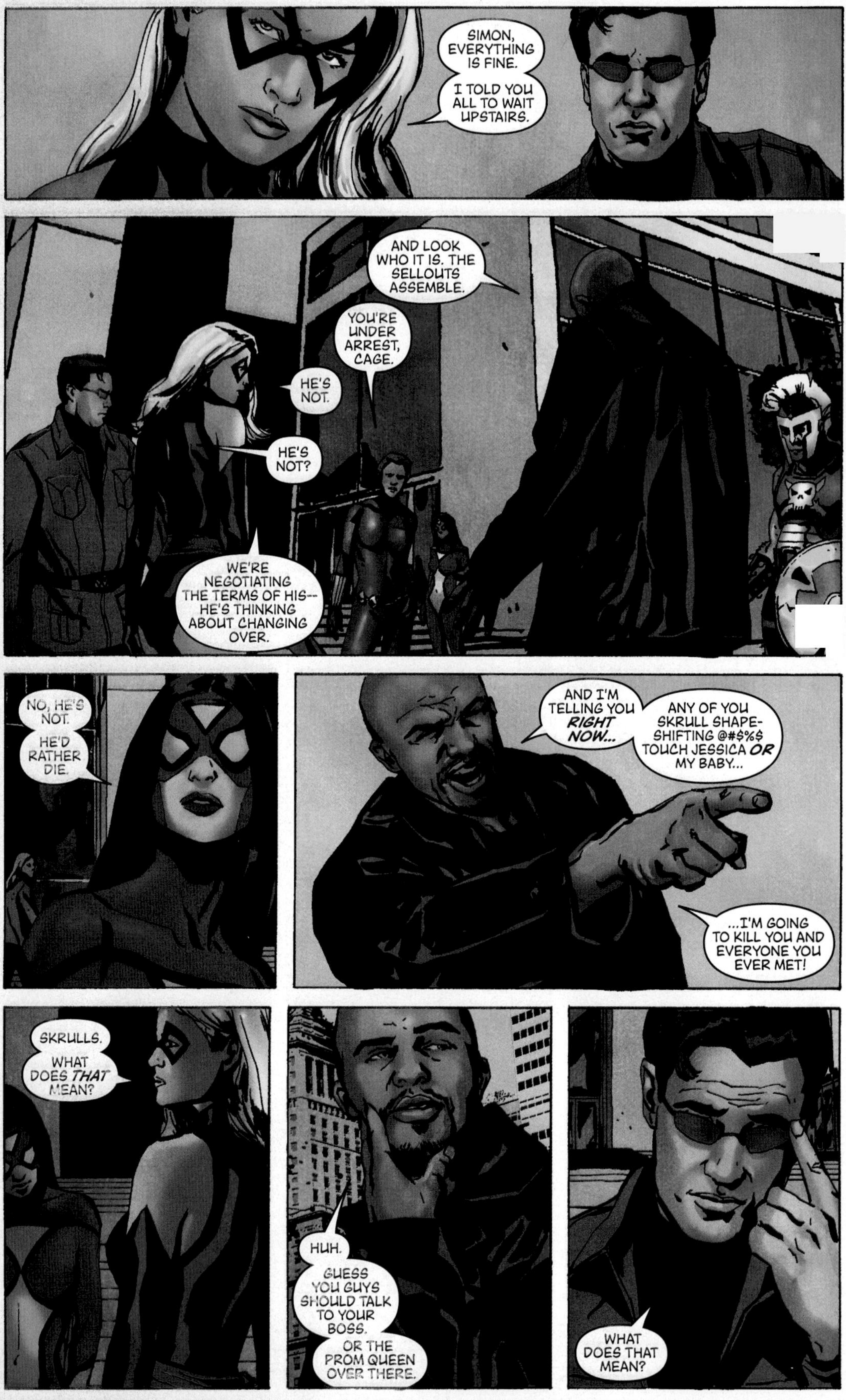
SIMON, EVERYTHING IS FINE.
I TOLD YOU ALL TO WAIT UPSTAIRS.
AND LOOK WHO IT IS. THE SELLOUTS ASSEMBLE.
YOU'RE UNDER ARREST, CAGE.
HE'S NOT.
HE'S NOT?
WE'RE NEGOTIATING THE TERMS OF HIS-- HE'S THINKING ABOUT CHANGING OVER.
NO, HE'S NOT.
HE'D RATHER DIE.
AND I'M TELLING YOU *RIGHT NOW...*
ANY OF YOU SKRULL SHAPE-SHIFTING @#$%$ TOUCH JESSICA *OR* MY BABY...
...I'M GOING TO KILL YOU AND EVERYONE YOU EVER MET!
SKRULLS.
WHAT DOES *THAT* MEAN?
HUH.
GUESS YOU GUYS SHOULD TALK TO YOUR BOSS.
OR THE PROM QUEEN OVER THERE.
WHAT DOES THAT MEAN?

HE'S WALKING? YOU'RE LETTING HIM WALK?

TEAM LEADER. MY CALL. I TOLD YOU--

I DON'T GET IT.

HE'S A FUGITIVE FROM--

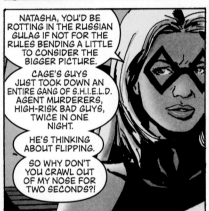

NATASHA, YOU'D BE ROTTING IN THE RUSSIAN GULAG IF NOT FOR THE RULES BENDING A LITTLE TO CONSIDER THE BIGGER PICTURE.

CAGE'S GUYS JUST TOOK DOWN AN ENTIRE GANG OF S.H.I.E.L.D. AGENT MURDERERS, HIGH-RISK BAD GUYS, TWICE IN ONE NIGHT.

HE'S THINKING ABOUT FLIPPING.

SO WHY DON'T YOU CRAWL OUT OF MY NOSE FOR TWO SECONDS?!

OKAY, UM... SKRULLS.

SHAPE-SHIFTING ALIENS.

HE'S TIRED.

I KNOW *WHAT* THEY ARE.

HE HASN'T SLEPT IN DAYS. I'M SORRY.

WHAT'S GOING ON?

SORRY?

SORRY.

THAT'S CLASSIFIED S.H.I.E.L.D. STUFF.

COME ON...

AND? WE'RE AGENTS. WE'RE AVENGERS.

I'M NOT THE ONE TO TALK TO. WAIT TILL TONY GETS BACK.

SKRULLS NOW?

I DON'T GET IT.

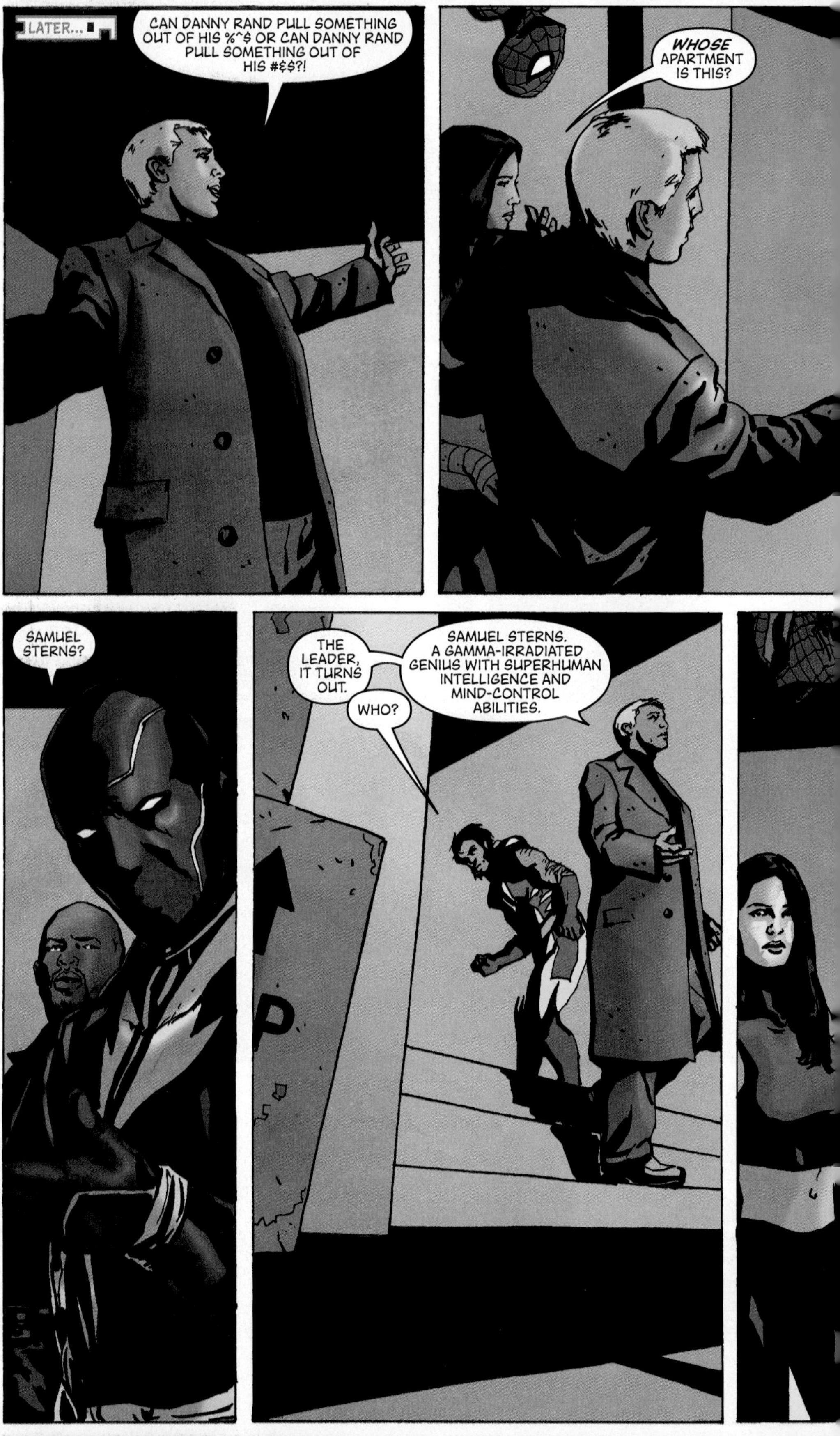
LATER...
CAN DANNY RAND PULL SOMETHING OUT OF HIS %^$ OR CAN DANNY RAND PULL SOMETHING OUT OF HIS #&$?!
WHOSE APARTMENT IS THIS?
SAMUEL STERNS?
THE LEADER, IT TURNS OUT.
WHO?
SAMUEL STERNS. A GAMMA-IRRADIATED GENIUS WITH SUPERHUMAN INTELLIGENCE AND MIND-CONTROL ABILITIES.

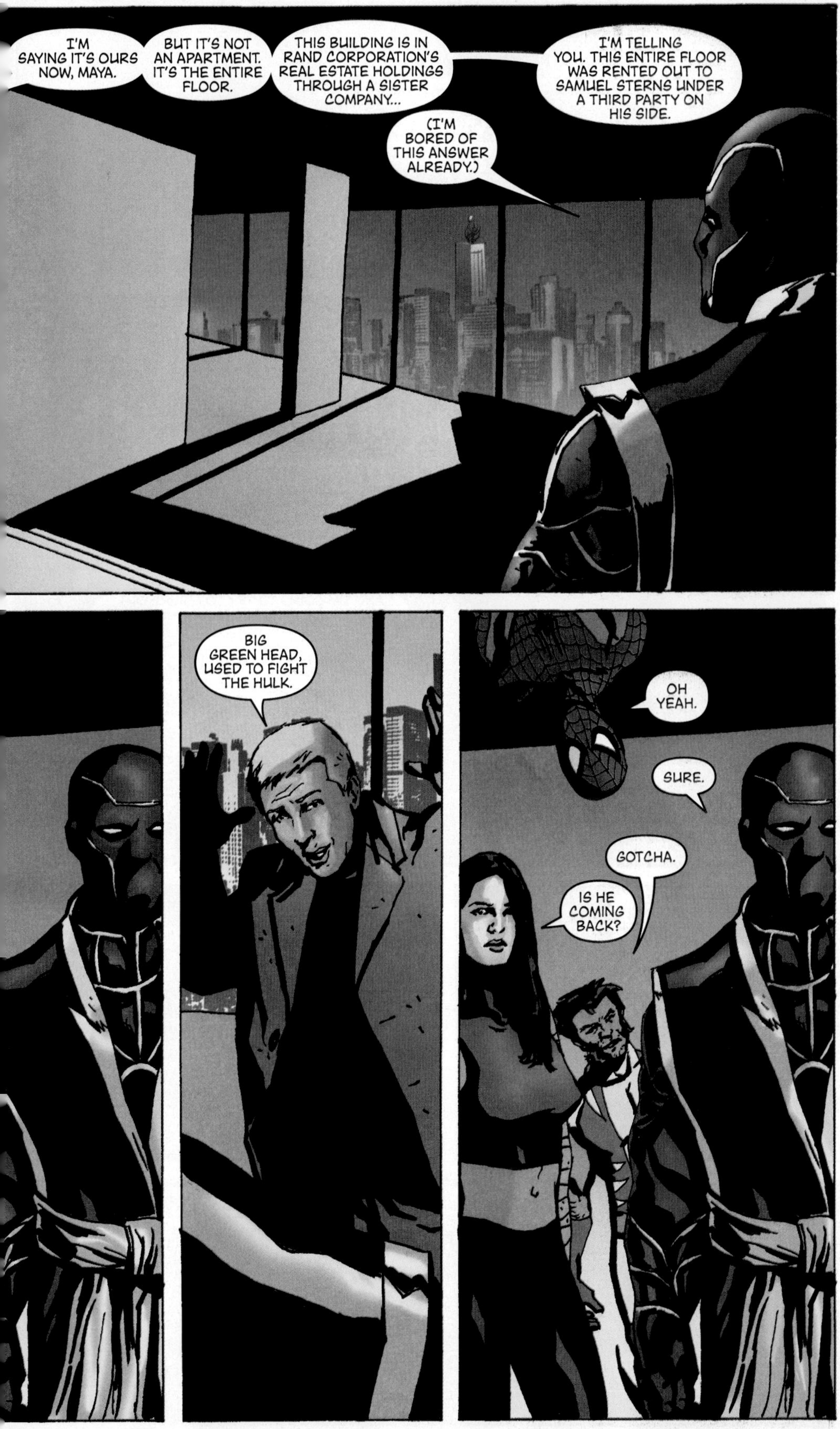
I'M SAYING IT'S OURS NOW, MAYA.
BUT IT'S NOT AN APARTMENT. IT'S THE ENTIRE FLOOR.
THIS BUILDING IS IN RAND CORPORATION'S REAL ESTATE HOLDINGS THROUGH A SISTER COMPANY...
I'M TELLING YOU. THIS ENTIRE FLOOR WAS RENTED OUT TO SAMUEL STERNS UNDER A THIRD PARTY ON HIS SIDE.
(I'M BORED OF THIS ANSWER ALREADY.)
BIG GREEN HEAD, USED TO FIGHT THE HULK.
OH YEAH.
SURE.
GOTCHA.
IS HE COMING BACK?

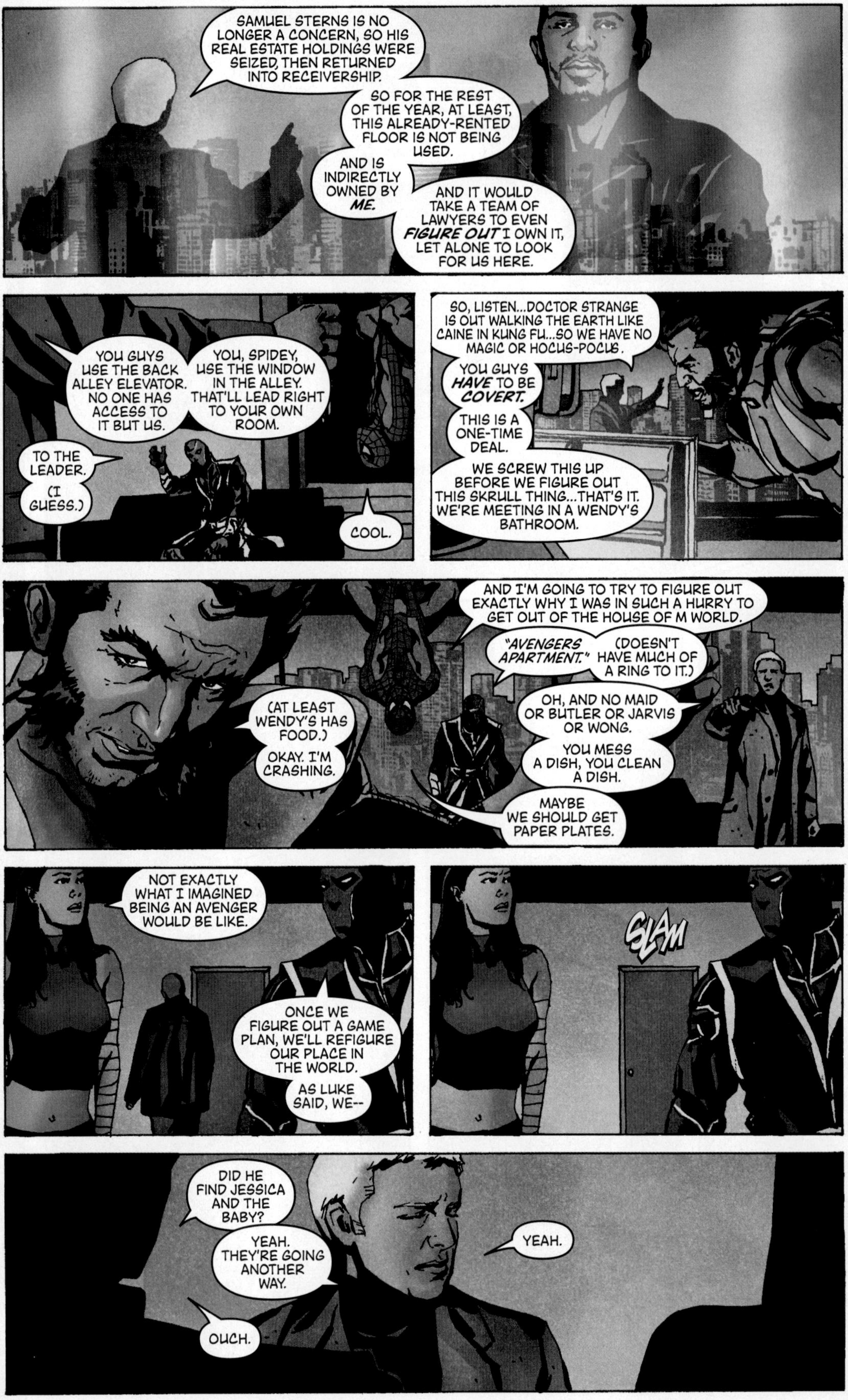
SAMUEL STERNS IS NO LONGER A CONCERN, SO HIS REAL ESTATE HOLDINGS WERE SEIZED, THEN RETURNED INTO RECEIVERSHIP.
SO FOR THE REST OF THE YEAR, AT LEAST, THIS ALREADY-RENTED FLOOR IS NOT BEING USED.
AND IS INDIRECTLY OWNED BY *ME.*
AND IT WOULD TAKE A TEAM OF LAWYERS TO EVEN *FIGURE OUT* I OWN IT, LET ALONE TO LOOK FOR US HERE.
YOU GUYS USE THE BACK ALLEY ELEVATOR. NO ONE HAS ACCESS TO IT BUT US.
YOU, SPIDEY, USE THE WINDOW IN THE ALLEY. THAT'LL LEAD RIGHT TO YOUR OWN ROOM.
TO THE LEADER.
(I GUESS.)
COOL.
SO, LISTEN...DOCTOR STRANGE IS OUT WALKING THE EARTH LIKE CAINE IN KUNG FU...SO WE HAVE NO MAGIC OR HOCUS-POCUS.
YOU GUYS *HAVE* TO BE *COVERT.*
THIS IS A ONE-TIME DEAL.
WE SCREW THIS UP BEFORE WE FIGURE OUT THIS SKRULL THING...THAT'S IT. WE'RE MEETING IN A WENDY'S BATHROOM.
AND I'M GOING TO TRY TO FIGURE OUT EXACTLY WHY I WAS IN SUCH A HURRY TO GET OUT OF THE HOUSE OF M WORLD.
"AVENGERS APARTMENT."
(DOESN'T HAVE MUCH OF A RING TO IT.)
(AT LEAST WENDY'S HAS FOOD.)
OKAY. I'M CRASHING.
OH, AND NO MAID OR BUTLER OR JARVIS OR WONG.
YOU MESS A DISH, YOU CLEAN A DISH.
MAYBE WE SHOULD GET PAPER PLATES.
NOT EXACTLY WHAT I IMAGINED BEING AN AVENGER WOULD BE LIKE.
ONCE WE FIGURE OUT A GAME PLAN, WE'LL REFIGURE OUR PLACE IN THE WORLD.
AS LUKE SAID, WE--
SLAM
DID HE FIND JESSICA AND THE BABY?
YEAH.
YEAH. THEY'RE GOING ANOTHER WAY.
OUCH.

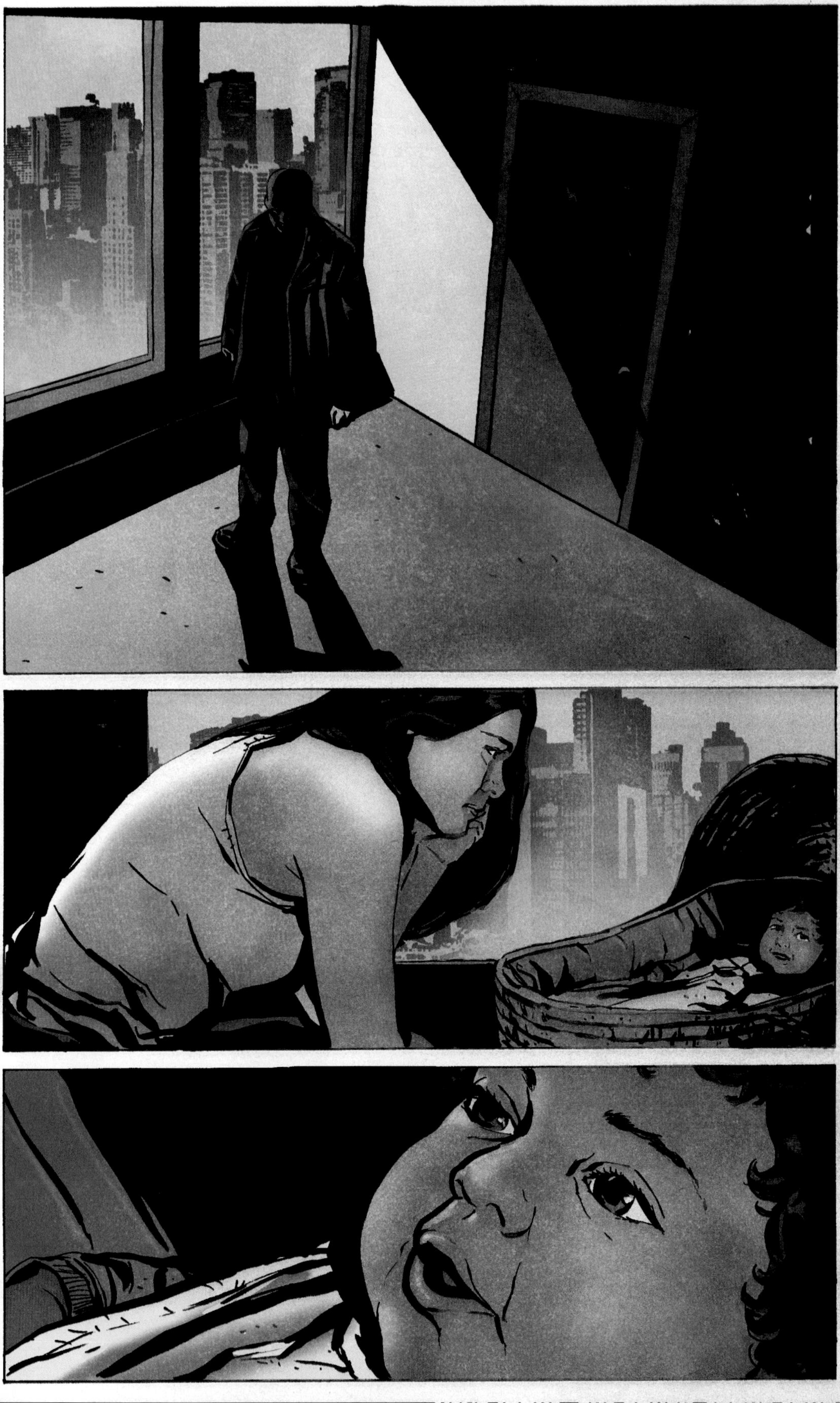

NEXT ISSUE: THE TRUTH ABOUT ECHO

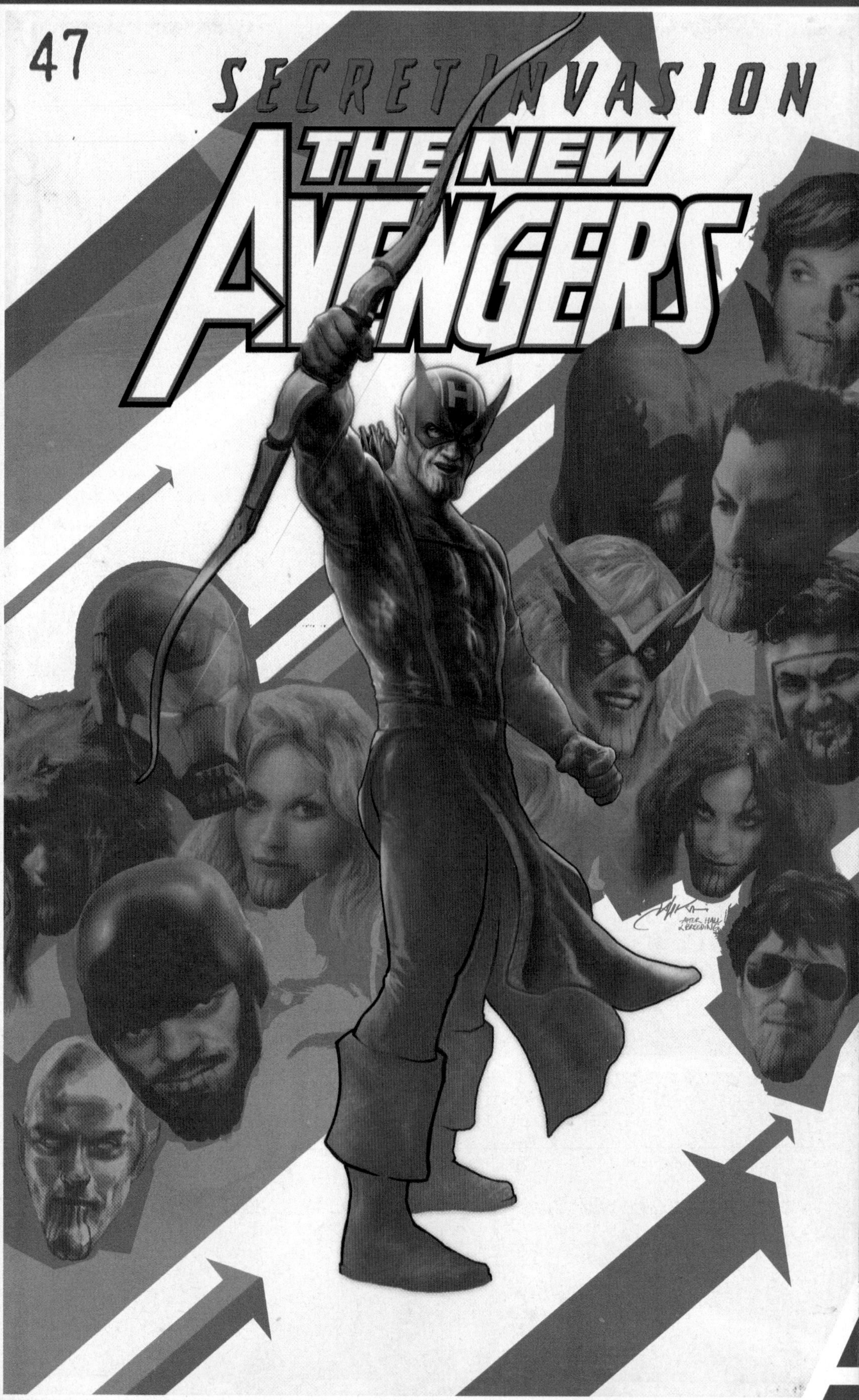

47
SECRET INVASION
THE NEW AVENGERS

And there came a day, a day unlike any other, when Earth's
Mightiest Heroes found themselves united against a common
threat! On that day, the Avengers were born, to fight the foes
no single super hero could withstand!

Previously in New Avengers

The shape-shifting alien race known as the Skrulls has invaded Earth. First they
deployed a well-planned Secret Invasion using their shape-shifting ability to seed
mistrust among the Avengers and other heroes around the world.

Now they have struck fast and hard, setting up camp and making their intentions
clear. The Earth is now part of the Skrull Empire.

Even though they've escaped the traps set for them, Earth's heroes, including the
Avengers, have been defeated both mentally and physically. They didn't even
know the extent of the invasion or which of them was — or could still be — a
Skrull agent.

Among the casualties of the growing paranoia is the marriage of Avenger Luke
Cage and Jessica Jones. Worried for the safety of their child, Jessica seeks shelter
at Avengers Tower, under the watchful eye of Stark's butler, Jarvis, to wait out the
worst of it.

BRIAN MICHAEL
BENDIS
WRITER

BILLY TAN &
MICHAEL GAYDOS
PENCILS

MATT BANNING & MICHAEL
GAYDOS
INKS

JUSTIN
PONSOR
COLORIST

RS & COMICRAFT'S ALBERT DESCHESNE
LETTERER

ALEKSI BRICLOT
COVER ARTIST

ANTHONY DIAL
PRODUCTION

JEANINE SCHAEFER
ASSOCIATE EDITOR

TOM BREVOORT
EDITOR

JOE QUESADA
EDITOR IN CHIEF

DAN BUCKLEY
PUBLISHER

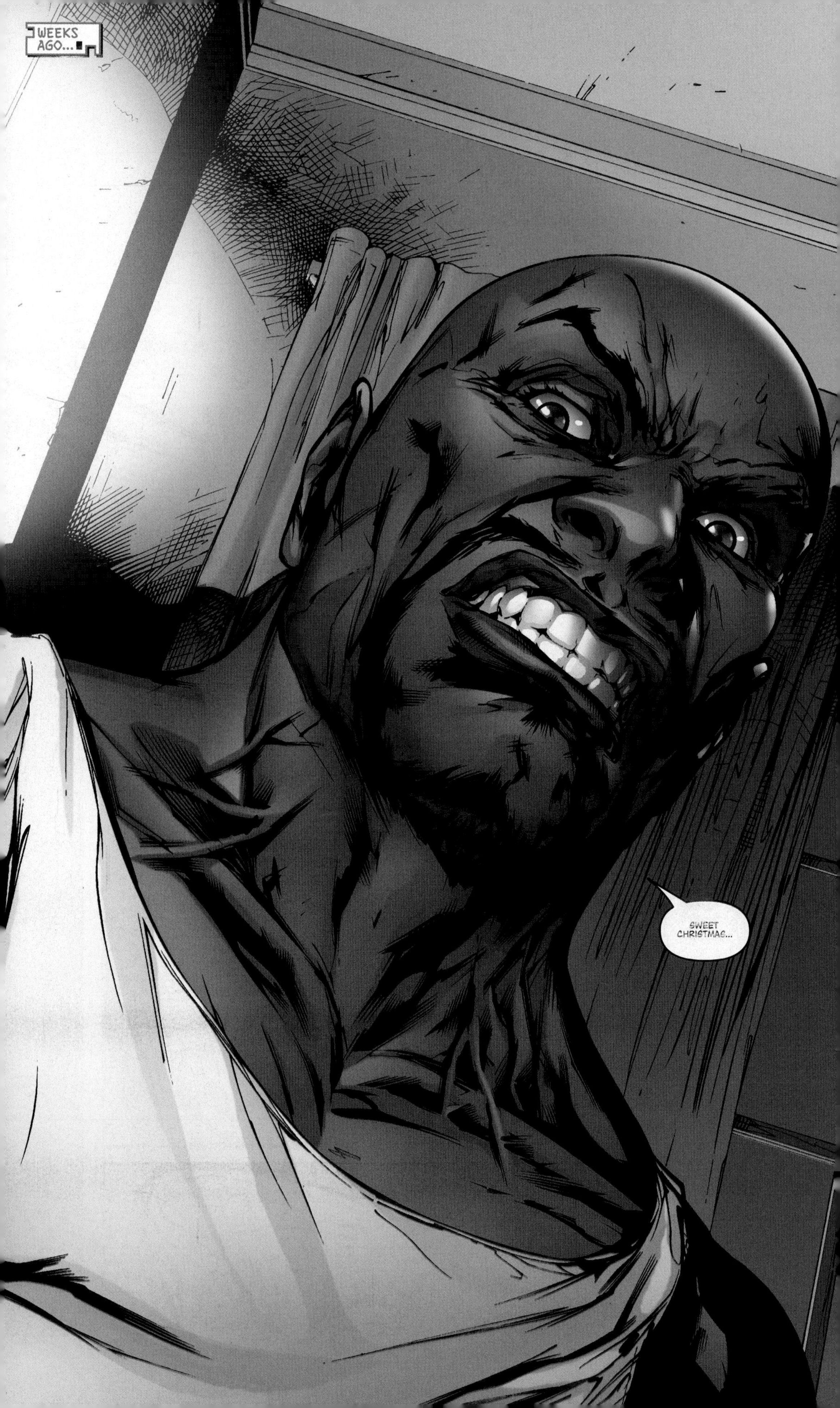
WEEKS AGO...
SWEET CHRISTMAS...

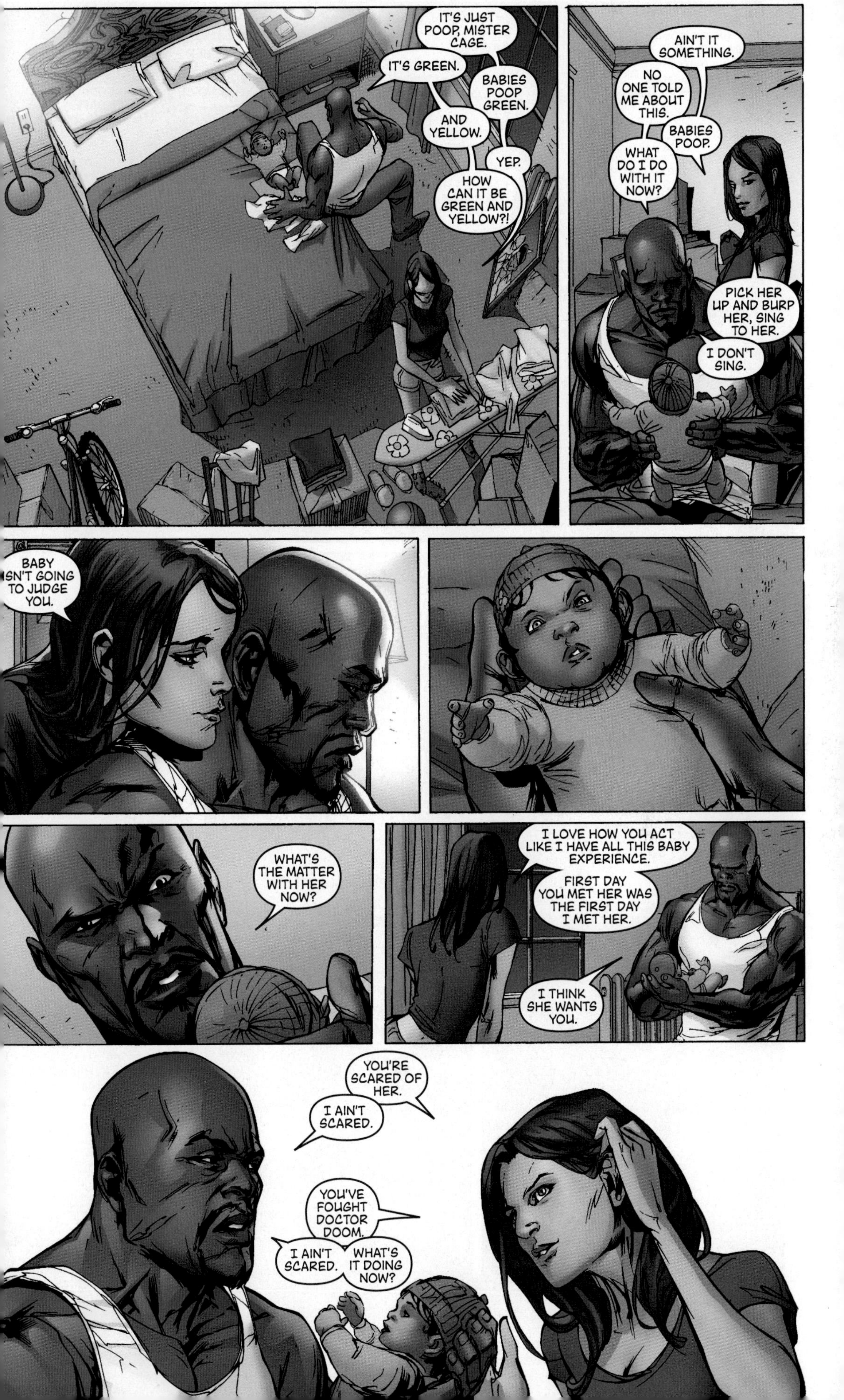

IT'S JUST POOP, MISTER CAGE.
IT'S GREEN.
BABIES POOP GREEN.
AND YELLOW.
YEP.
HOW CAN IT BE GREEN AND YELLOW?!
AIN'T IT SOMETHING.
NO ONE TOLD ME ABOUT THIS.
BABIES POOP.
WHAT DO I DO WITH IT NOW?
PICK HER UP AND BURP HER, SING TO HER.
I DON'T SING.
BABY SN'T GOING TO JUDGE YOU.
WHAT'S THE MATTER WITH HER NOW?
I LOVE HOW YOU ACT LIKE I HAVE ALL THIS BABY EXPERIENCE.
FIRST DAY YOU MET HER WAS THE FIRST DAY I MET HER.
I THINK SHE WANTS YOU.
YOU'RE SCARED OF HER.
I AIN'T SCARED.
YOU'VE FOUGHT DOCTOR DOOM.
I AIN'T SCARED.
WHAT'S IT DOING NOW?

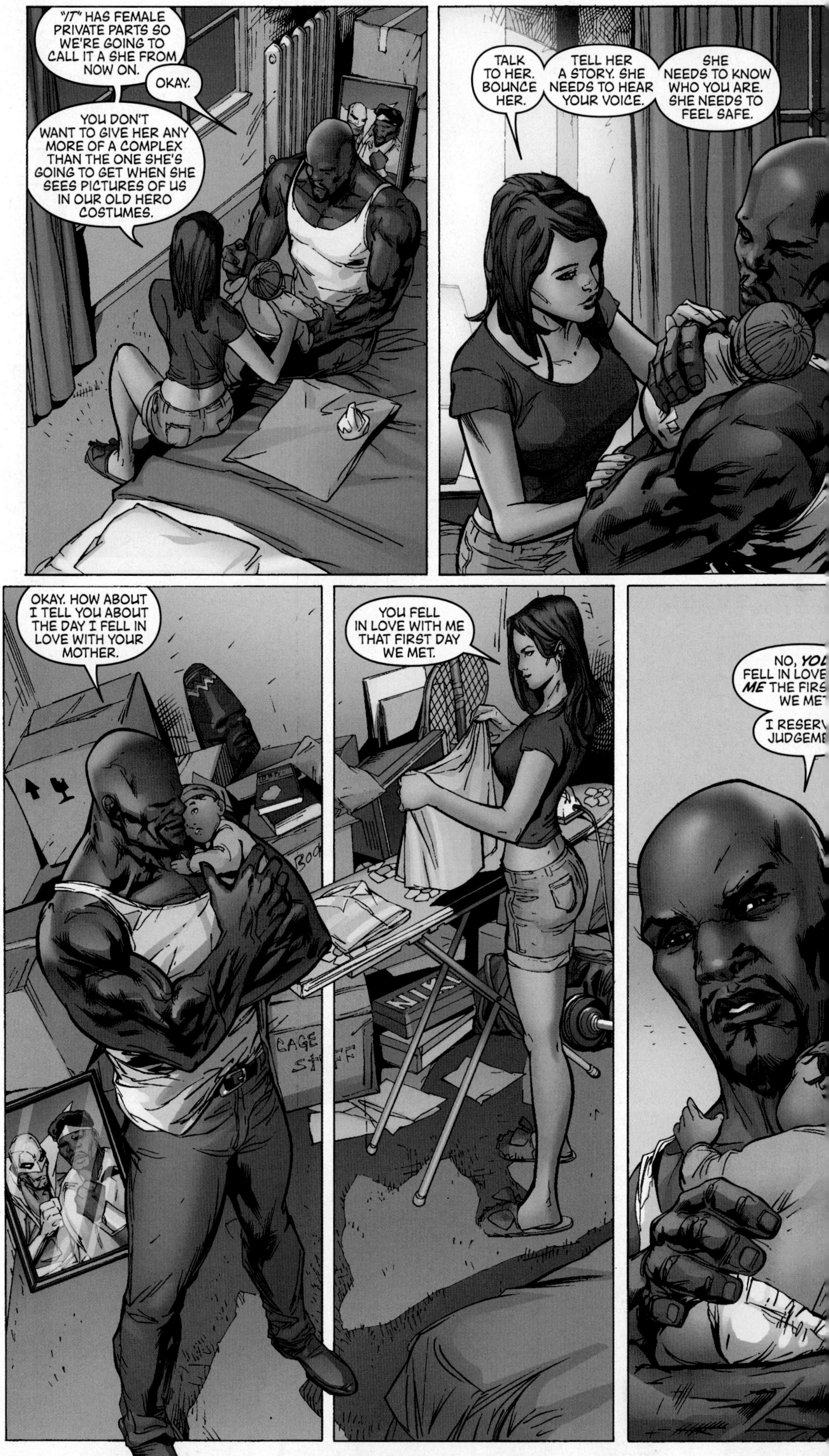
"IT" HAS FEMALE PRIVATE PARTS SO WE'RE GOING TO CALL IT A SHE FROM NOW ON.
OKAY.
YOU DON'T WANT TO GIVE HER ANY MORE OF A COMPLEX THAN THE ONE SHE'S GOING TO GET WHEN SHE SEES PICTURES OF US IN OUR OLD HERO COSTUMES.
TALK TO HER. BOUNCE HER.
TELL HER A STORY. SHE NEEDS TO HEAR YOUR VOICE.
SHE NEEDS TO KNOW WHO YOU ARE. SHE NEEDS TO FEEL SAFE.
OKAY. HOW ABOUT I TELL YOU ABOUT THE DAY I FELL IN LOVE WITH YOUR MOTHER.
CAGE STUFF
YOU FELL IN LOVE WITH ME THAT FIRST DAY WE MET.
NO, YO FELL IN LOVE ME THE FIRS WE MET
I RESERV JUDGEM

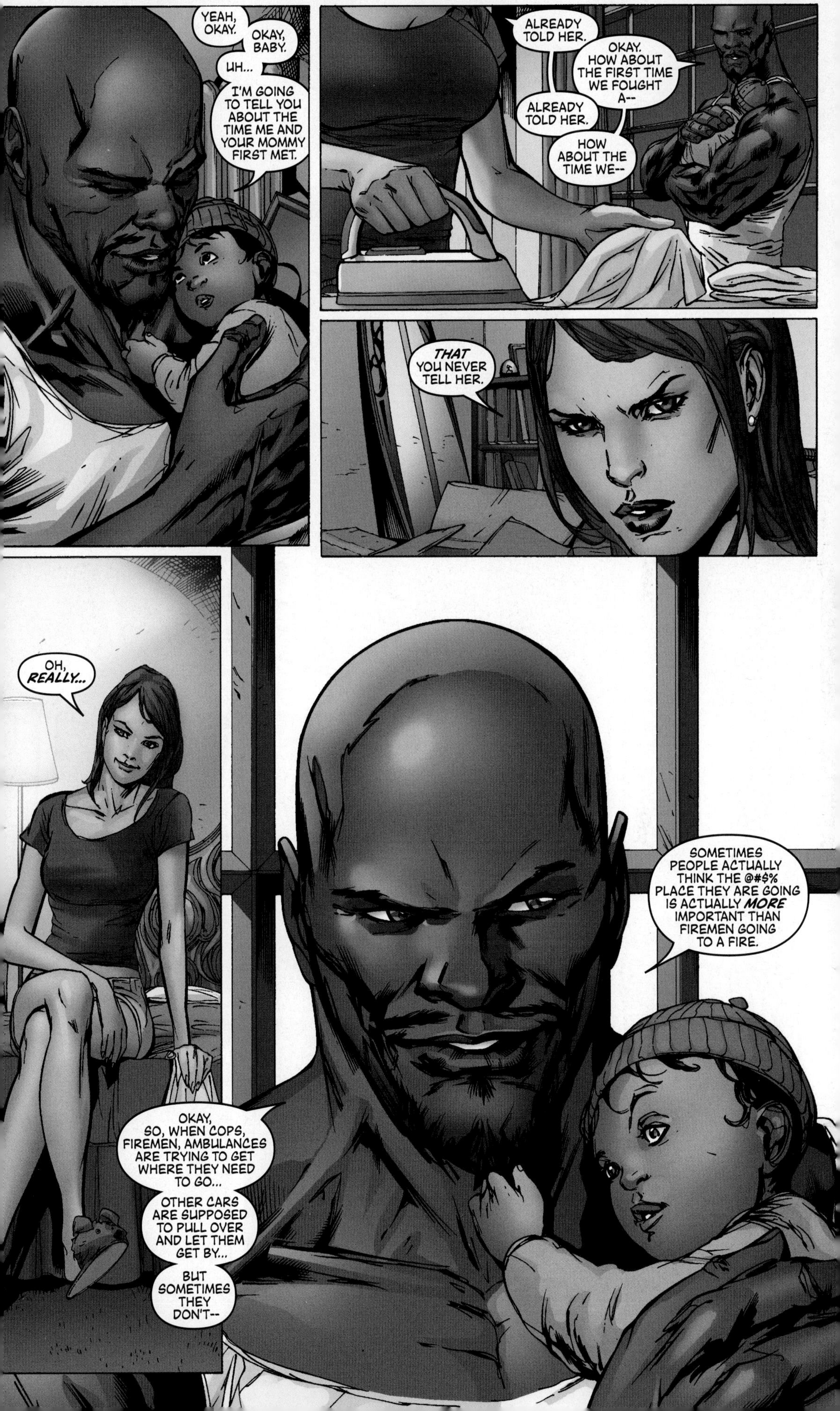
YEAH, OKAY.
OKAY, BABY.
UH...
I'M GOING TO TELL YOU ABOUT THE TIME ME AND YOUR MOMMY FIRST MET.
ALREADY TOLD HER.
OKAY. HOW ABOUT THE FIRST TIME WE FOUGHT A--
ALREADY TOLD HER.
HOW ABOUT THE TIME WE--
THAT YOU NEVER TELL HER.
OH, REALLY...
OKAY, SO, WHEN COPS, FIREMEN, AMBULANCES ARE TRYING TO GET WHERE THEY NEED TO GO...
OTHER CARS ARE SUPPOSED TO PULL OVER AND LET THEM GET BY...
BUT SOMETIMES THEY DON'T--
SOMETIMES PEOPLE ACTUALLY THINK THE @#$% PLACE THEY ARE GOING IS ACTUALLY MORE IMPORTANT THAN FIREMEN GOING TO A FIRE.

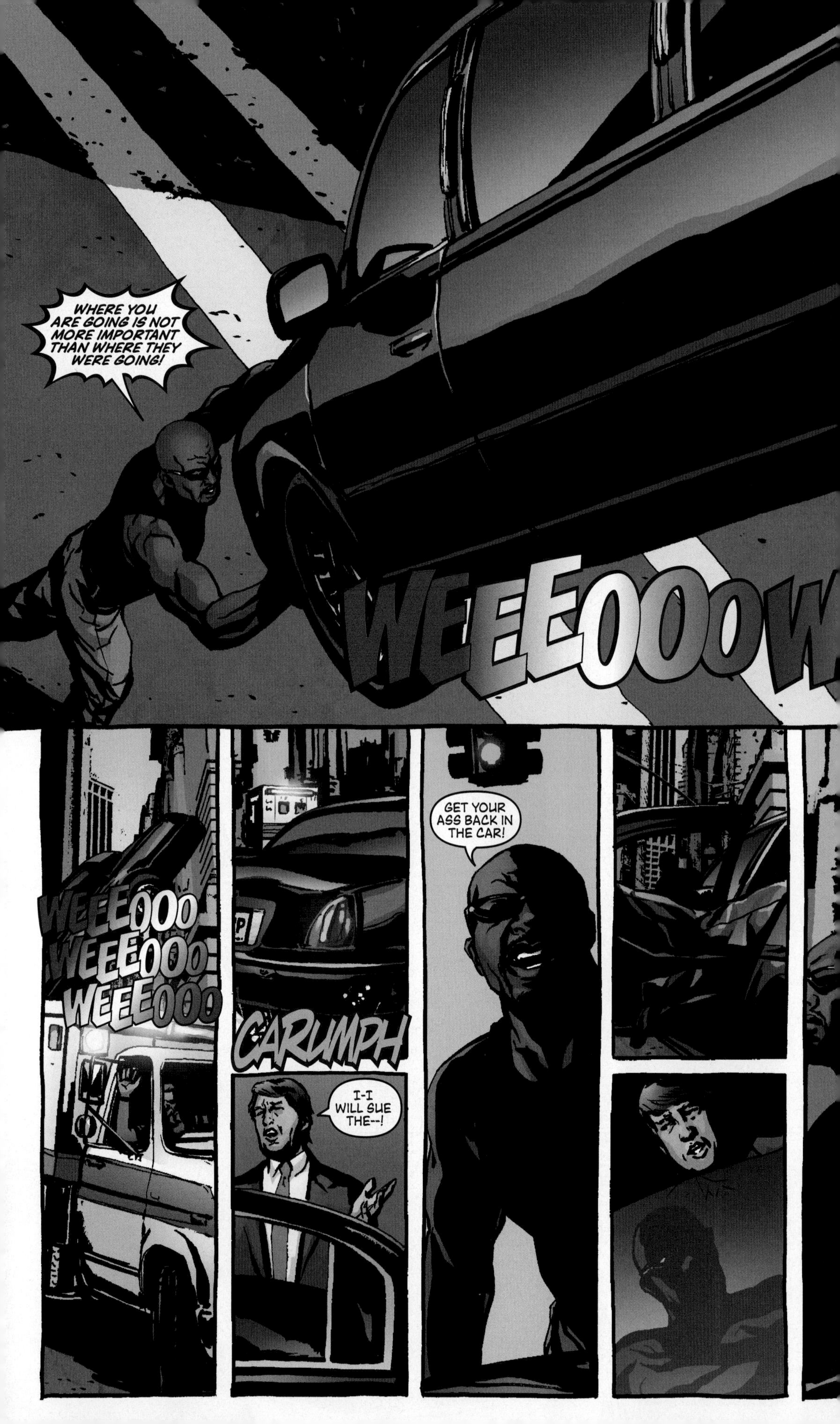
WHERE YOU ARE GOING IS NOT MORE IMPORTANT THAN WHERE THEY WERE GOING!
WEEEOOOW
WEEEOOO
WEEEOOO
WEEEOOO
CARUMPH
I-I WILL SUE THE--!
GET YOUR ASS BACK IN THE CAR!

EOOOWEEEOOOWEE

ABOUT TIME!

YOU ARE THE MAN!

CLAP CLAP CLAP CLAP

CLAP CLAP CLAP

JESSICA JONES.

YOU REMEMBER MY NAME.

TOLD YOU I WASN'T EVER GOING TO FORGET IT.

IT'S BEEN A WHILE.

GUESS IT HAS.

WHAT ARE YOU DOING IN MY NEIGHBORHOOD?

I WAS COMING TO SEE *YOU*, ACTUALLY.

WHAT?

I NEED TO HIRE YOU.

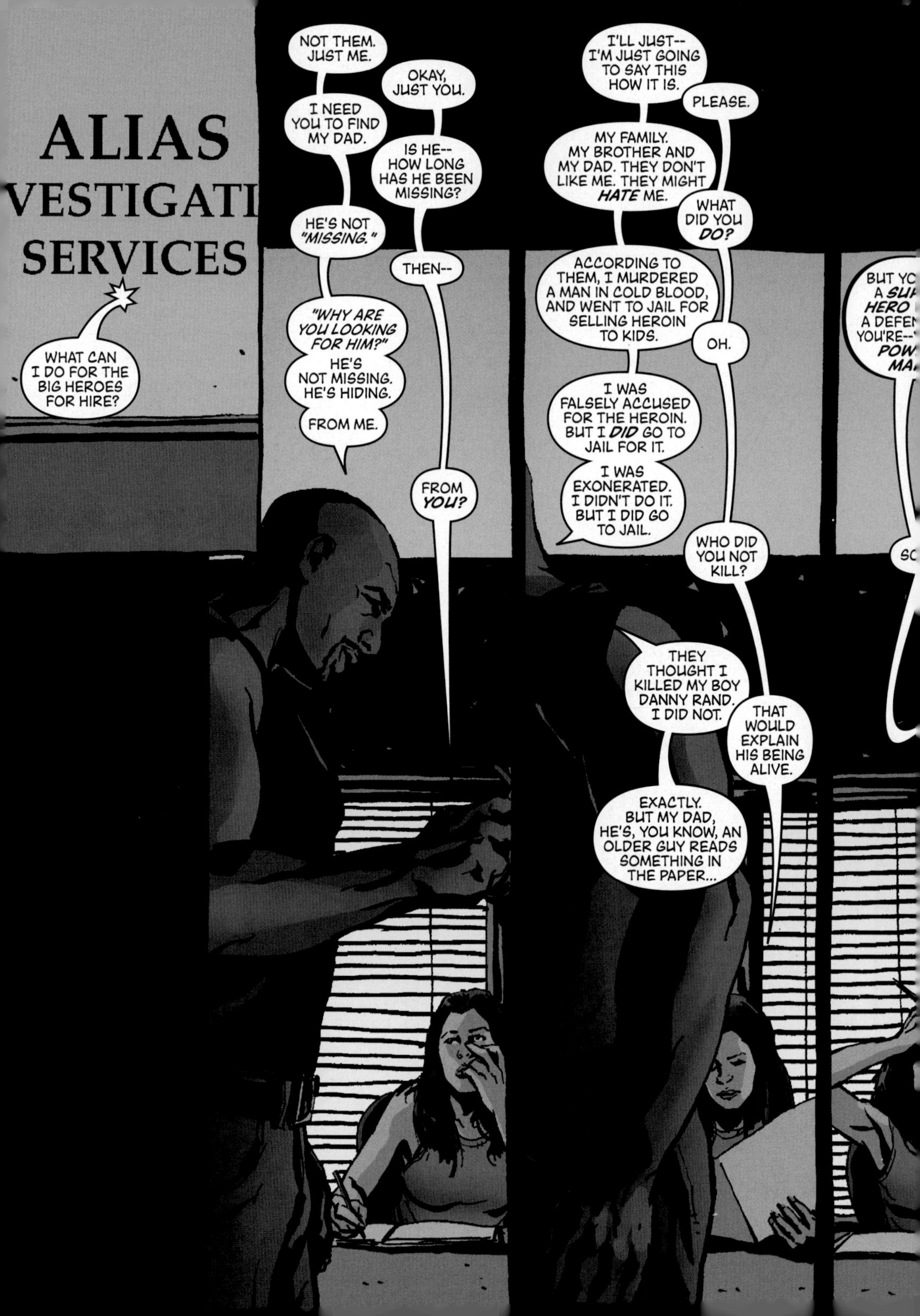
ALIAS
SERVICES
WHAT CAN I DO FOR THE BIG HEROES FOR HIRE?
NOT THEM. JUST ME.
OKAY, JUST YOU.
I NEED YOU TO FIND MY DAD.
IS HE-- HOW LONG HAS HE BEEN MISSING?
HE'S NOT "MISSING."
THEN--
"WHY ARE YOU LOOKING FOR HIM?"
HE'S NOT MISSING. HE'S HIDING.
FROM ME.
FROM YOU?
I'LL JUST-- I'M JUST GOING TO SAY THIS HOW IT IS.
PLEASE.
MY FAMILY. MY BROTHER AND MY DAD. THEY DON'T LIKE ME. THEY MIGHT HATE ME.
WHAT DID YOU DO?
ACCORDING TO THEM, I MURDERED A MAN IN COLD BLOOD, AND WENT TO JAIL FOR SELLING HEROIN TO KIDS.
OH.
I WAS FALSELY ACCUSED FOR THE HEROIN. BUT I DID GO TO JAIL FOR IT.
I WAS EXONERATED. I DIDN'T DO IT. BUT I DID GO TO JAIL.
WHO DID YOU NOT KILL?
THEY THOUGHT I KILLED MY BOY DANNY RAND. I DID NOT.
THAT WOULD EXPLAIN HIS BEING ALIVE.
EXACTLY. BUT MY DAD, HE'S, YOU KNOW, AN OLDER GUY READS SOMETHING IN THE PAPER...

DOESN'T
ENOUGH
KNOW IT
T TRUE.

THERE.
CK AND
WHITE.

AND
VENT TO
FOR THE
G THING.
T'S ALL
KNOWS
OF ME.

NO. YOU
SEE--

THEY'RE--WHAT
YOU'RE SAYING IS--
THEY'RE KIND OF GOING
OUT OF THEIR WAY TO
TELL YOU TO LEAVE
THEM ALONE.

RESPECT
IT. MAYBE
THEY'LL COME
AROUND.

I JUST WANT TO
LOOK MY DAD IN THE
EYE AND TELL HIM WHO
I REALLY AM. I WANT HIM
TO *HEAR* ME. I JUST
WANT HIM TO
HEAR ME.

WELL,
TO BE HONEST,
I SORTA HIRED
DAKOTA NORTH
FIRST.

OH.

SHE'S
KIND OF
A WACKY
CHICK.

I KNOW,
RIGHT?

EVEN FOR
US IN OUR CIRCLES.
SOMETHING WRONG
WITH HER.

HAT--THAT
N'T HAVING
POSITIVE
FFECT ON
HIM.

N FACT,
HINK IT DID
OPPOSITE.
THINK IT
ARRASSES
#$%^ OUT
OF HIM.

THANK YOU.
EVERYONE'S ALL
IN LOVE WITH
HER AND I'M LIKE,
HELLO?

AND I
COULDN'T FIND
JESSICA DREW,
SO...

I
THOUGHT,
HEY...

AND AS
AS I CAN
L, I THINK
THINKS
AT'S THE
LIE.

THINK HE
KS MY NEW
IS THE LIE
COVER UP
BAD GUY
THINKS I
ALLY AM.

HE MAY
NOT BE
ABLE TO.

I JUST
WANT TO SAY
THE WORDS.
I WANT TO
KNOW THAT
I DID.

O, SO MY
ROTHER...

E KEEPS
NG MY DAD
MOVING HIM
OUND AND
Y'RE HIDING
ROM ME.

ERY TIME
ATCH UP TO
EM SOME-
HING GOES
WRONG.

WELL,
I'M GLAD I
WAS ON THE LIST
SOMEWHERE.

WELL,
AYBE, AND
NOW THIS IS
RD TO HEAR,
IT MAYBE
JST LEAVE
THEM
ALONE.

OKAY,
OKAY...LISTEN,
I'M FLATTERED
YOU THOUGHT
OF ME.

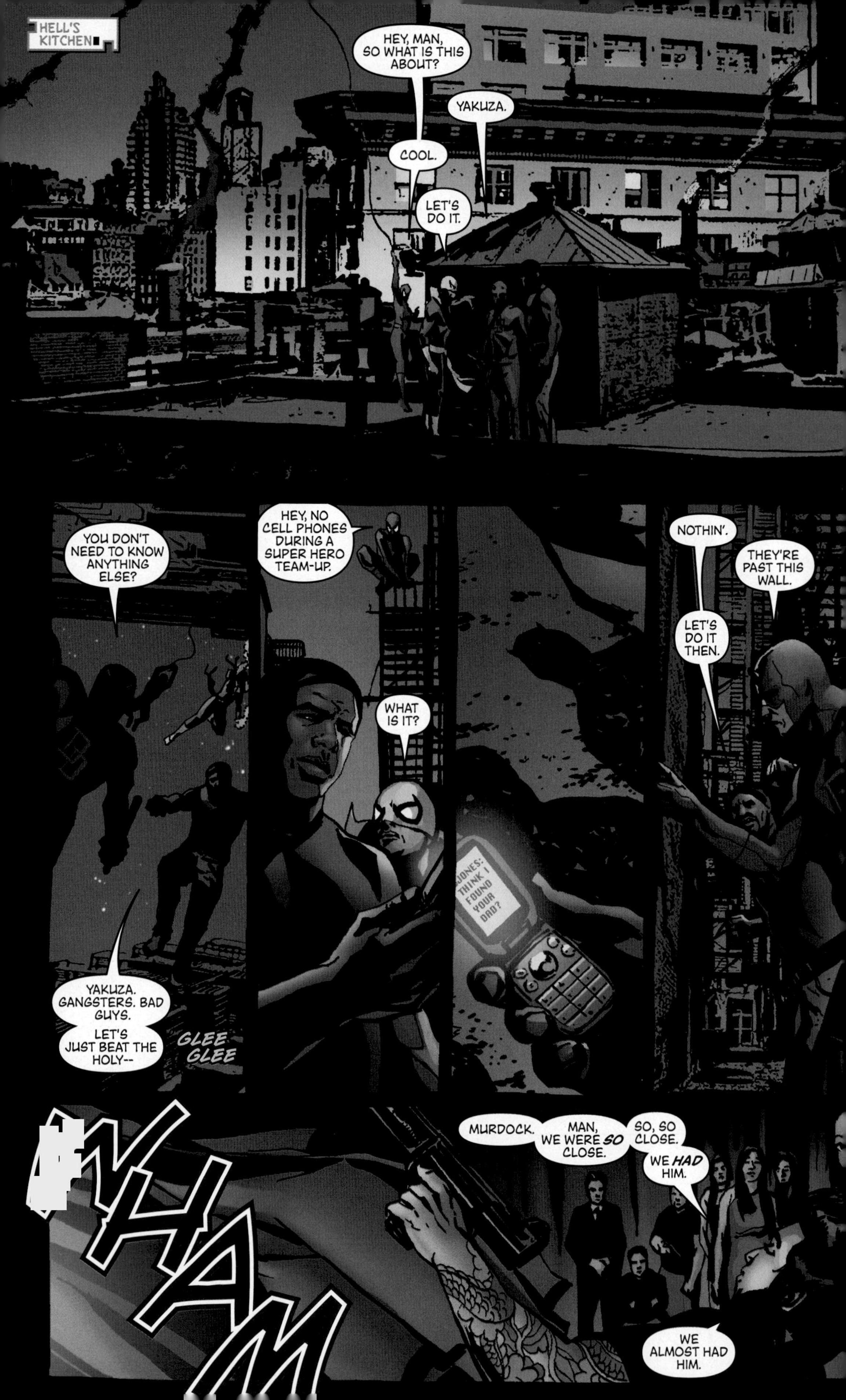

HELL'S KITCHEN
HEY, MAN, SO WHAT IS THIS ABOUT?
YAKUZA.
COOL.
LET'S DO IT.
YOU DON'T NEED TO KNOW ANYTHING ELSE?
YAKUZA. GANGSTERS. BAD GUYS.
LET'S JUST BEAT THE HOLY--
GLEE GLEE
HEY, NO CELL PHONES DURING A SUPER HERO TEAM-UP.
WHAT IS IT?
JONES: THINK I FOUND YOUR DAD?
NOTHIN'.
THEY'RE PAST THIS WALL.
LET'S DO IT THEN.
WHAM
MURDOCK.
MAN, WE WERE *SO* CLOSE.
SO, SO CLOSE.
WE *HAD* HIM.
WE ALMOST HAD HIM.

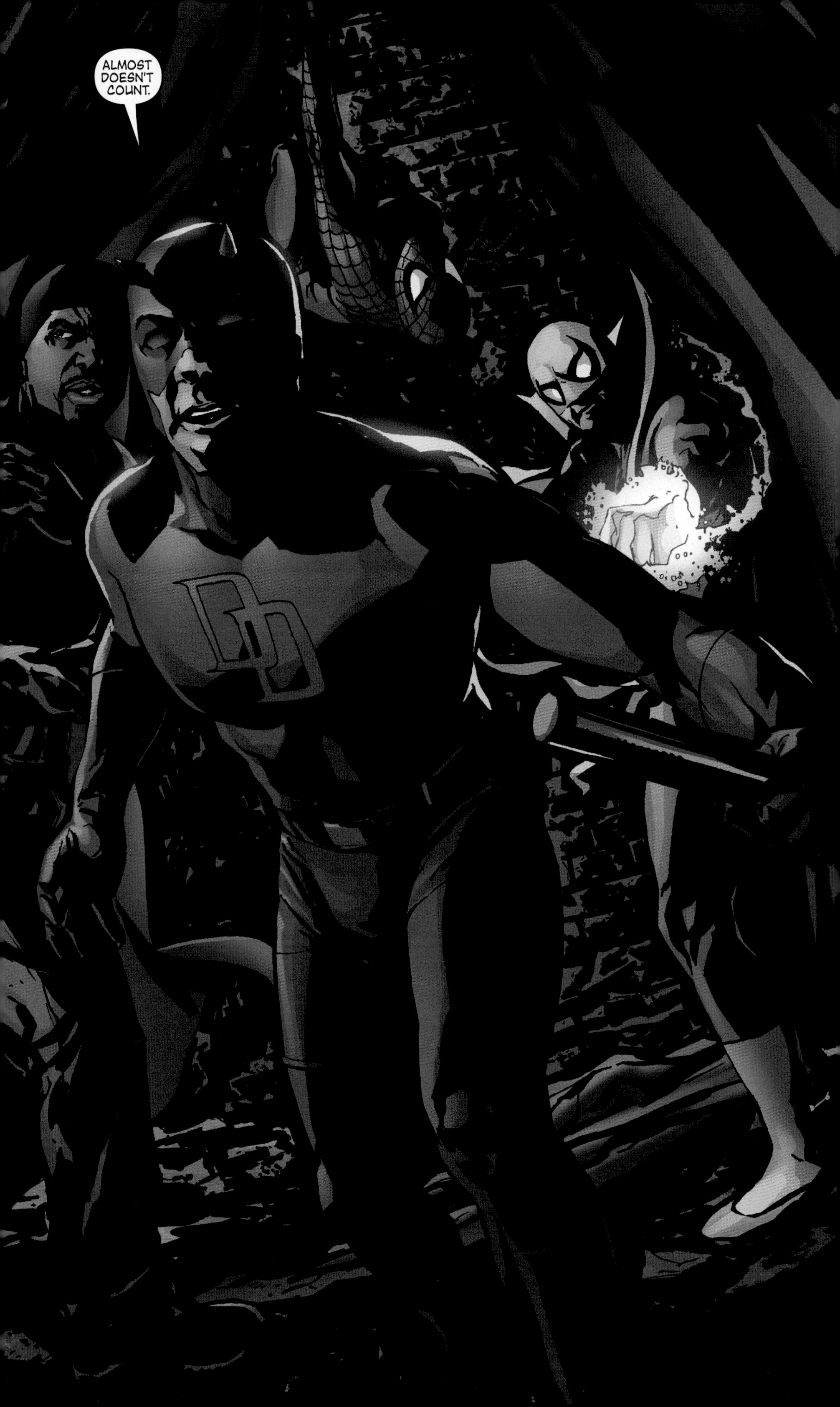
ALMOST DOESN'T COUNT.

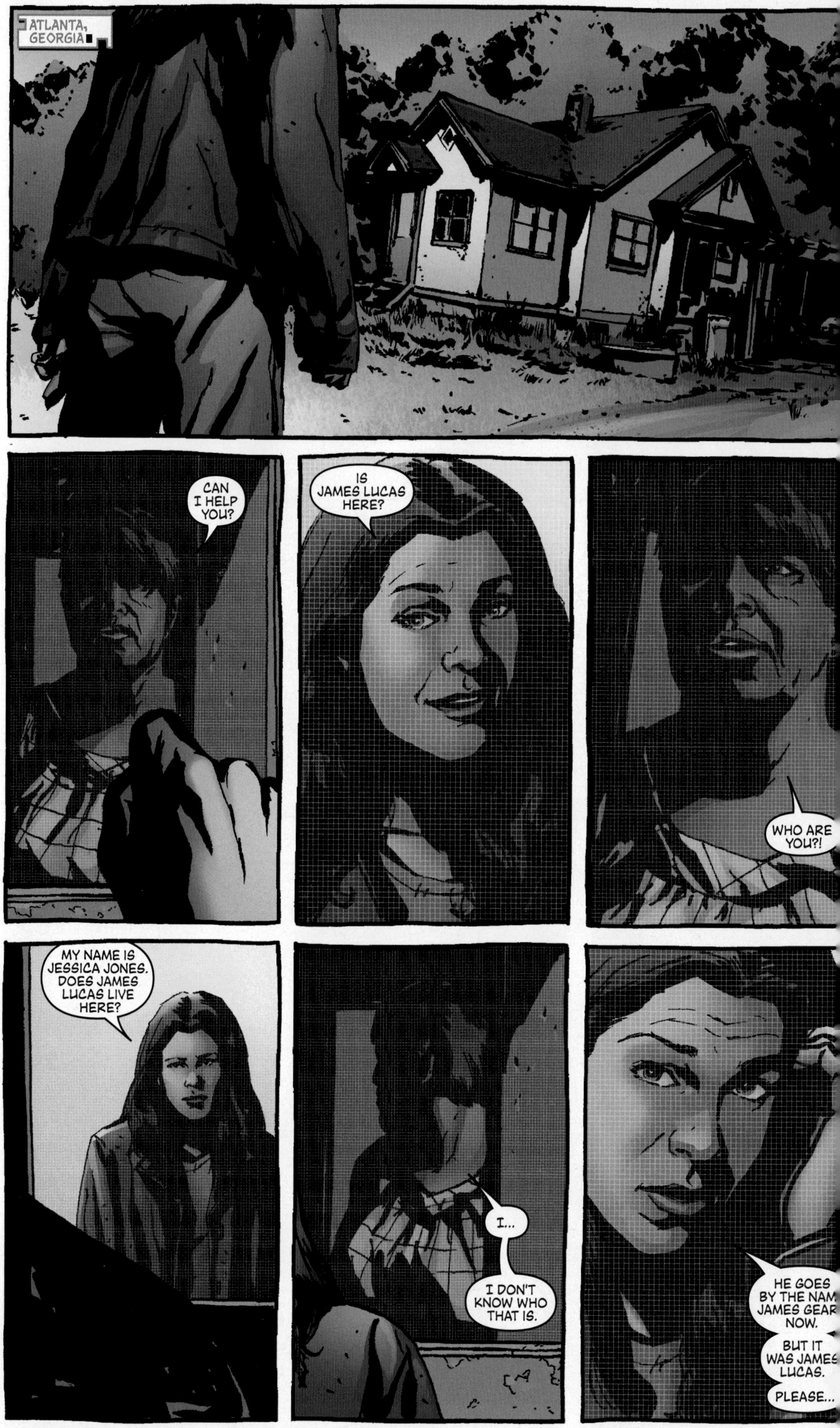
ATLANTA, GEORGIA
CAN I HELP YOU?
IS JAMES LUCAS HERE?
WHO ARE YOU?!
MY NAME IS JESSICA JONES. DOES JAMES LUCAS LIVE HERE?
I...
I DON'T KNOW WHO THAT IS.
HE GOES BY THE NAM JAMES GEAR NOW.
BUT IT WAS JAMES LUCAS.
PLEASE...

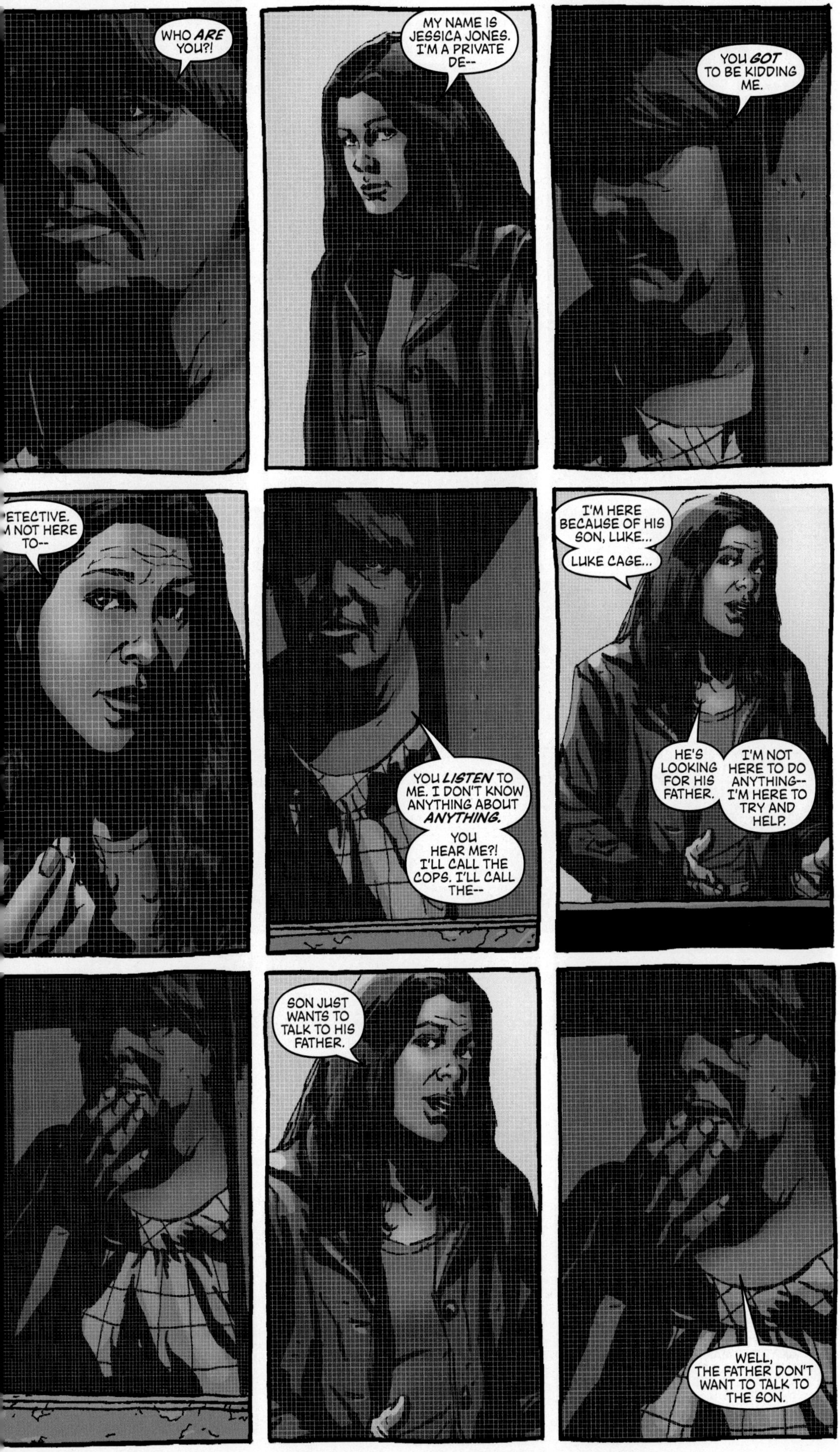
WHO ARE YOU?!
MY NAME IS JESSICA JONES. I'M A PRIVATE DE--
YOU GOT TO BE KIDDING ME.
ETECTIVE. M NOT HERE TO--
YOU LISTEN TO ME. I DON'T KNOW ANYTHING ABOUT ANYTHING.
YOU HEAR ME?! I'LL CALL THE COPS. I'LL CALL THE--
I'M HERE BECAUSE OF HIS SON, LUKE...
LUKE CAGE...
HE'S LOOKING FOR HIS FATHER.
I'M NOT HERE TO DO ANYTHING-- I'M HERE TO TRY AND HELP.
SON JUST WANTS TO TALK TO HIS FATHER.
WELL, THE FATHER DON'T WANT TO TALK TO THE SON.

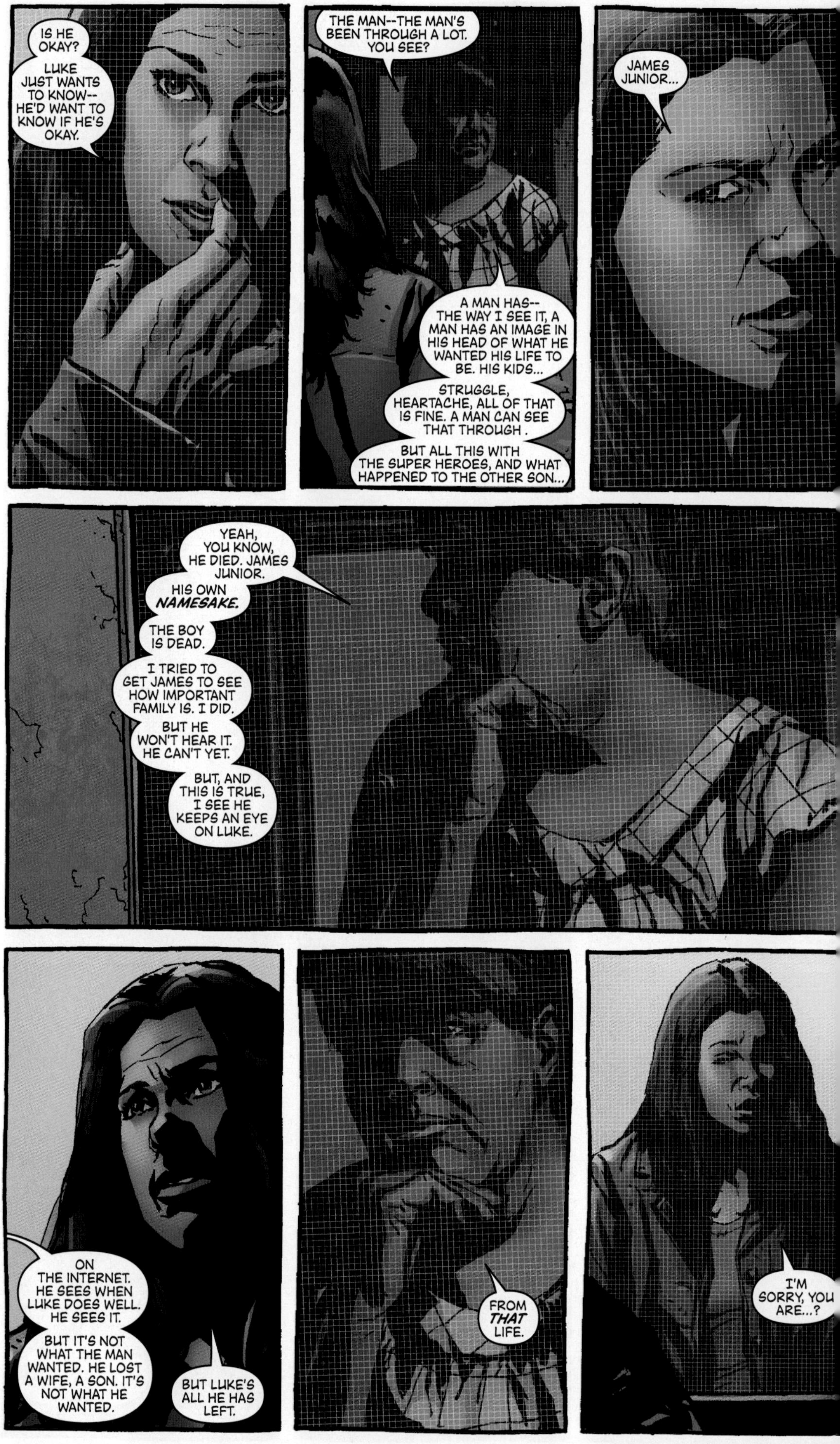
IS HE OKAY?
LUKE JUST WANTS TO KNOW-- HE'D WANT TO KNOW IF HE'S OKAY.
THE MAN--THE MAN'S BEEN THROUGH A LOT. YOU SEE?
A MAN HAS-- THE WAY I SEE IT, A MAN HAS AN IMAGE IN HIS HEAD OF WHAT HE WANTED HIS LIFE TO BE. HIS KIDS...
STRUGGLE, HEARTACHE, ALL OF THAT IS FINE. A MAN CAN SEE THAT THROUGH .
BUT ALL THIS WITH THE SUPER HEROES, AND WHAT HAPPENED TO THE OTHER SON...
JAMES JUNIOR...
YEAH, YOU KNOW, HE DIED. JAMES JUNIOR.
HIS OWN *NAMESAKE.*
THE BOY IS DEAD.
I TRIED TO GET JAMES TO SEE HOW IMPORTANT FAMILY IS. I DID.
BUT HE WON'T HEAR IT. HE CAN'T YET.
BUT, AND THIS IS TRUE, I SEE HE KEEPS AN EYE ON LUKE.
ON THE INTERNET. HE SEES WHEN LUKE DOES WELL. HE SEES IT.
BUT IT'S NOT WHAT THE MAN WANTED. HE LOST A WIFE, A SON. IT'S NOT WHAT HE WANTED.
BUT LUKE'S ALL HE HAS LEFT.
FROM *THAT* LIFE.
I'M SORRY, YOU ARE...?

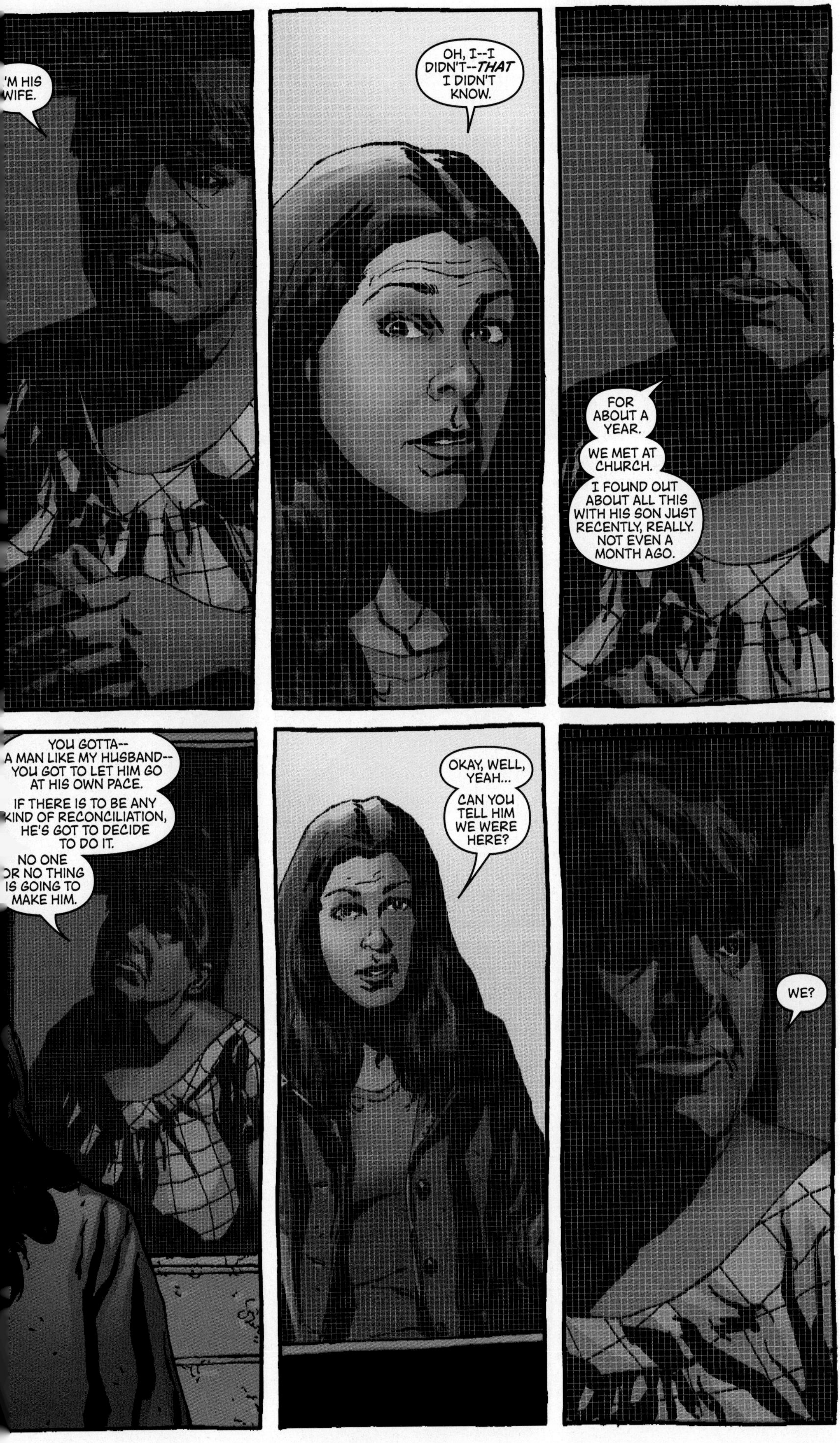
'M HIS WIFE.
OH, I--I DIDN'T--THAT I DIDN'T KNOW.
FOR ABOUT A YEAR.
WE MET AT CHURCH.
I FOUND OUT ABOUT ALL THIS WITH HIS SON JUST RECENTLY, REALLY. NOT EVEN A MONTH AGO.
YOU GOTTA-- A MAN LIKE MY HUSBAND-- YOU GOT TO LET HIM GO AT HIS OWN PACE.
IF THERE IS TO BE ANY KIND OF RECONCILIATION, HE'S GOT TO DECIDE TO DO IT.
NO ONE OR NO THING IS GOING TO MAKE HIM.
OKAY, WELL, YEAH...
CAN YOU TELL HIM WE WERE HERE?
WE?

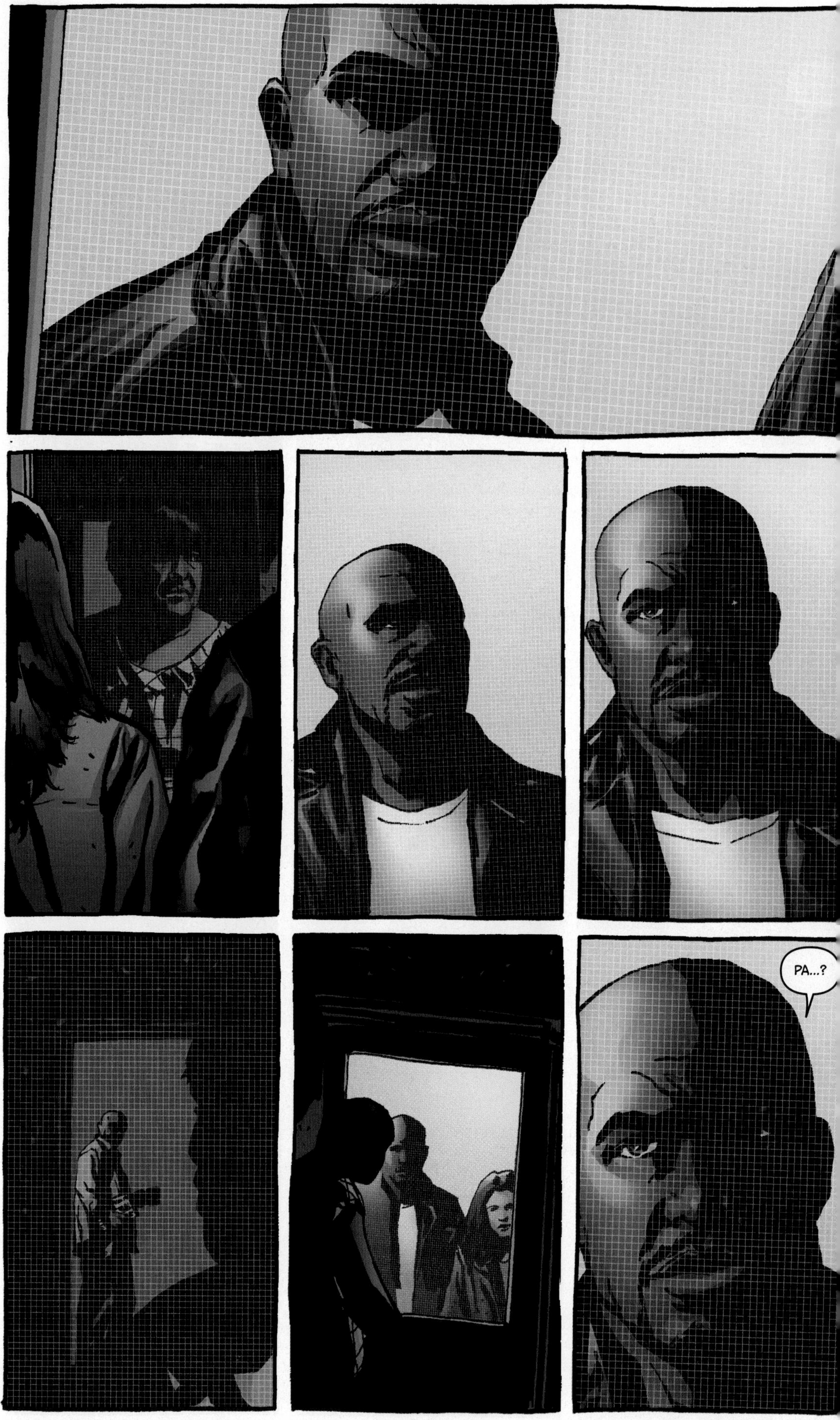
PA...?

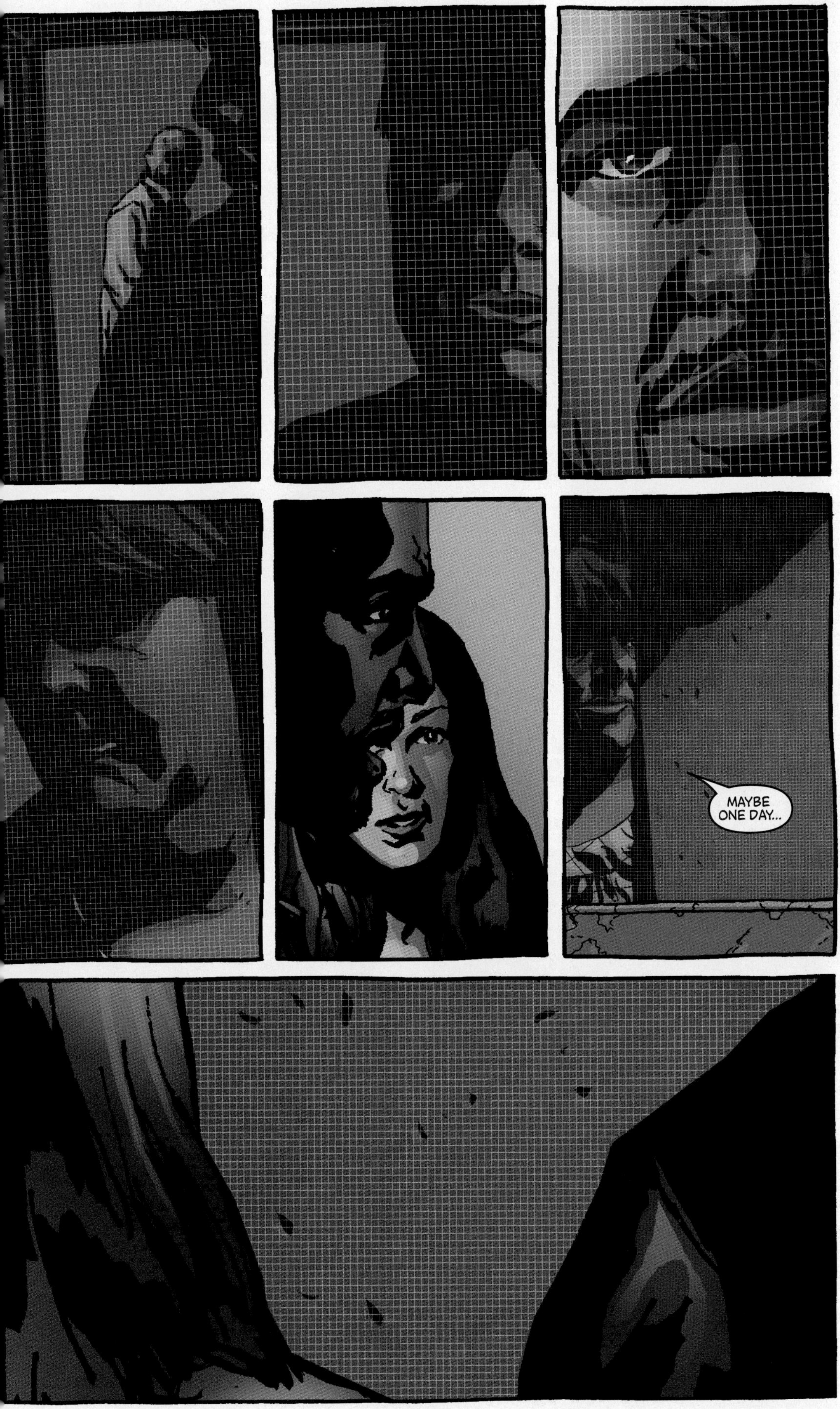
MAYBE
ONE DAY...

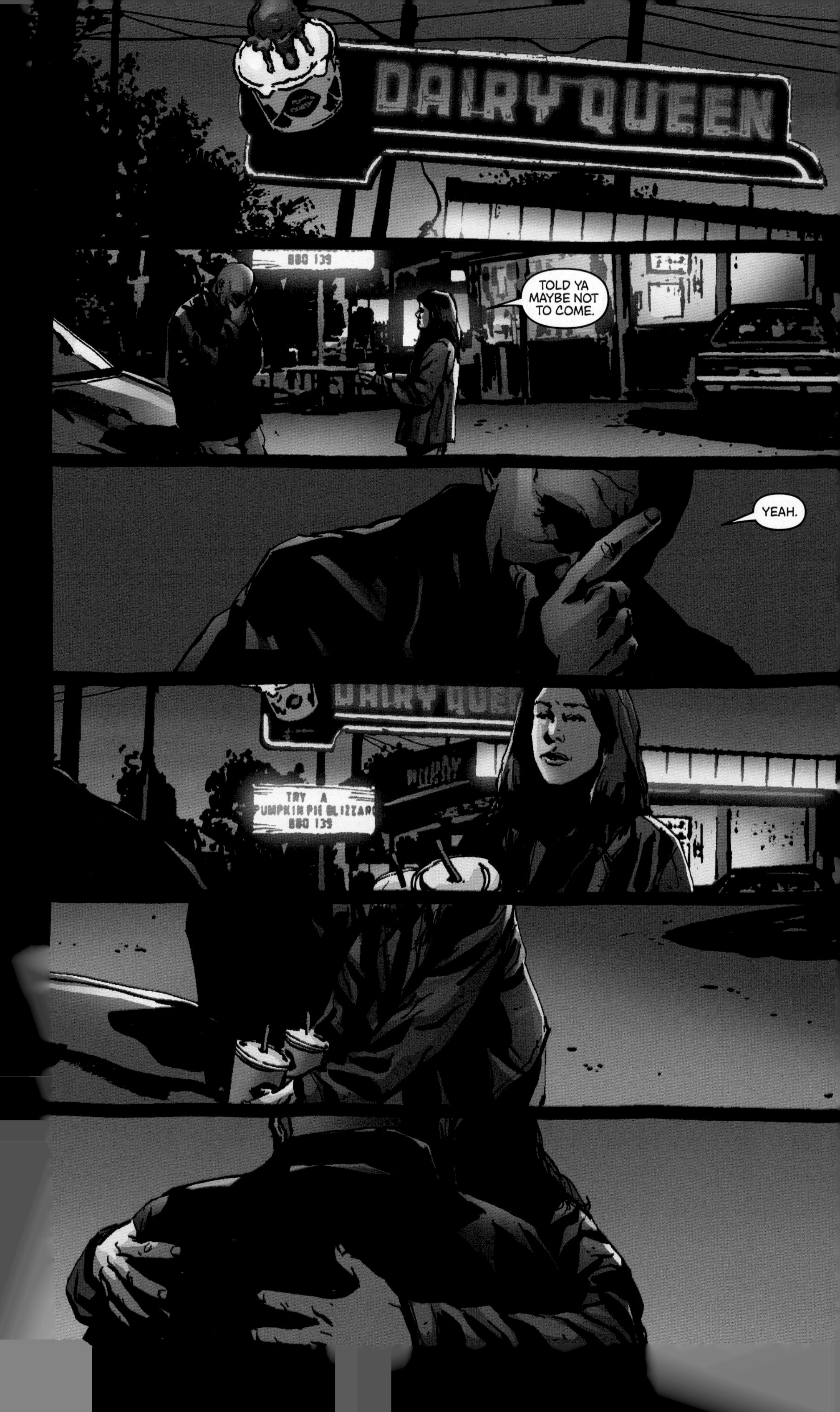
DAIRY QUEEN
TOLD YA MAYBE NOT TO COME.
YEAH.

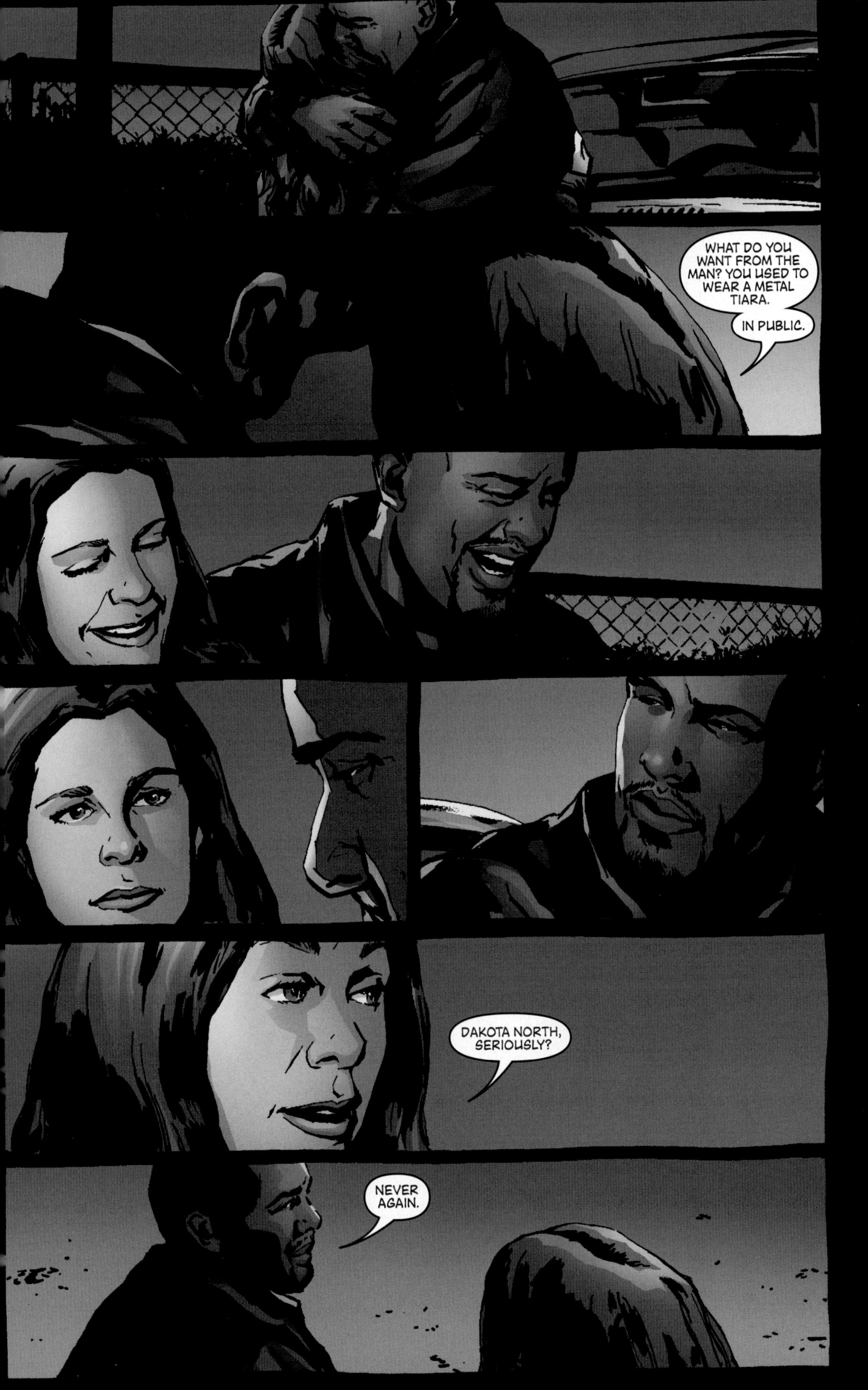
WHAT DO YOU WANT FROM THE MAN? YOU USED TO WEAR A METAL TIARA.
IN PUBLIC.
DAKOTA NORTH, SERIOUSLY?
NEVER AGAIN.

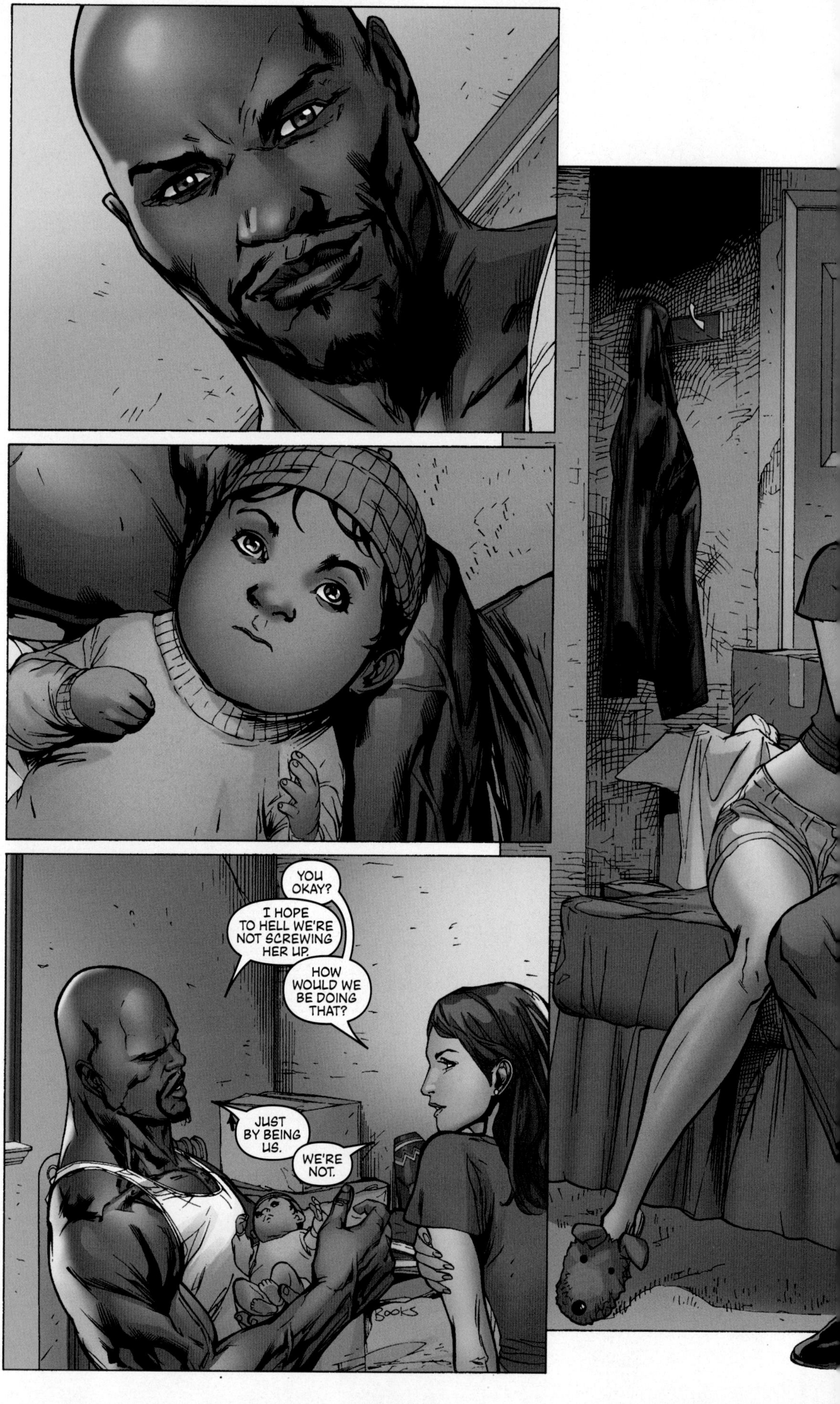
YOU OKAY?
I HOPE TO HELL WE'RE NOT SCREWING HER UP.
HOW WOULD WE BE DOING THAT?
JUST BY BEING US.
WE'RE NOT.
BOOKS

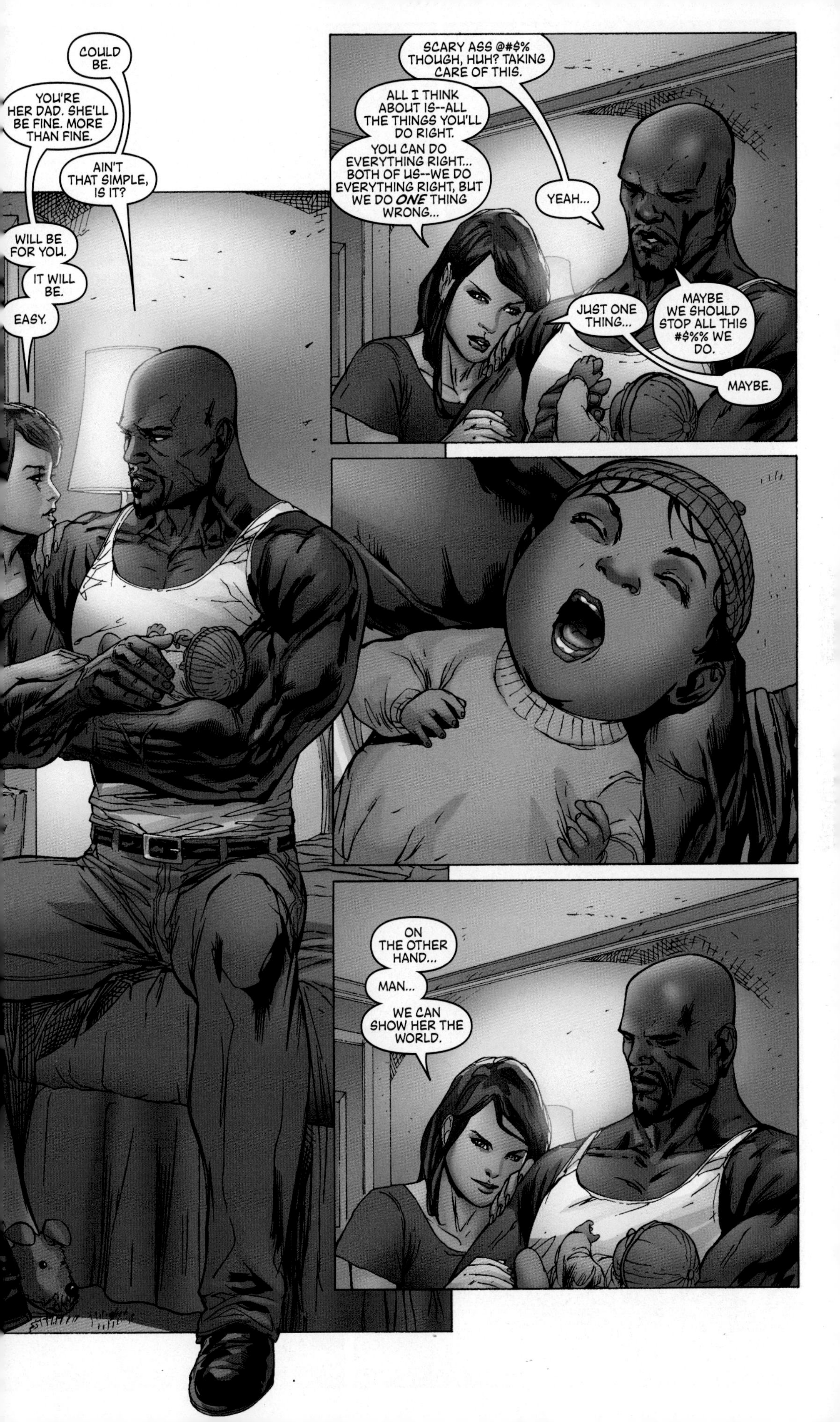
COULD BE.
YOU'RE HER DAD. SHE'LL BE FINE. MORE THAN FINE.
AIN'T THAT SIMPLE, IS IT?
WILL BE FOR YOU.
IT WILL BE.
EASY.
SCARY ASS @#$% THOUGH, HUH? TAKING CARE OF THIS.
ALL I THINK ABOUT IS--ALL THE THINGS YOU'LL DO RIGHT.
YOU CAN DO EVERYTHING RIGHT... BOTH OF US--WE DO EVERYTHING RIGHT, BUT WE DO ONE THING WRONG...
YEAH...
JUST ONE THING...
MAYBE WE SHOULD STOP ALL THIS #$%% WE DO.
MAYBE.
ON THE OTHER HAND...
MAN...
WE CAN SHOW HER THE WORLD.

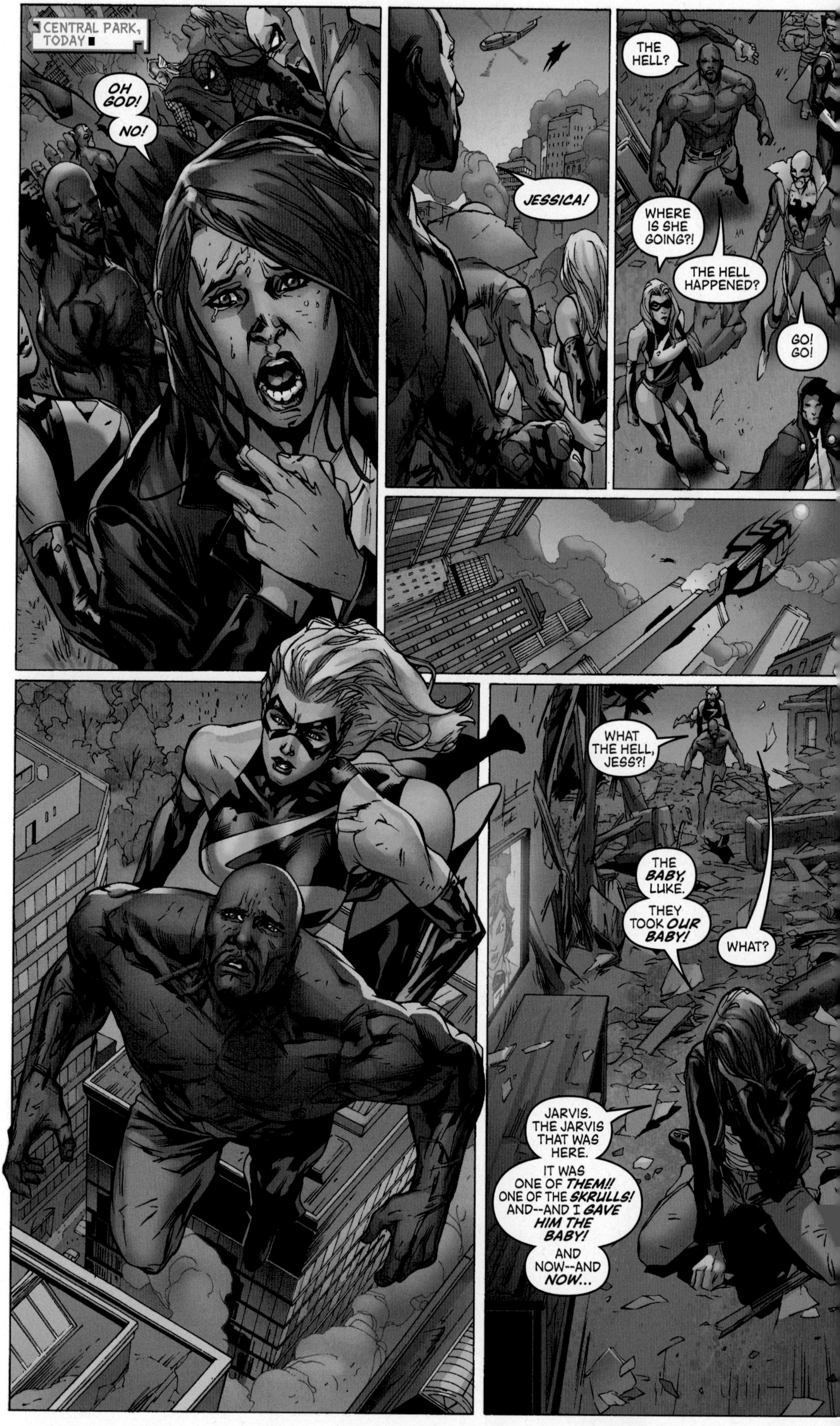
CENTRAL PARK, TODAY
OH GOD!
NO!
JESSICA!
THE HELL?
WHERE IS SHE GOING?!
THE HELL HAPPENED?
GO! GO!
WHAT THE HELL, JESS?!
THE BABY, LUKE.
THEY TOOK OUR BABY!
WHAT?
JARVIS. THE JARVIS THAT WAS HERE.
IT WAS ONE OF THEM!! ONE OF THE SKRULLS! AND--AND I GAVE HIM THE BABY!
AND NOW--AND NOW...

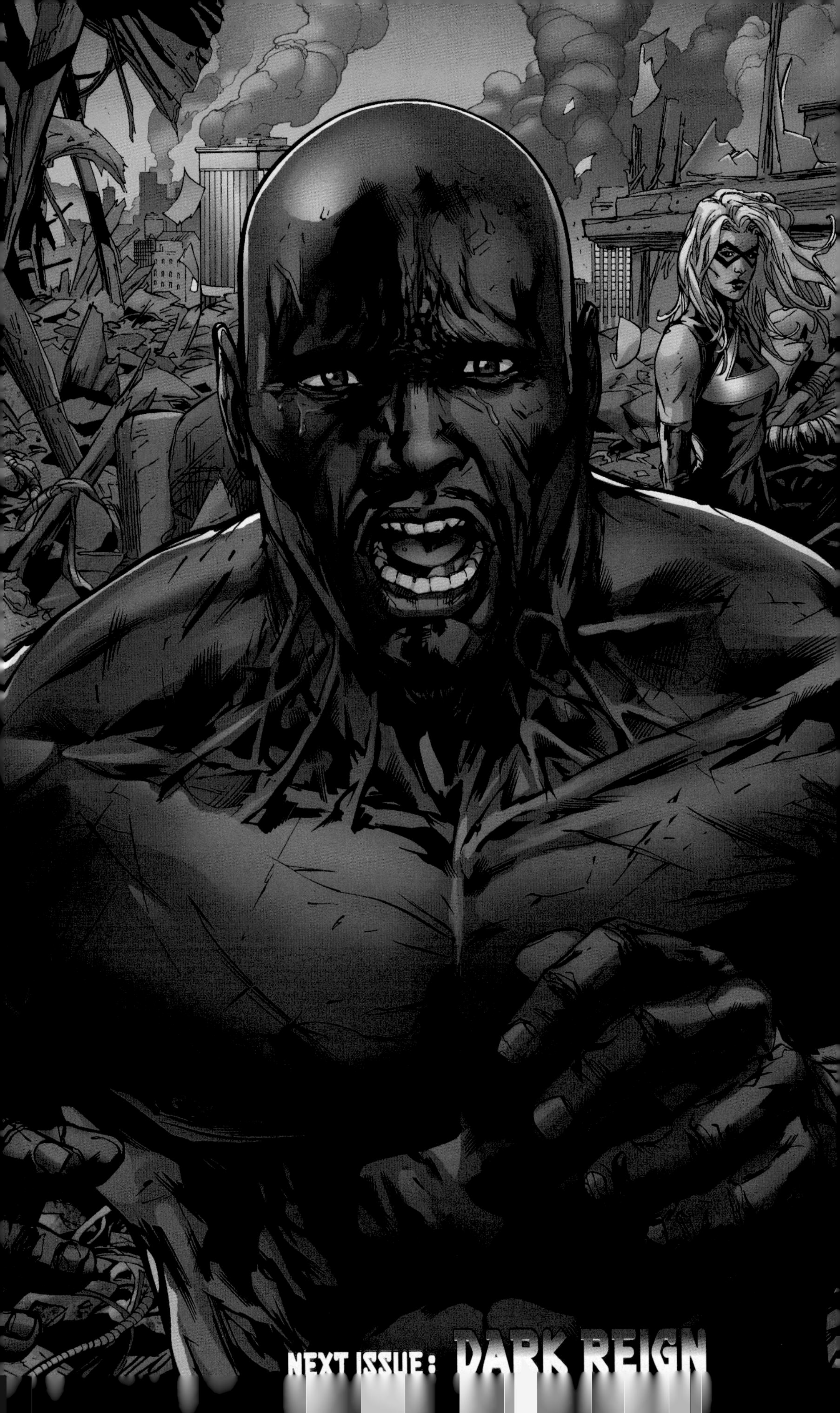
NEXT ISSUE: DARK REIGN

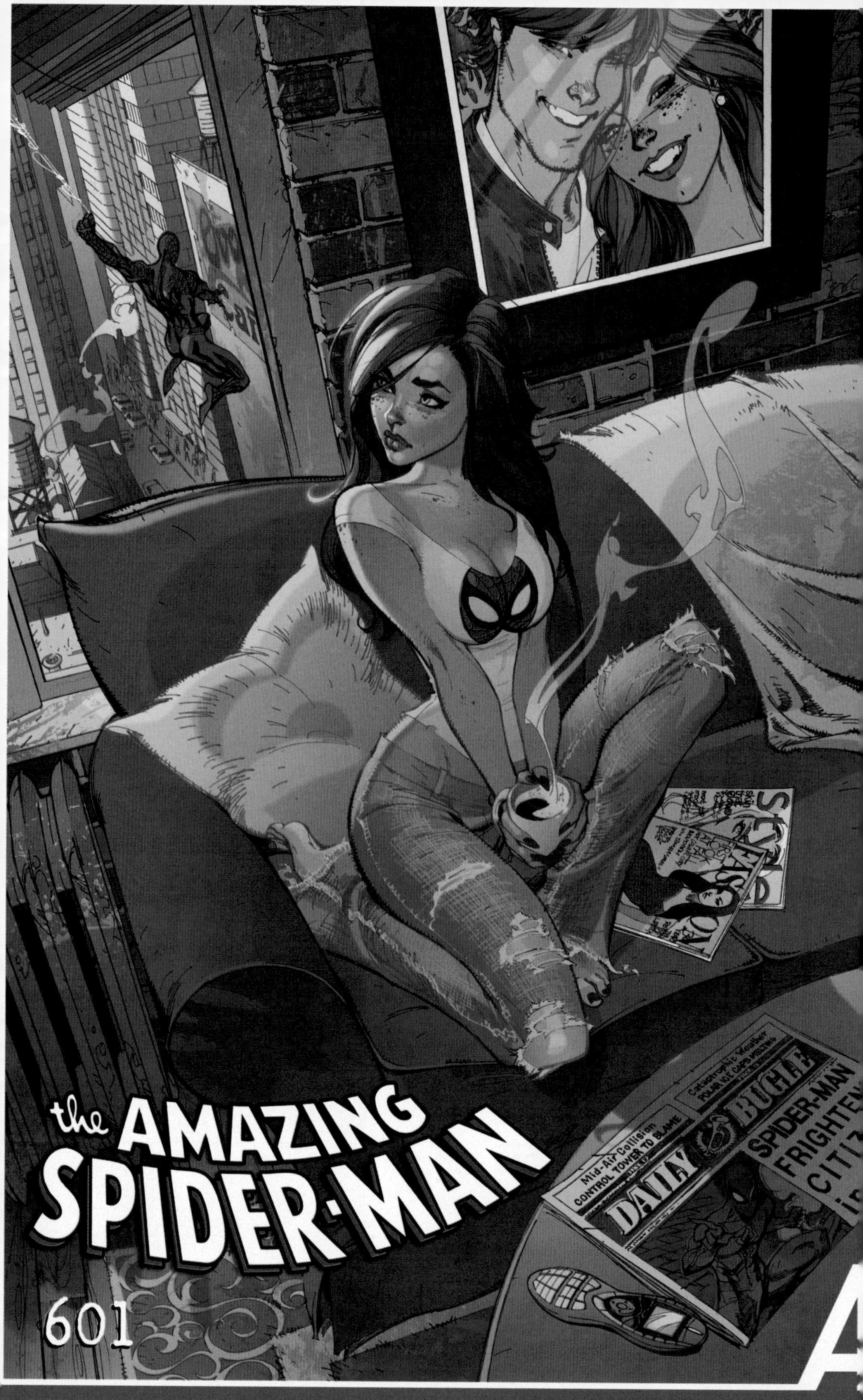

the AMAZING
SPIDER-MAN
601
Mid-Air Collision
CONTROL TOWER TO BLAME
Catastrophic Weather
POLAR ICE CAPS MELTING
DAILY
SPIDER-MAN

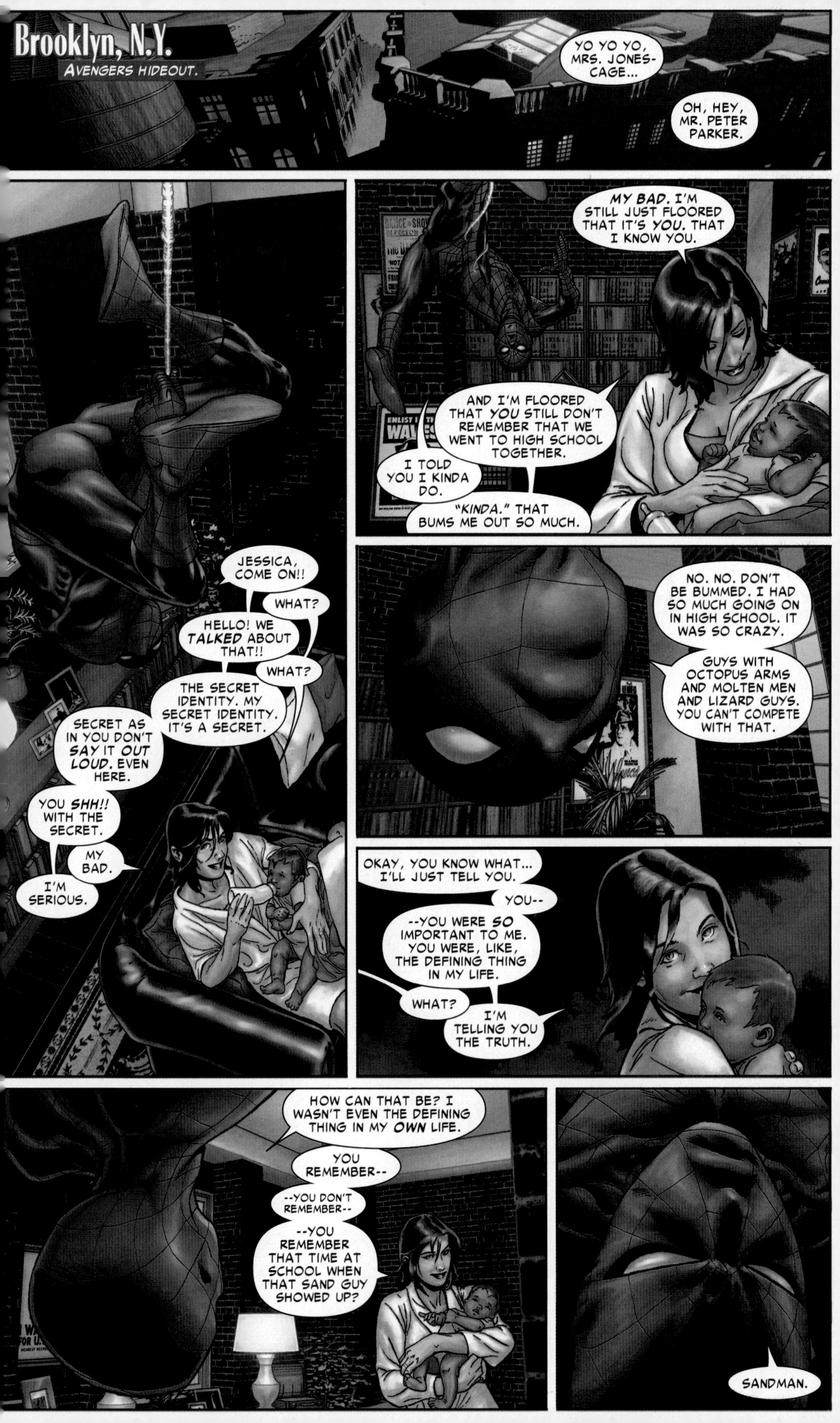
Brooklyn, N.Y.
Avengers hideout.
YO YO YO, MRS. JONES-CAGE...
OH, HEY, MR. PETER PARKER.
JESSICA, COME ON!!
WHAT?
HELLO! WE TALKED ABOUT THAT!!
WHAT?
THE SECRET IDENTITY. MY SECRET IDENTITY. IT'S A SECRET.
SECRET AS IN YOU DON'T SAY IT OUT LOUD. EVEN HERE.
YOU SHH!! WITH THE SECRET.
MY BAD.
I'M SERIOUS.
MY BAD. I'M STILL JUST FLOORED THAT IT'S YOU. THAT I KNOW YOU.
AND I'M FLOORED THAT YOU STILL DON'T REMEMBER THAT WE WENT TO HIGH SCHOOL TOGETHER.
I TOLD YOU I KINDA DO.
"KINDA." THAT BUMS ME OUT SO MUCH.
NO. NO. DON'T BE BUMMED. I HAD SO MUCH GOING ON IN HIGH SCHOOL. IT WAS SO CRAZY.
GUYS WITH OCTOPUS ARMS AND MOLTEN MEN AND LIZARD GUYS. YOU CAN'T COMPETE WITH THAT.
OKAY, YOU KNOW WHAT... I'LL JUST TELL YOU.
YOU--
--YOU WERE SO IMPORTANT TO ME. YOU WERE, LIKE, THE DEFINING THING IN MY LIFE.
WHAT?
I'M TELLING YOU THE TRUTH.
HOW CAN THAT BE? I WASN'T EVEN THE DEFINING THING IN MY OWN LIFE.
YOU REMEMBER--
--YOU DON'T REMEMBER--
--YOU REMEMBER THAT TIME AT SCHOOL WHEN THAT SAND GUY SHOWED UP?
SANDMAN.

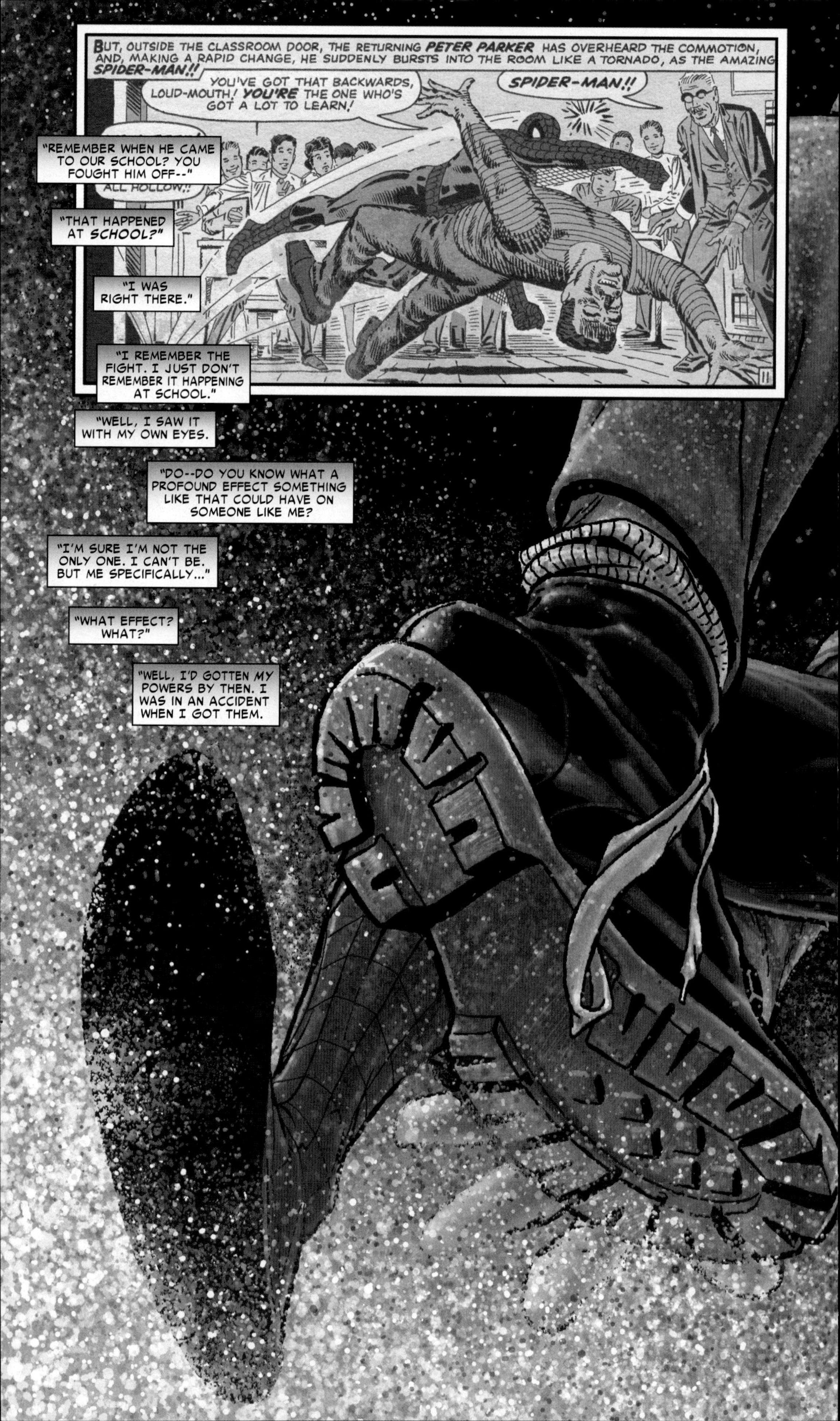
BUT, OUTSIDE THE CLASSROOM DOOR, THE RETURNING PETER PARKER HAS OVERHEARD THE COMMOTION, AND, MAKING A RAPID CHANGE, HE SUDDENLY BURSTS INTO THE ROOM LIKE A TORNADO, AS THE AMAZING SPIDER-MAN!!
YOU'VE GOT THAT BACKWARDS, LOUD-MOUTH! YOU'RE THE ONE WHO'S GOT A LOT TO LEARN!
SPIDER-MAN!!
"REMEMBER WHEN HE CAME TO OUR SCHOOL? YOU FOUGHT HIM OFF--"
"THAT HAPPENED AT SCHOOL?"
"I WAS RIGHT THERE."
"I REMEMBER THE FIGHT. I JUST DON'T REMEMBER IT HAPPENING AT SCHOOL."
"WELL, I SAW IT WITH MY OWN EYES.
"DO--DO YOU KNOW WHAT A PROFOUND EFFECT SOMETHING LIKE THAT COULD HAVE ON SOMEONE LIKE ME?
"I'M SURE I'M NOT THE ONLY ONE. I CAN'T BE. BUT ME SPECIFICALLY..."
"WHAT EFFECT? WHAT?"
"WELL, I'D GOTTEN MY POWERS BY THEN. I WAS IN AN ACCIDENT WHEN I GOT THEM.

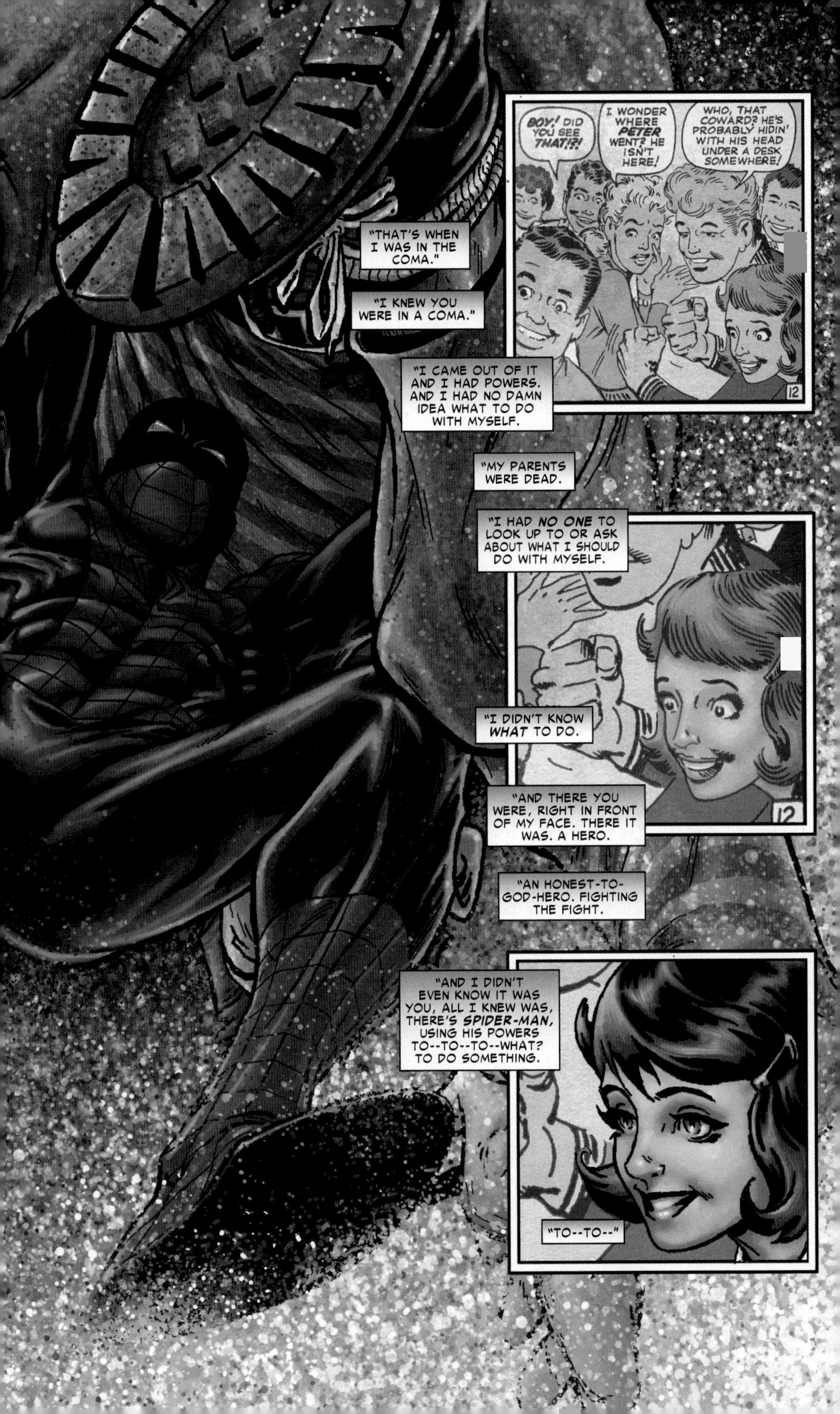
BOY! DID YOU SEE THAT!?!
I WONDER WHERE PETER WENT? HE ISN'T HERE!
WHO, THAT COWARD? HE'S PROBABLY HIDIN' WITH HIS HEAD UNDER A DESK SOMEWHERE!
12
"THAT'S WHEN I WAS IN THE COMA."
"I KNEW YOU WERE IN A COMA."
"I CAME OUT OF IT AND I HAD POWERS. AND I HAD NO DAMN IDEA WHAT TO DO WITH MYSELF.
"MY PARENTS WERE DEAD.
"I HAD NO ONE TO LOOK UP TO OR ASK ABOUT WHAT I SHOULD DO WITH MYSELF.
"I DIDN'T KNOW WHAT TO DO.
12
"AND THERE YOU WERE, RIGHT IN FRONT OF MY FACE. THERE IT WAS. A HERO.
"AN HONEST-TO-GOD-HERO. FIGHTING THE FIGHT.
"AND I DIDN'T EVEN KNOW IT WAS YOU, ALL I KNEW WAS, THERE'S SPIDER-MAN, USING HIS POWERS TO--TO--TO--WHAT? TO DO SOMETHING.
"TO--TO--"

I DON'T KNOW THE WORDS I'M LOOKING FOR.

I DO...

WITH GREAT POWER THERE MUST ALSO COME GREAT RESPONSIBILITY.

OH, THAT'S GOOD.

I KNOW.

THAT'S--THAT'S-- DID YOU JUST MAKE THAT UP?

NO. NO, I KIND OF LIVE MY LIFE BY IT.

THAT'S WHAT I NEEDED!

WHEN I WAS A KID...I NEEDED SOMEONE LIKE YOU TO SHOW ME THAT.

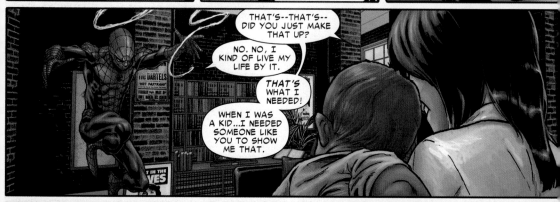

"I MADE MY FIRST COSTUME BECAUSE OF YOU."

"WOW."

"AND I DIDN'T EVEN KNOW ABOUT THIS 'POWER AND RESPONSIBILITY' THING."

"I KNEW IT IN THEORY, BUT I DIDN'T HAVE THE WORDS."

IT'S GOOD, RIGHT?

CAN I USE IT?

YOU CAN.

THAT'S SOMETHING TO TELL MY KID. THAT'S SOMETHING YOU COULD LIVE BY.

AND I DO LIVE BY IT.

ON MY BETTER DAYS...

YOU COULD START A RELIGION BASED ON THAT!

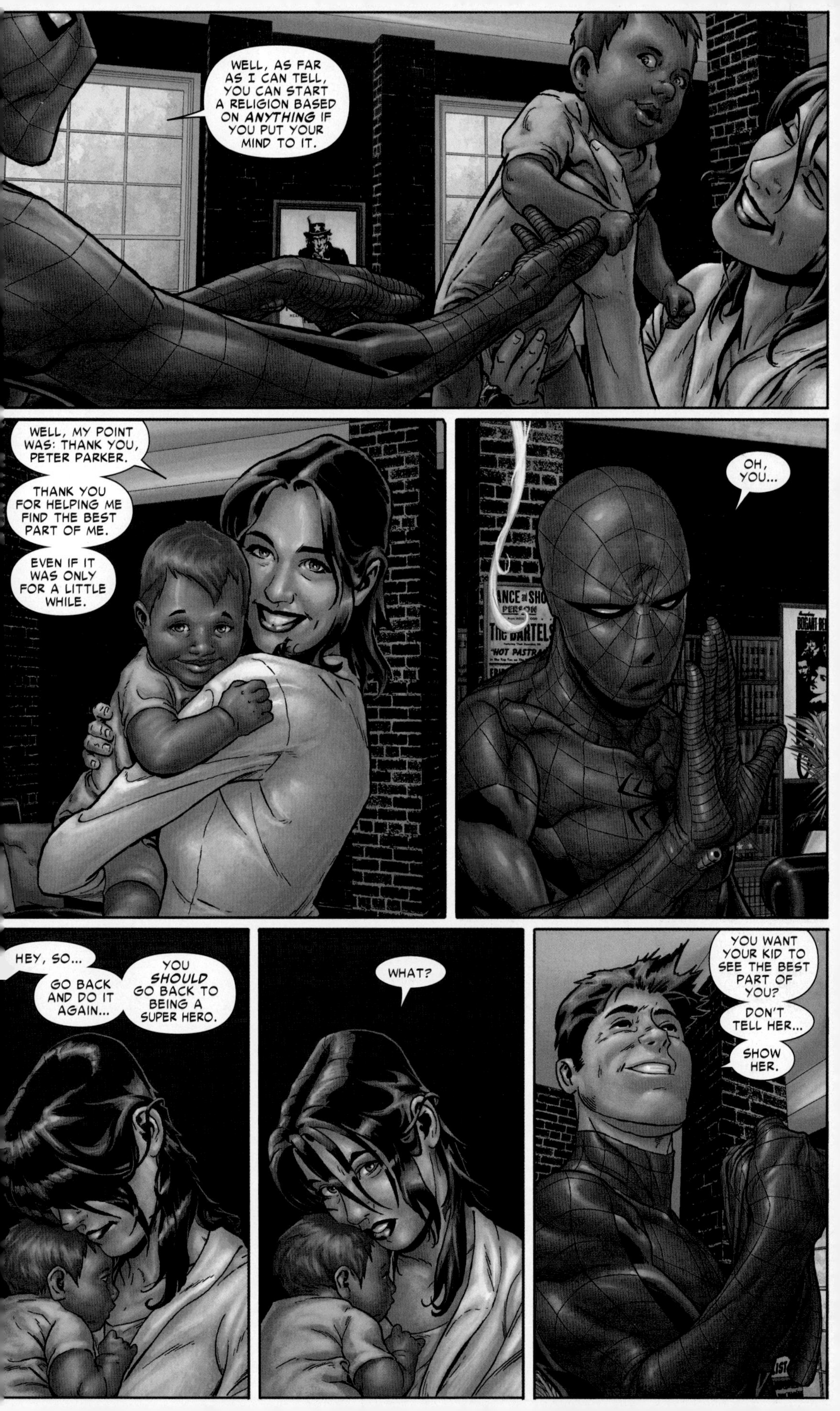
WELL, AS FAR AS I CAN TELL, YOU CAN START A RELIGION BASED ON *ANYTHING* IF YOU PUT YOUR MIND TO IT.
WELL, MY POINT WAS: THANK YOU, PETER PARKER.
THANK YOU FOR HELPING ME FIND THE BEST PART OF ME.
EVEN IF IT WAS ONLY FOR A LITTLE WHILE.
OH, YOU...
HEY, SO...
GO BACK AND DO IT AGAIN...
YOU *SHOULD* GO BACK TO BEING A SUPER HERO.
WHAT?
YOU WANT YOUR KID TO SEE THE BEST PART OF YOU?
DON'T TELL HER...
SHOW HER.

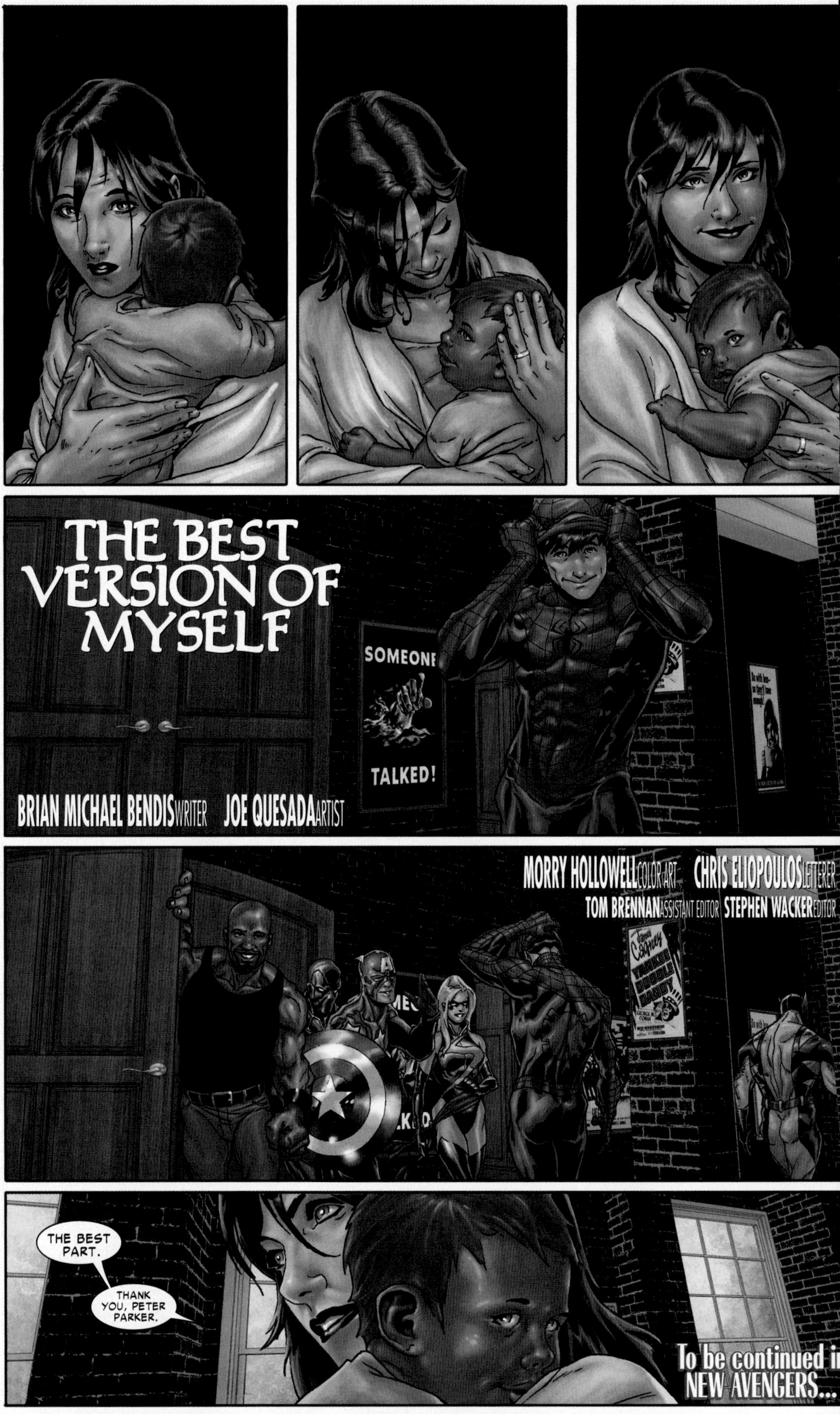
THE BEST VERSION OF MYSELF
SOMEONE
TALKED!
BRIAN MICHAEL BENDIS WRITER JOE QUESADA ARTIST
MORRY HOLLOWELL COLOR ART CHRIS ELIOPOULOS LETTERER
TOM BRENNAN ASSISTANT EDITOR STEPHEN WACKER EDITOR
THE BEST PART.
THANK YOU, PETER PARKER.
To be continued in NEW AVENGERS...

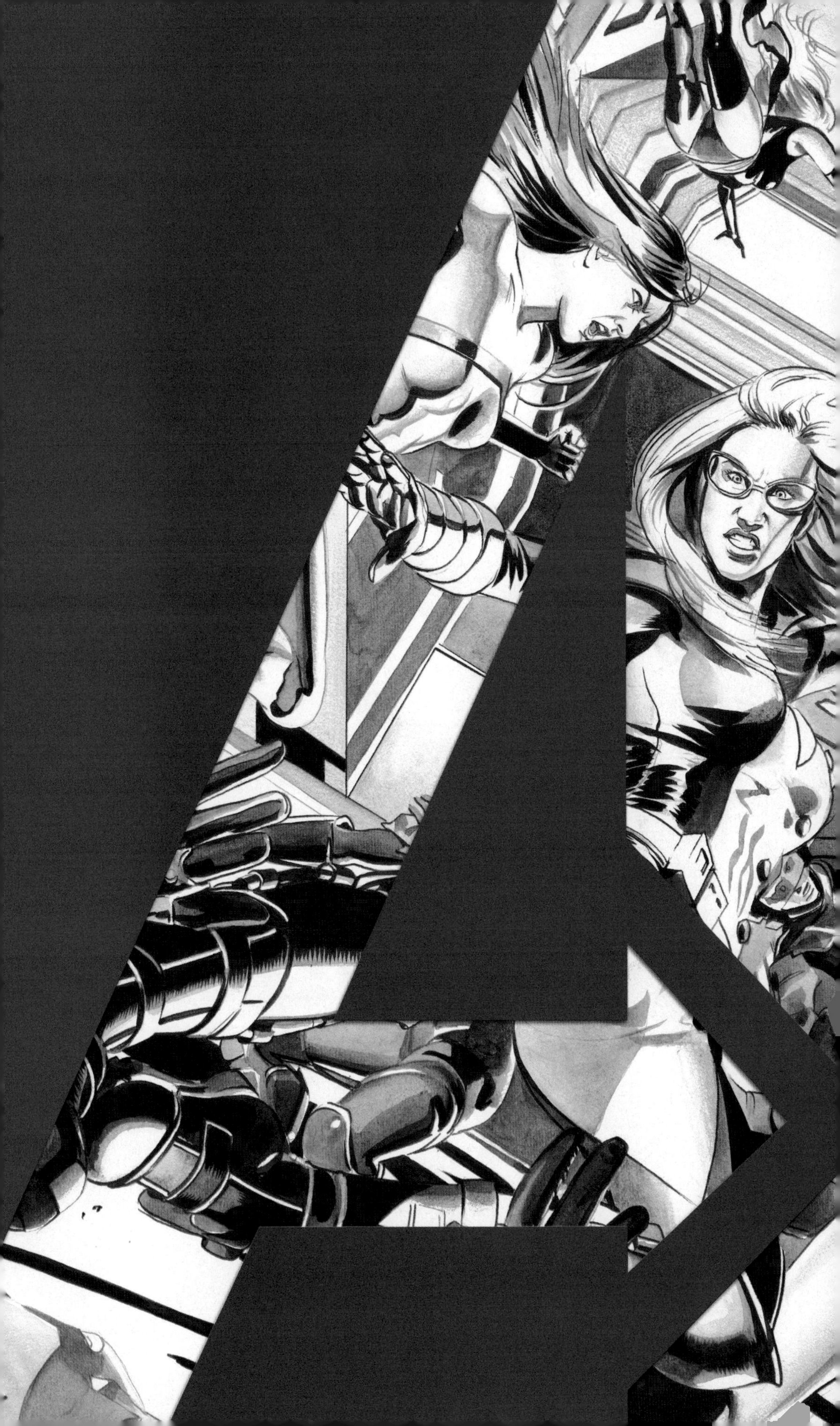

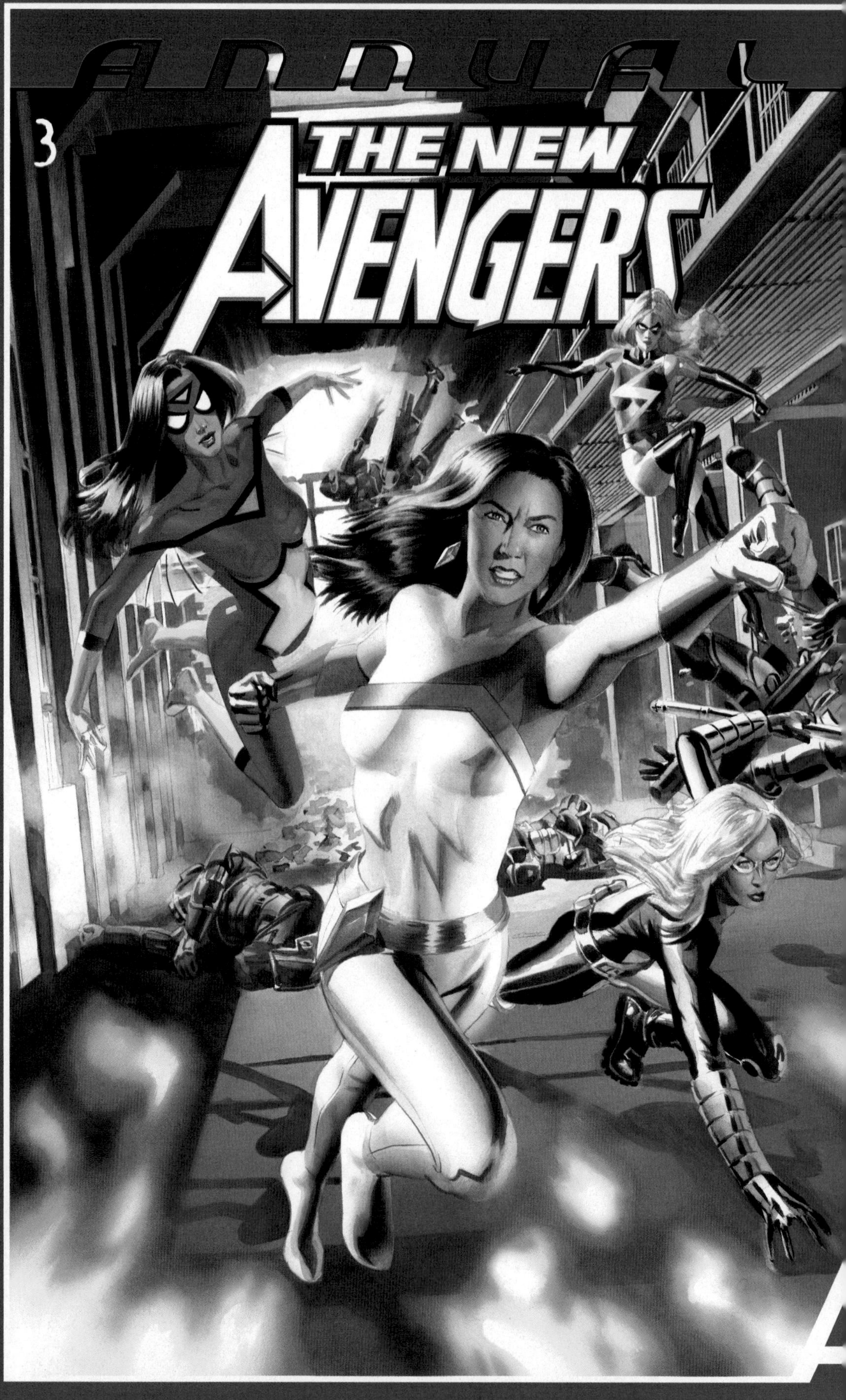
ANNUAL
3
THE NEW AVENGERS

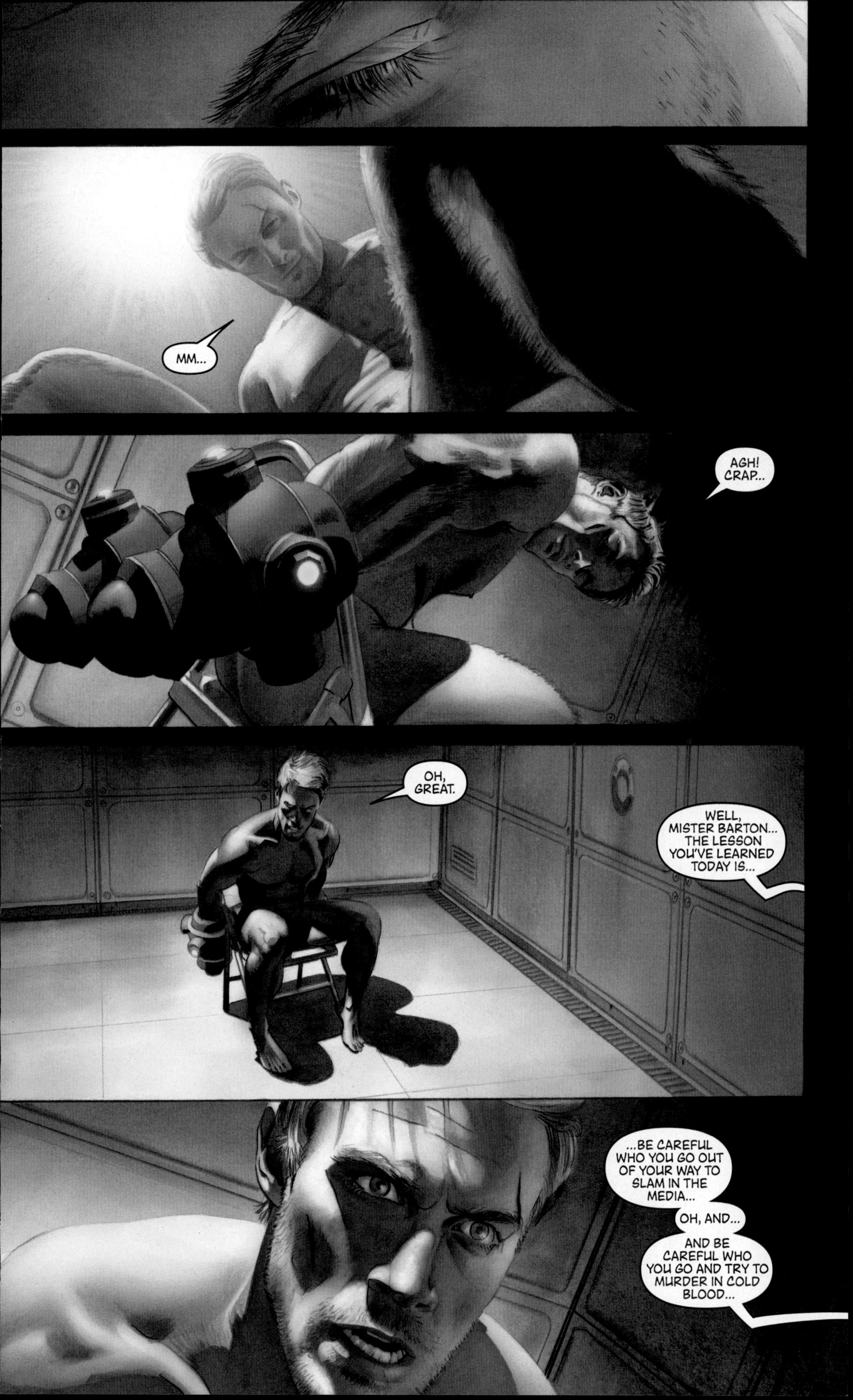
MM...
AGH! CRAP...
OH, GREAT.
WELL, MISTER BARTON... THE LESSON YOU'VE LEARNED TODAY IS...
...BE CAREFUL WHO YOU GO OUT OF YOUR WAY TO SLAM IN THE MEDIA...
OH, AND...
AND BE CAREFUL WHO YOU GO AND TRY TO MURDER IN COLD BLOOD...

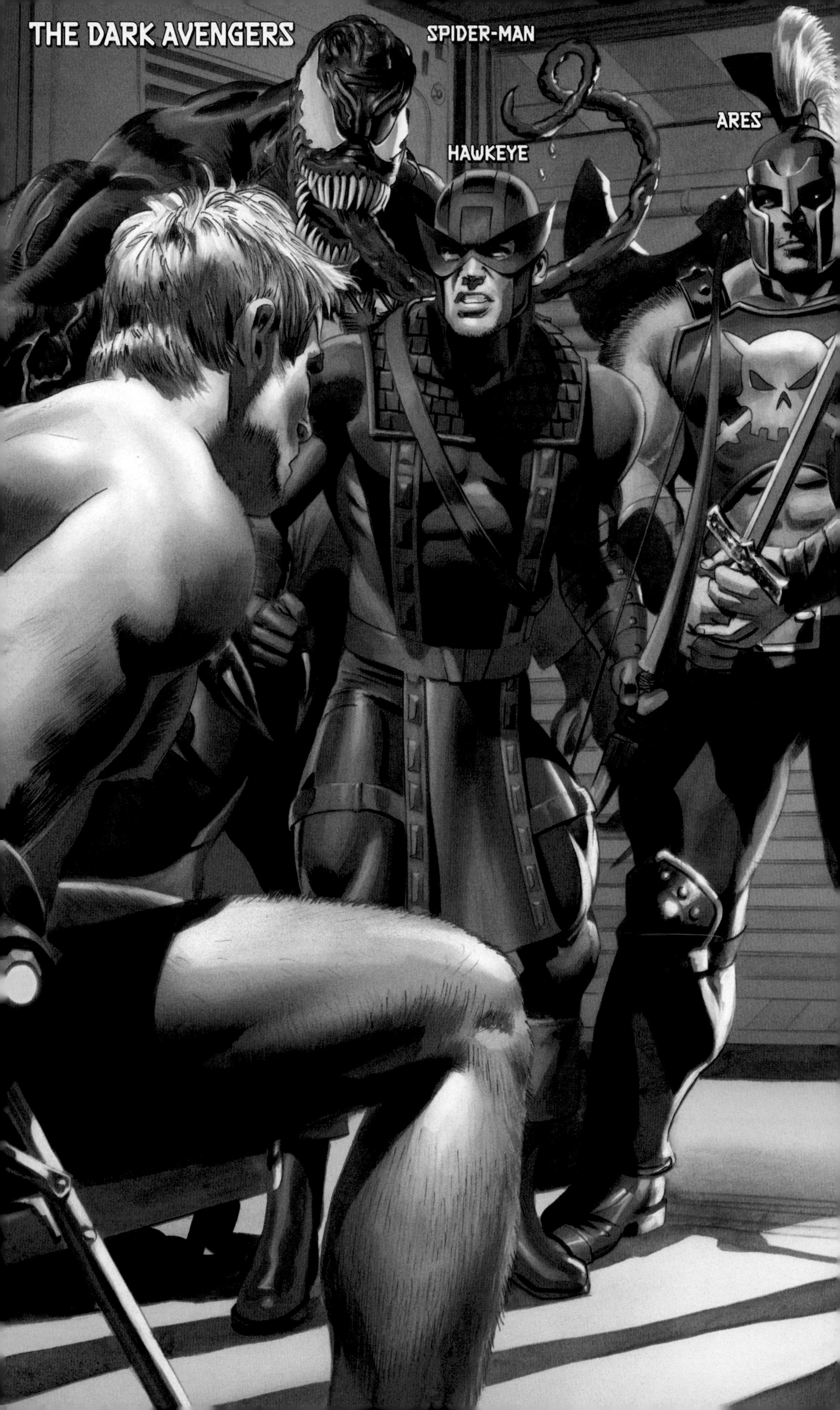
THE DARK AVENGERS
SPIDER-MAN
HAWKEYE
ARES

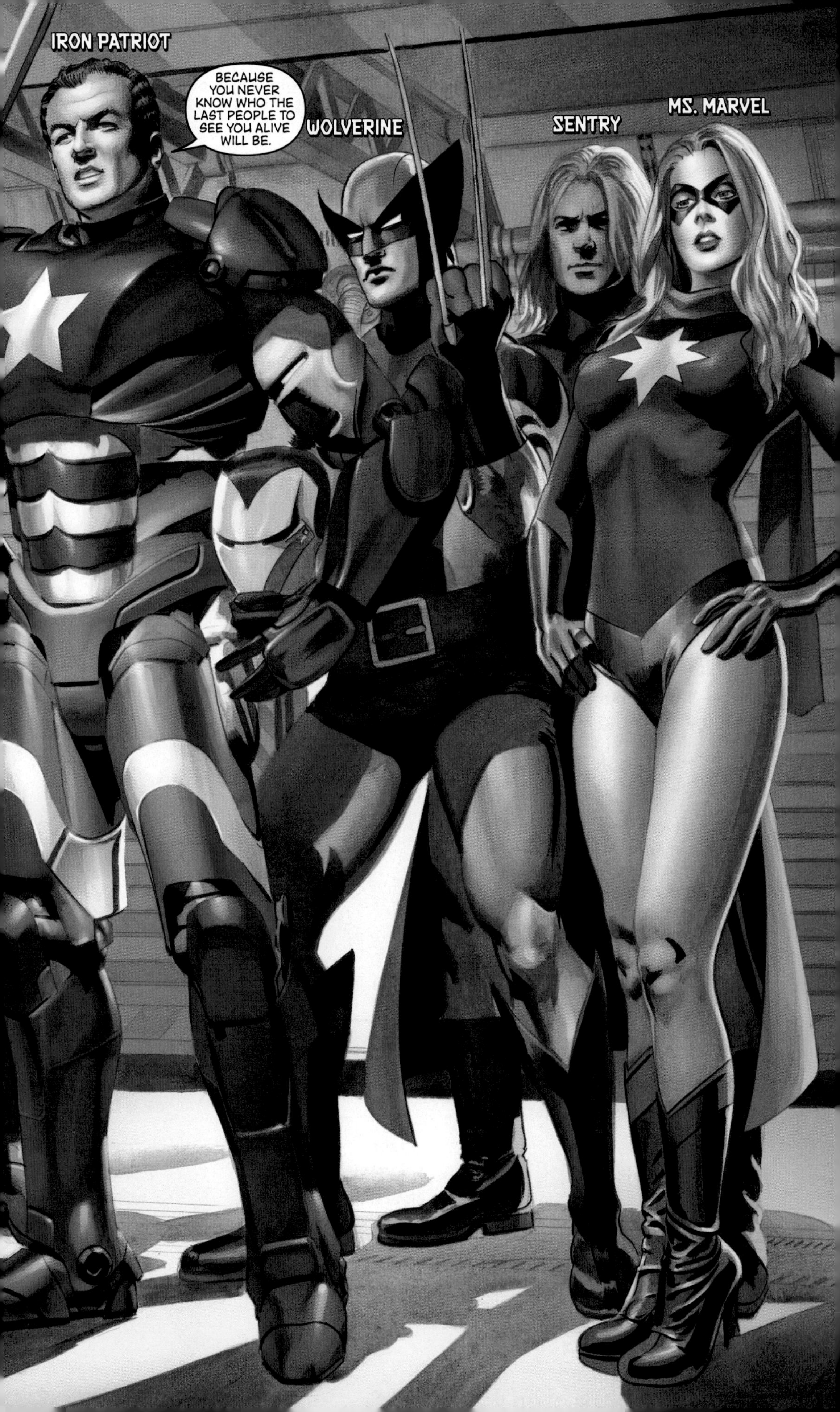
IRON PATRIOT
BECAUSE YOU NEVER KNOW WHO THE LAST PEOPLE TO SEE YOU ALIVE WILL BE.
WOLVERINE
SENTRY
MS. MARVEL

And there came a day, a day unlike any other, when Earth's Mightiest Heroes found themselves uni[?] against a common threat! On that day, the Avengers were born, to fight the foes no single super h[?] could withstand!

THE NEW AVENGERS

The Avengers are on the run! Until they can be sure who's on their side, Spider-Man, Captain America, Luke Cage, Ronin, Mockingbird, Spider-Woman and Ms. Marvel are using Captain America's hideout in Brooklyn as a safe house. Collectively they try to keep the values of the Avengers name alive even though they're living on the wrong side of the law.

Norman Osborn is the new political and media darling and director of H.A.M.M.E.R., the national peacekeeping task force, which includes his own team of Avengers.

Clint Barton aka Hawkeye aka Ronin went to the media and outed Norman as the twisted Green Goblin. When that didn't work, he abandoned his team and went to kill Norman himself. He failed.

BRIAN MICHAEL BENDIS
WRITER

MIKE MAYHEW
ARTIST

ANDY TROY
COLOR ART

RS & COMICRAFT'S ALBERT DESCHESNE
LETTERER

MIKE MAYHEW
COVER ARTIST

TAYLOR ESPOSITO
PRODUCTION

LAUREN SANKOVITCH
ASSOCIATE EDITOR

TOM BREVOORT
EDITOR

JOE QUESADA
EDITOR IN CHIEF

DAN BUCKLEY
PUBLISHER

ALAN FINE
EXECUTIVE PRODUCER

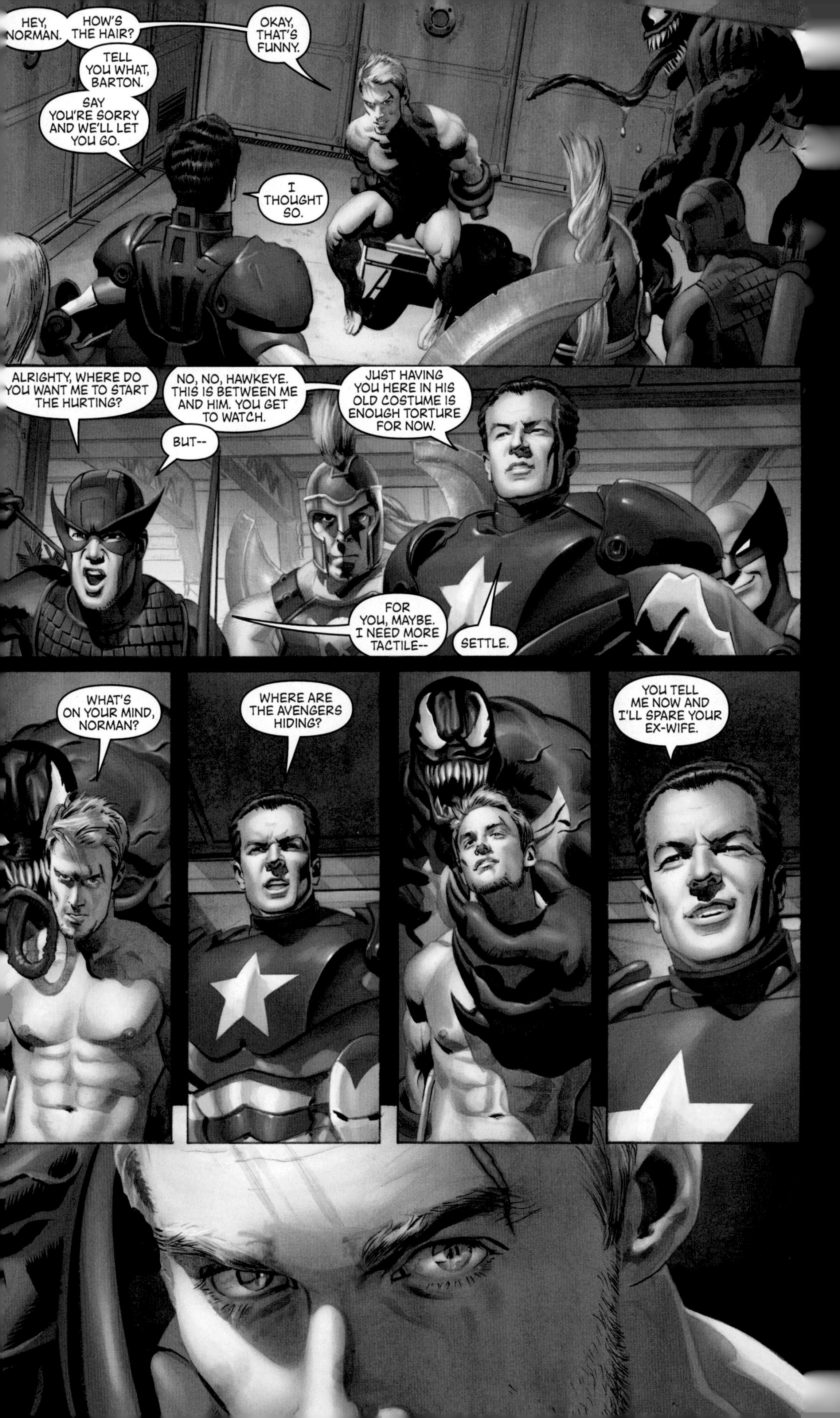
HEY, NORMAN.
HOW'S THE HAIR?
OKAY, THAT'S FUNNY.
TELL YOU WHAT, BARTON.
SAY YOU'RE SORRY AND WE'LL LET YOU GO.
I THOUGHT SO.
ALRIGHTY, WHERE DO YOU WANT ME TO START THE HURTING?
NO, NO, HAWKEYE. THIS IS BETWEEN ME AND HIM. YOU GET TO WATCH.
BUT--
JUST HAVING YOU HERE IN HIS OLD COSTUME IS ENOUGH TORTURE FOR NOW.
FOR YOU, MAYBE. I NEED MORE TACTILE--
SETTLE.
WHAT'S ON YOUR MIND, NORMAN?
WHERE ARE THE AVENGERS HIDING?
YOU TELL ME NOW AND I'LL SPARE YOUR EX-WIFE.

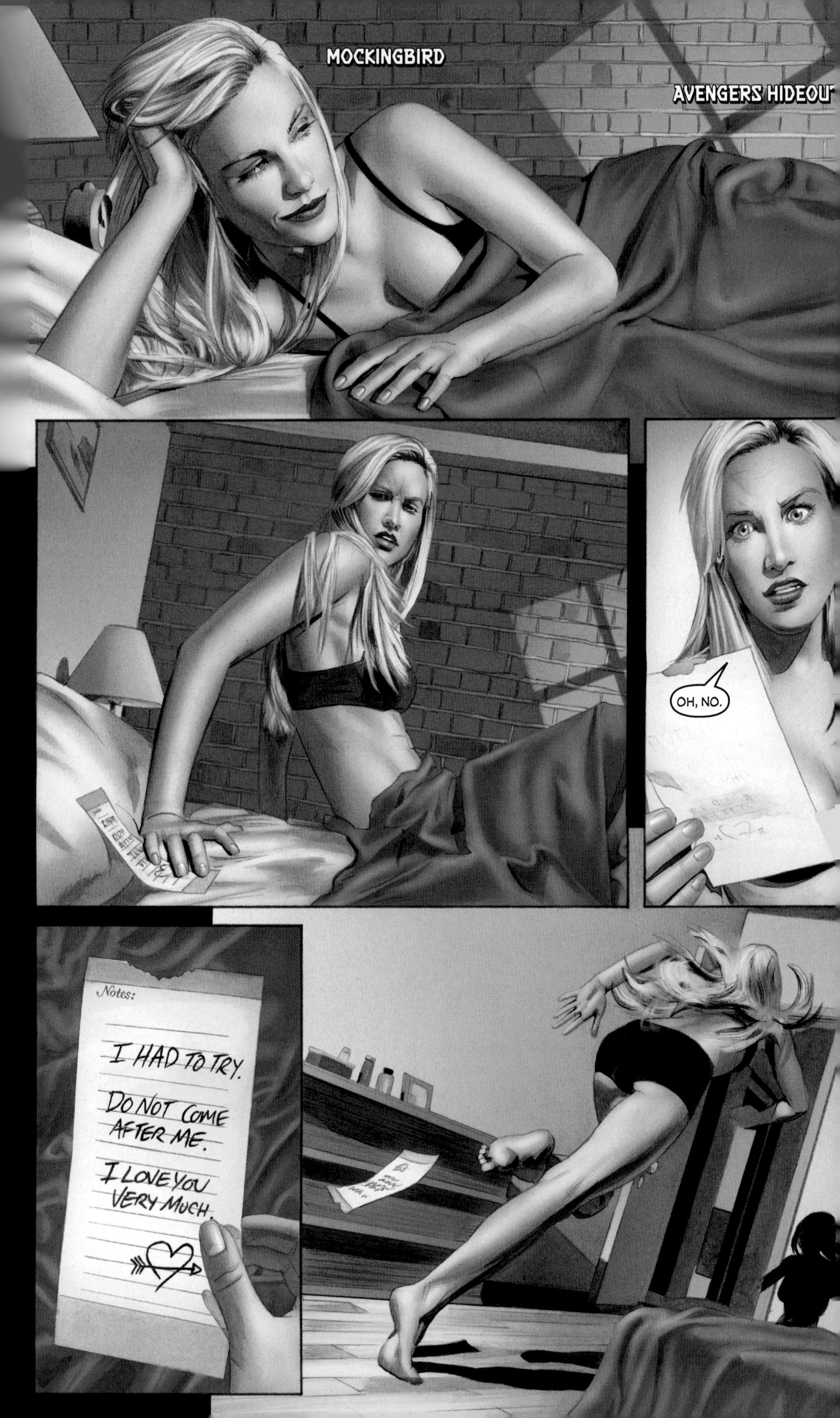
MOCKINGBIRD
AVENGERS HIDEOUT
OH, NO.
Notes:
I HAD TO TRY.
DO NOT COME AFTER ME.
I LOVE YOU VERY MUCH.

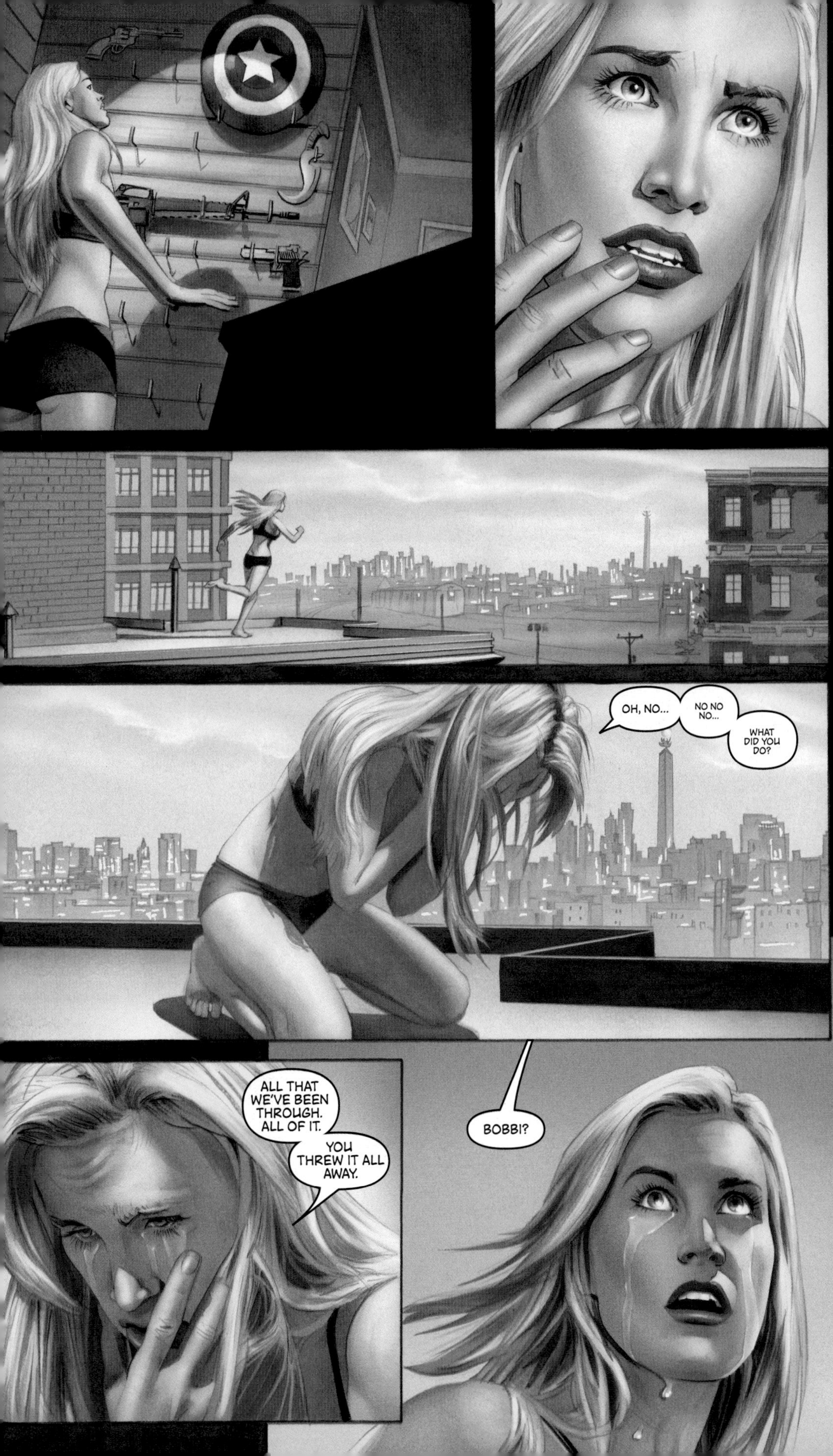
OH, NO...
NO NO NO...
WHAT DID YOU DO?
ALL THAT WE'VE BEEN THROUGH. ALL OF IT.
YOU THREW IT ALL AWAY.
BOBBI?

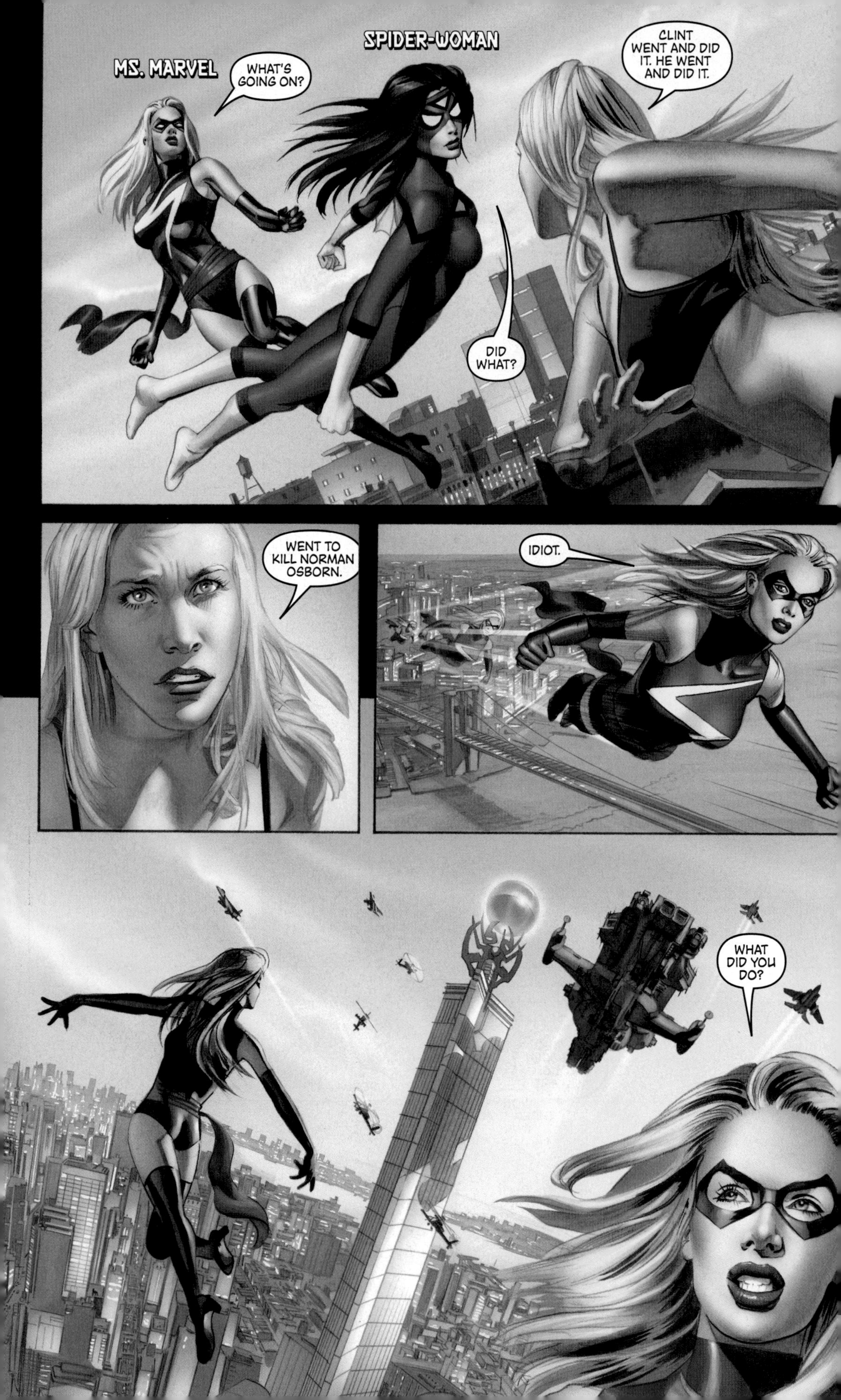

MS. MARVEL
SPIDER-WOMAN
WHAT'S GOING ON?
CLINT WENT AND DID IT. HE WENT AND DID IT.
DID WHAT?
WENT TO KILL NORMAN OSBORN.
IDIOT.
WHAT DID YOU DO?

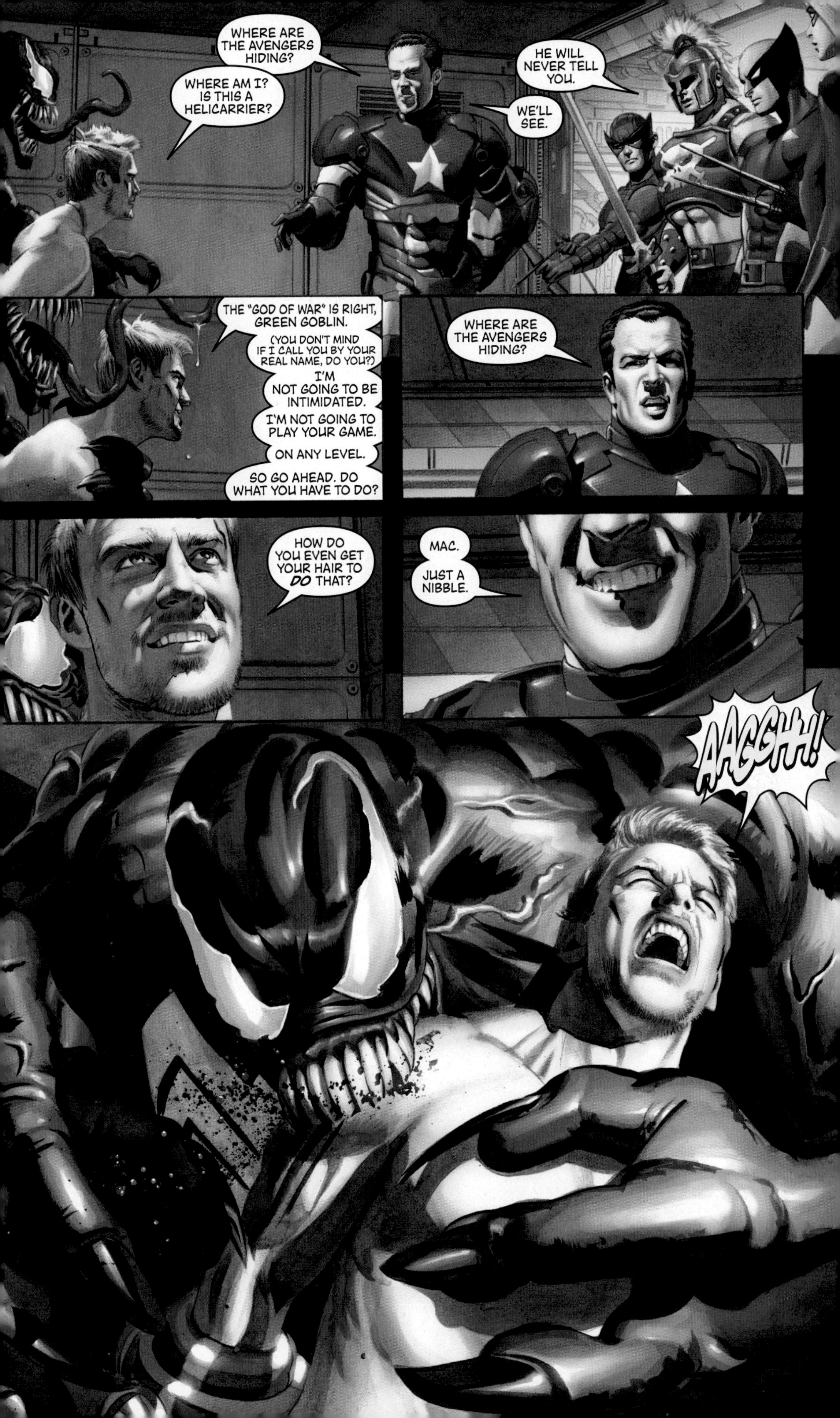
WHERE ARE THE AVENGERS HIDING?
WHERE AM I? IS THIS A HELICARRIER?
HE WILL NEVER TELL YOU.
WE'LL SEE.
THE "GOD OF WAR" IS RIGHT, GREEN GOBLIN.
(YOU DON'T MIND IF I CALL YOU BY YOUR REAL NAME, DO YOU?)
I'M NOT GOING TO BE INTIMIDATED.
I'M NOT GOING TO PLAY YOUR GAME.
ON ANY LEVEL.
SO GO AHEAD. DO WHAT YOU HAVE TO DO?
WHERE ARE THE AVENGERS HIDING?
HOW DO YOU EVEN GET YOUR HAIR TO *DO* THAT?
MAC.
JUST A NIBBLE.
AAGGHH!

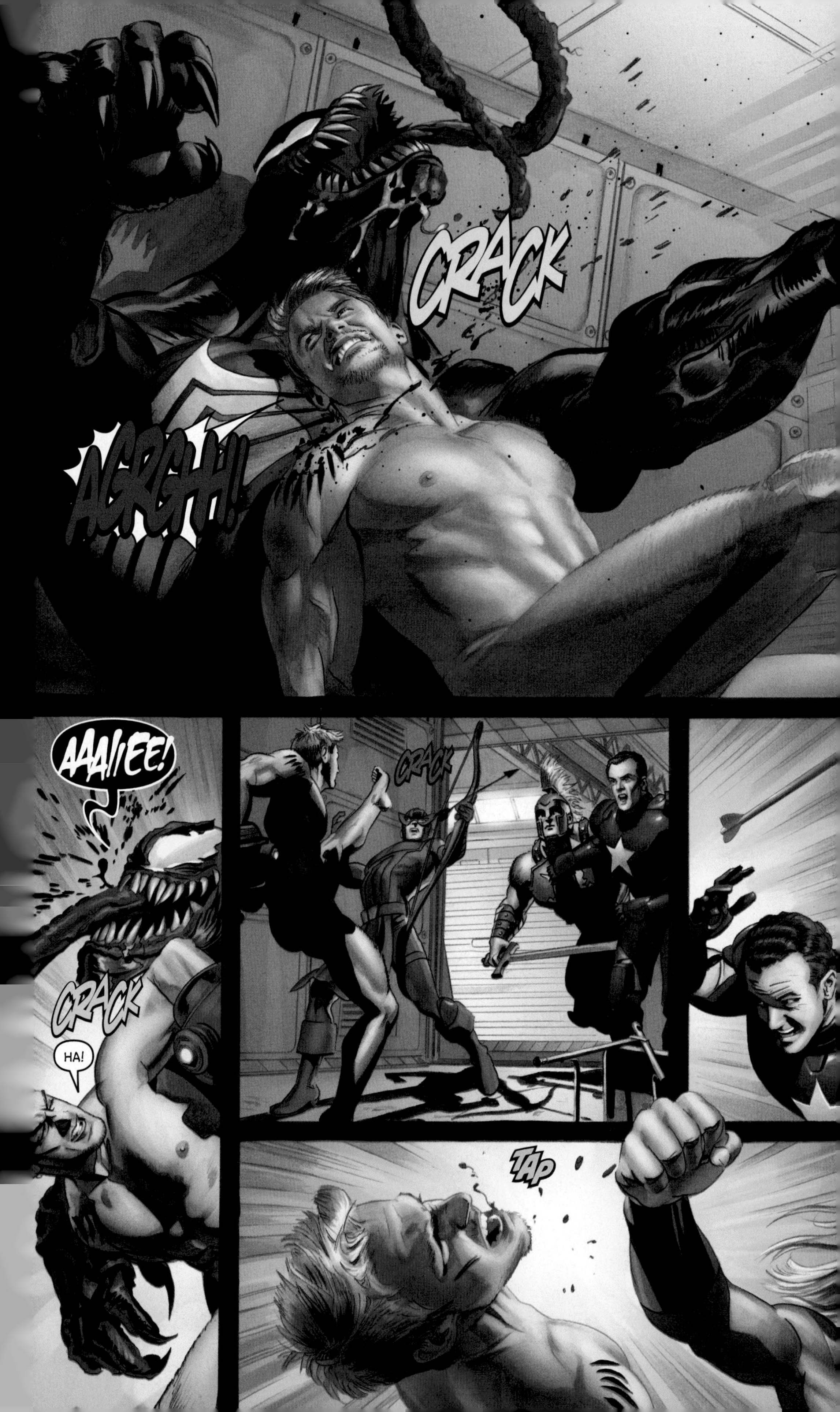
CRACK
AGRGH!
AAAIIEE!
CRACK
HA!
CRACK
TAP

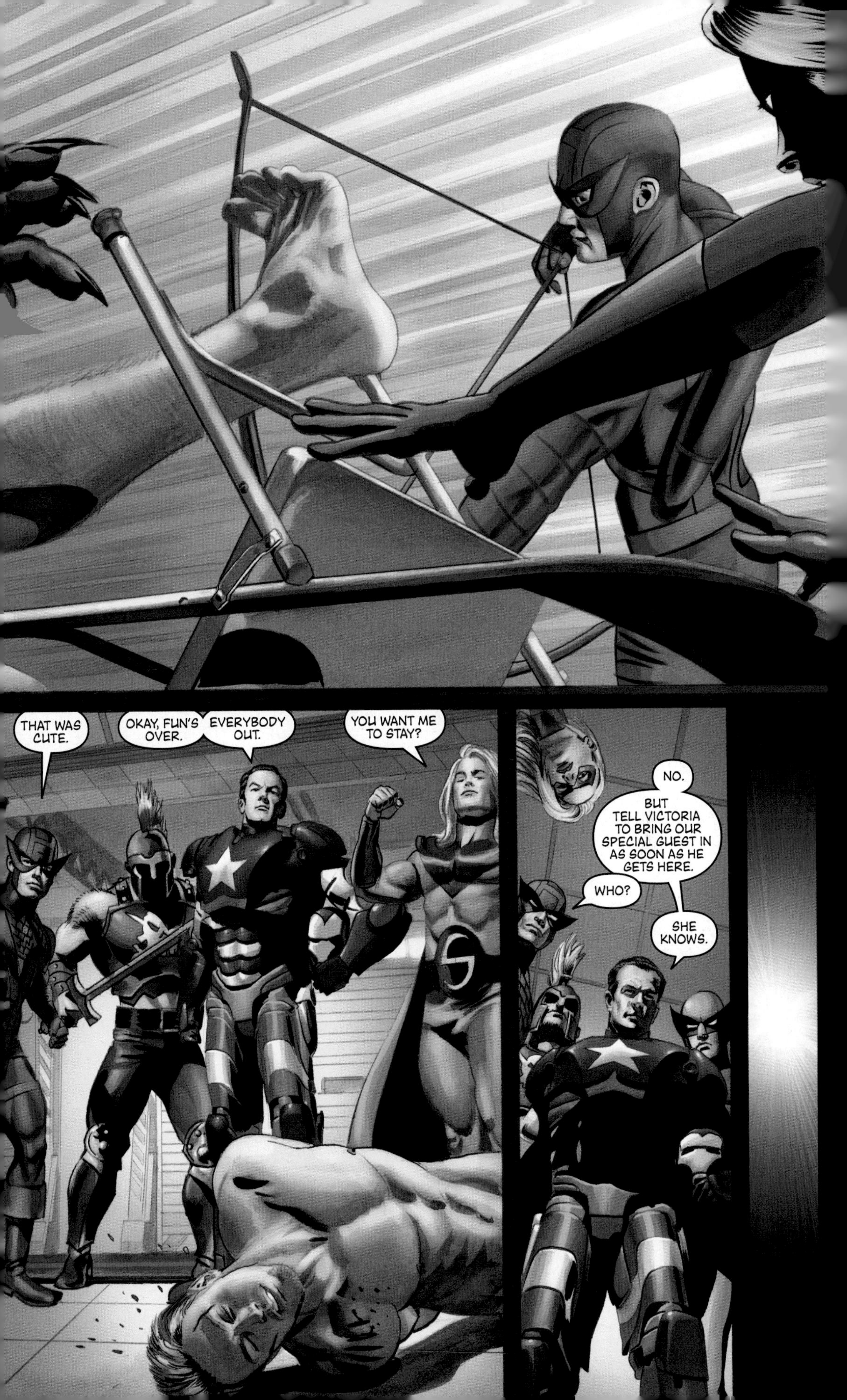
THAT WAS CUTE.
OKAY, FUN'S OVER.
EVERYBODY OUT.
YOU WANT ME TO STAY?
NO.
BUT TELL VICTORIA TO BRING OUR SPECIAL GUEST IN AS SOON AS HE GETS HERE.
WHO?
SHE KNOWS.

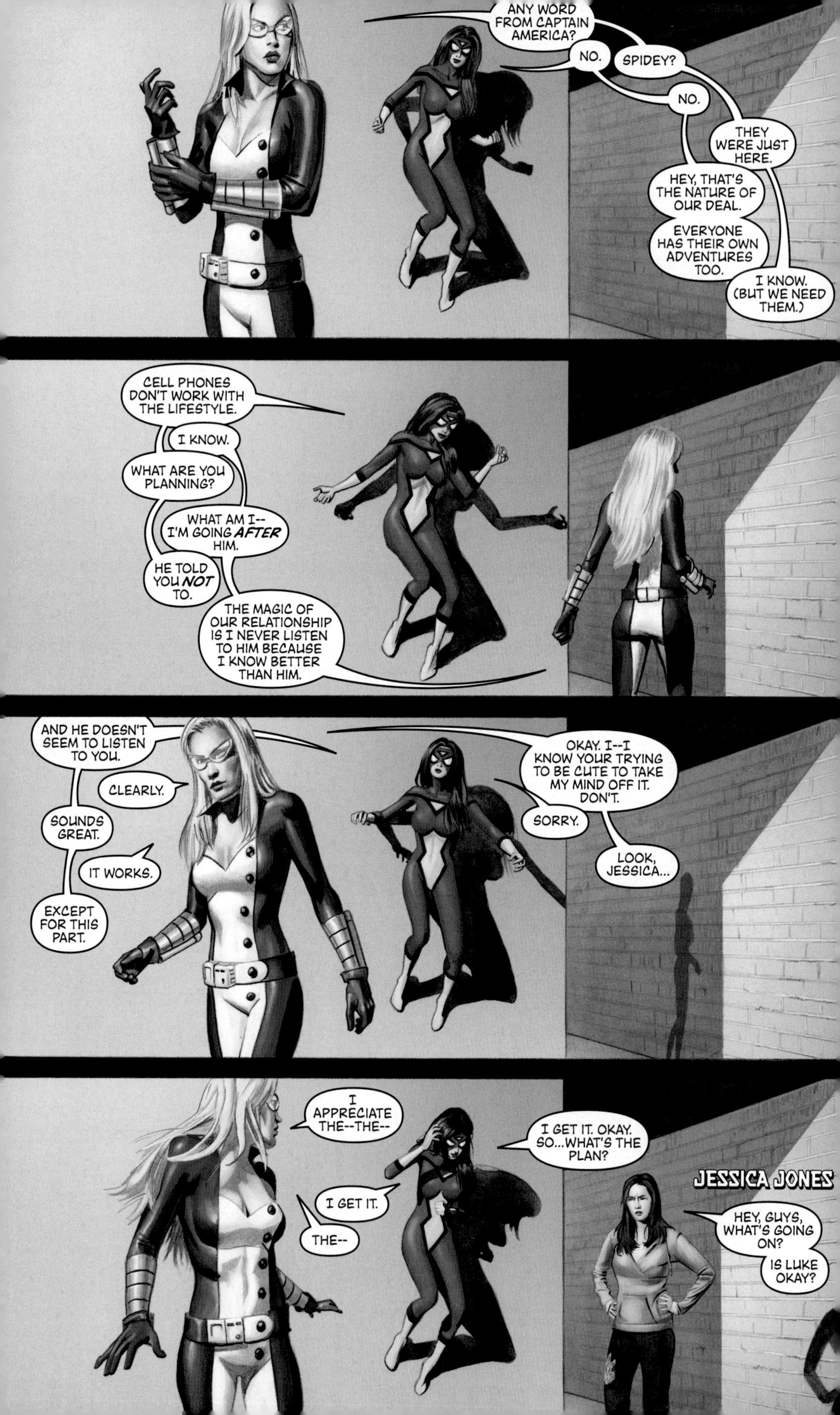
ANY WORD FROM CAPTAIN AMERICA?
NO.
SPIDEY?
NO.
THEY WERE JUST HERE.
HEY, THAT'S THE NATURE OF OUR DEAL.
EVERYONE HAS THEIR OWN ADVENTURES TOO.
I KNOW. (BUT WE NEED THEM.)
CELL PHONES DON'T WORK WITH THE LIFESTYLE.
I KNOW.
WHAT ARE YOU PLANNING?
WHAT AM I-- I'M GOING AFTER HIM.
HE TOLD YOU NOT TO.
THE MAGIC OF OUR RELATIONSHIP IS I NEVER LISTEN TO HIM BECAUSE I KNOW BETTER THAN HIM.
AND HE DOESN'T SEEM TO LISTEN TO YOU.
CLEARLY.
SOUNDS GREAT.
IT WORKS.
EXCEPT FOR THIS PART.
OKAY. I--I KNOW YOUR TRYING TO BE CUTE TO TAKE MY MIND OFF IT. DON'T.
SORRY.
LOOK, JESSICA...
I APPRECIATE THE--THE--
I GET IT.
THE--
I GET IT. OKAY. SO...WHAT'S THE PLAN?
JESSICA JONES
HEY, GUYS, WHAT'S GOING ON?
IS LUKE OKAY?

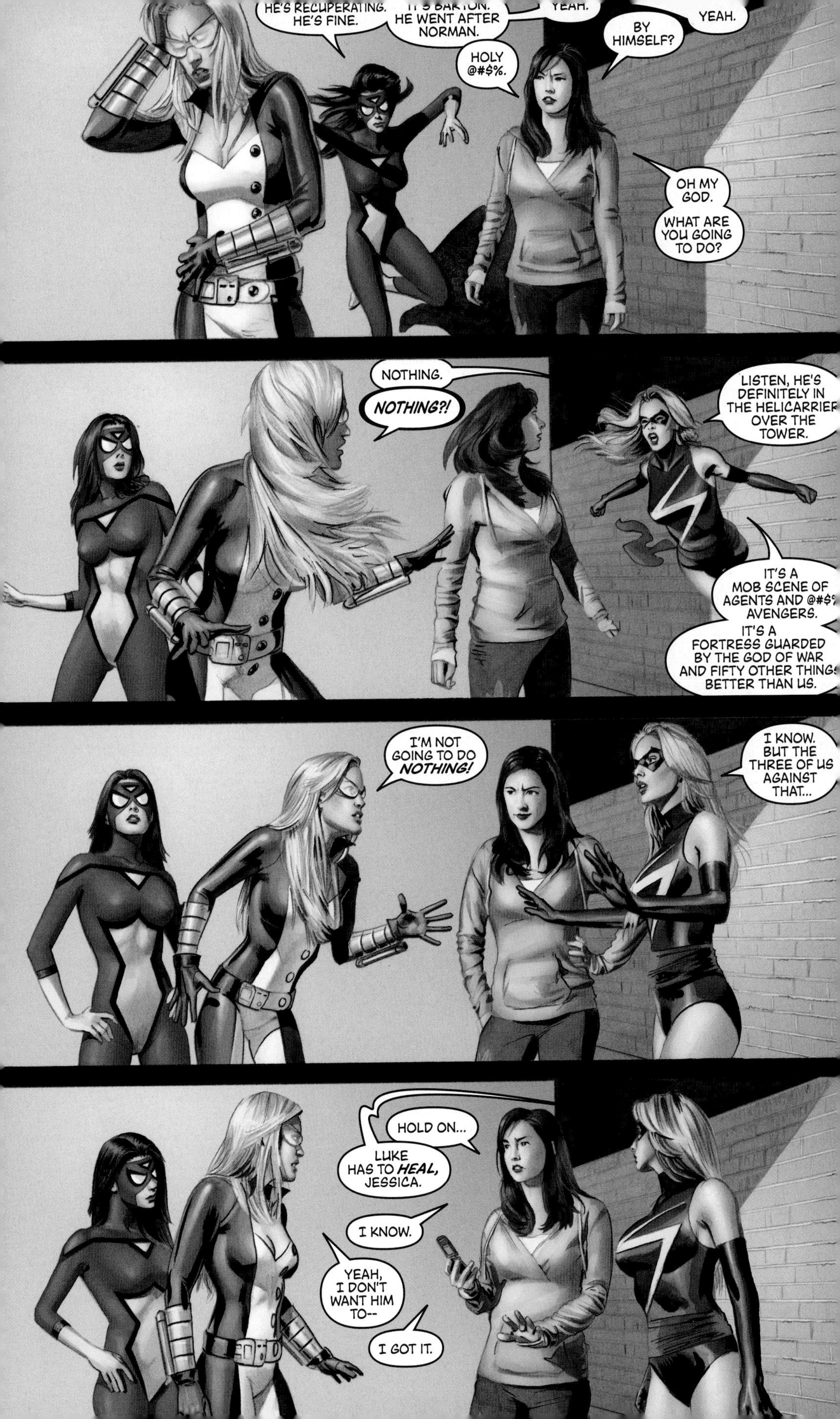
HE'S RECUPERATING. HE'S FINE.
HE WENT AFTER NORMAN.
YEAH.
HOLY @#$%.
BY HIMSELF?
YEAH.
OH MY GOD.
WHAT ARE YOU GOING TO DO?
NOTHING.
NOTHING?!
LISTEN, HE'S DEFINITELY IN THE HELICARRIE
OVER THE TOWER.
IT'S A MOB SCENE OF AGENTS AND @#$
AVENGERS.
IT'S A FORTRESS GUARDED BY THE GOD OF WAR AND FIFTY OTHER THING
BETTER THAN US.
I'M NOT GOING TO DO *NOTHING!*
I KNOW. BUT THE THREE OF US AGAINST THAT...
HOLD ON...
LUKE HAS TO *HEAL,* JESSICA.
I KNOW.
YEAH, I DON'T WANT HIM TO--
I GOT IT.

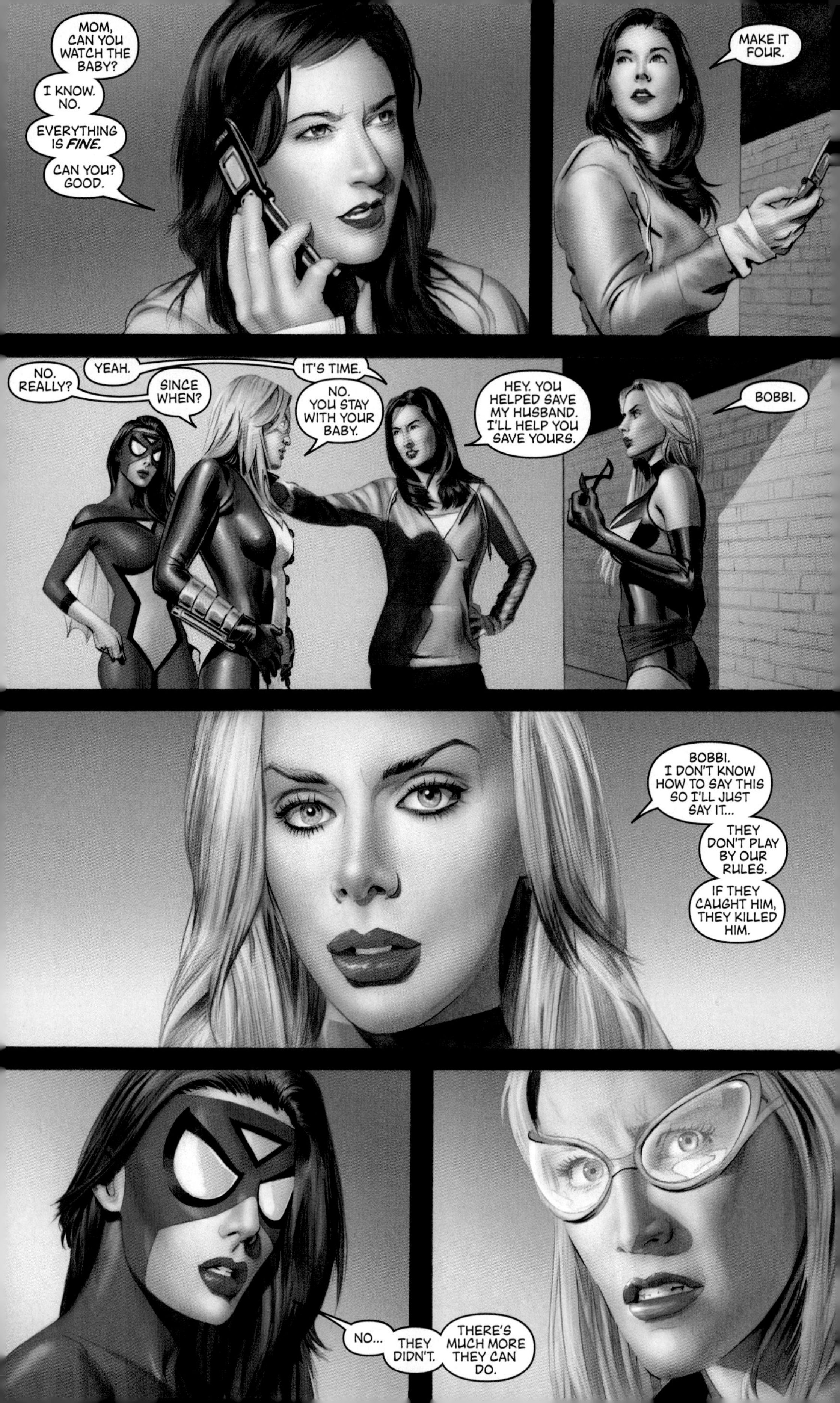
MOM, CAN YOU WATCH THE BABY?
I KNOW. NO.
EVERYTHING IS *FINE.*
CAN YOU? GOOD.
MAKE IT FOUR.
NO. REALLY?
YEAH.
SINCE WHEN?
IT'S TIME.
NO. YOU STAY WITH YOUR BABY.
HEY. YOU HELPED SAVE MY HUSBAND. I'LL HELP YOU SAVE YOURS.
BOBBI.
BOBBI. I DON'T KNOW HOW TO SAY THIS SO I'LL JUST SAY IT...
THEY DON'T PLAY BY OUR RULES.
IF THEY CAUGHT HIM, THEY KILLED HIM.
NO...
THEY DIDN'T.
THERE'S MUCH MORE THEY CAN DO.

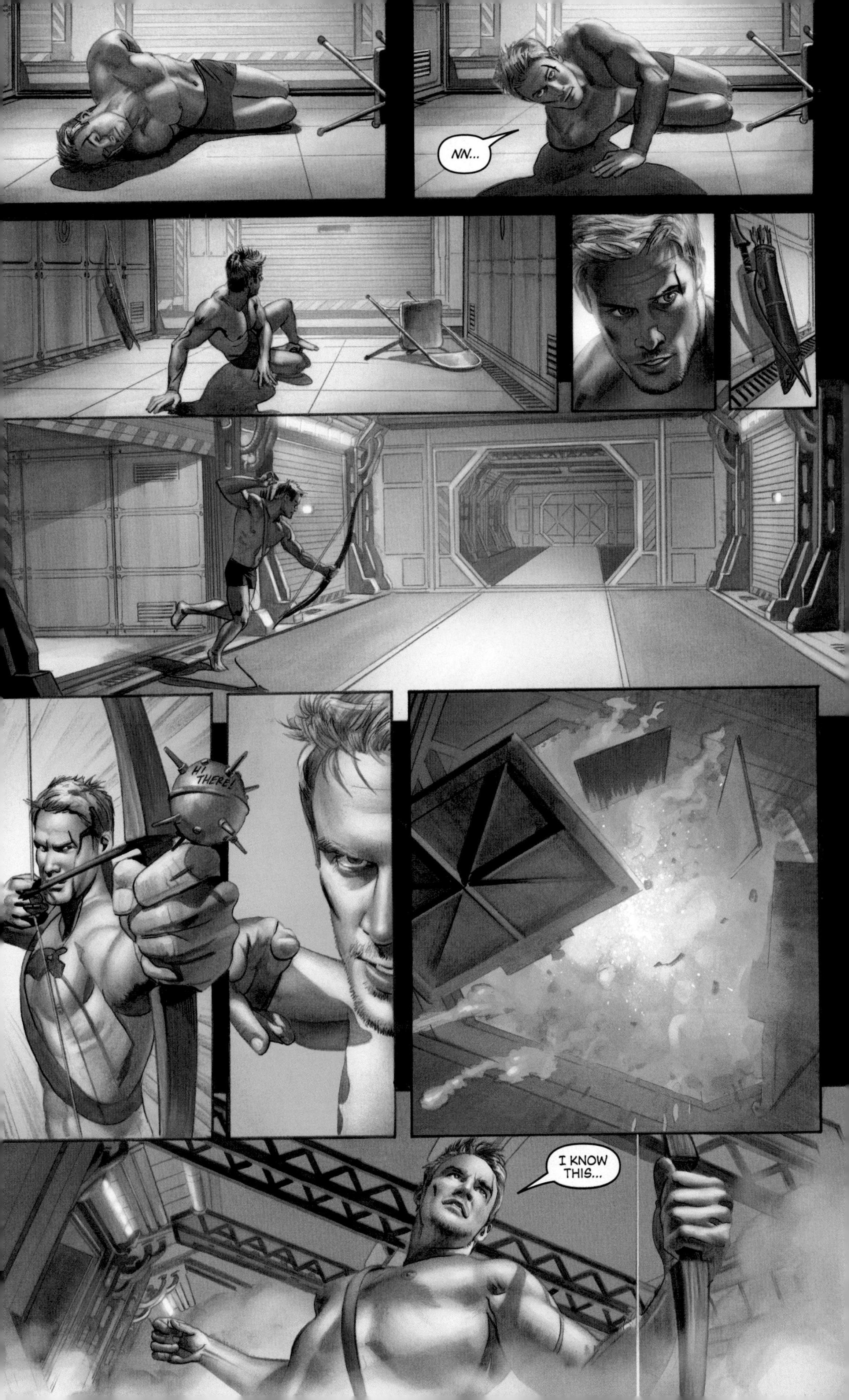
NN...
HI THERE!
I KNOW THIS...

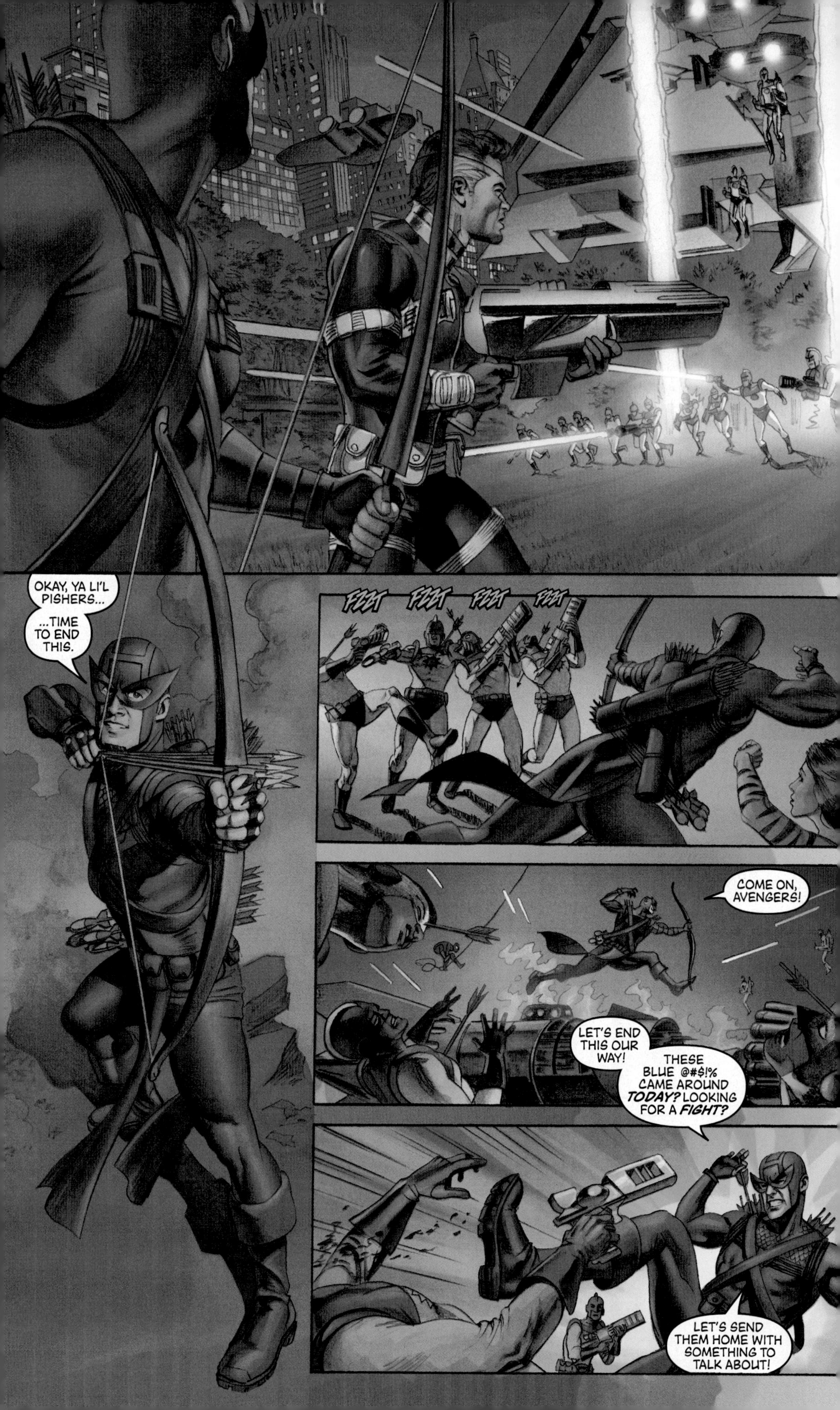
OKAY, YA LI'L PISHERS...
...TIME TO END THIS.
FZZT FZZT FZZT FZZT
COME ON, AVENGERS!
LET'S END THIS OUR WAY!
THESE BLUE @#$!% CAME AROUND *TODAY?* LOOKING FOR A *FIGHT?*
LET'S SEND THEM HOME WITH SOMETHING TO TALK ABOUT!

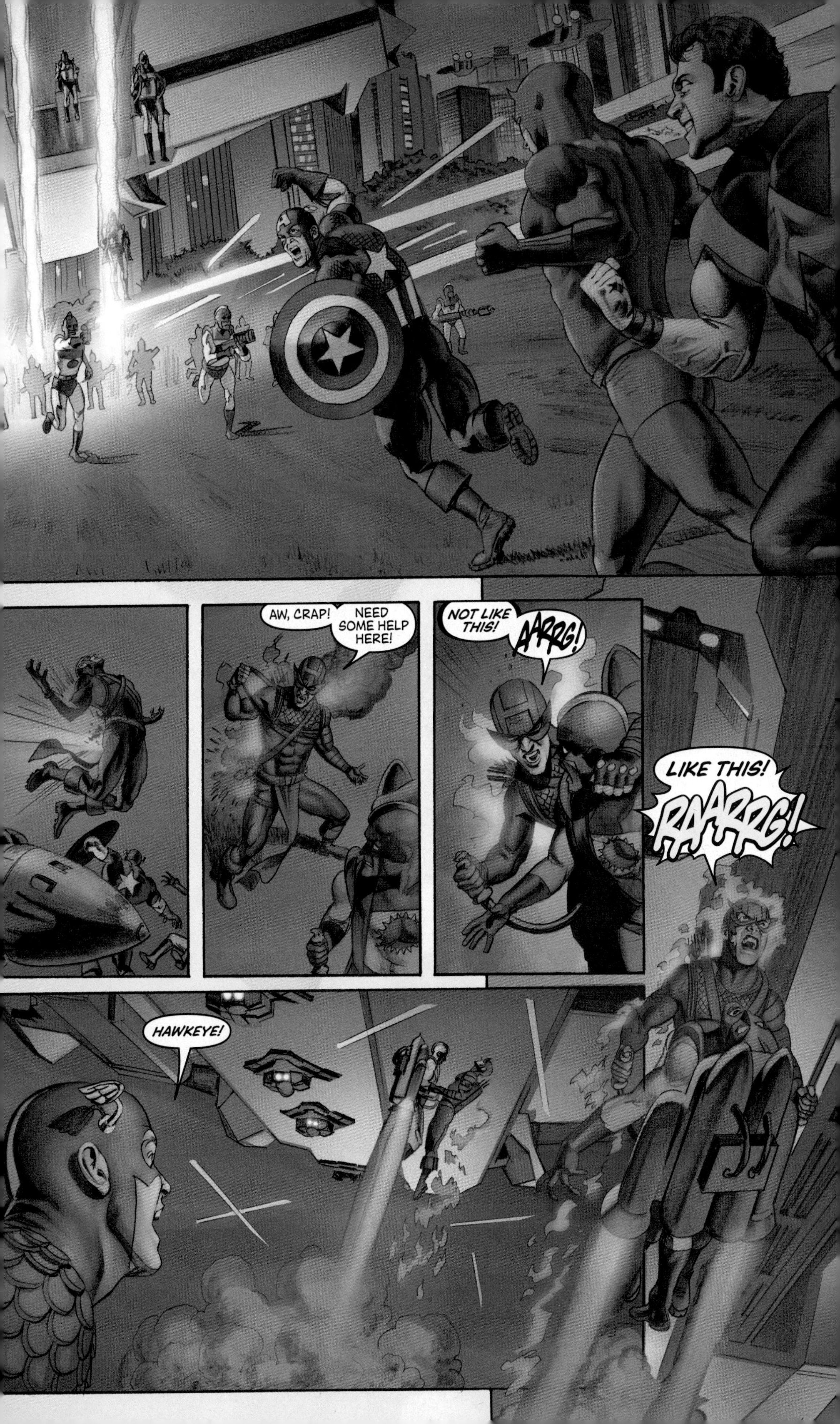
AW, CRAP!
NEED SOME HELP HERE!
NOT LIKE THIS!
AARRG!
LIKE THIS!
RAARRG!
HAWKEYE!

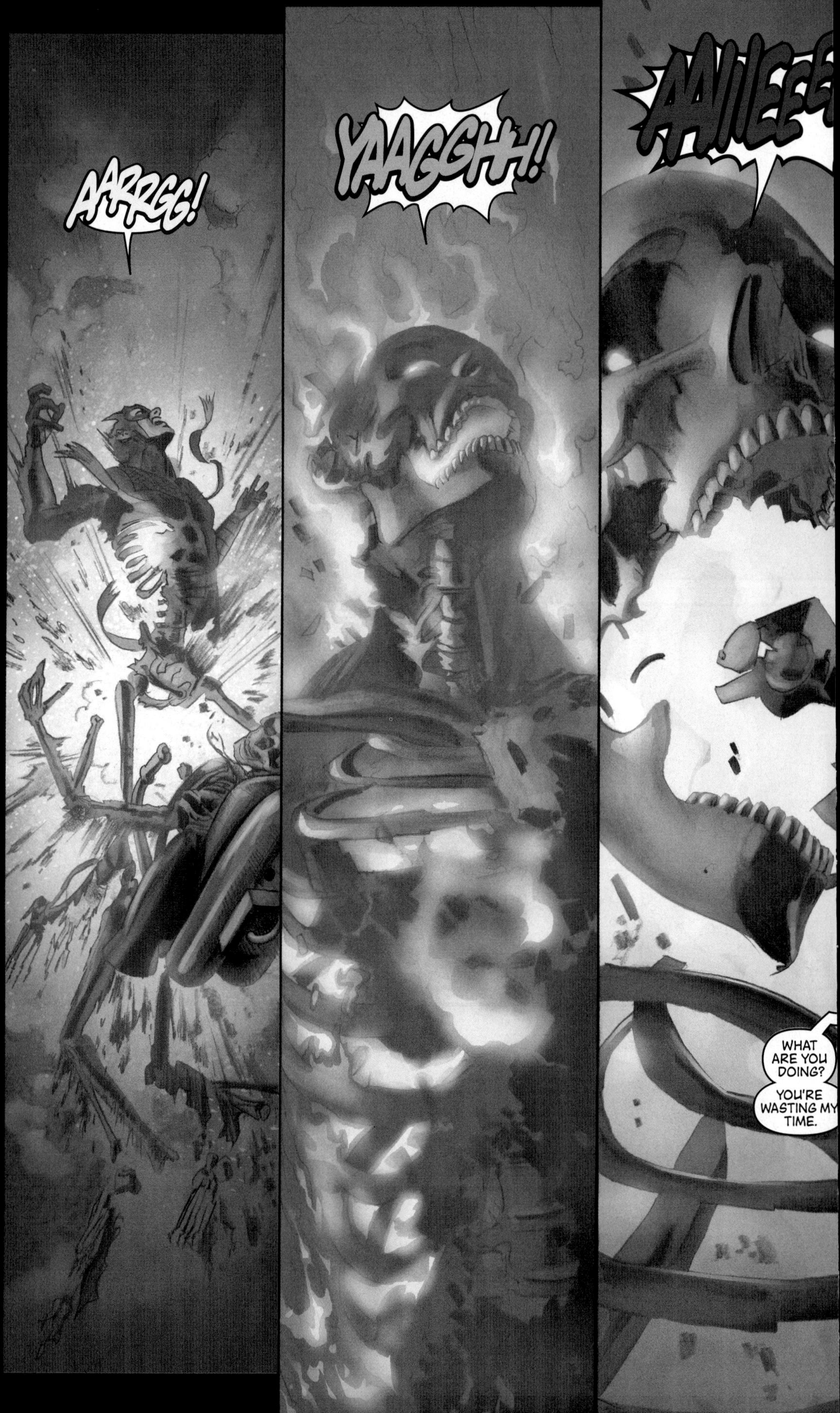
AARRGG!
YAAGGHH!
AAIIEEE
WHAT ARE YOU DOING?
YOU'RE WASTING MY TIME.

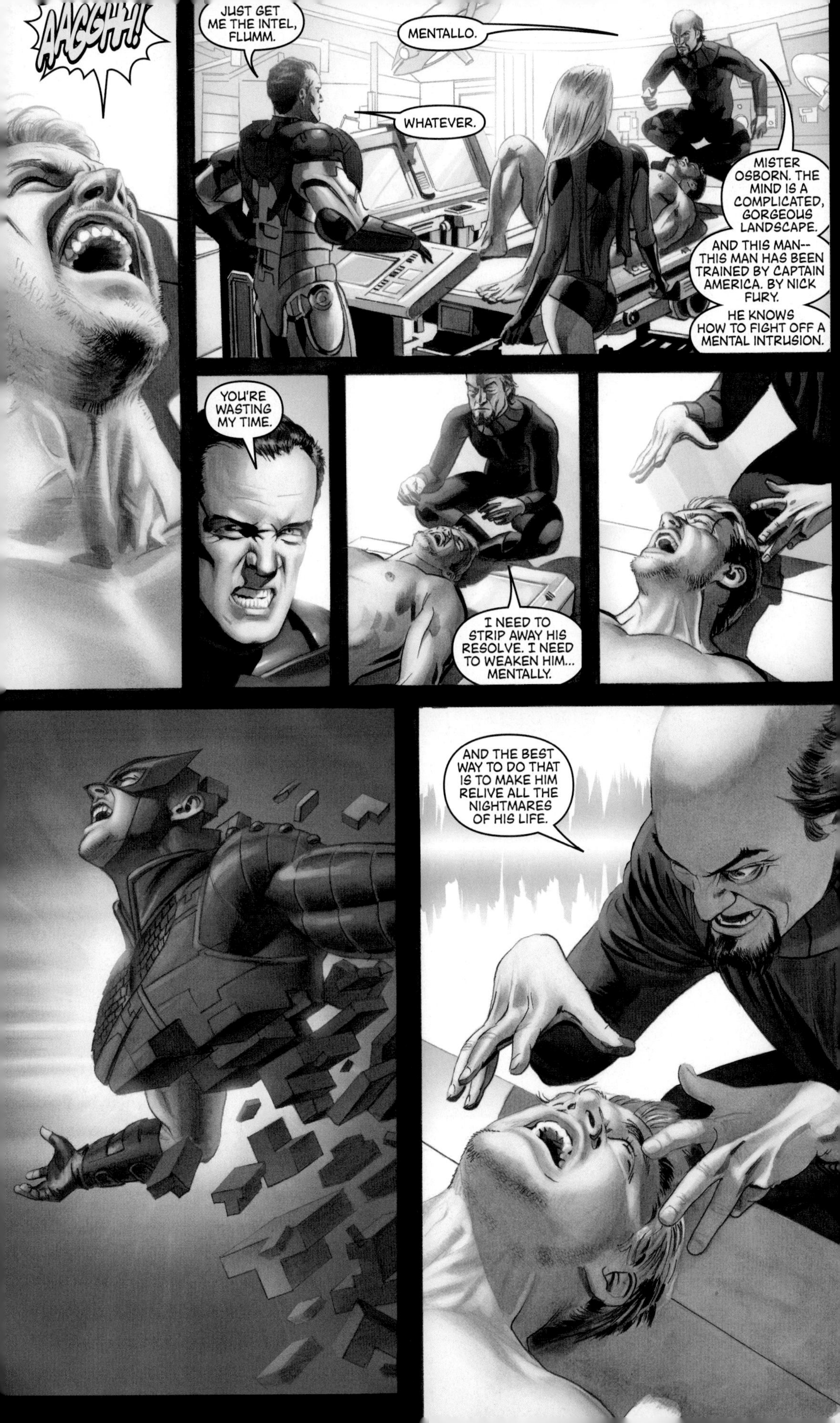
AAGGHH!
JUST GET ME THE INTEL, FLUMM.
MENTALLO.
WHATEVER.
MISTER OSBORN. THE MIND IS A COMPLICATED, GORGEOUS LANDSCAPE.
AND THIS MAN-- THIS MAN HAS BEEN TRAINED BY CAPTAIN AMERICA. BY NICK FURY.
HE KNOWS HOW TO FIGHT OFF A MENTAL INTRUSION.
YOU'RE WASTING MY TIME.
I NEED TO STRIP AWAY HIS RESOLVE. I NEED TO WEAKEN HIM... MENTALLY.
AND THE BEST WAY TO DO THAT IS TO MAKE HIM RELIVE ALL THE NIGHTMARES OF HIS LIFE.

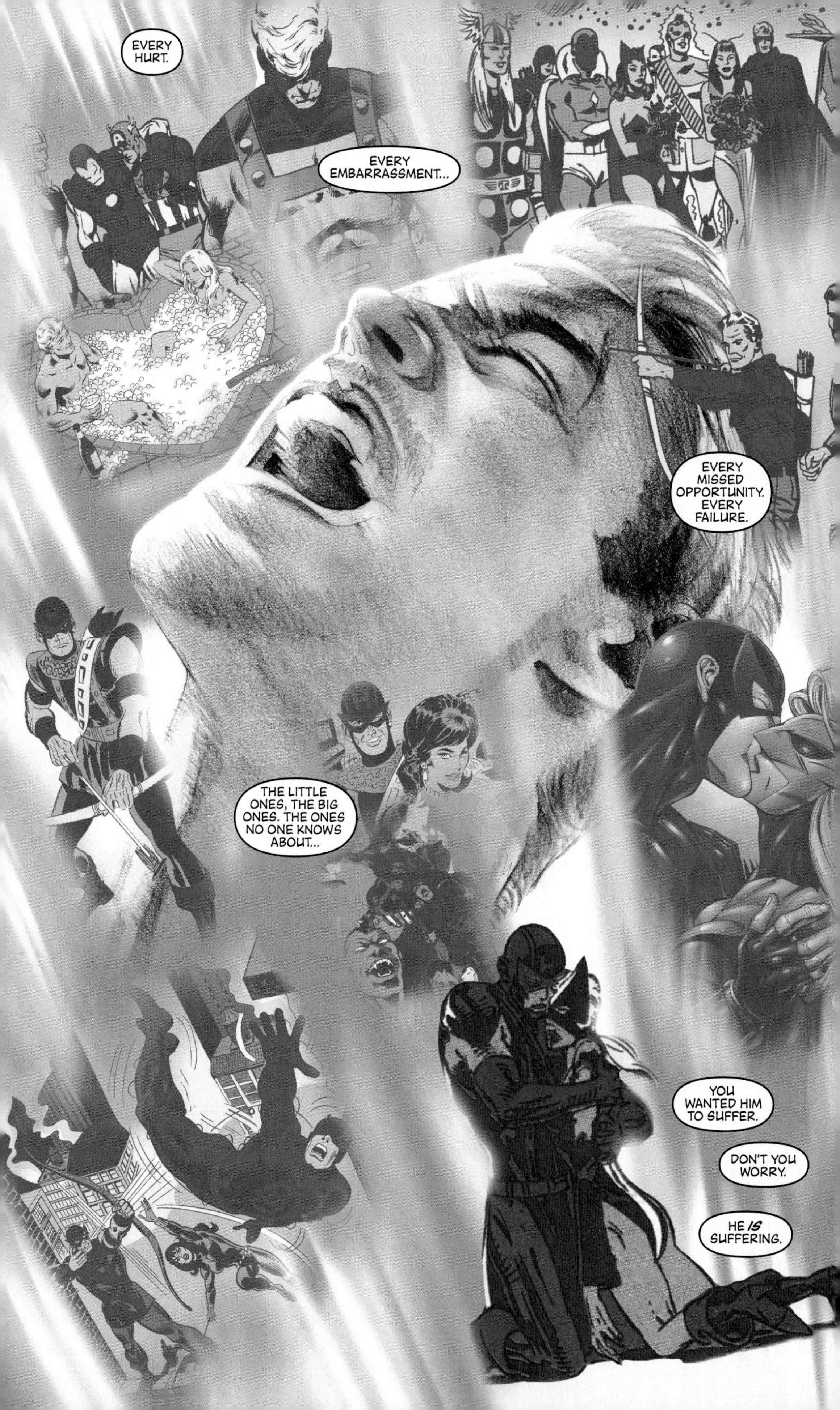
EVERY HURT.
EVERY EMBARRASSMENT...
EVERY MISSED OPPORTUNITY. EVERY FAILURE.
THE LITTLE ONES, THE BIG ONES. THE ONES NO ONE KNOWS ABOUT...
YOU WANTED HIM TO SUFFER.
DON'T YOU WORRY.
HE *IS* SUFFERING.

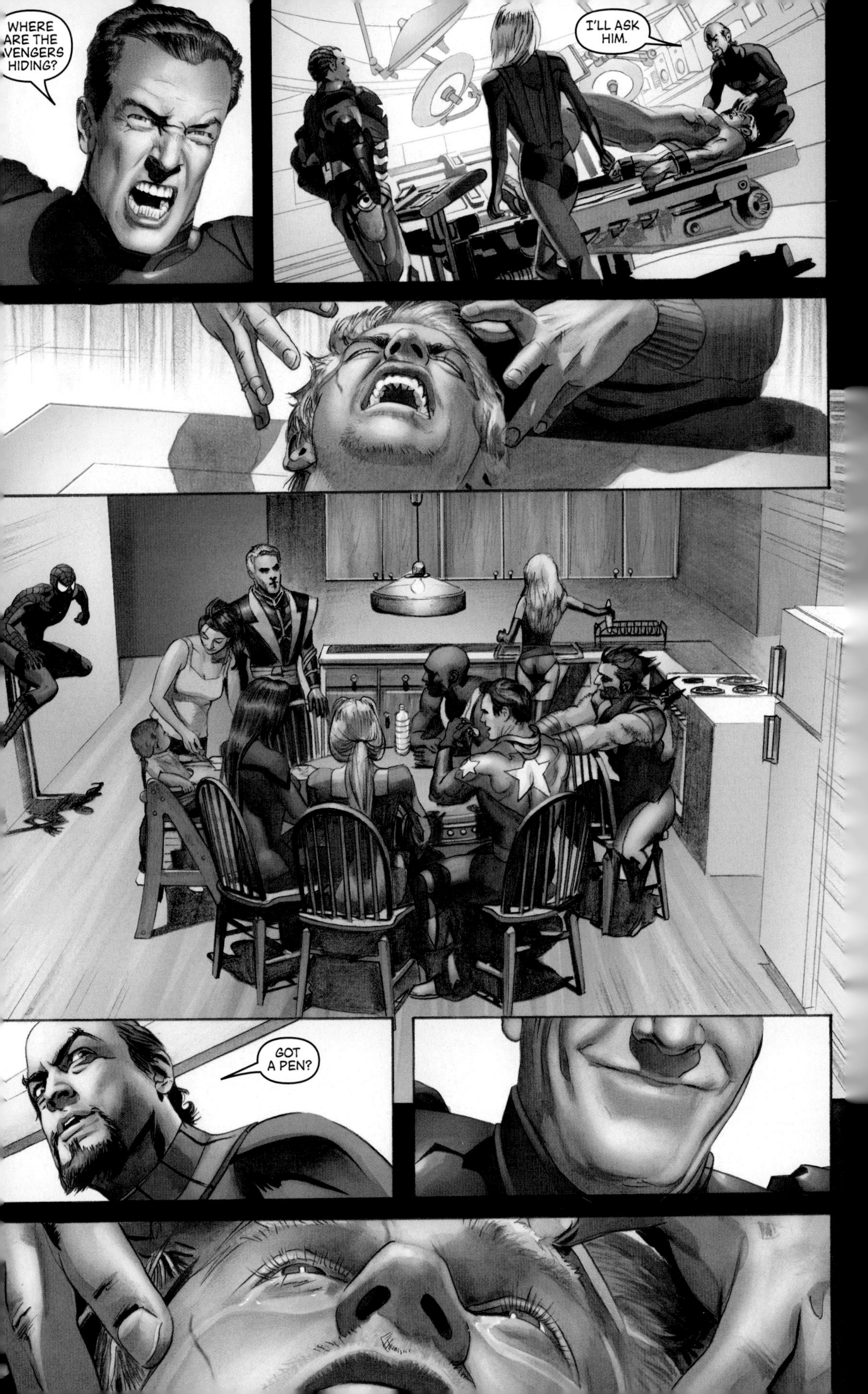
WHERE ARE THE VENGERS HIDING?
I'LL ASK HIM.
GOT A PEN?

BROOKLYN.

WHAT DOES THE ARMOR SAY, NORMY?

NOTHING. IT SCANS CLEAN.

THERE'S NO ONE THERE?

NO, THE BUILDING IS *CLOAKED*. AS IN I CAN'T SCAN IT.

IT MEAN THEY A *ABSOLUT* IN THER

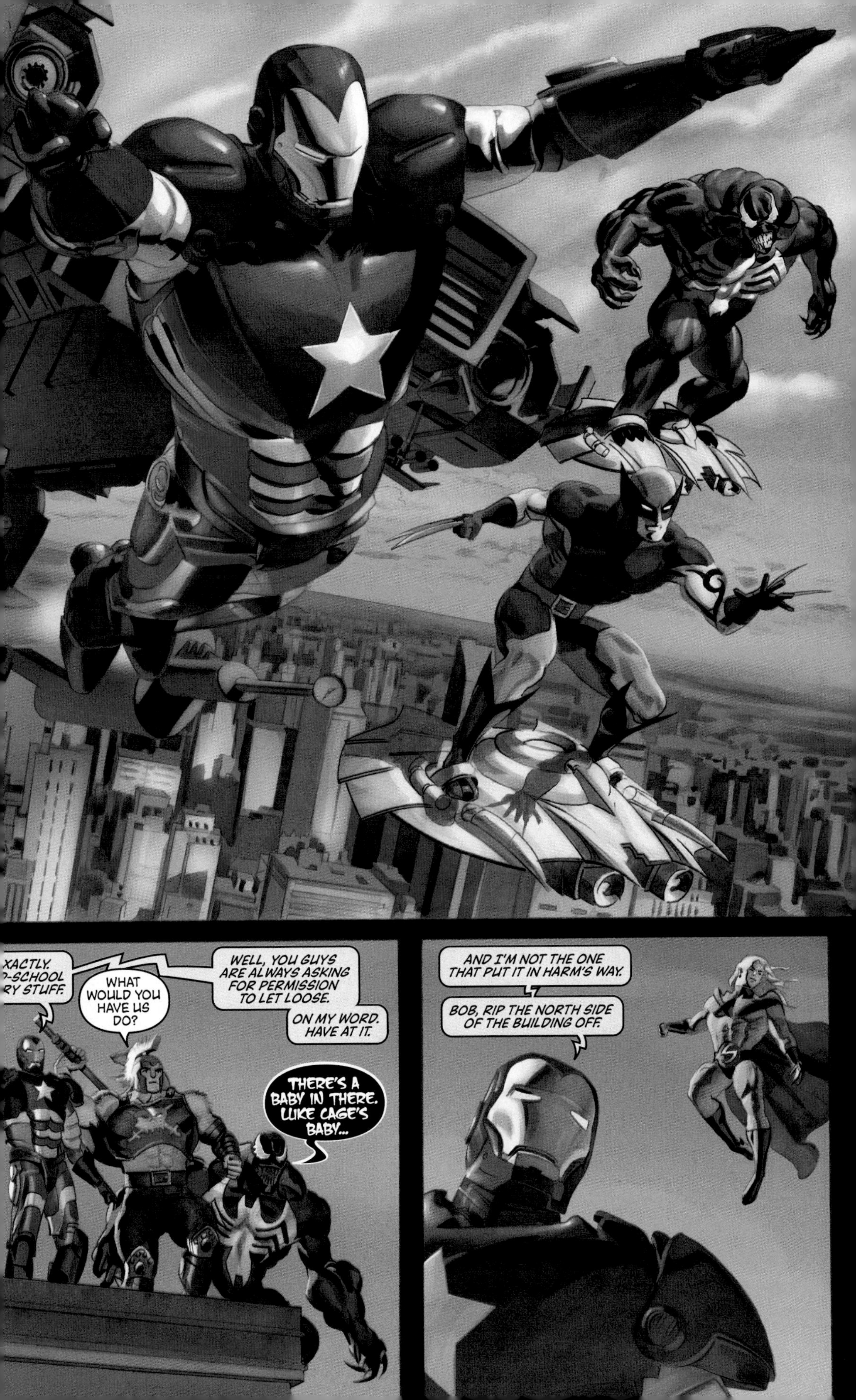
XACTLY. -SCHOOL RY STUFF.
WHAT WOULD YOU HAVE US DO?
WELL, YOU GUYS ARE ALWAYS ASKING FOR PERMISSION TO LET LOOSE.
ON MY WORD. HAVE AT IT.
THERE'S A BABY IN THERE. LUKE CAGE'S BABY...
AND I'M NOT THE ONE THAT PUT IT IN HARM'S WAY.
BOB, RIP THE NORTH SIDE OF THE BUILDING OFF.

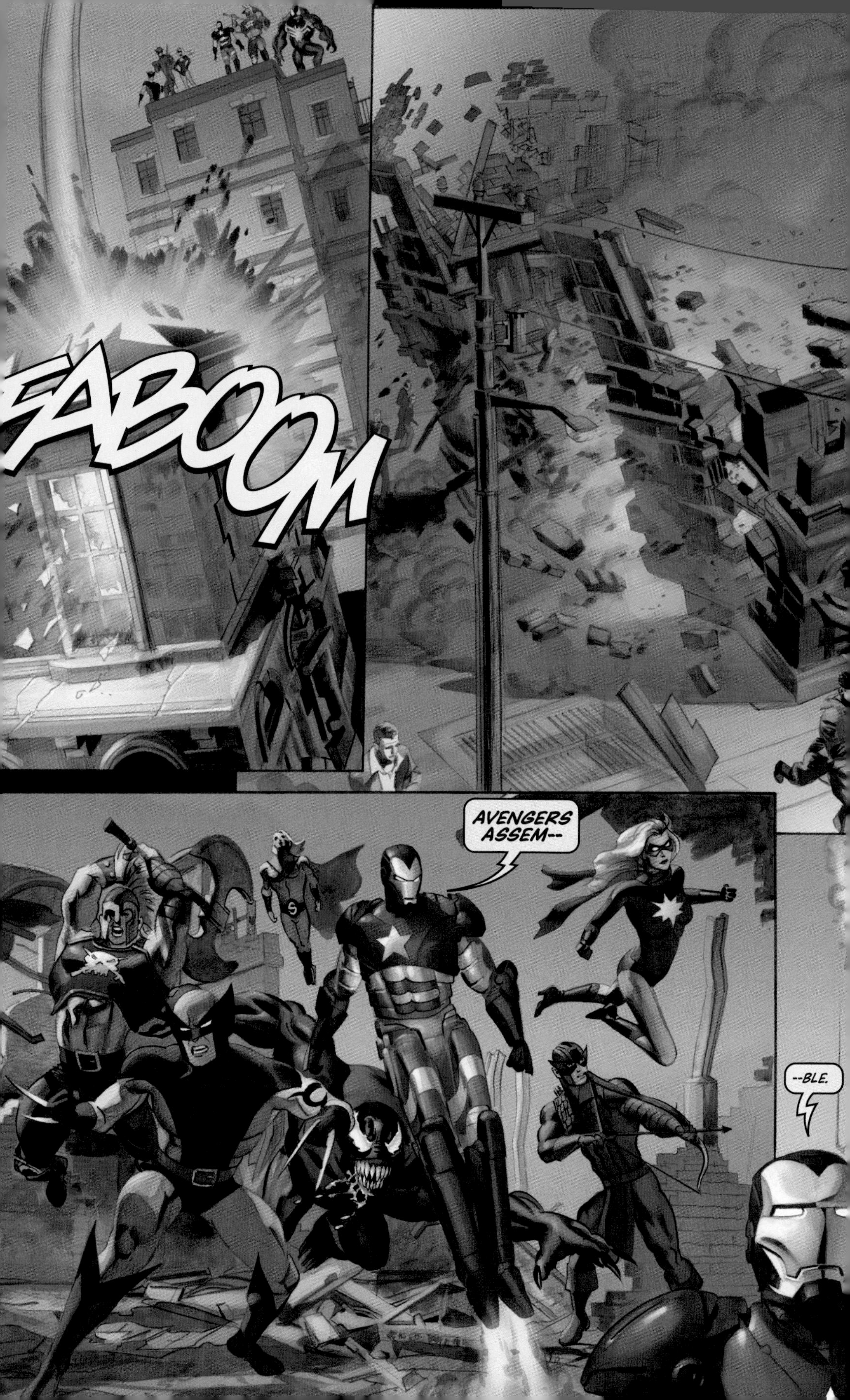
KABOOM
AVENGERS ASSEM--
--BLE.

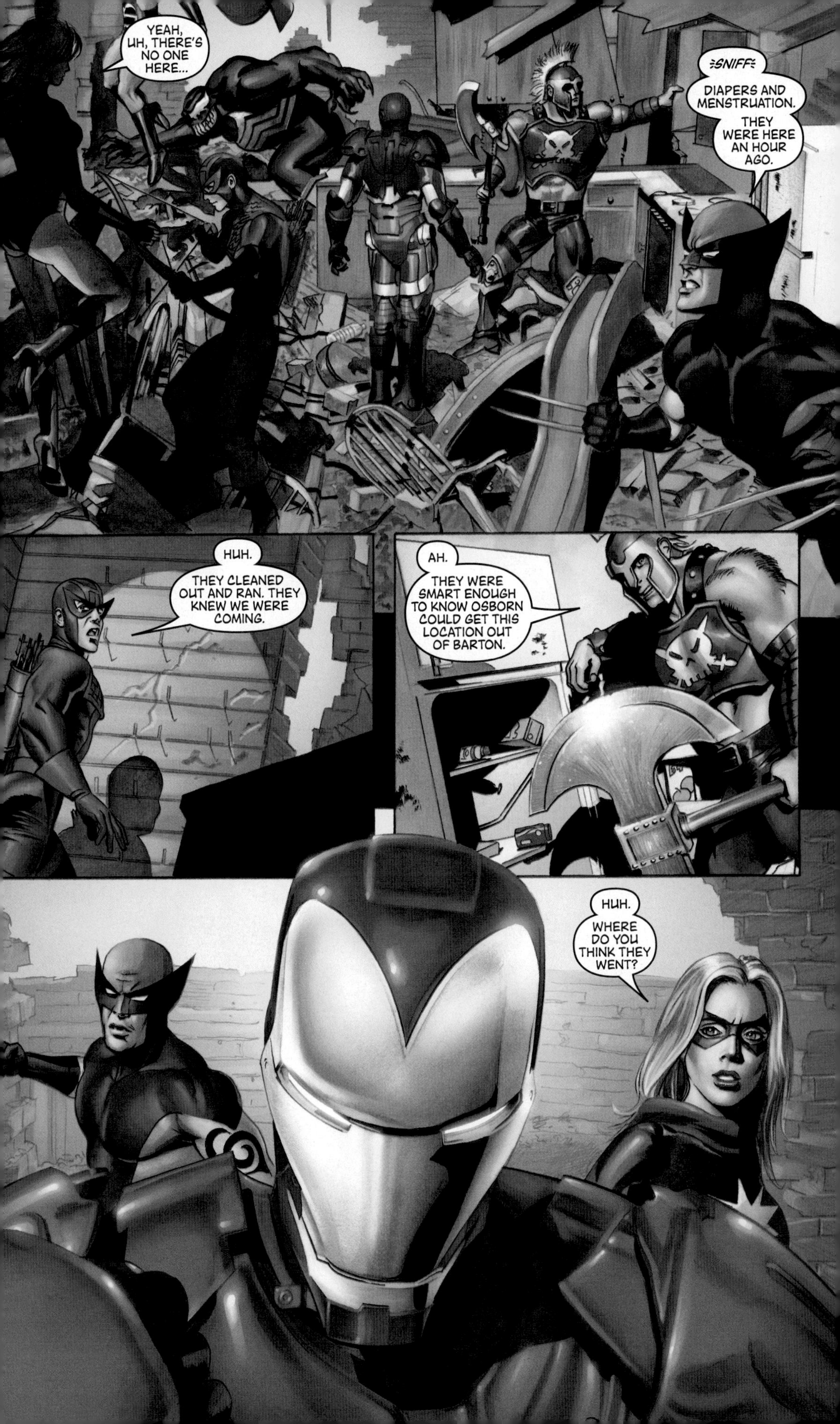
YEAH, UH, THERE'S NO ONE HERE...
SNIFF
DIAPERS AND MENSTRUATION.
THEY WERE HERE AN HOUR AGO.
HUH.
THEY CLEANED OUT AND RAN. THEY KNEW WE WERE COMING.
AH.
THEY WERE SMART ENOUGH TO KNOW OSBORN COULD GET THIS LOCATION OUT OF BARTON.
HUH.
WHERE DO YOU THINK THEY WENT?

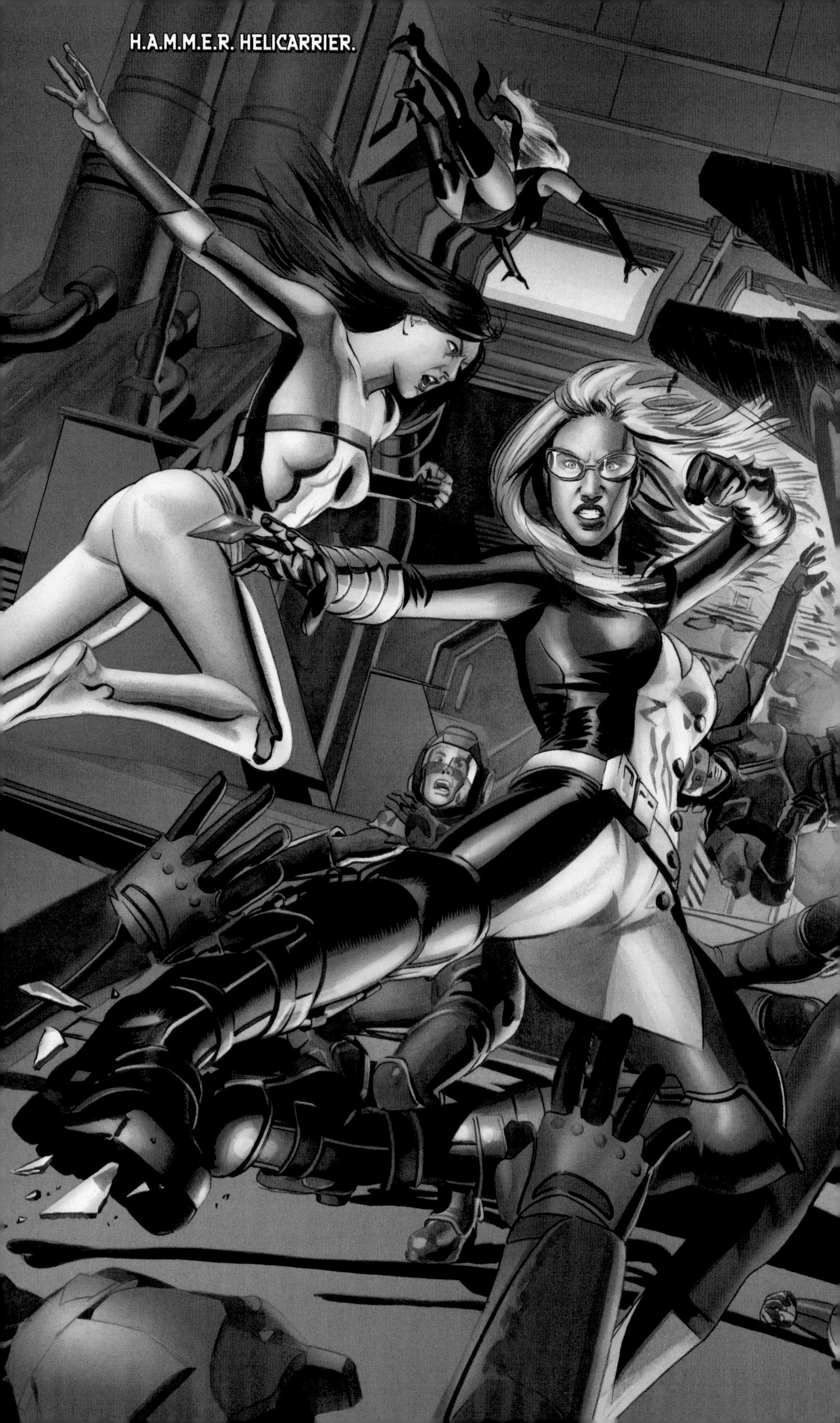
H.A.M.M.E.R. HELICARRIER.

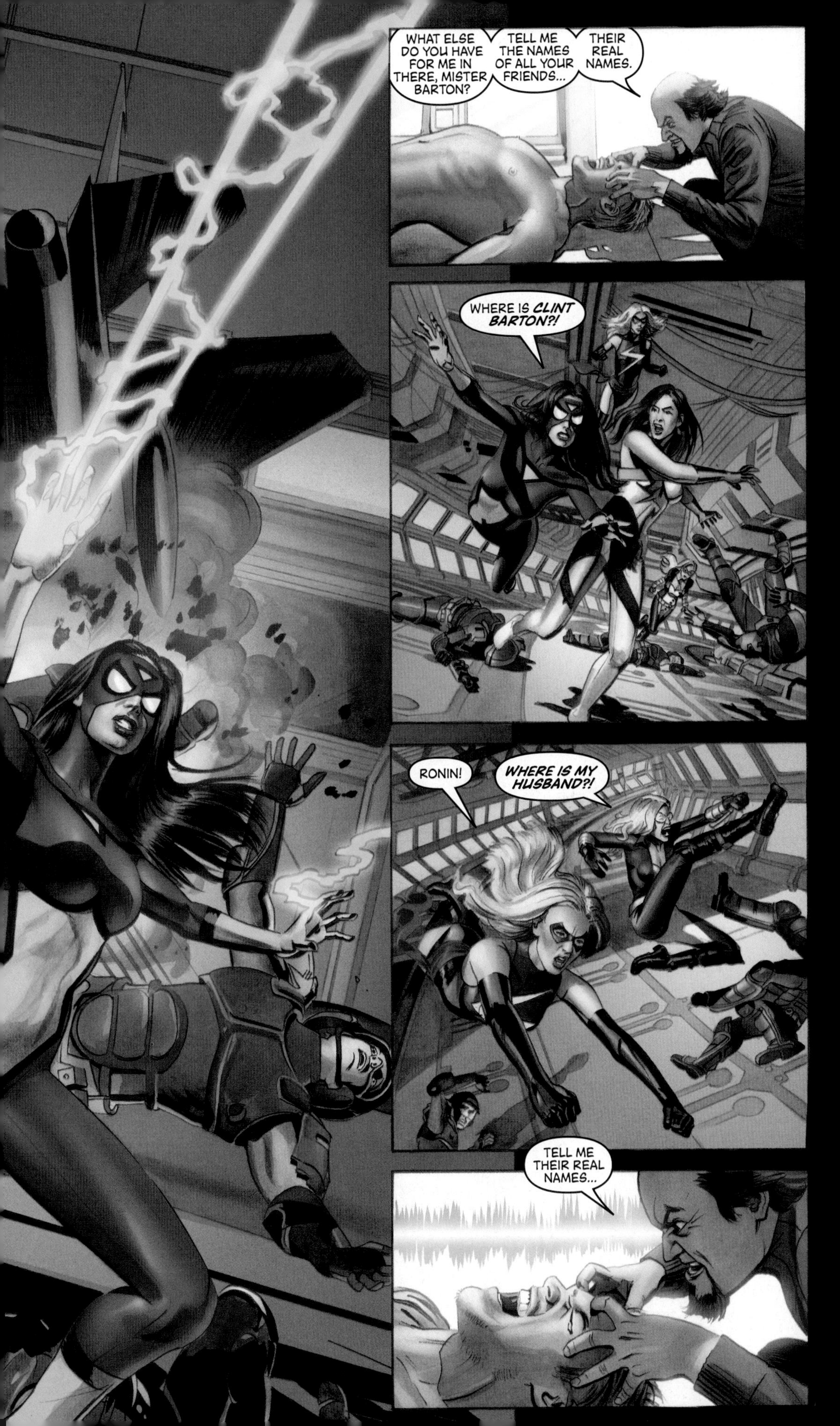
WHAT ELSE DO YOU HAVE FOR ME IN THERE, MISTER BARTON?
TELL ME THE NAMES OF ALL YOUR FRIENDS...
THEIR REAL NAMES.
WHERE IS CLINT BARTON?!
RONIN!
WHERE IS MY HUSBAND?!
TELL ME THEIR REAL NAMES...

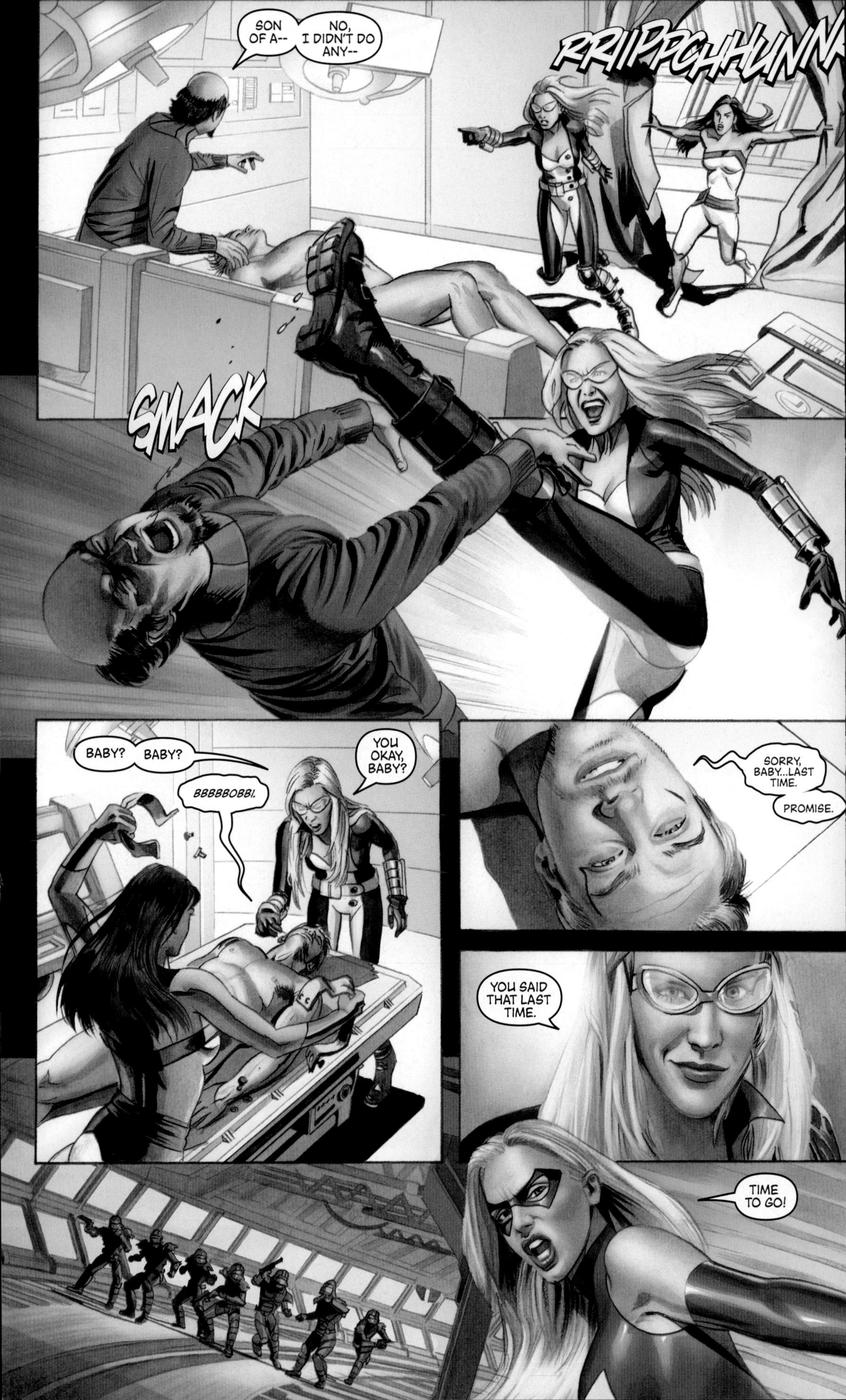
SON OF A--
NO, I DIDN'T DO ANY--
RRIIPPCHHUNNK
SMACK
BABY? BABY?
YOU OKAY, BABY?
BBBBBOBBI.
SORRY, BABY...LAST TIME.
PROMISE.
YOU SAID THAT LAST TIME.
TIME TO GO!

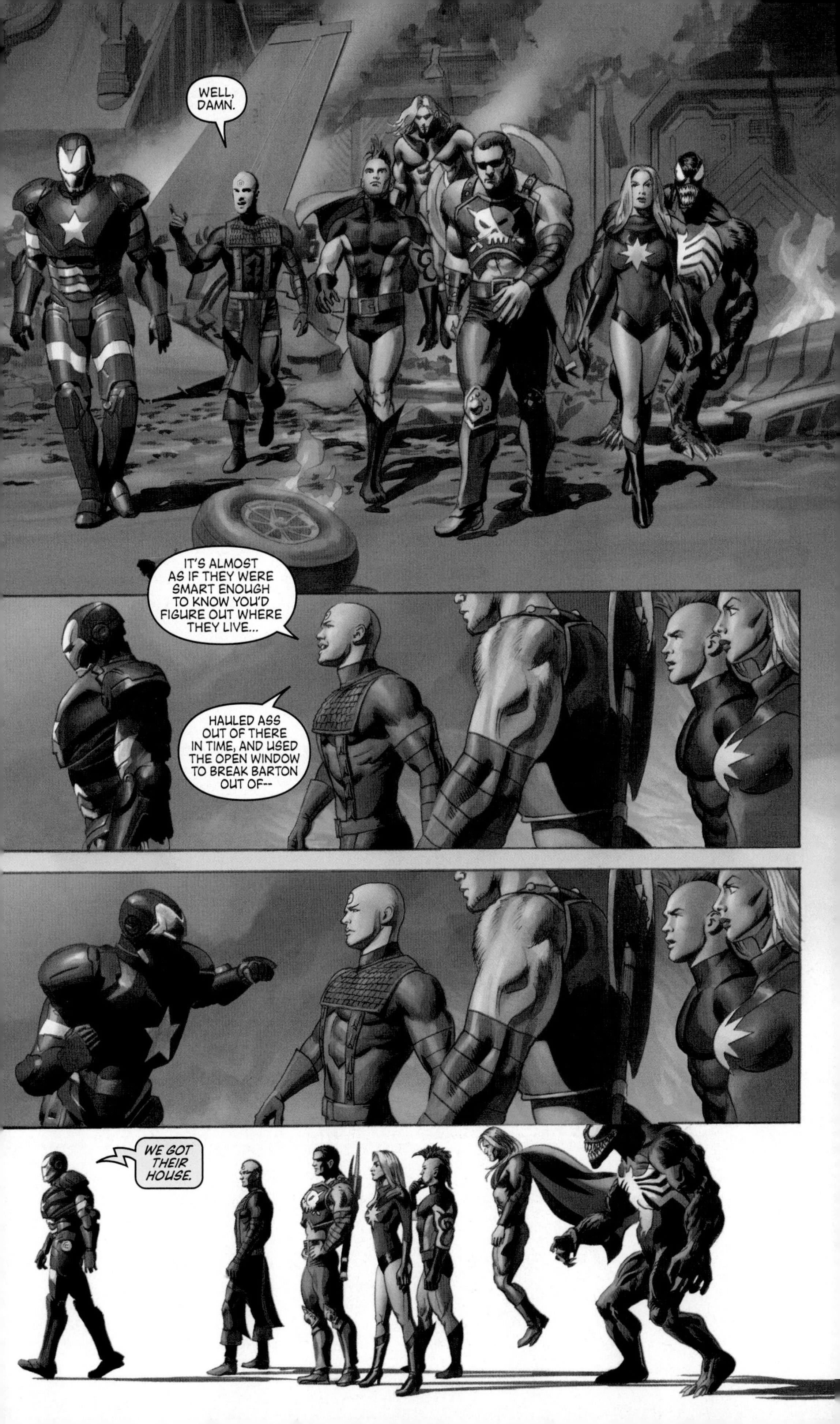
WELL, DAMN.
IT'S ALMOST AS IF THEY WERE SMART ENOUGH TO KNOW YOU'D FIGURE OUT WHERE THEY LIVE...
HAULED ASS OUT OF THERE IN TIME, AND USED THE OPEN WINDOW TO BREAK BARTON OUT OF--
WE GOT THEIR HOUSE.

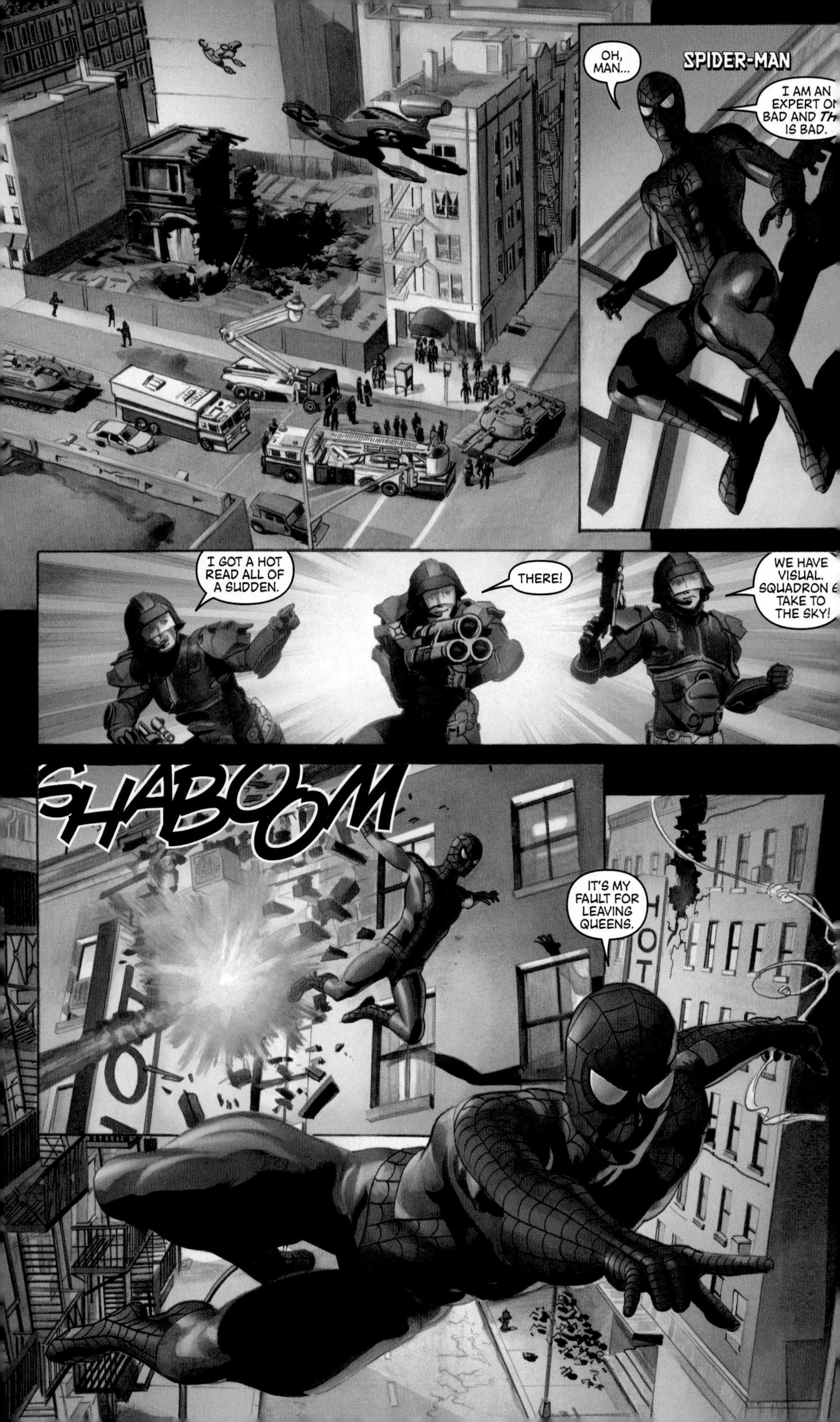

OH, MAN...
SPIDER-MAN
I AM AN EXPERT O BAD AND TH IS BAD.
I GOT A HOT READ ALL OF A SUDDEN.
THERE!
WE HAVE VISUAL. SQUADRON 6 TAKE TO THE SKY!
SHABOOM
IT'S MY FAULT FOR LEAVING QUEENS.

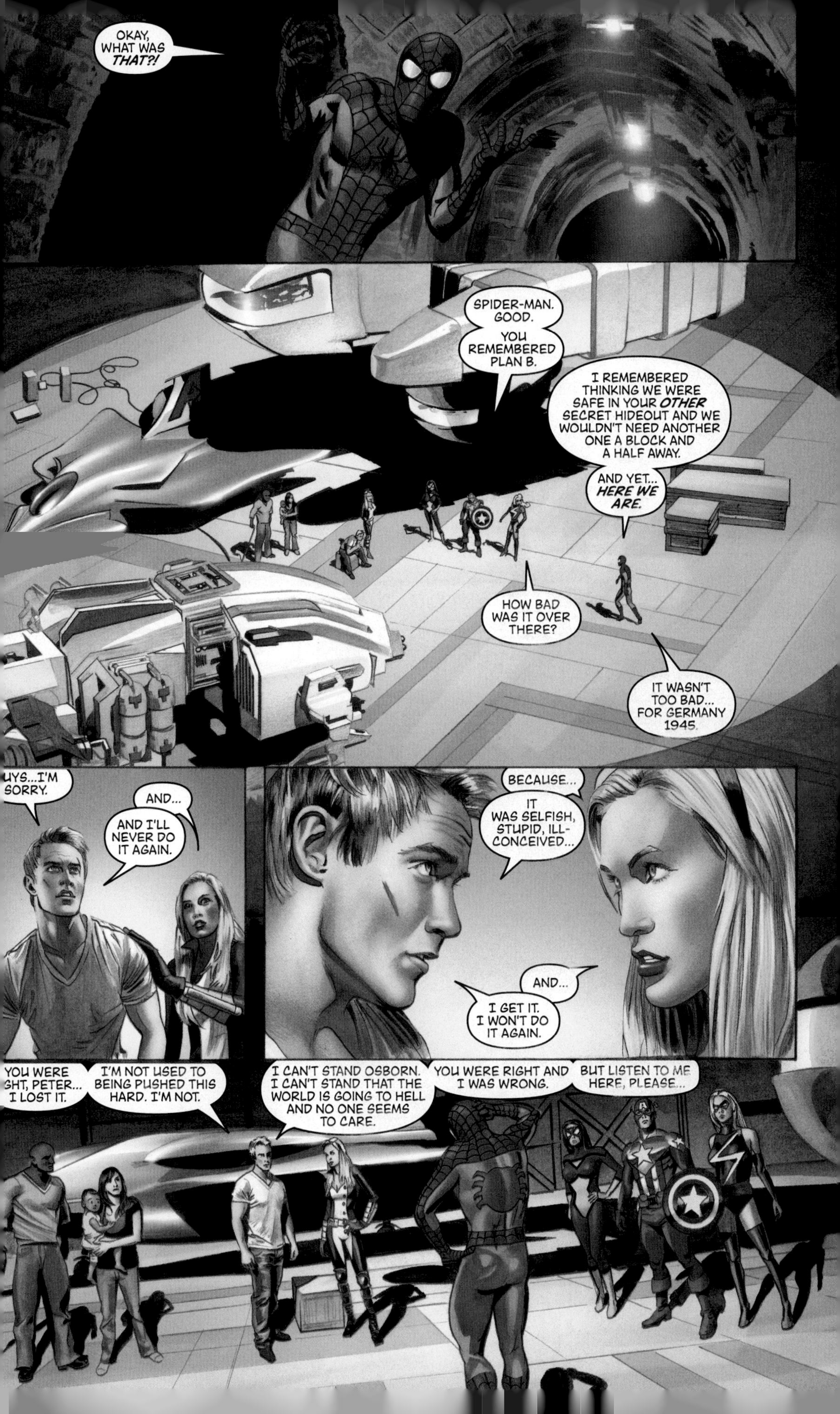
OKAY, WHAT WAS THAT?!
SPIDER-MAN. GOOD. YOU REMEMBERED PLAN B.
I REMEMBERED THINKING WE WERE SAFE IN YOUR OTHER SECRET HIDEOUT AND WE WOULDN'T NEED ANOTHER ONE A BLOCK AND A HALF AWAY.
AND YET... HERE WE ARE.
HOW BAD WAS IT OVER THERE?
IT WASN'T TOO BAD... FOR GERMANY 1945.
UYS...I'M SORRY.
AND...
AND I'LL NEVER DO IT AGAIN.
BECAUSE...
IT WAS SELFISH, STUPID, ILL-CONCEIVED...
AND...
I GET IT. I WON'T DO IT AGAIN.
YOU WERE GHT, PETER... I LOST IT.
I'M NOT USED TO BEING PUSHED THIS HARD. I'M NOT.
I CAN'T STAND OSBORN. I CAN'T STAND THAT THE WORLD IS GOING TO HELL AND NO ONE SEEMS TO CARE.
YOU WERE RIGHT AND I WAS WRONG.
BUT LISTEN TO ME HERE, PLEASE...

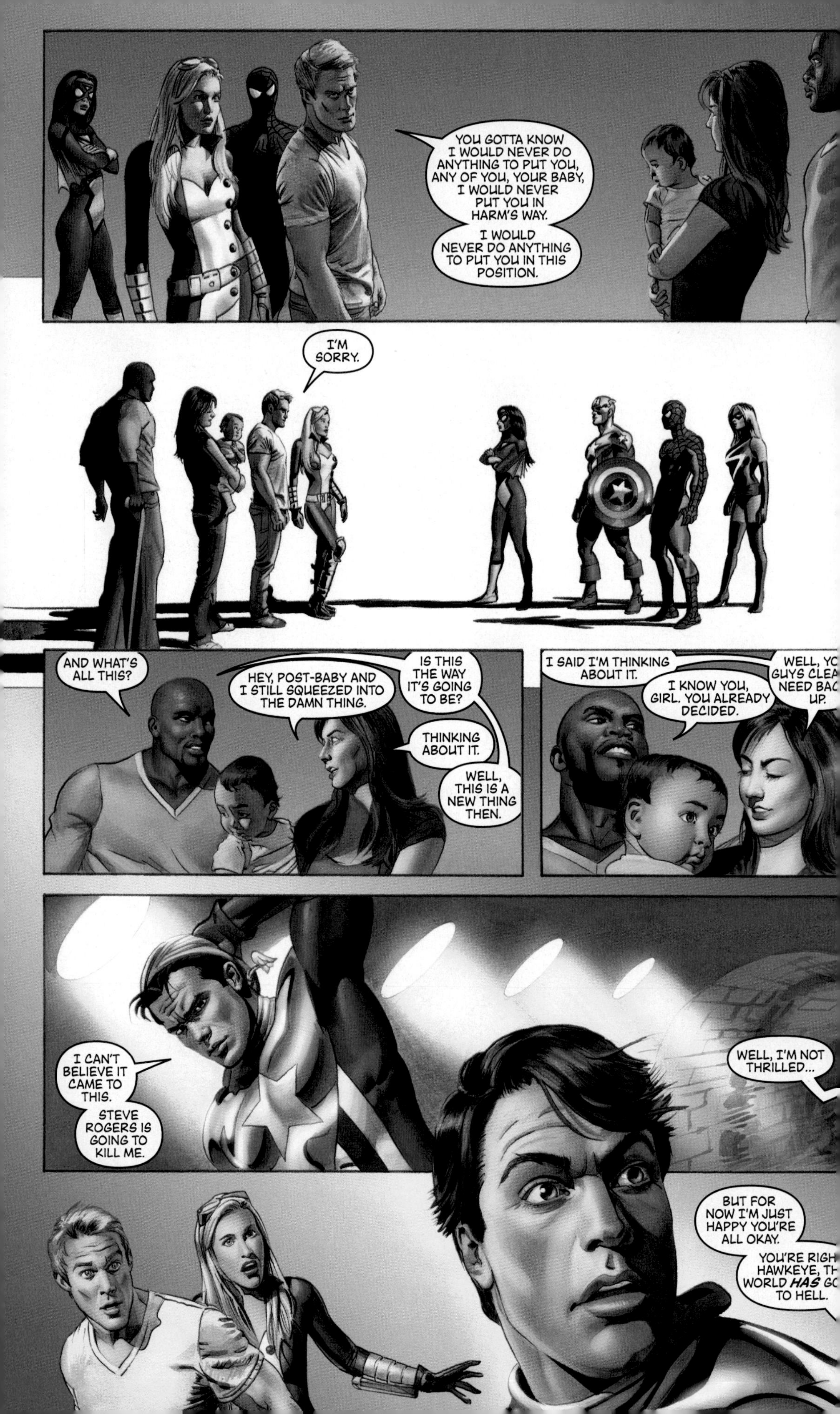
YOU GOTTA KNOW I WOULD NEVER DO ANYTHING TO PUT YOU, ANY OF YOU, YOUR BABY, I WOULD NEVER PUT YOU IN HARM'S WAY.
I WOULD NEVER DO ANYTHING TO PUT YOU IN THIS POSITION.
I'M SORRY.
AND WHAT'S ALL THIS?
HEY, POST-BABY AND I STILL SQUEEZED INTO THE DAMN THING.
IS THIS THE WAY IT'S GOING TO BE?
THINKING ABOUT IT.
WELL, THIS IS A NEW THING THEN.
I SAID I'M THINKING ABOUT IT.
I KNOW YOU, GIRL. YOU ALREADY DECIDED.
WELL, YO
GUYS CLEA
NEED BAC
UP.
I CAN'T BELIEVE IT CAME TO THIS.
STEVE ROGERS IS GOING TO KILL ME.
WELL, I'M NOT THRILLED...
BUT FOR NOW I'M JUST HAPPY YOU'RE ALL OKAY.
YOU'RE RIGH
HAWKEYE, TH
WORLD *HAS* GO
TO HELL.

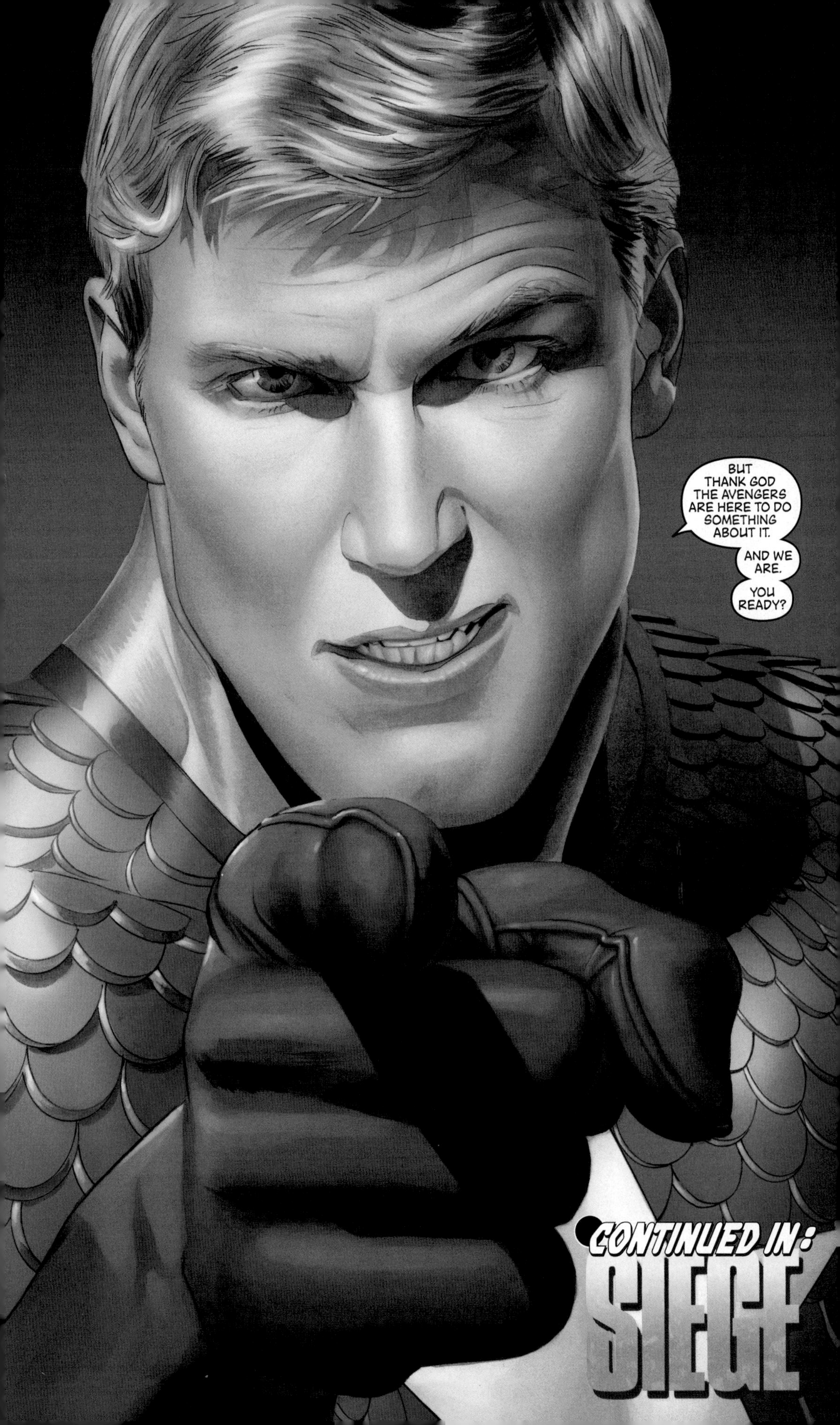
BUT THANK GOD THE AVENGERS ARE HERE TO DO SOMETHING ABOUT IT.
AND WE ARE.
YOU READY?
CONTINUED IN:
SIEGE

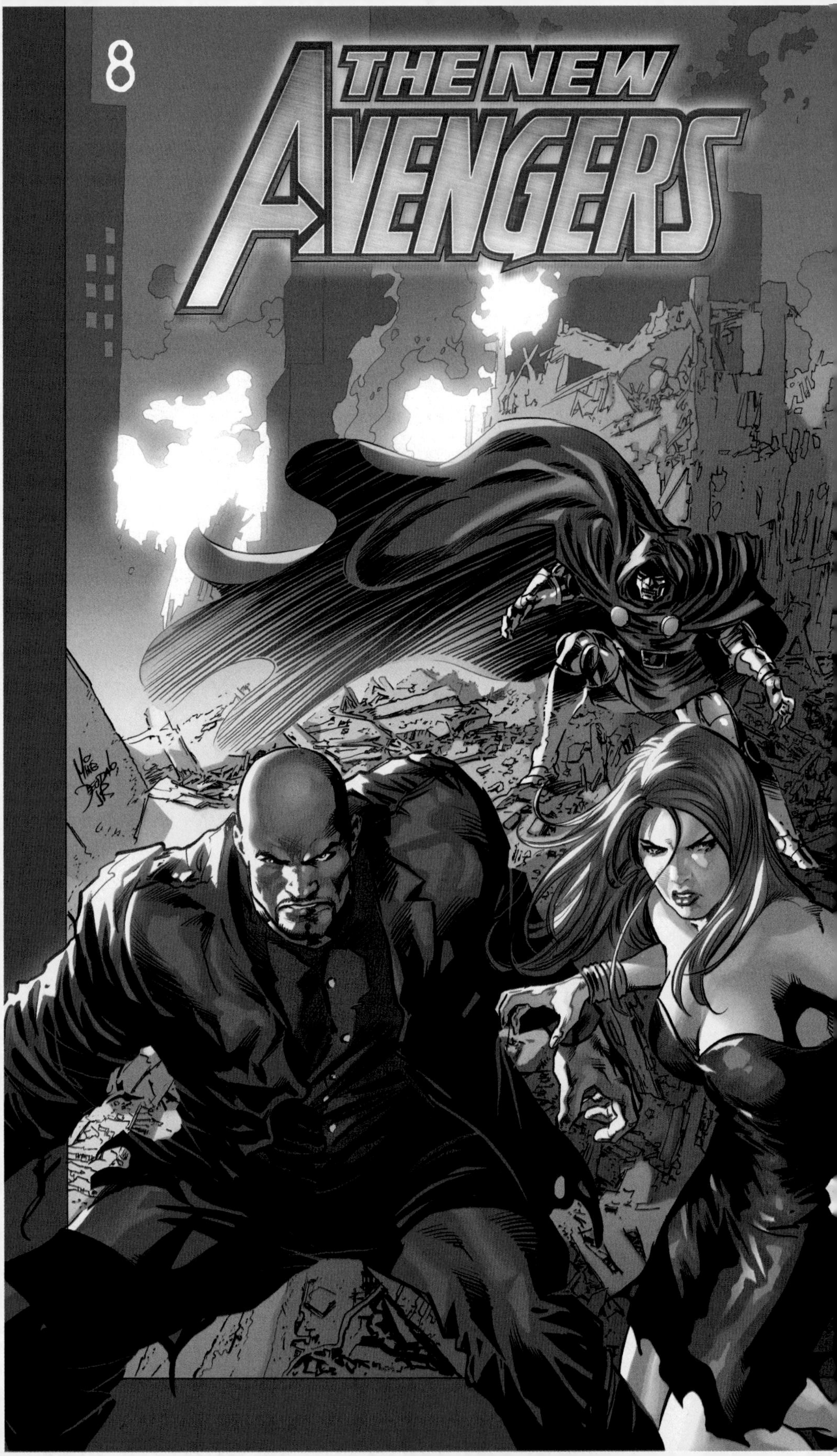
8
THE NEW
AVENGERS

EARTH'S MIGHTIEST
IEROES, UNITED
AINST A COMMON
EAT! ON THAT DAY
E AVENGERS WERE
RN, TO FIGHT FOES
IT NO SINGLE HERO
COULD
WITHSTAND!

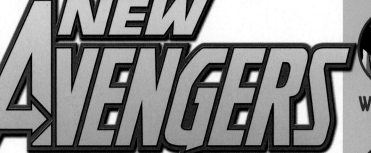

NEW AVENGERS

WOLVERINE

.UKE
:AGE

DR.
STRANGE

MS.
ARVEL

MOCKINGBIRD

HING

JESSICA
JONES

RON
FIST

VICTORIA
HAND

IDER-
MAN

SQUIRREL
GIRL

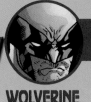

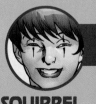

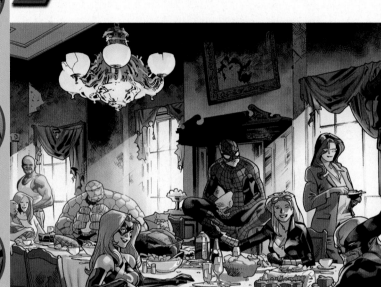

AVENGERS COMMANDER STEVE ROGERS HAS GIVEN LUKE CAGE, JESSICA JONES, MS. MARVEL, MOCKINGBIRD, SPIDER-MAN, WOLVERINE, AND THE THING THE KEYS TO AVENGERS MANSION, A LIAISON IN THE CONTROVERSIAL FORM OF VICTORIA HAND, AND FREE REIN TO PROTECT THE WORLD ANY WAY THEY SEE FIT.

AFTER SAVING THE WORLD FROM A MAGICAL EXTRADIMENSIONAL THREAT AT THE COST OF SORCERER SUPREME DOCTOR VOODOO'S LIFE, SURVIVING THE PERILS OF HIRING A NANNY FOR THE CAGES' INFANT DAUGHTER AND WELCOMING DR. STRANGE'S HIGH-STRUNG ASSISTANT WONG INTO THE MANSION, THE NEW AVENGERS ARE READY FOR A LITTLE TIME OFF...

RIAN MICHAEL BENDIS — WRITER
DANIEL ACUÑA — ART
VC'S JOE CARAMAGNA — LETTERS & PRODUCTION
MIKE DEODATO & RAIN BEREDO — COVER ART
LAUREN INKOVITCH — ASSOCIATE EDITOR
TOM BREVOORT — EDITOR
JOE QUESADA — EDITOR IN CHIEF
DAN BUCKLEY — PUBLISHER
ALAN FINE — EXEC. PRODUCER
SPECIAL THANKS TO DIEGO OLMOS & SANTI ARCAS

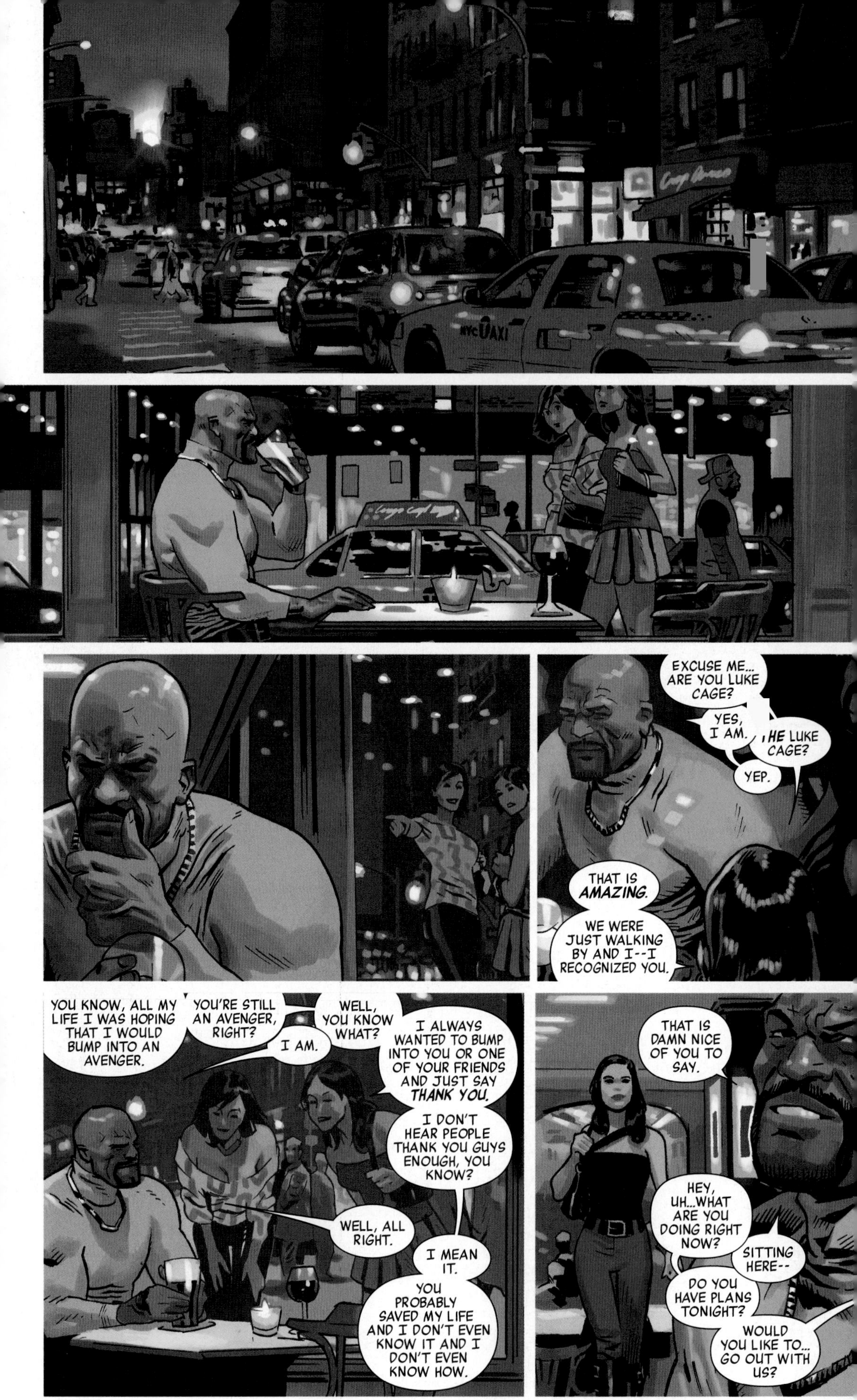

EXCUSE ME... ARE YOU LUKE CAGE?
YES, I AM.
THE LUKE CAGE?
YEP.
THAT IS AMAZING.
WE WERE JUST WALKING BY AND I--I RECOGNIZED YOU.
YOU KNOW, ALL MY LIFE I WAS HOPING THAT I WOULD BUMP INTO AN AVENGER.
YOU'RE STILL AN AVENGER, RIGHT?
I AM.
WELL, YOU KNOW WHAT?
I ALWAYS WANTED TO BUMP INTO YOU OR ONE OF YOUR FRIENDS AND JUST SAY THANK YOU.
I DON'T HEAR PEOPLE THANK YOU GUYS ENOUGH, YOU KNOW?
WELL, ALL RIGHT.
I MEAN IT.
YOU PROBABLY SAVED MY LIFE AND I DON'T EVEN KNOW IT AND I DON'T EVEN KNOW HOW.
THAT IS DAMN NICE OF YOU TO SAY.
HEY, UH...WHAT ARE YOU DOING RIGHT NOW?
SITTING HERE--
DO YOU HAVE PLANS TONIGHT?
WOULD YOU LIKE TO... GO OUT WITH US?

I'M WAITING FOR MY WIFE.

UGH! A WIFE! THAT IS *TOO* BAD.

BUT A GOOD ANSWER.

YOU ARE SO LUCKY.

ACTUALLY, I'M THE LUCKY ONE.

ANOTHER GOOD ANSWER.

YOU-- YOU GUYS-- YOU GUYS HAVE A GREAT EVENING.

NOT MY FIRST RODEO.

LOOK AT YOU. YOU REALLY ENJOYED THAT.

I WAS JUST THINKING OF HOW MUCH I SAVED YOU.

SAVED ME?

WHAT A HORRIBLE LIFE YOU USED TO LEAD...SKANK HO AFTER SKANK HO...

THANK YOU FOR SAVING ME.

IT WAS AWFUL.

YOU'RE WELCOME.

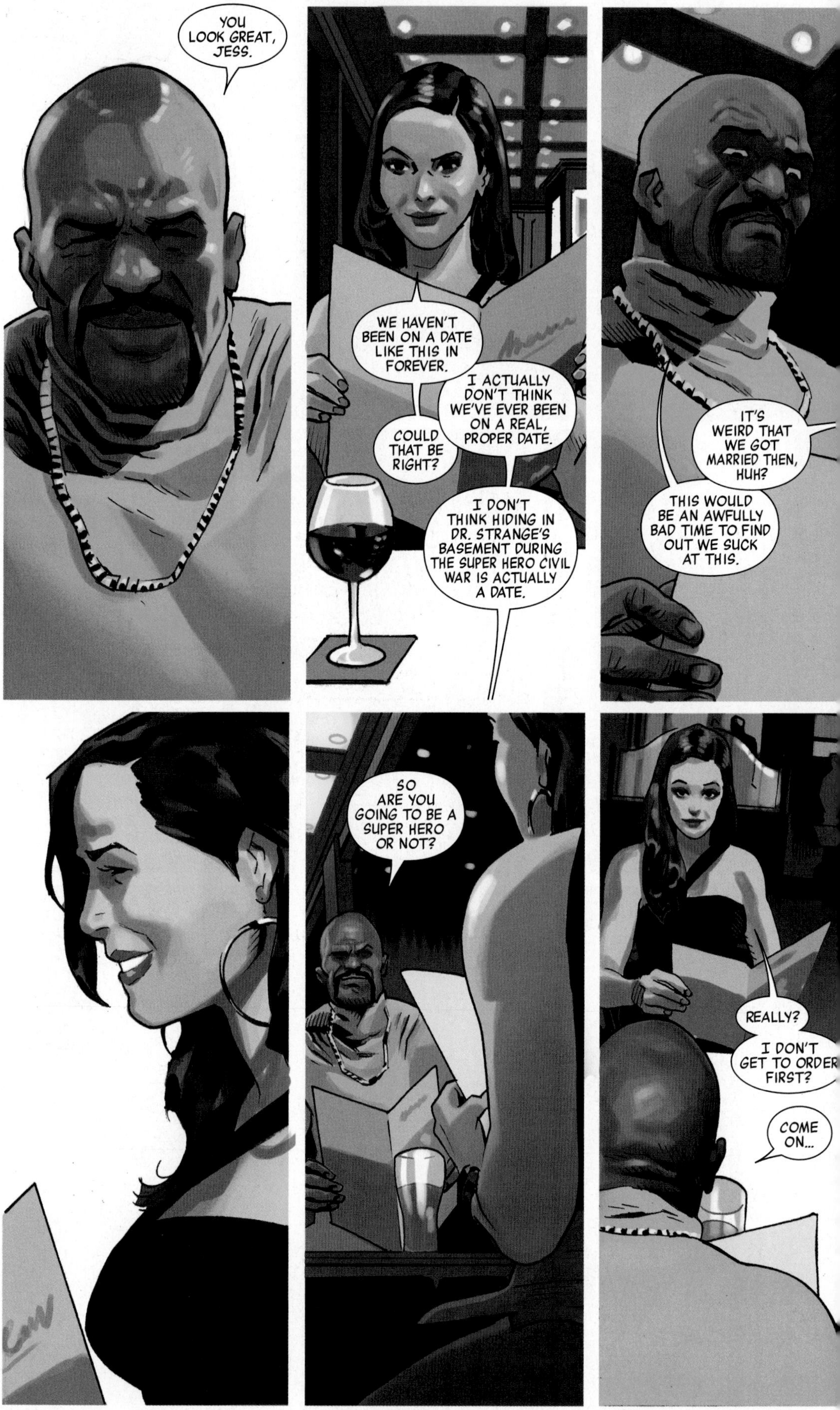
YOU LOOK GREAT, JESS.
WE HAVEN'T BEEN ON A DATE LIKE THIS IN FOREVER.
COULD THAT BE RIGHT?
I ACTUALLY DON'T THINK WE'VE EVER BEEN ON A REAL, PROPER DATE.
I DON'T THINK HIDING IN DR. STRANGE'S BASEMENT DURING THE SUPER HERO CIVIL WAR IS ACTUALLY A DATE.
IT'S WEIRD THAT WE GOT MARRIED THEN, HUH?
THIS WOULD BE AN AWFULLY BAD TIME TO FIND OUT WE SUCK AT THIS.
SO ARE YOU GOING TO BE A SUPER HERO OR NOT?
REALLY?
I DON'T GET TO ORDER FIRST?
COME ON...

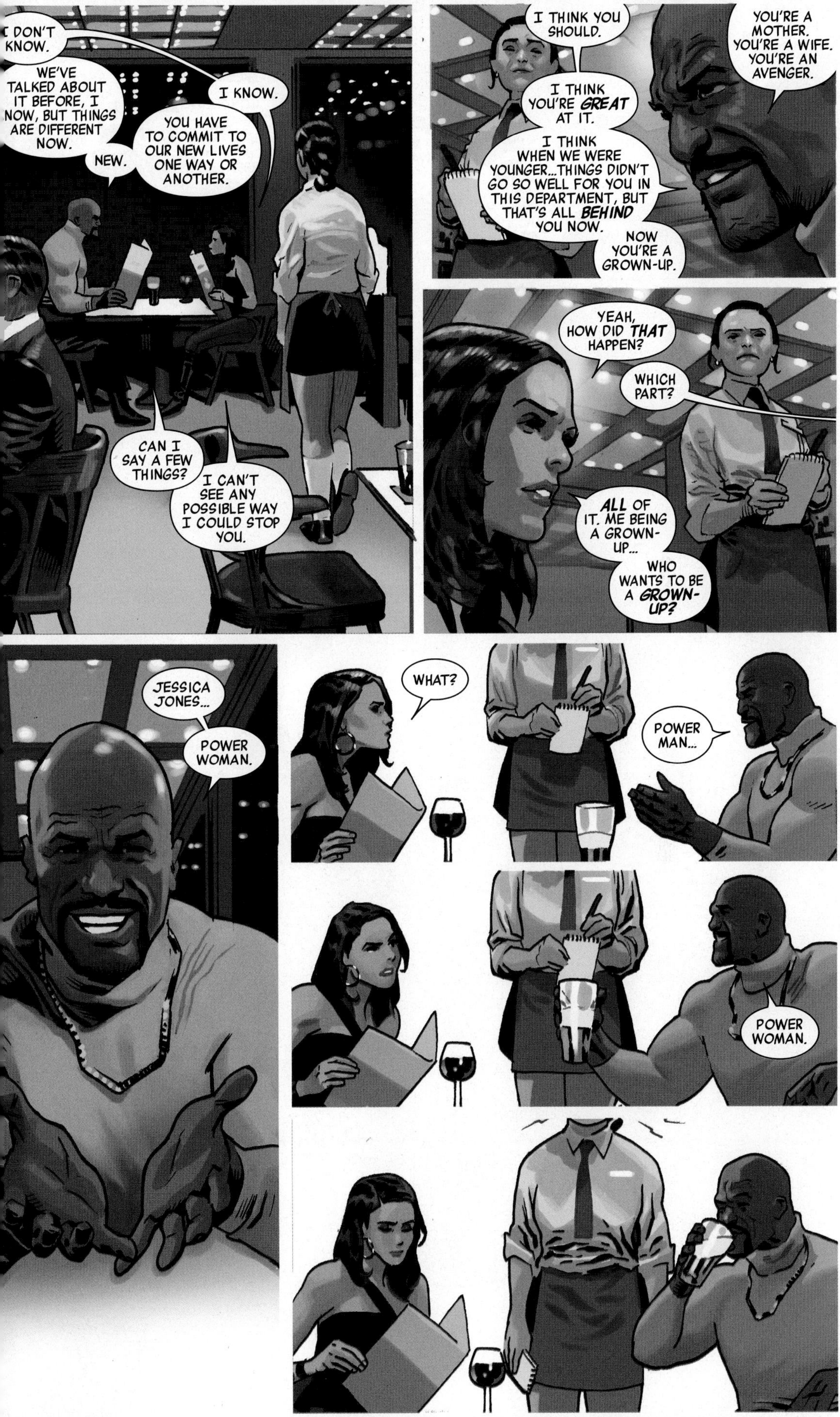
I DON'T KNOW.
WE'VE TALKED ABOUT IT BEFORE, I KNOW, BUT THINGS ARE DIFFERENT NOW.
NEW.
I KNOW.
YOU HAVE TO COMMIT TO OUR NEW LIVES ONE WAY OR ANOTHER.
CAN I SAY A FEW THINGS?
I CAN'T SEE ANY POSSIBLE WAY I COULD STOP YOU.
I THINK YOU SHOULD.
YOU'RE A MOTHER. YOU'RE A WIFE. YOU'RE AN AVENGER.
I THINK YOU'RE GREAT AT IT.
I THINK WHEN WE WERE YOUNGER...THINGS DIDN'T GO SO WELL FOR YOU IN THIS DEPARTMENT, BUT THAT'S ALL BEHIND YOU NOW.
NOW YOU'RE A GROWN-UP.
YEAH, HOW DID THAT HAPPEN?
WHICH PART?
ALL OF IT. ME BEING A GROWN-UP...
WHO WANTS TO BE A GROWN-UP?
JESSICA JONES...
POWER WOMAN.
WHAT?
POWER MAN...
POWER WOMAN.

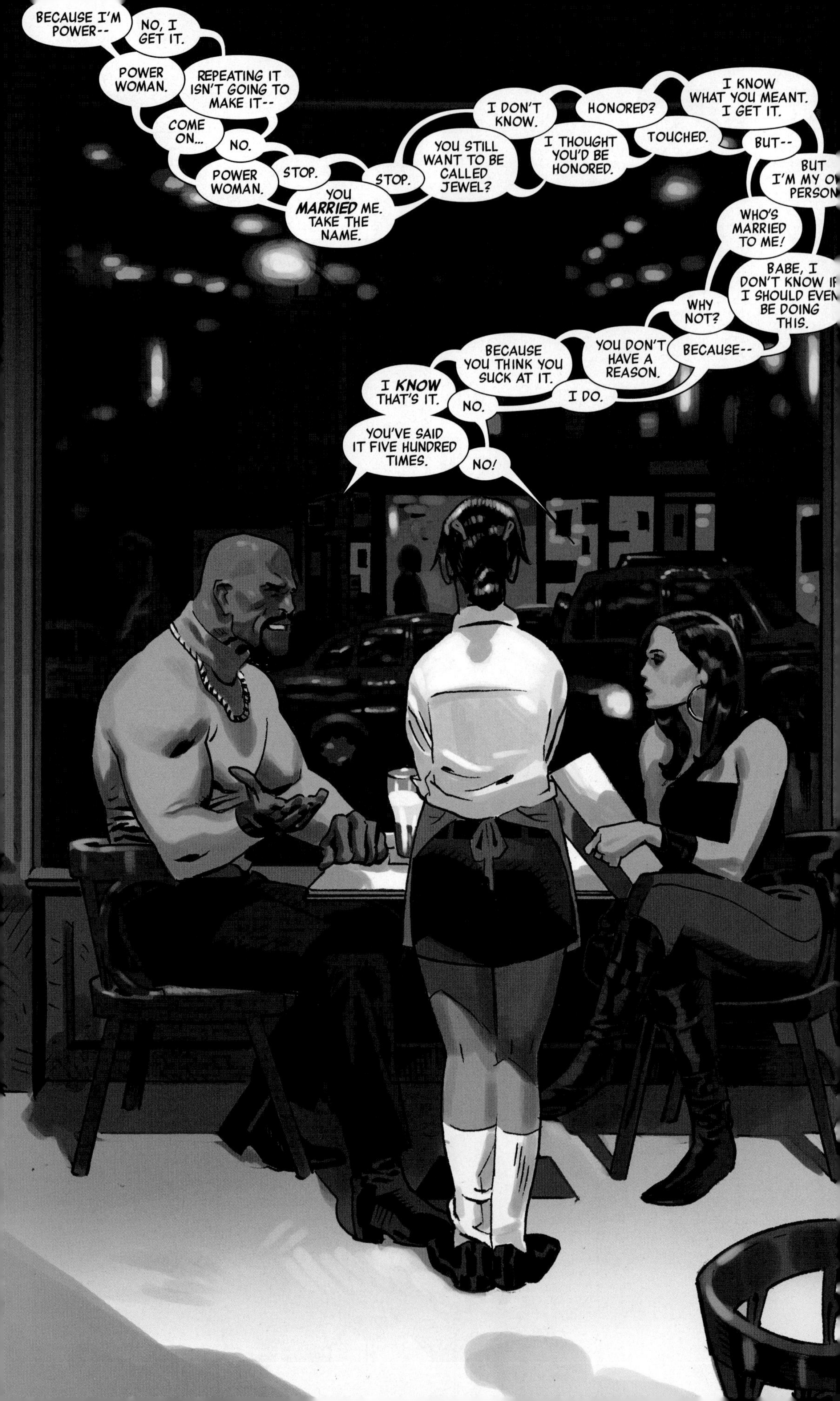
BECAUSE I'M POWER--
NO, I GET IT.
POWER WOMAN.
REPEATING IT ISN'T GOING TO MAKE IT--
COME ON...
NO.
POWER WOMAN.
STOP.
YOU *MARRIED* ME. TAKE THE NAME.
STOP.
YOU STILL WANT TO BE CALLED JEWEL?
I DON'T KNOW.
I THOUGHT YOU'D BE HONORED.
HONORED?
TOUCHED.
I KNOW WHAT YOU MEANT. I GET IT.
BUT--
BUT I'M MY O
PERSON
WHO'S MARRIED TO ME!
BABE, I DON'T KNOW I
I SHOULD EVEN
BE DOING THIS.
WHY NOT?
BECAUSE--
YOU DON'T HAVE A REASON.
I DO.
BECAUSE YOU THINK YOU SUCK AT IT.
NO.
I *KNOW* THAT'S IT.
YOU'VE SAID IT FIVE HUNDRED TIMES.
NO!

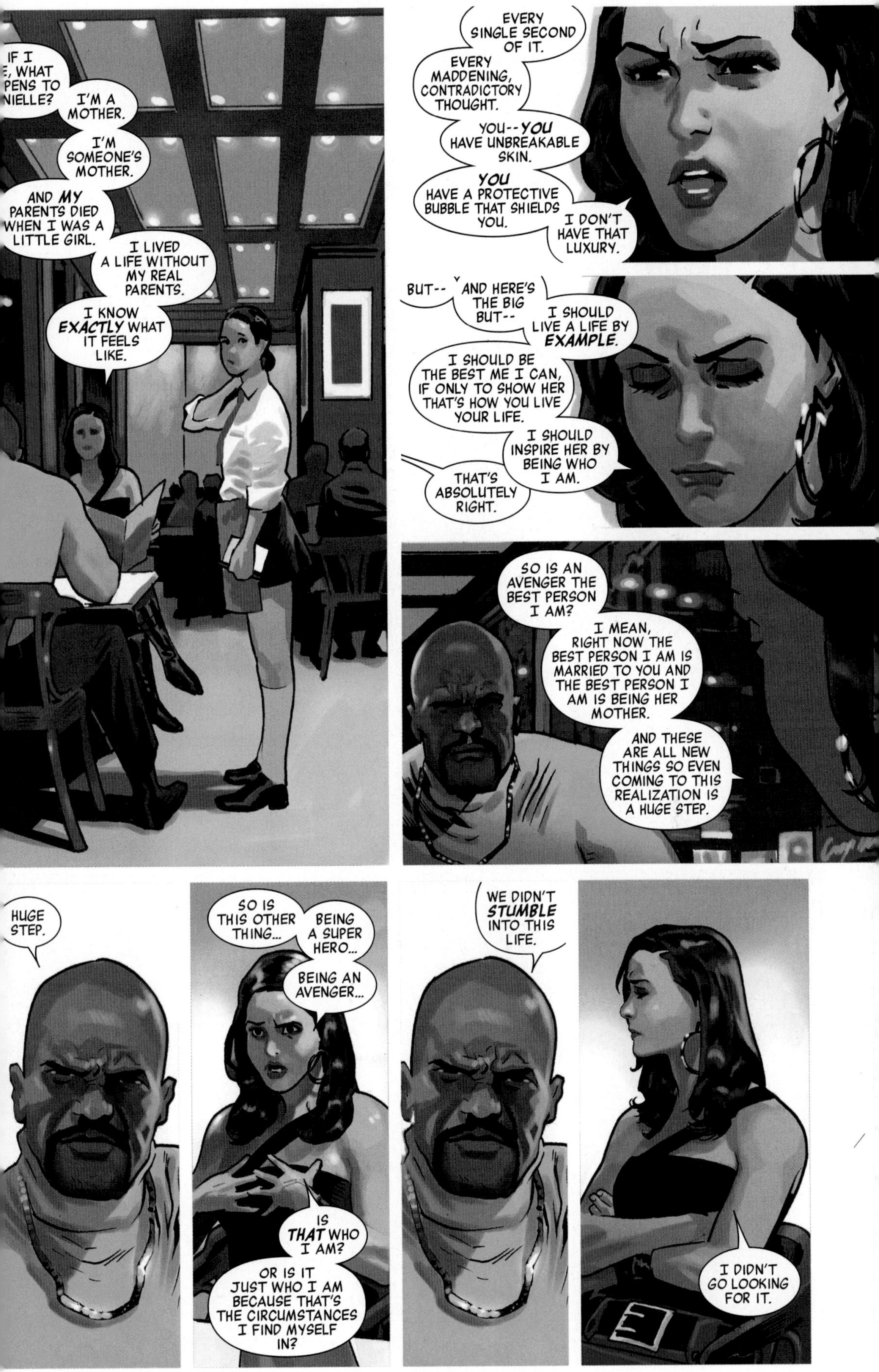
IF I
E, WHAT
PENS TO
NIELLE?
I'M A MOTHER.
I'M SOMEONE'S MOTHER.
AND MY PARENTS DIED WHEN I WAS A LITTLE GIRL.
I LIVED A LIFE WITHOUT MY REAL PARENTS.
I KNOW EXACTLY WHAT IT FEELS LIKE.
EVERY SINGLE SECOND OF IT.
EVERY MADDENING, CONTRADICTORY THOUGHT.
YOU--YOU HAVE UNBREAKABLE SKIN.
YOU HAVE A PROTECTIVE BUBBLE THAT SHIELDS YOU.
I DON'T HAVE THAT LUXURY.
BUT--
AND HERE'S THE BIG BUT--
I SHOULD LIVE A LIFE BY EXAMPLE.
I SHOULD BE THE BEST ME I CAN, IF ONLY TO SHOW HER THAT'S HOW YOU LIVE YOUR LIFE.
I SHOULD INSPIRE HER BY BEING WHO I AM.
THAT'S ABSOLUTELY RIGHT.
SO IS AN AVENGER THE BEST PERSON I AM?
I MEAN, RIGHT NOW THE BEST PERSON I AM IS MARRIED TO YOU AND THE BEST PERSON I AM IS BEING HER MOTHER.
AND THESE ARE ALL NEW THINGS SO EVEN COMING TO THIS REALIZATION IS A HUGE STEP.
HUGE STEP.
SO IS THIS OTHER THING...
BEING A SUPER HERO...
BEING AN AVENGER...
IS THAT WHO I AM?
OR IS IT JUST WHO I AM BECAUSE THAT'S THE CIRCUMSTANCES I FIND MYSELF IN?
WE DIDN'T STUMBLE INTO THIS LIFE.
I DIDN'T GO LOOKING FOR IT.

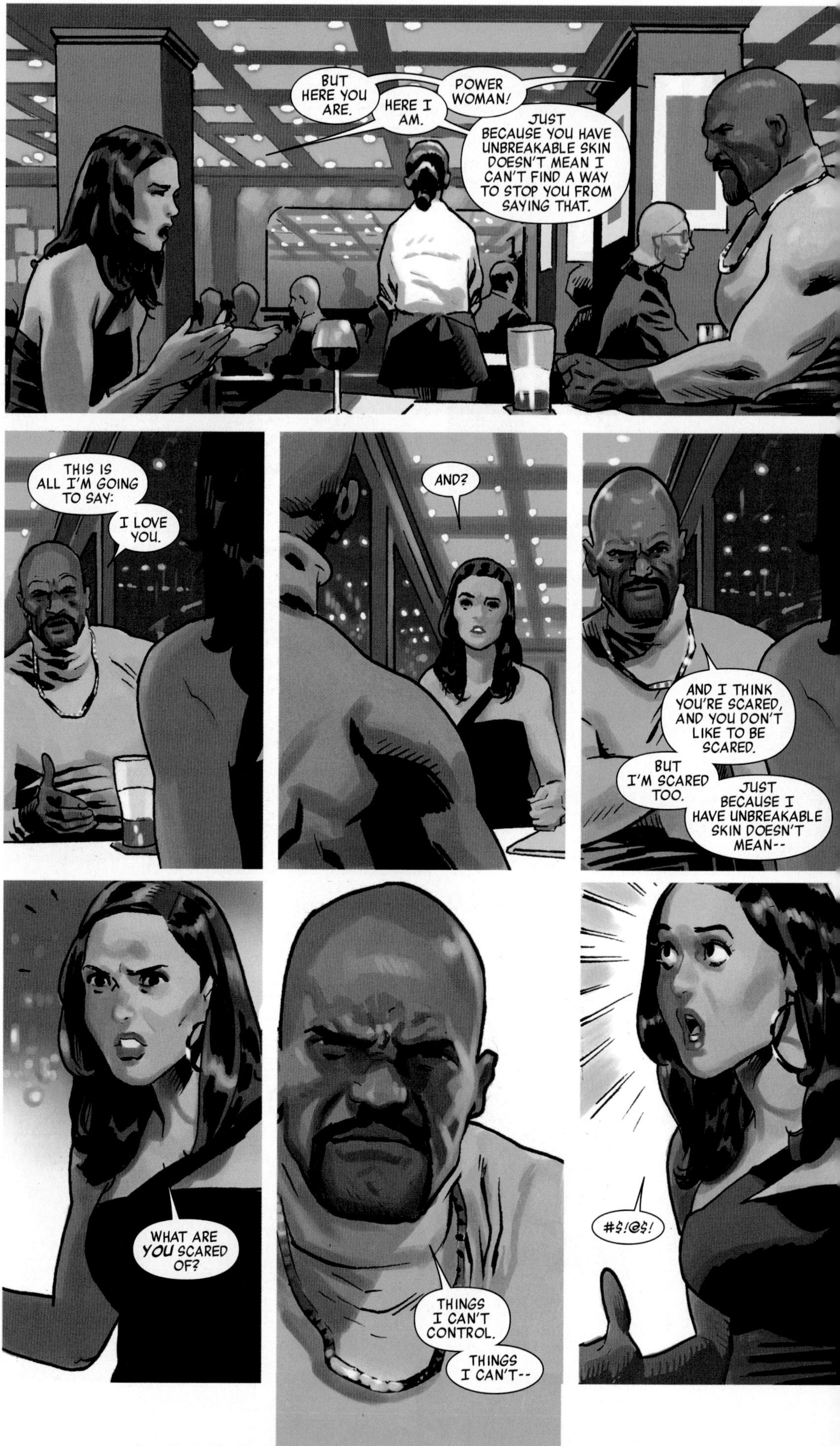
BUT HERE YOU ARE.
HERE I AM.
POWER WOMAN!
JUST BECAUSE YOU HAVE UNBREAKABLE SKIN DOESN'T MEAN I CAN'T FIND A WAY TO STOP YOU FROM SAYING THAT.
THIS IS ALL I'M GOING TO SAY:
I LOVE YOU.
AND?
AND I THINK YOU'RE SCARED, AND YOU DON'T LIKE TO BE SCARED.
BUT I'M SCARED TOO.
JUST BECAUSE I HAVE UNBREAKABLE SKIN DOESN'T MEAN--
WHAT ARE *YOU* SCARED OF?
THINGS I CAN'T CONTROL.
THINGS I CAN'T--
#$!@$!

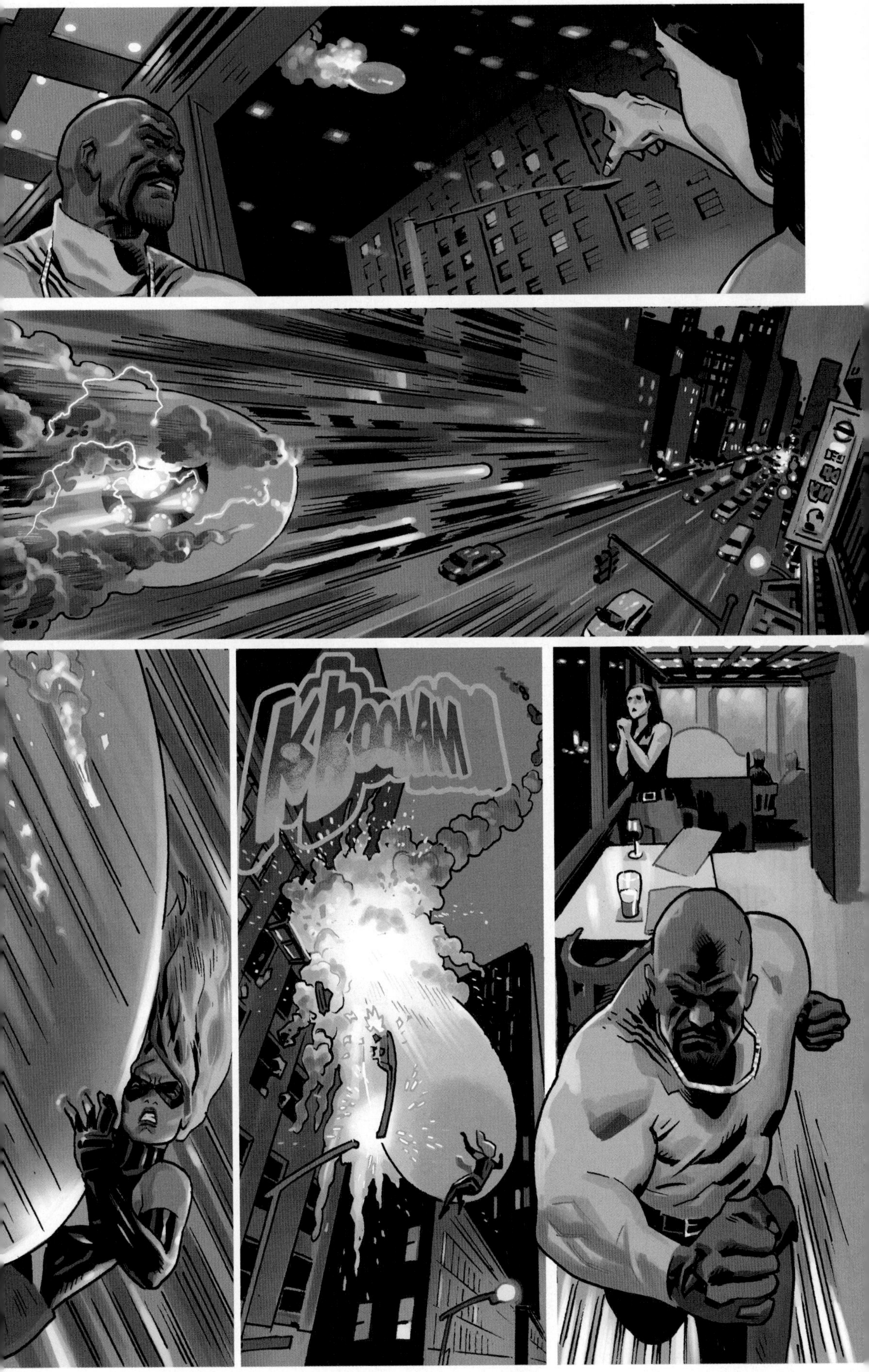
KBOOMM

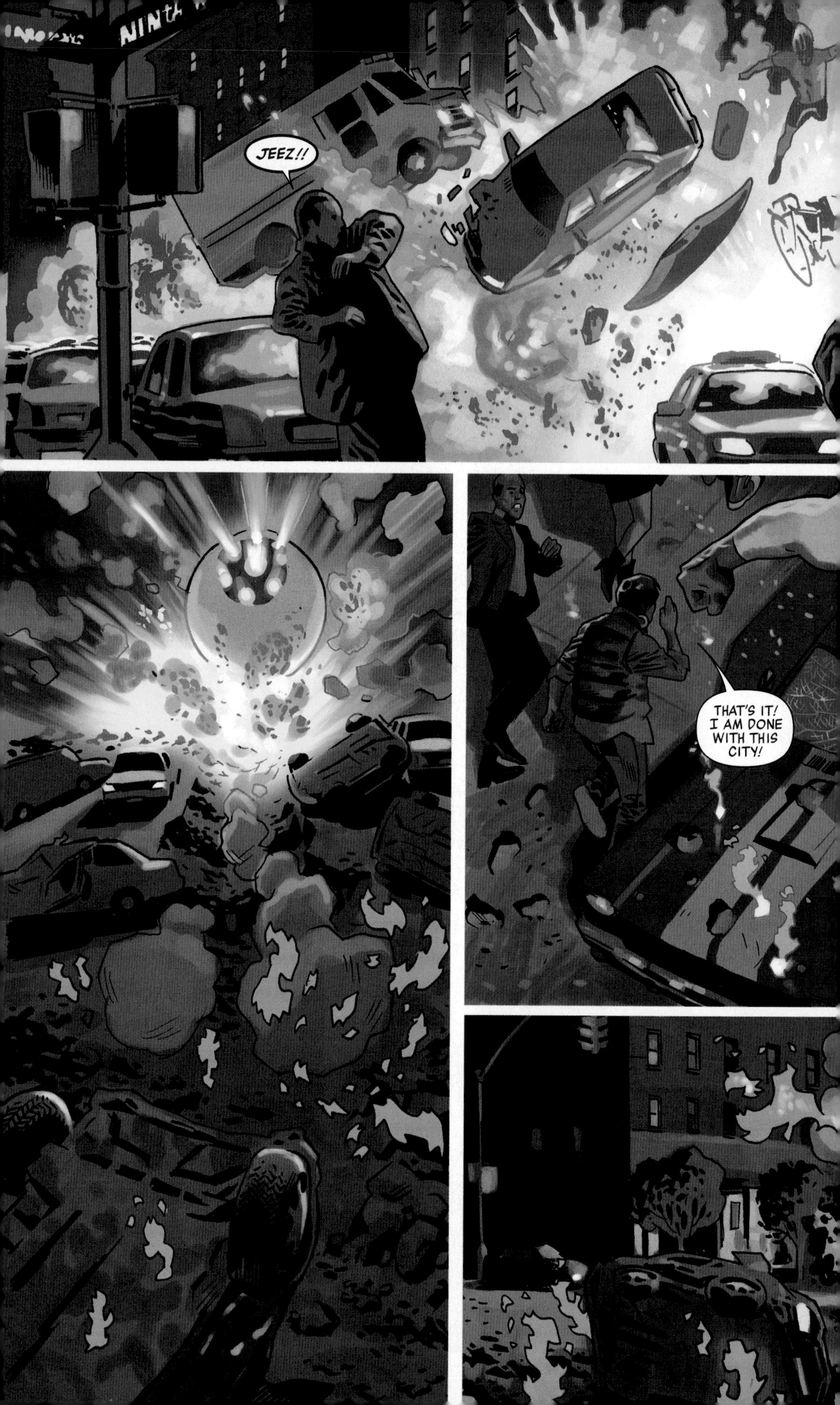
JEEZ!!
THAT'S IT! I AM DONE WITH THIS CITY!

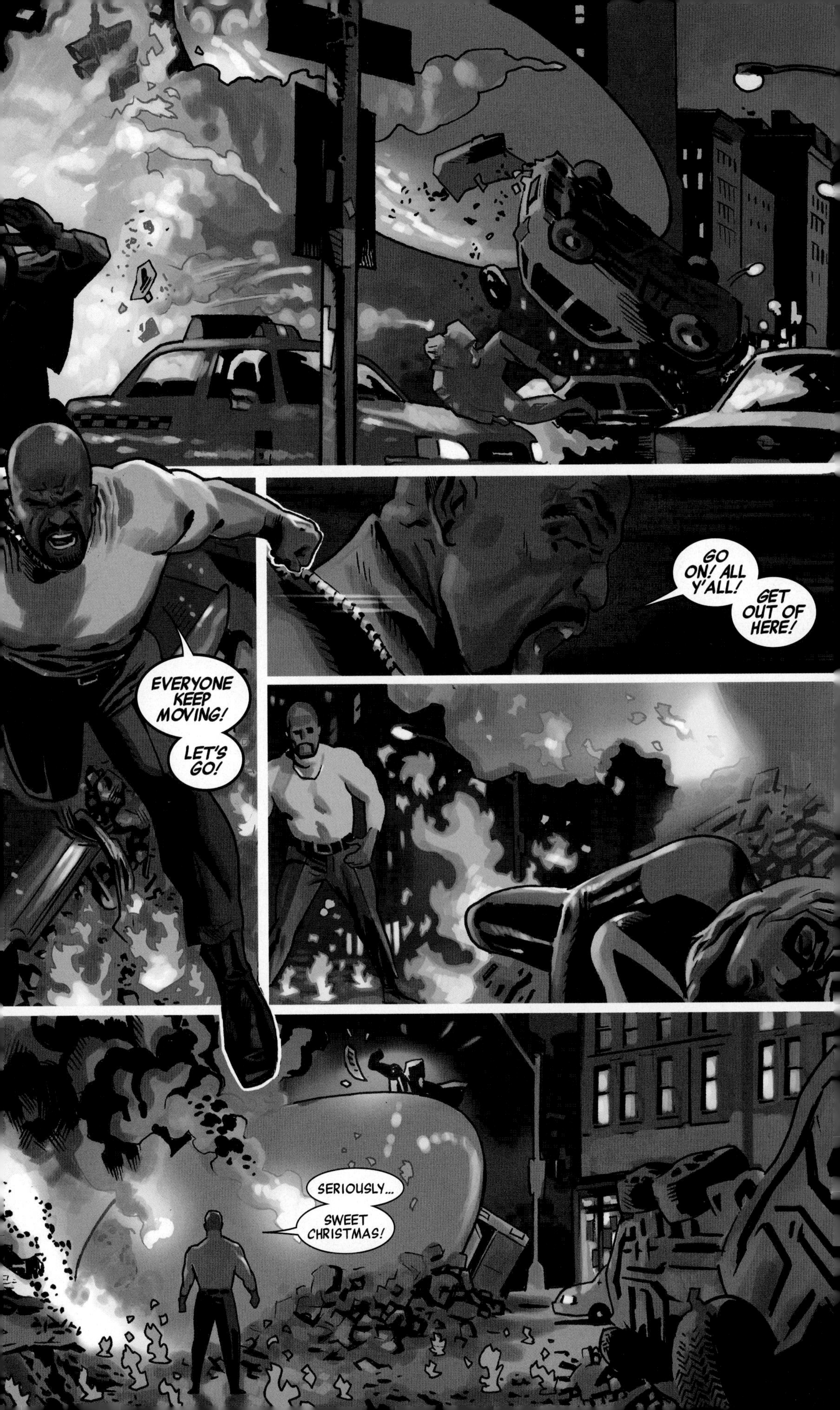
EVERYONE KEEP MOVING!
LET'S GO!
GO ON! ALL Y'ALL!
GET OUT OF HERE!
SERIOUSLY...
SWEET CHRISTMAS!

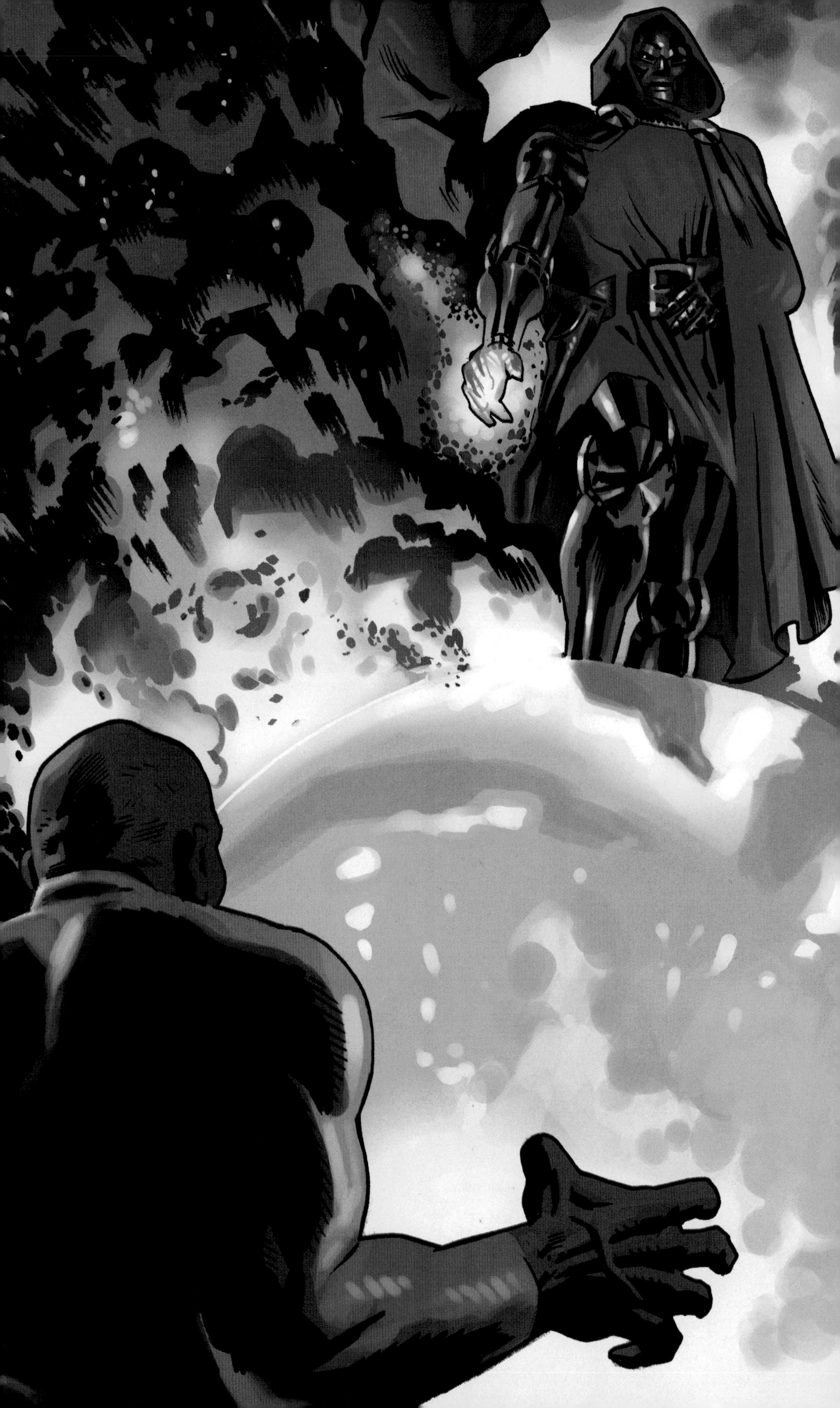

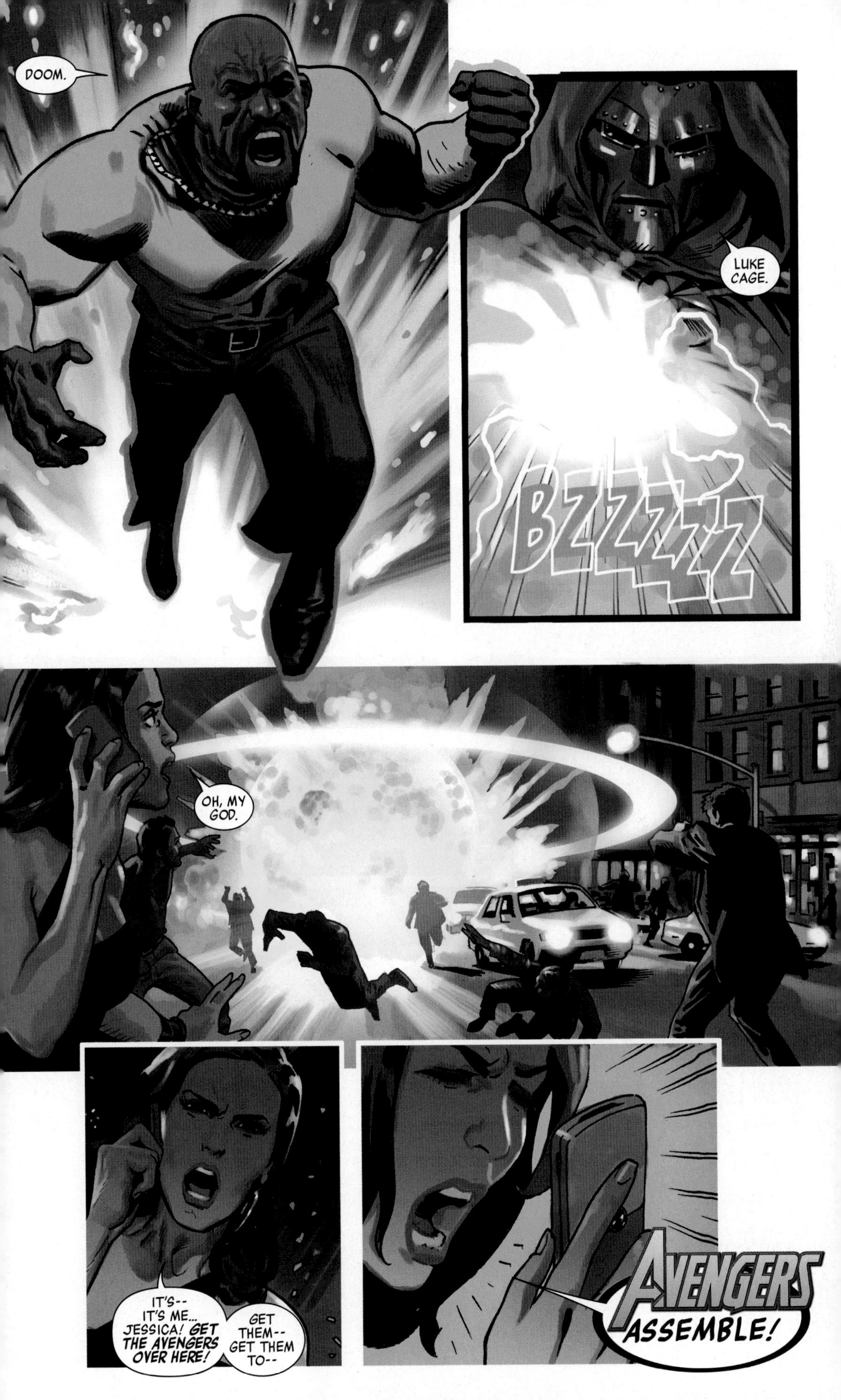
DOOM.
LUKE CAGE.
BZZZZZZ
OH, MY GOD.
IT'S-- IT'S ME... JESSICA! GET THE AVENGERS OVER HERE!
GET THEM-- GET THEM TO--
AVENGERS ASSEMBLE!

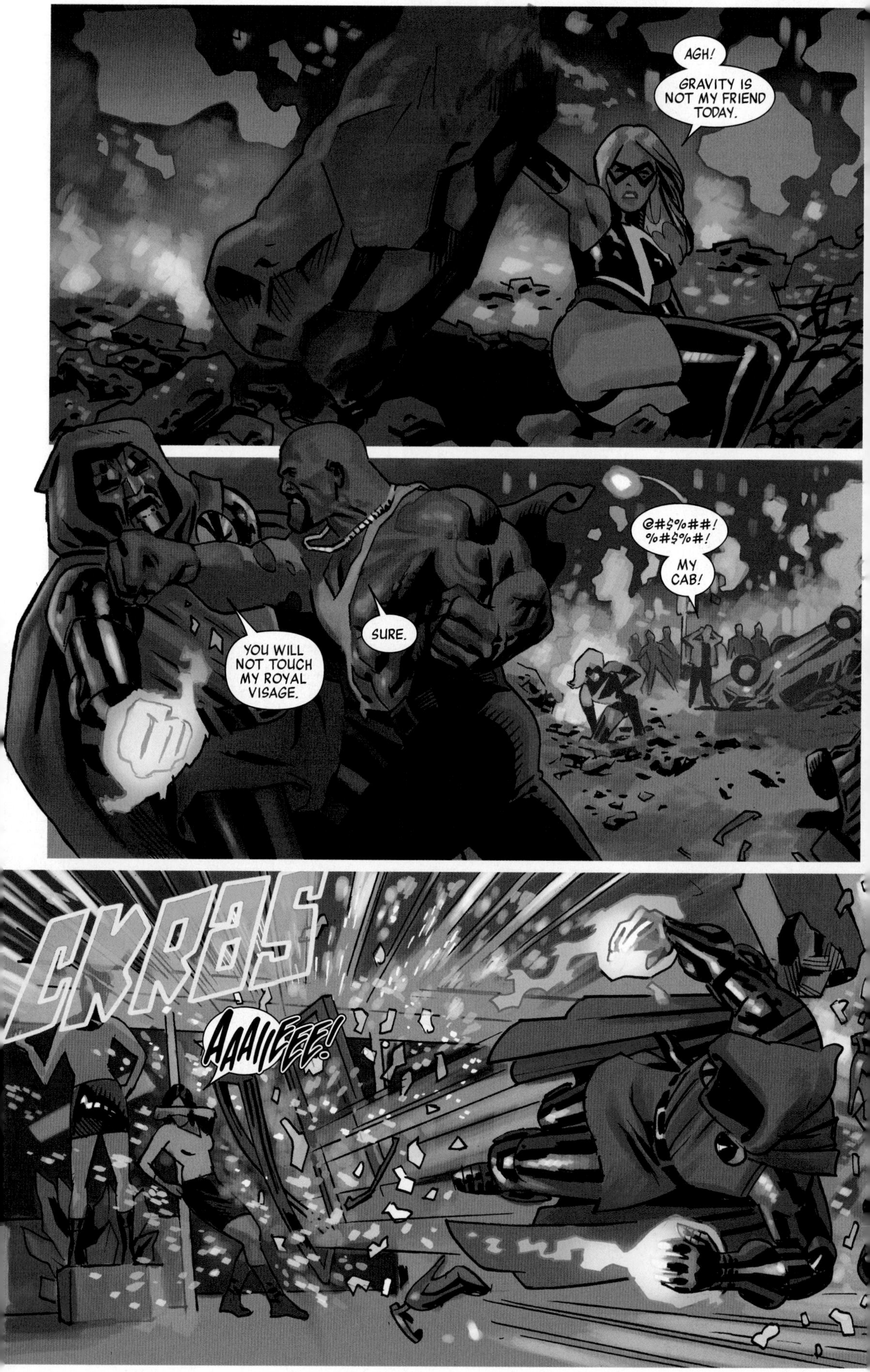
AGH!
GRAVITY IS NOT MY FRIEND TODAY.
YOU WILL NOT TOUCH MY ROYAL VISAGE.
SURE.
@#$%##! %#$%#!
MY CAB!
AAAIIEEE!

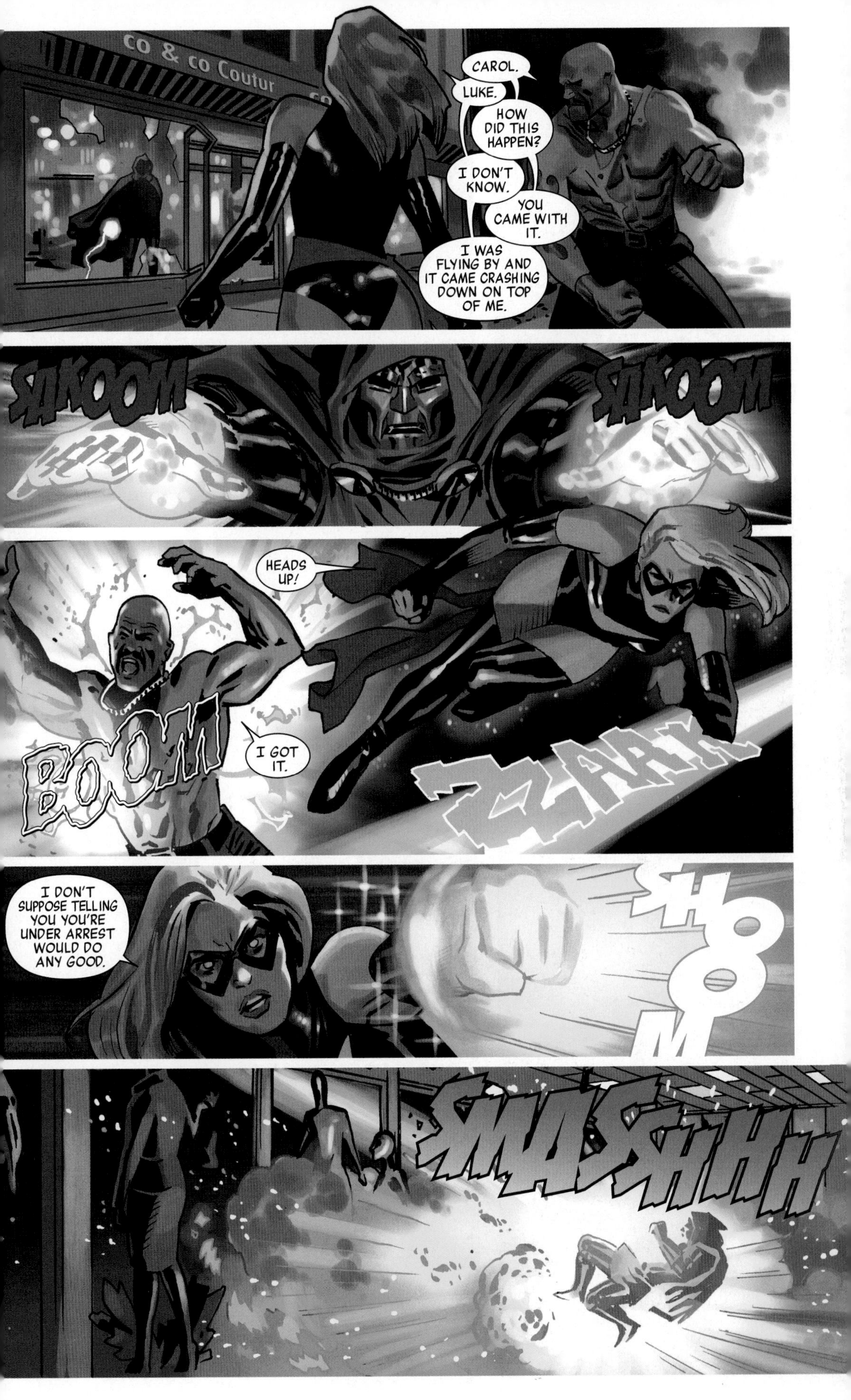
co & co Coutur
CAROL.
LUKE.
HOW DID THIS HAPPEN?
I DON'T KNOW.
YOU CAME WITH IT.
I WAS FLYING BY AND IT CAME CRASHING DOWN ON TOP OF ME.
HEADS UP!
BOOM
I GOT IT.
I DON'T SUPPOSE TELLING YOU YOU'RE UNDER ARREST WOULD DO ANY GOOD.
SHOOM
SMASHHH

HOW'S THE DATE GOING?

I CAN'T GET THROUGH TO HER.

I TOLD YOU, LET IT BE.

LET HER FIGURE OUT WHAT SHE WANTS ON HER OWN.

WHAT'S THE PLAN?

STALL HIM UNTIL THE REST OF THE AVENGERS GET HERE.

THAT IS A TERRIBLE PLAN.

OR WE COULD JUST LEAVE.

DAMN!

I'VE GOT TO SAY, DOOM... YOU ARE NOT YOUR USUAL CHATTY SELF.

WHERE'S ALL THE PROPAGANDA YOU LIKE TO THROW AT US WHILE YOU WHIP UP YOUR MAGIC WHAMMIES?

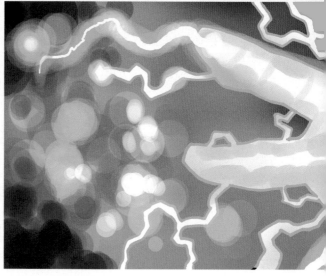

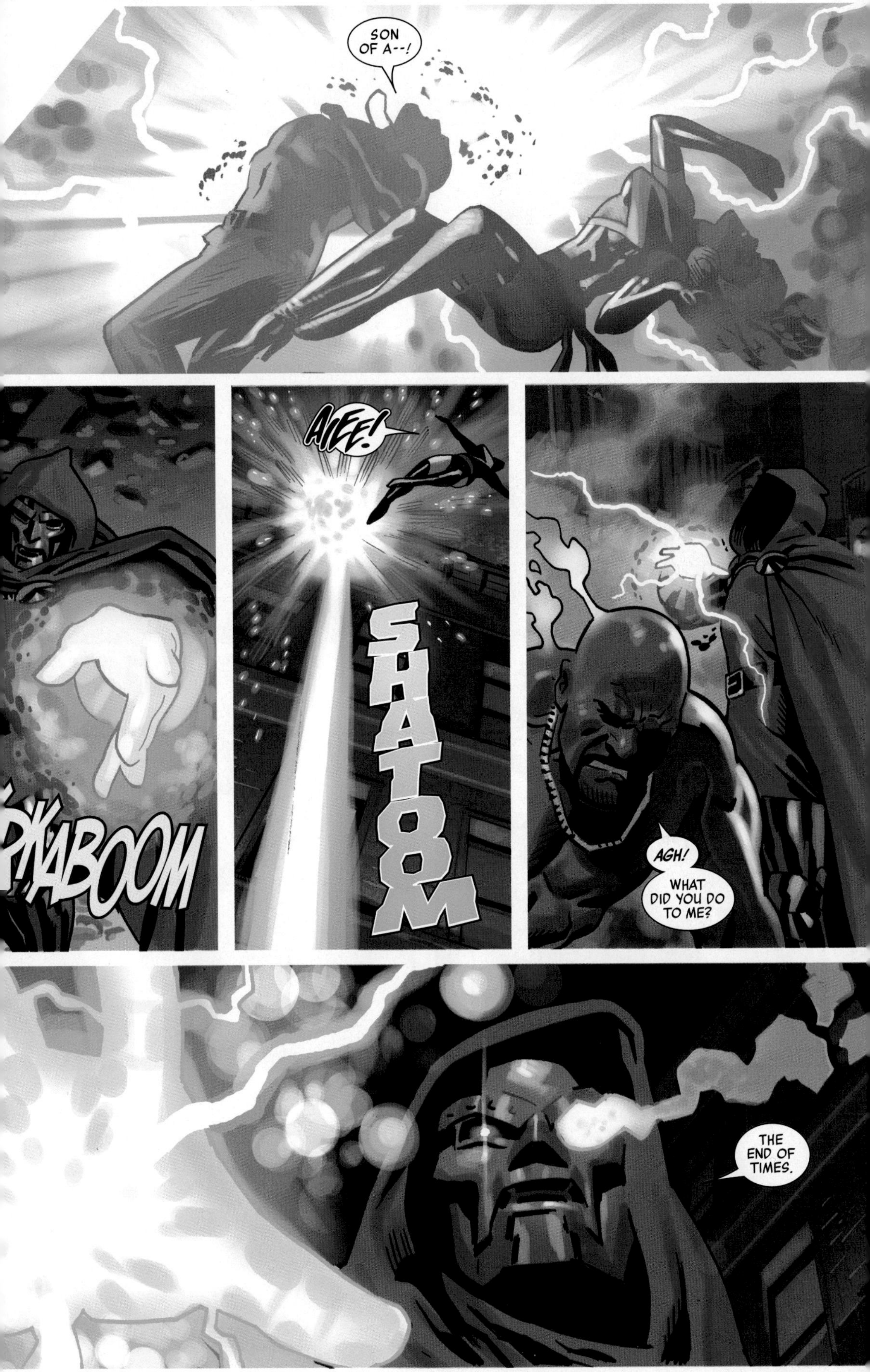
SON OF A--!
AIEE!
PKABOOM
SHATOOM
AGH!
WHAT DID YOU DO TO ME?
THE END OF TIMES.

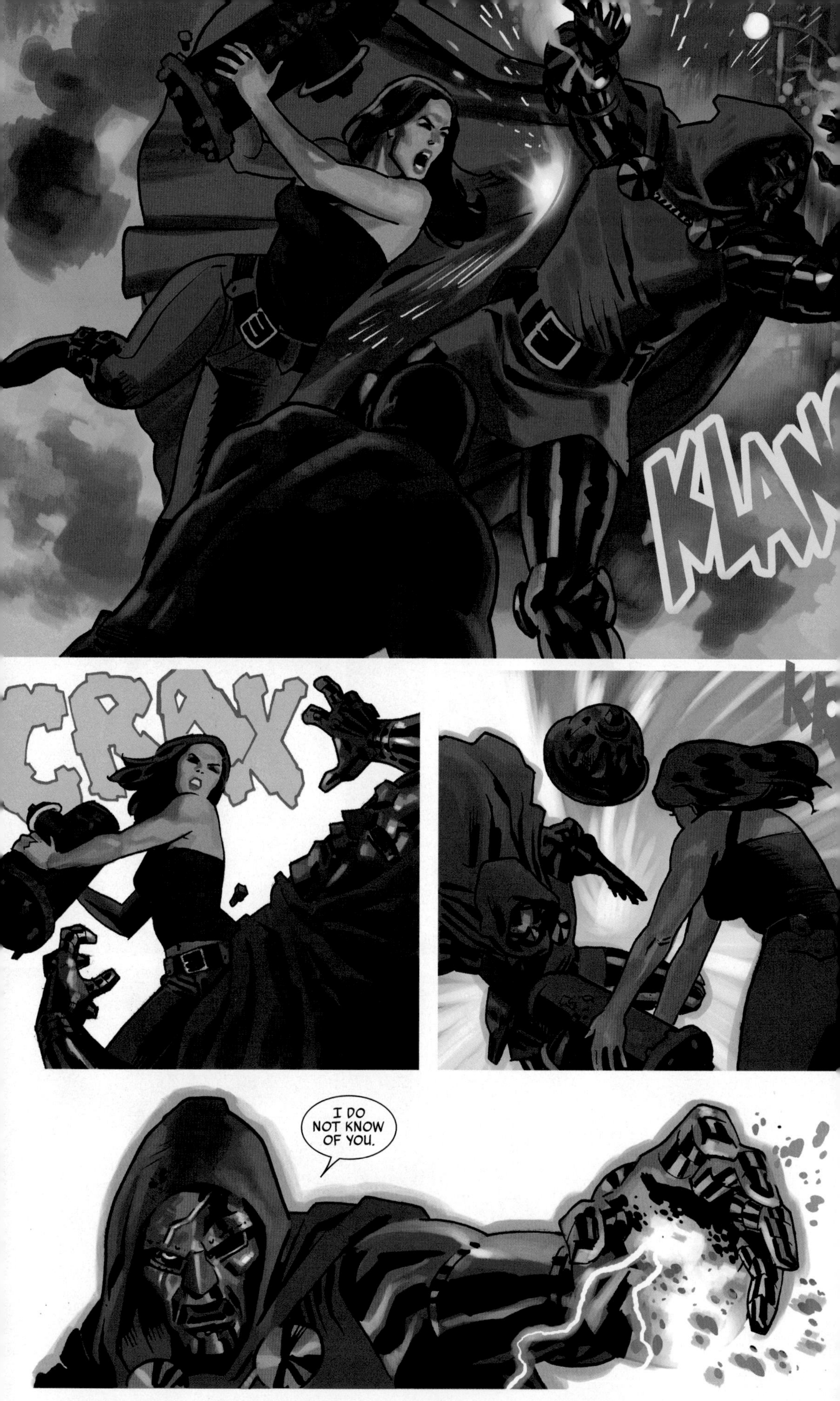
KLAN
CRAX
I DO NOT KNOW OF YOU.

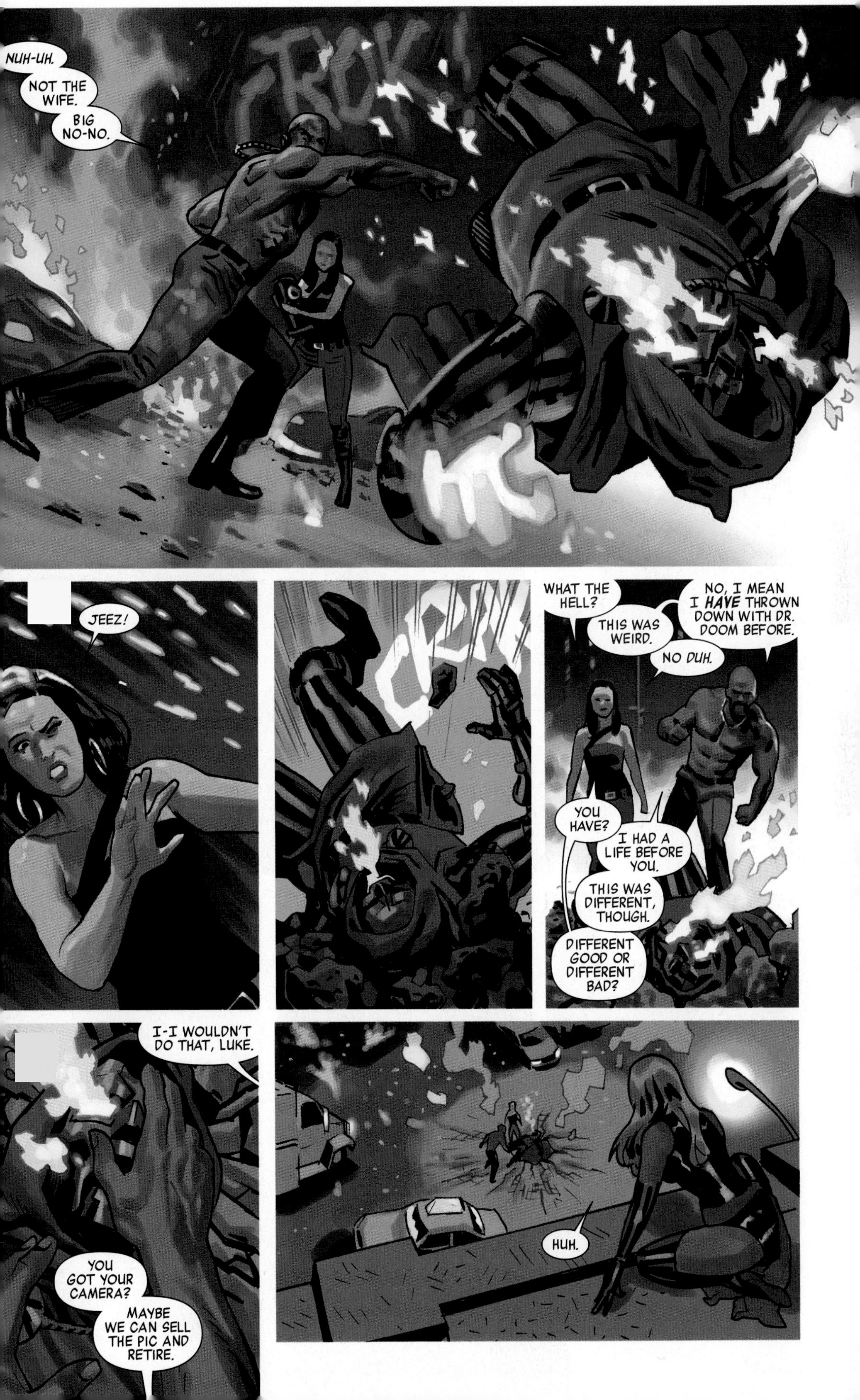
NUH-UH.
NOT THE WIFE.
BIG NO-NO.
CROK!
JEEZ!
CRON
WHAT THE HELL?
THIS WAS WEIRD.
NO, I MEAN I HAVE THROWN DOWN WITH DR. DOOM BEFORE.
NO DUH.
YOU HAVE?
I HAD A LIFE BEFORE YOU.
THIS WAS DIFFERENT, THOUGH.
DIFFERENT GOOD OR DIFFERENT BAD?
I-I WOULDN'T DO THAT, LUKE.
YOU GOT YOUR CAMERA?
MAYBE WE CAN SELL THE PIC AND RETIRE.
HUH.

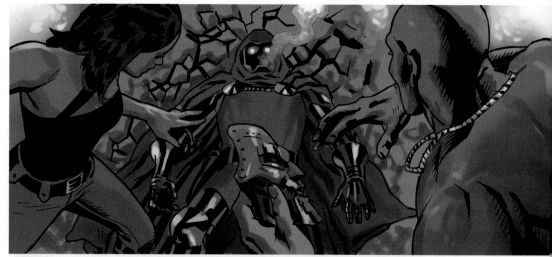

WHAT THE *WHAT?*

IT AIN'T EVEN HIM?

THEN WHAT IS IT?

HOW THE HELL SHOULD I KNOW?

YOU'RE POWER MAN.

IT'S-- IT'S LIKE A--A DOOMBOT.

WHAT THE HELL IS A *DOOMBOT?*

YOU USED TO BE A DETECTIVE. WHAT DOES IT SOUND LIKE?

A ROBOT MADE TO LOOK LIKE DOCTOR DOOM THAT DOCTOR DOOM MADE BECAUSE HE'S CRAZY IN LOVE WITH HIMSELF?

BINGO.

WHAT IS IT DOING *HERE?*

AGAIN: YOU DO REALIZE I HAVE NOT LEFT YOUR SIDE ALL DAY.

THERE'S NOTHING GOING ON HERE THAT I KNOW THAT YOU DON'T.

I'M TALKING OUT LOUD.

I'M THINKING IT OUT...

YOU'RE LOOKING RIGHT AT ME WHEN YOU DO IT. IT MAKES ME THINK YOU'RE TALKING TO ME.

WELL, THAT'S YOUR BUSINESS.

YOU'RE JUST MAD BECAUSE YOU THOUGHT *YOU* BEAT UP DR. DOOM AND YOU WERE ALL PROUD OF YOURSELF.

YOU'RE JUST MAD BECAUSE YOU THOUGHT YOU GOT BEAT UP BY DR. DOOM AND NOW REALIZE YOU JUST GOT BEAT UP BY A *ROBOT* OF DR. DOOM.

LOOK WHAT A GOOD TIME YOU'RE HAVING...

YOU OWE ME A DINNER, MISTER.

YO GABBA GABBA, LOOK AT WHAT YOU ALL DID!

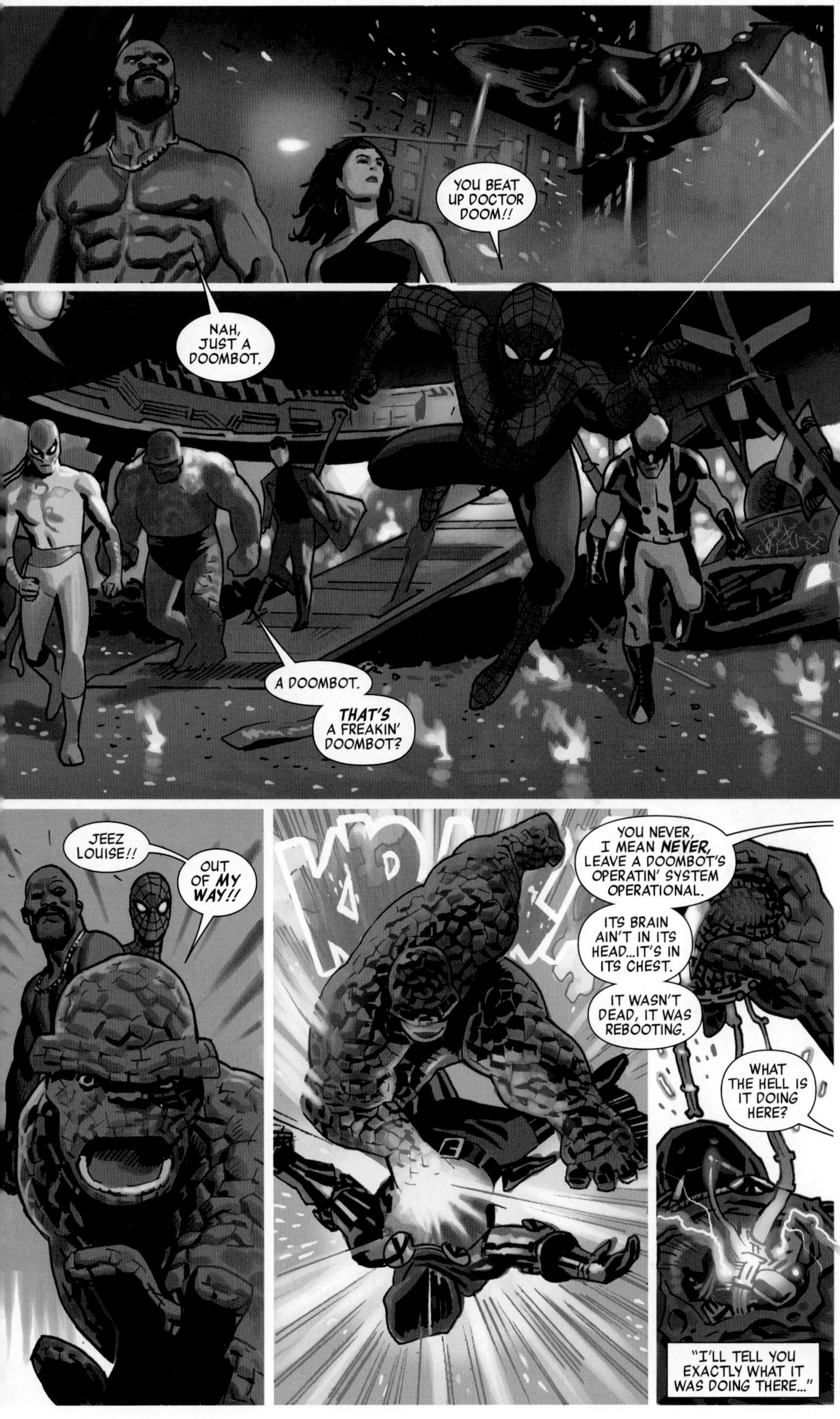
YOU BEAT UP DOCTOR DOOM!!
NAH, JUST A DOOMBOT.
A DOOMBOT.
THAT'S A FREAKIN' DOOMBOT?
JEEZ LOUISE!!
OUT OF MY WAY!!
YOU NEVER, I MEAN NEVER, LEAVE A DOOMBOT'S OPERATIN' SYSTEM OPERATIONAL.
ITS BRAIN AIN'T IN ITS HEAD...IT'S IN ITS CHEST.
IT WASN'T DEAD, IT WAS REBOOTING.
WHAT THE HELL IS IT DOING HERE?
"I'LL TELL YOU EXACTLY WHAT IT WAS DOING THERE..."

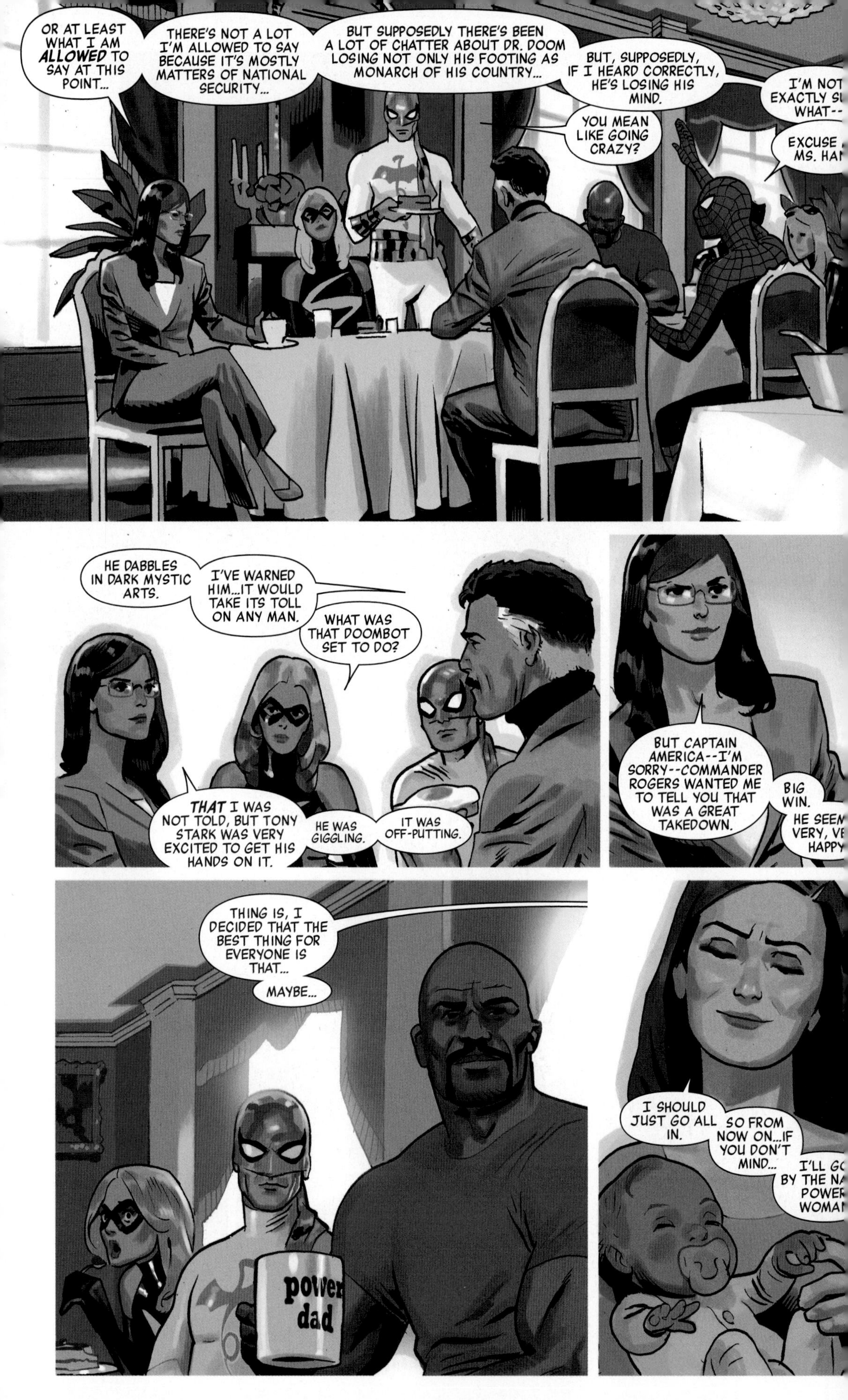

OR AT LEAST WHAT I AM **ALLOWED** TO SAY AT THIS POINT...
THERE'S NOT A LOT I'M ALLOWED TO SAY BECAUSE IT'S MOSTLY MATTERS OF NATIONAL SECURITY...
BUT SUPPOSEDLY THERE'S BEEN A LOT OF CHATTER ABOUT DR. DOOM LOSING NOT ONLY HIS FOOTING AS MONARCH OF HIS COUNTRY...
BUT, SUPPOSEDLY, IF I HEARD CORRECTLY, HE'S LOSING HIS MIND.
YOU MEAN LIKE GOING CRAZY?
I'M NOT EXACTLY S WHAT--
EXCUSE MS. HA
HE DABBLES IN DARK MYSTIC ARTS.
I'VE WARNED HIM...IT WOULD TAKE ITS TOLL ON ANY MAN.
WHAT WAS THAT DOOMBOT SET TO DO?
THAT I WAS NOT TOLD, BUT TONY STARK WAS VERY EXCITED TO GET HIS HANDS ON IT.
HE WAS GIGGLING.
IT WAS OFF-PUTTING.
BUT CAPTAIN AMERICA--I'M SORRY--COMMANDER ROGERS WANTED ME TO TELL YOU THAT WAS A GREAT TAKEDOWN.
BIG WIN.
HE SEEM VERY, V HAPPY
THING IS, I DECIDED THAT THE BEST THING FOR EVERYONE IS THAT...
MAYBE...
power dad
I SHOULD JUST GO ALL IN.
SO FROM NOW ON...IF YOU DON'T MIND...
I'LL G BY THE N POWER WOMA

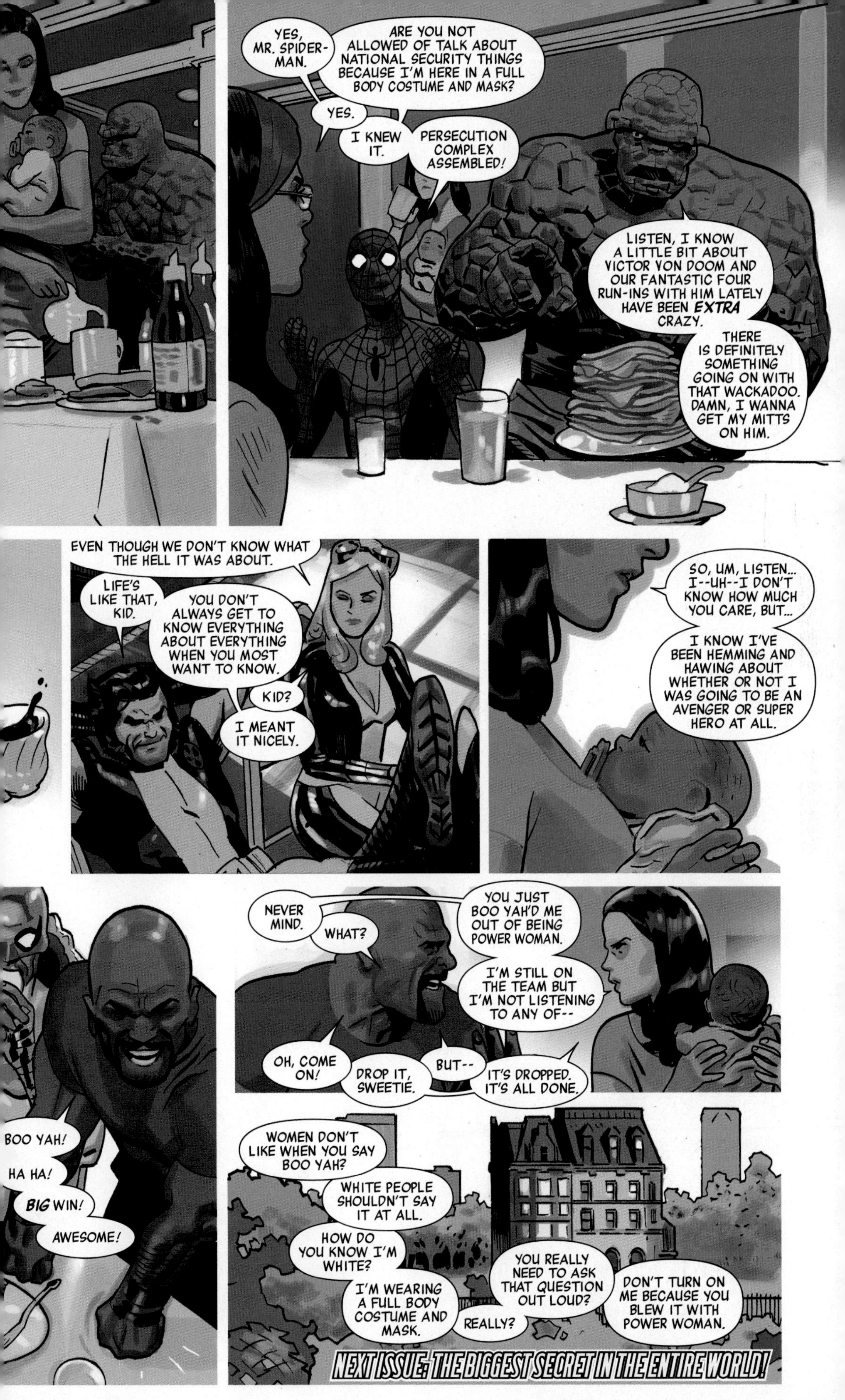
ARE YOU NOT ALLOWED OF TALK ABOUT NATIONAL SECURITY THINGS BECAUSE I'M HERE IN A FULL BODY COSTUME AND MASK?
YES, MR. SPIDER-MAN.
YES.
I KNEW IT.
PERSECUTION COMPLEX ASSEMBLED!
LISTEN, I KNOW A LITTLE BIT ABOUT VICTOR VON DOOM AND OUR FANTASTIC FOUR RUN-INS WITH HIM LATELY HAVE BEEN EXTRA CRAZY.
THERE IS DEFINITELY SOMETHING GOING ON WITH THAT WACKADOO. DAMN, I WANNA GET MY MITTS ON HIM.
EVEN THOUGH WE DON'T KNOW WHAT THE HELL IT WAS ABOUT.
LIFE'S LIKE THAT, KID.
YOU DON'T ALWAYS GET TO KNOW EVERYTHING ABOUT EVERYTHING WHEN YOU MOST WANT TO KNOW.
KID?
I MEANT IT NICELY.
SO, UM, LISTEN... I--UH--I DON'T KNOW HOW MUCH YOU CARE, BUT...
I KNOW I'VE BEEN HEMMING AND HAWING ABOUT WHETHER OR NOT I WAS GOING TO BE AN AVENGER OR SUPER HERO AT ALL.
BOO YAH!
HA HA!
BIG WIN!
AWESOME!
YOU JUST BOO YAH'D ME OUT OF BEING POWER WOMAN.
WHAT?
NEVER MIND.
I'M STILL ON THE TEAM BUT I'M NOT LISTENING TO ANY OF--
OH, COME ON!
DROP IT, SWEETIE.
BUT--
IT'S DROPPED. IT'S ALL DONE.
WOMEN DON'T LIKE WHEN YOU SAY BOO YAH?
WHITE PEOPLE SHOULDN'T SAY IT AT ALL.
HOW DO YOU KNOW I'M WHITE?
I'M WEARING A FULL BODY COSTUME AND MASK.
REALLY?
YOU REALLY NEED TO ASK THAT QUESTION OUT LOUD?
DON'T TURN ON ME BECAUSE YOU BLEW IT WITH POWER WOMAN.
NEXT ISSUE: THE BIGGEST SECRET IN THE ENTIRE WORLD!

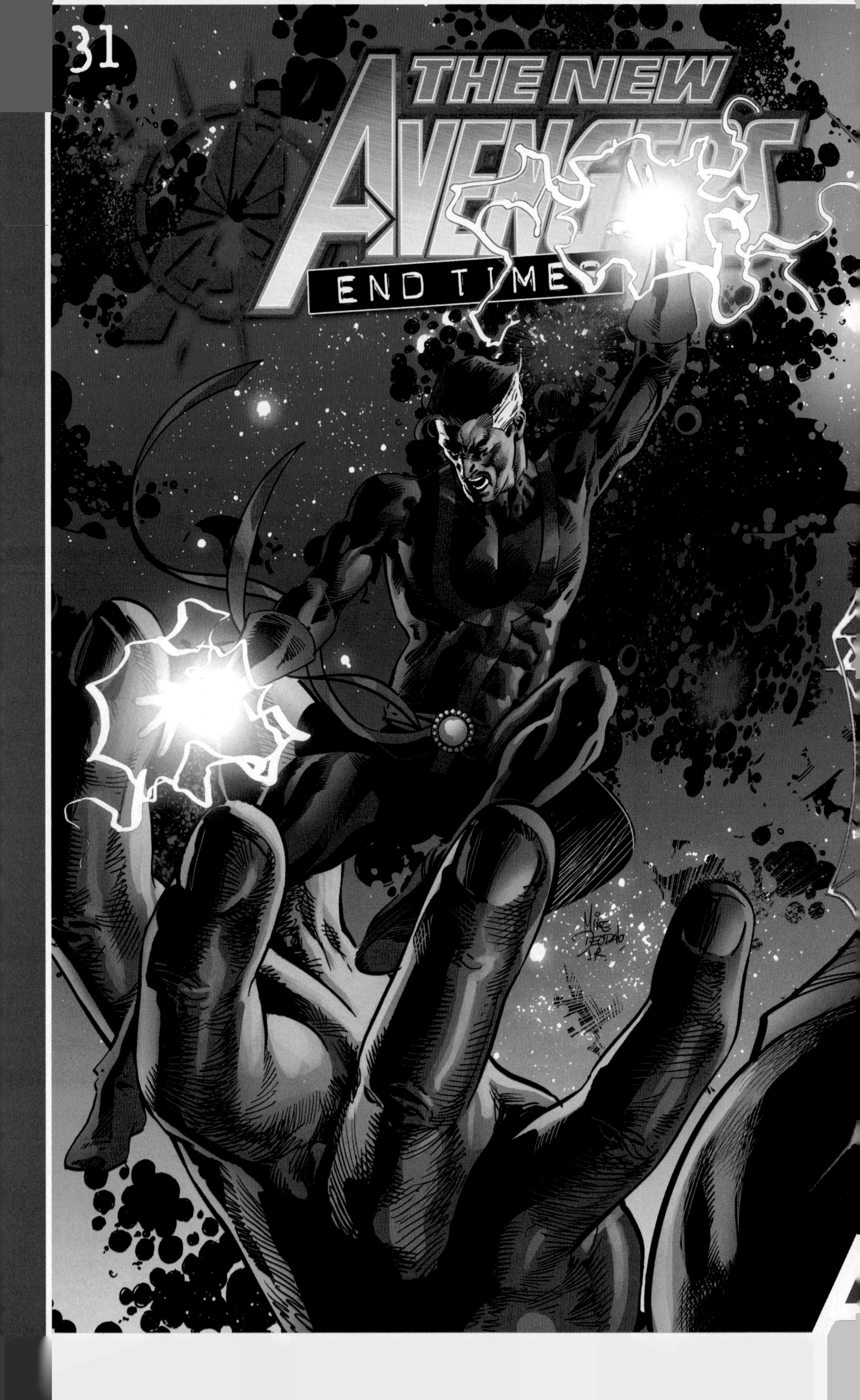

31
THE NEW AVENGERS
END TIMES
MIKE DEODATO JR.

ARTH'S MIGHTIEST HEROES, UNITED AINST A COMMON EAT! ON THAT DAY E AVENGERS WERE RN, TO FIGHT FOES IT NO SINGLE HERO COULD WITHSTAND!

NEW AVENGERS

LUKE CAGE

PTAIN ARVEL

HING

IRON FIST

PIDER-MAN

WOLVERINE

DR. STRANGE

MOCKINGBIRD

JESSICA JONES

VICTORIA HAND

DAREDEVIL

AVENGERS COMMANDER STEVE ROGERS GAVE LUKE CAGE, JESSICA JONES, MS. MARVEL, MOCKINGBIRD, DAREDEVIL, SPIDER-MAN, DR. STRANGE, WOLVERINE, IRON FIST AND THE THING THE KEYS TO AVENGERS MANSION, A LIAISON IN THE CONTROVERSIAL FORM OF VICTORIA HAND, AND FREE REIN TO PROTECT THE WORLD ANY WAY THEY SEE FIT.

THE CATASTROPHIC PHOENIX FORCE RETURNED, EVENTUALLY MANIFESTING FULLY IN THE X-MEN LEADER CYCLOPS, WHO BECAME THE DARK PHOENIX. ALTHOUGH THE AVENGERS ALLIED WITH THE X-MEN TO STOP CYCLOPS AND DISPEL THE PHOENIX FORCE, IT PROVED ONE BRUSH WITH A WORLD-DESTROYING FORCE TOO MANY FOR TEAM LEADER AND NEW FAMILY MAN LUKE CAGE, WHO HAS OPTED TO LEAVE THE TEAM.

IAN MICHAEL BENDIS WRITER
MICHAEL GAYDOS ARTIST
RAIN BEREDO COLOR ART
VC'S JOE CARAMAGNA LETTERS & PRODUCTION
BRANDON PETERSON COVER ARTIST
JAKE THOMAS ASSISTANT EDITOR
TOM BREVOORT WITH LAUREN SANKOVITCH EDITORS
AXEL ALONSO EDITOR IN CHIEF
JOE QUESADA CHIEF CREATIVE OFFICER
DAN BUCKLEY PUBLISHER
ALAN FINE EXEC. PRODUCER

NEW ORLEANS.

WHAT THE HELL AM I LOOKING AT?

HEY, YO, DOCTOR STRANGE... IT'S DAIMON HELLSTORM.

SON OF SATAN.

ANYWAY, I SEE YOU'RE BUSY BEATING UP MUTANTS FOR TRYING TO MAKE THE WORLD A BETTER PLACE...

BUT WHEN YOU'RE *DONE*, I WAS WONDERI IF I COULD GET Y TO TAKE A LOOK SOME FUNKY SURG COMING OUT OF T ASTRAL PLANE

IF IT'S YOU DOING IT, THAT'S FINE...

...BUT YOU'VE ALWAYS BEEN A MORE CONTROLLED SORT OF SORCERER.

THESE SEEM VIOLENT.

WITHOUT A SORCERER SUPREME IN THIS DIMENSION I DON'T LIKE THESE KIND OF MAGIC ANOMALIES.

KNOCK KNOCK

THE HELL--?

WHO IS IT?

DAIMON HELLSTORM?

THE FIRE INCANTATION OF ILLUMINATION.

YEAH?

IT'S VICTORIA HAND.

FROM AVENGERS MANSION.

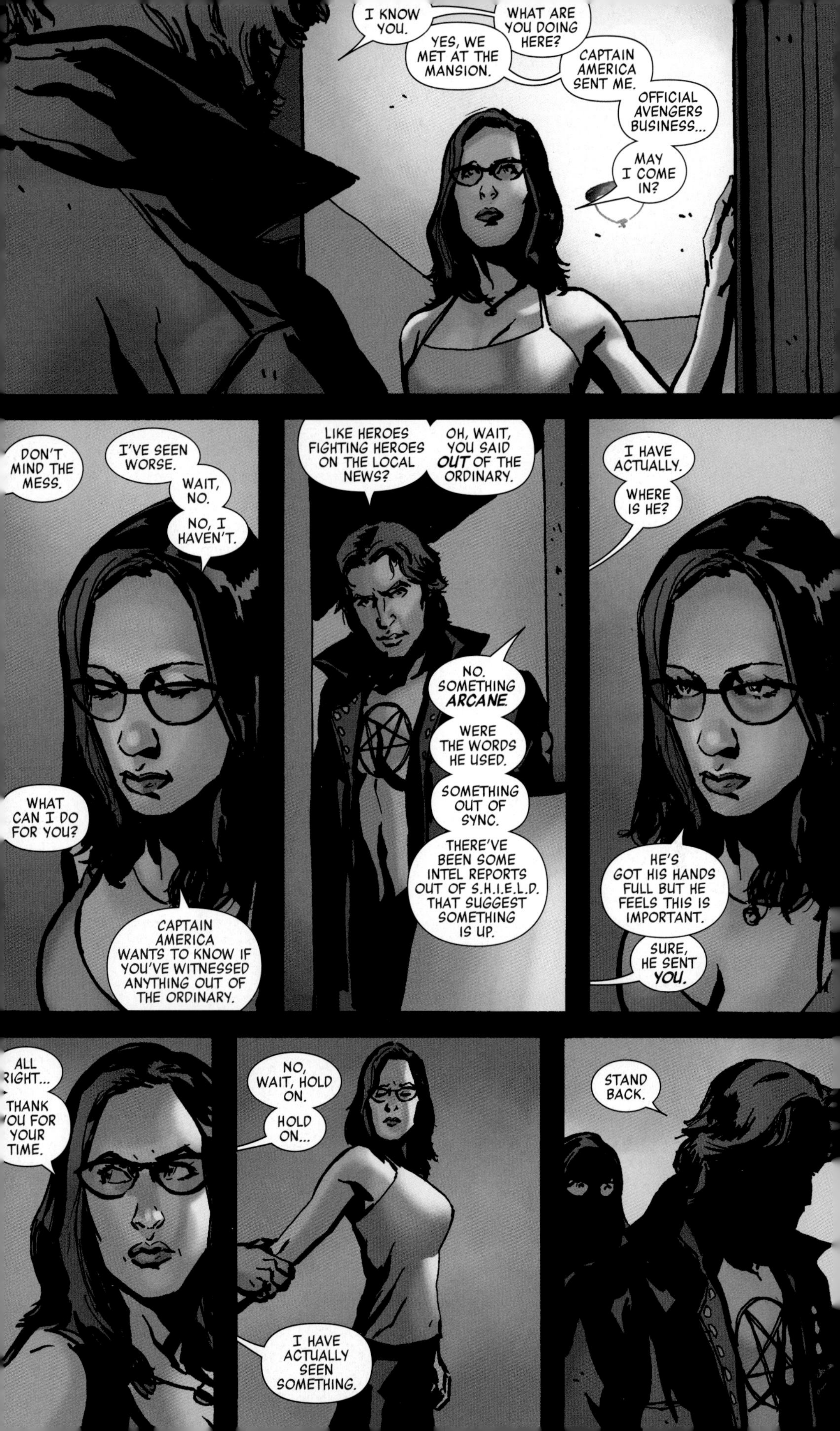

I KNOW YOU.
WHAT ARE YOU DOING HERE?
YES, WE MET AT THE MANSION.
CAPTAIN AMERICA SENT ME.
OFFICIAL AVENGERS BUSINESS...
MAY I COME IN?
DON'T MIND THE MESS.
I'VE SEEN WORSE.
WAIT, NO.
NO, I HAVEN'T.
WHAT CAN I DO FOR YOU?
CAPTAIN AMERICA WANTS TO KNOW IF YOU'VE WITNESSED ANYTHING OUT OF THE ORDINARY.
LIKE HEROES FIGHTING HEROES ON THE LOCAL NEWS?
OH, WAIT, YOU SAID *OUT* OF THE ORDINARY.
NO. SOMETHING ***ARCANE***.
WERE THE WORDS HE USED.
SOMETHING OUT OF SYNC.
THERE'VE BEEN SOME INTEL REPORTS OUT OF S.H.I.E.L.D. THAT SUGGEST SOMETHING IS UP.
I HAVE ACTUALLY.
WHERE IS HE?
HE'S GOT HIS HANDS FULL BUT HE FEELS THIS IS IMPORTANT.
SURE, HE SENT ***YOU.***
ALL RIGHT...
THANK YOU FOR YOUR TIME.
NO, WAIT, HOLD ON.
HOLD ON...
I HAVE ACTUALLY SEEN SOMETHING.
STAND BACK.

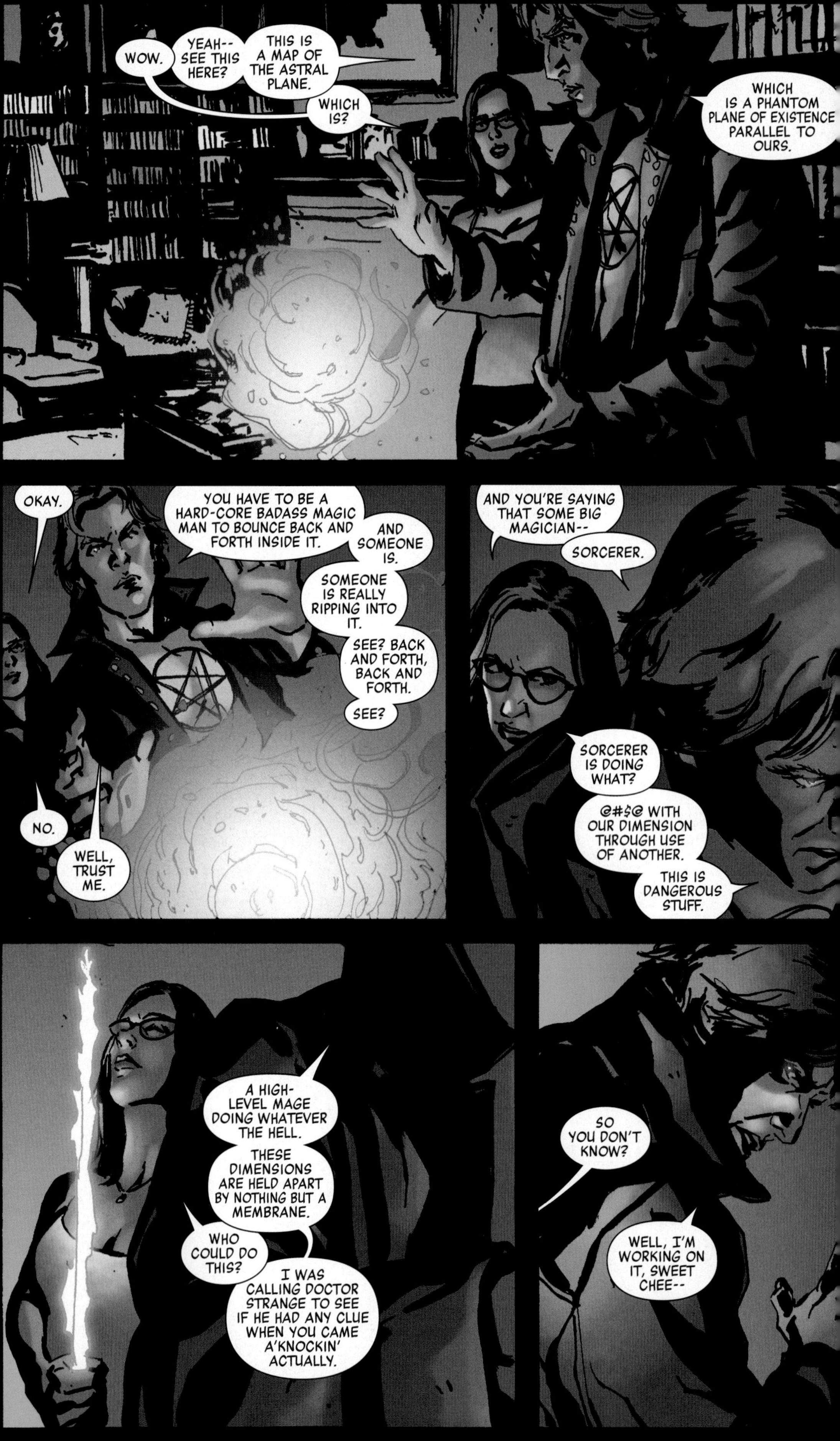
WOW.
YEAH-- SEE THIS HERE?
THIS IS A MAP OF THE ASTRAL PLANE.
WHICH IS?
WHICH IS A PHANTOM PLANE OF EXISTENCE PARALLEL TO OURS.
OKAY.
YOU HAVE TO BE A HARD-CORE BADASS MAGIC MAN TO BOUNCE BACK AND FORTH INSIDE IT.
AND SOMEONE IS.
SOMEONE IS REALLY RIPPING INTO IT.
SEE? BACK AND FORTH, BACK AND FORTH.
SEE?
NO.
WELL, TRUST ME.
AND YOU'RE SAYING THAT SOME BIG MAGICIAN--
SORCERER.
SORCERER IS DOING WHAT?
@#$@ WITH OUR DIMENSION THROUGH USE OF ANOTHER.
THIS IS DANGEROUS STUFF.
A HIGH-LEVEL MAGE DOING WHATEVER THE HELL.
THESE DIMENSIONS ARE HELD APART BY NOTHING BUT A MEMBRANE.
WHO COULD DO THIS?
I WAS CALLING DOCTOR STRANGE TO SEE IF HE HAD ANY CLUE WHEN YOU CAME A'KNOCKIN' ACTUALLY.
SO YOU DON'T KNOW?
WELL, I'M WORKING ON IT, SWEET CHEE--

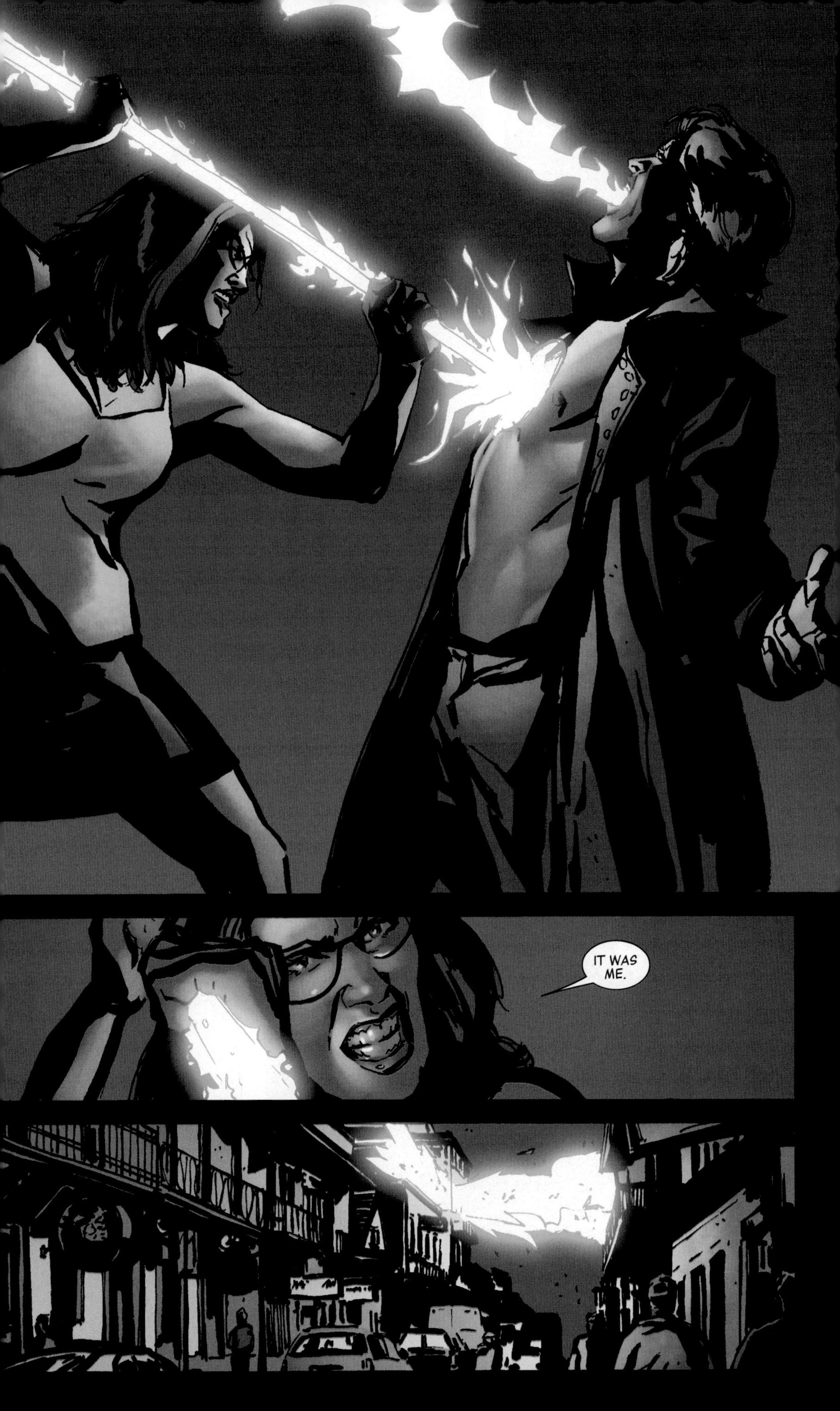
IT WAS ME.

WHAT?!

YOU'RE SHOCKED BY THIS?

THIS IS YOUR HOUSE.

WELL, NOT REALLY.

YOU OWN THIS PLACE?!

WE BOUGHT IT OFF OF TONY STARK FOR A DOLLAR.

IT WAS MORE OF A SYMBOLIC GESTURE.

SOUND LIKE YO OWN T HOUSE

WELL, W AIN'T RAIS OUR BABY HERE, THAT DAMN SU

YOU DRAG ME INTO THE AVENGERS AND NOW YOU'RE LEAVING?

PLACE IS FINE TO RAISE A KID. I GREW UP IN A PLACE JUST LIKE IT, AND I TURNED OUT FINE.

WHA GO O

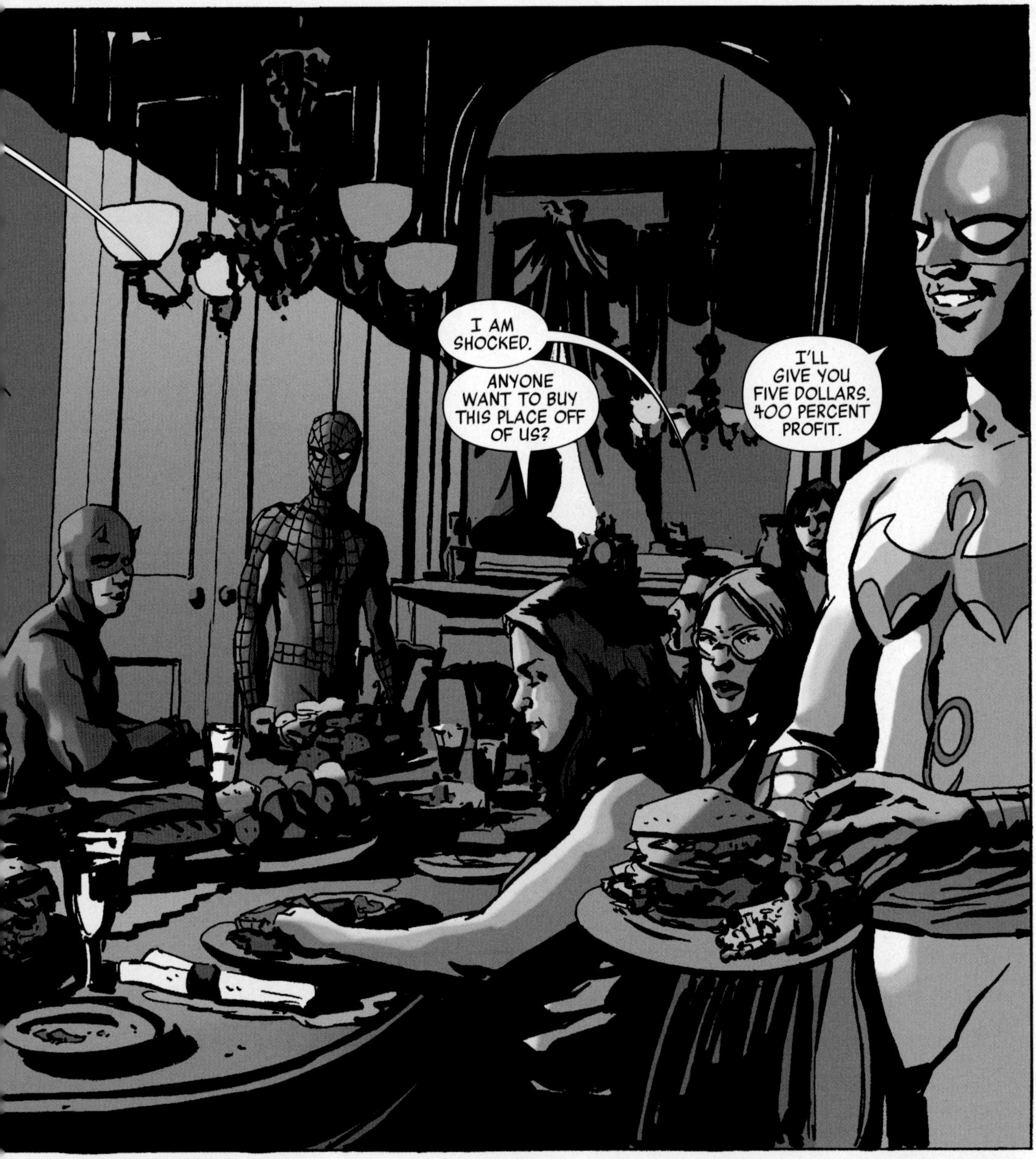
I AM SHOCKED.
ANYONE WANT TO BUY THIS PLACE OFF OF US?
I'LL GIVE YOU FIVE DOLLARS. 400 PERCENT PROFIT.

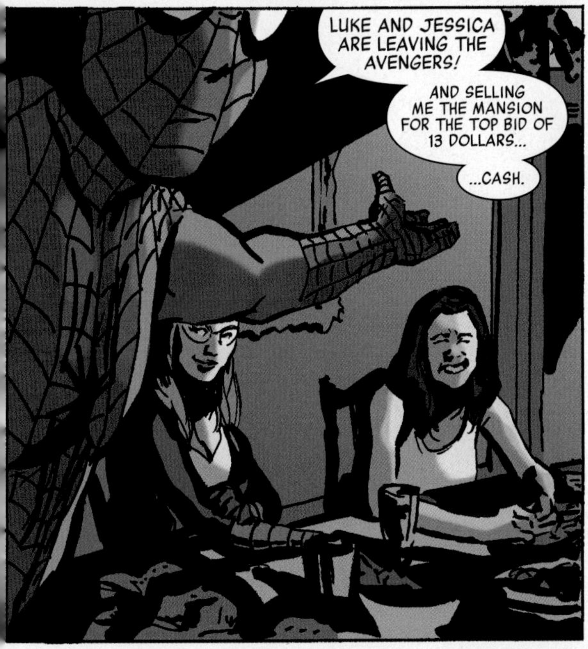
LUKE AND JESSICA ARE LEAVING THE AVENGERS!
AND SELLING ME THE MANSION FOR THE TOP BID OF 13 DOLLARS...
...CASH.

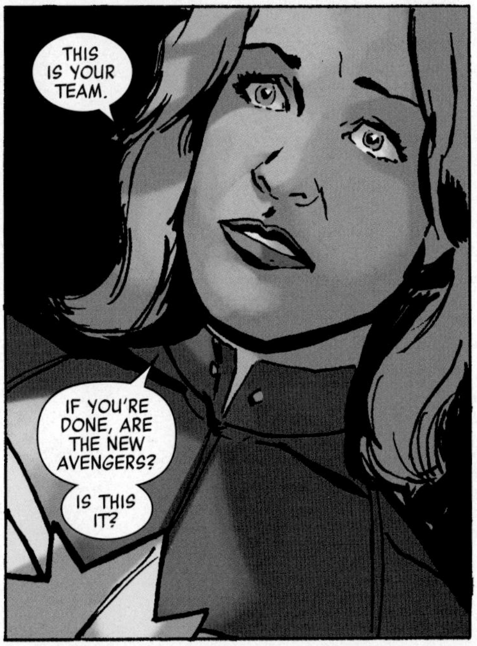
THIS IS YOUR TEAM.
IF YOU'RE DONE, ARE THE NEW AVENGERS?
IS THIS IT?

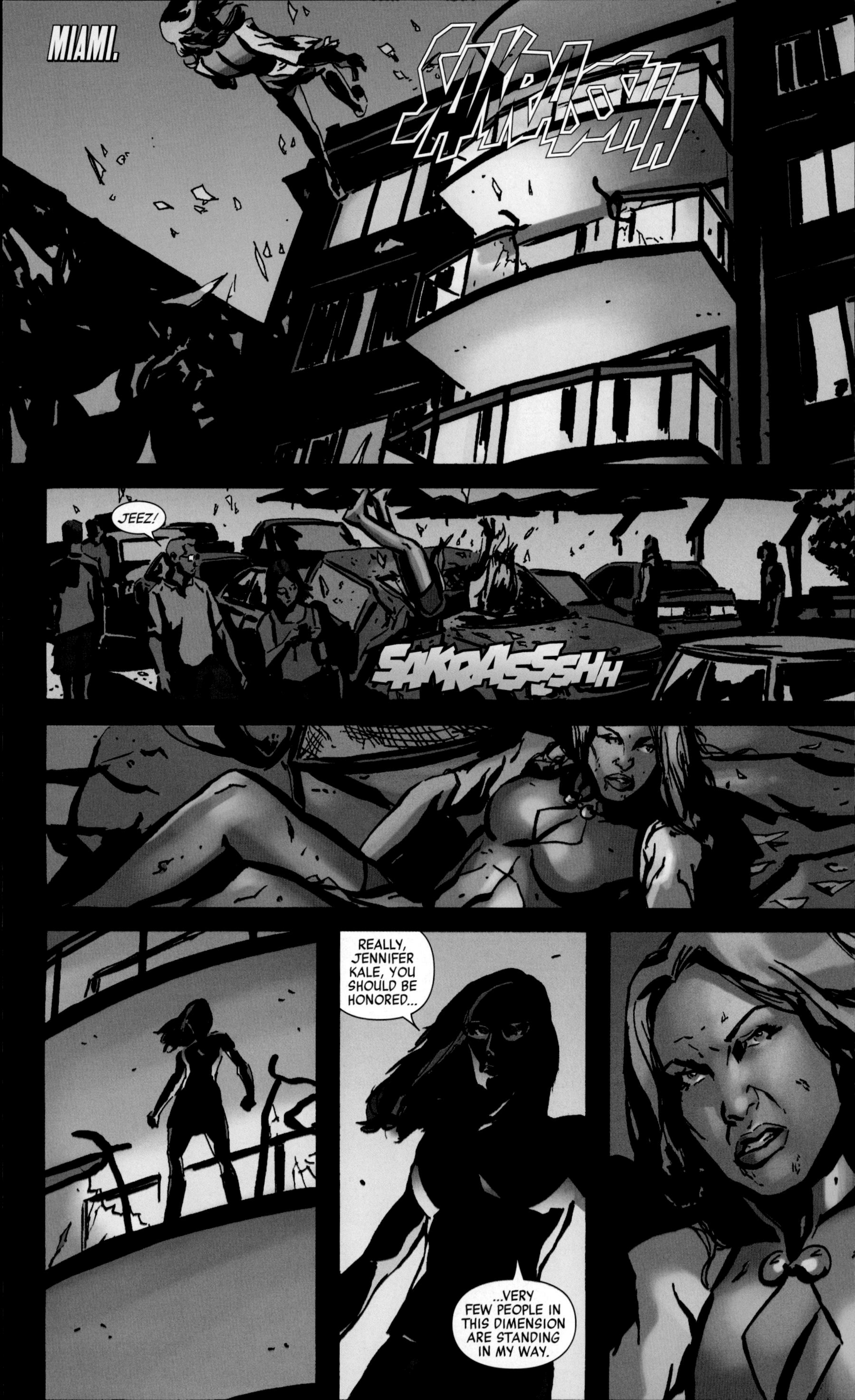
MIAMI.
JEEZ!
SAKRASSSHH
REALLY, JENNIFER KALE, YOU SHOULD BE HONORED...
...VERY FEW PEOPLE IN THIS DIMENSION ARE STANDING IN MY WAY.

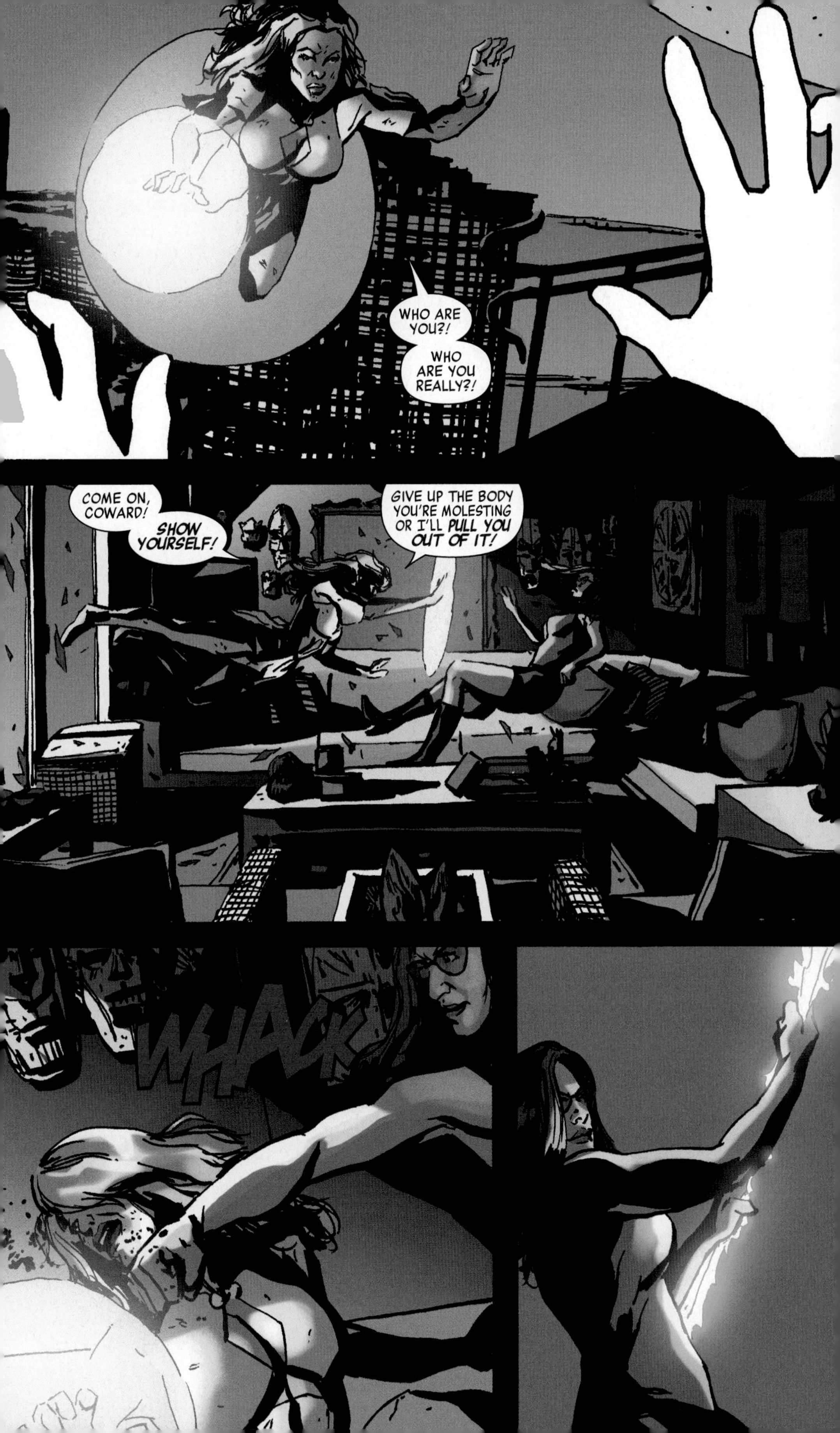
WHO ARE YOU?!
WHO ARE YOU REALLY?!
COME ON, COWARD!
SHOW YOURSELF!
GIVE UP THE BODY YOU'RE MOLESTING OR I'LL PULL YOU OUT OF IT!
WHACK

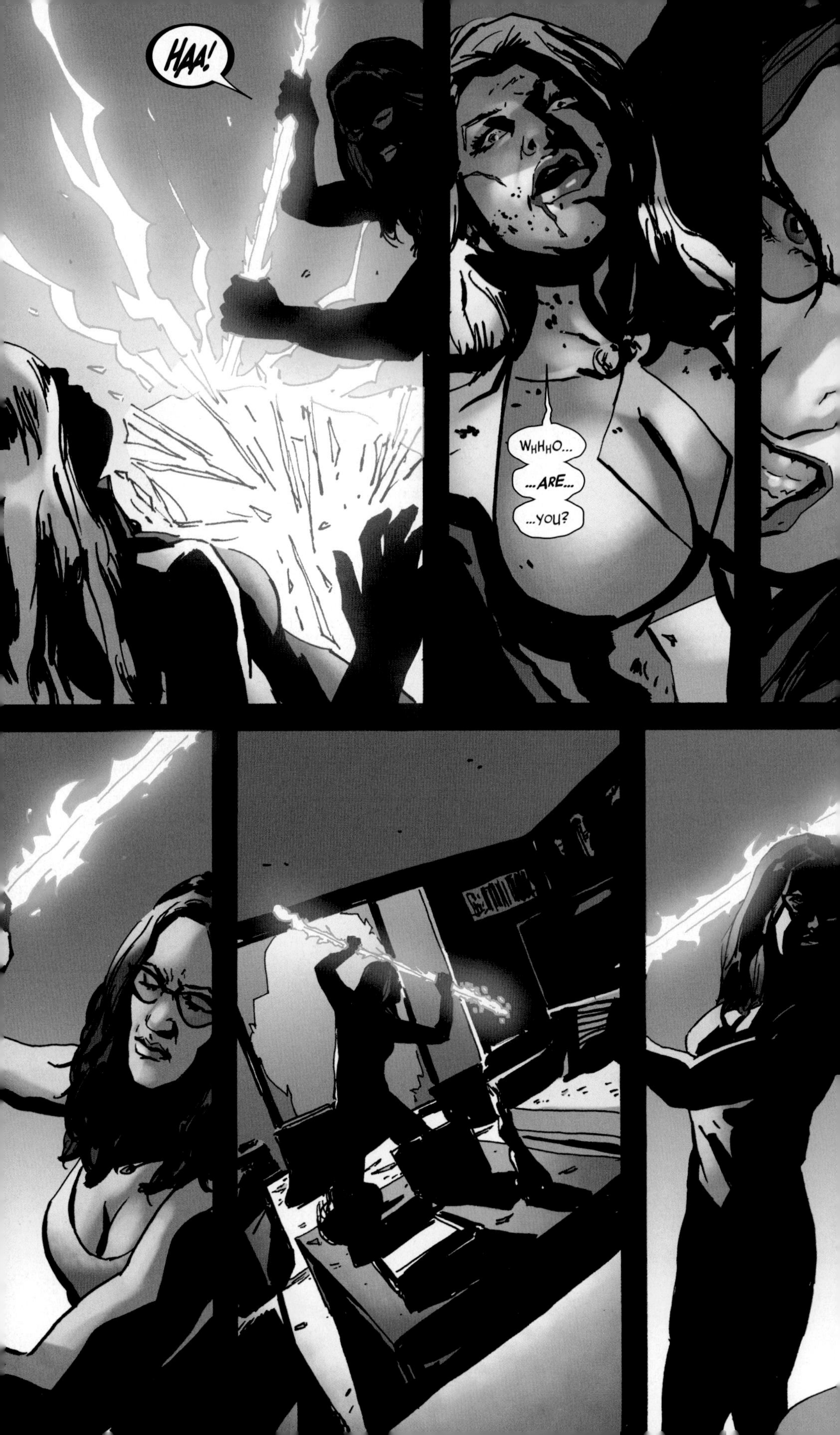
HAA!
WHHHO...
...ARE...
...YOU?

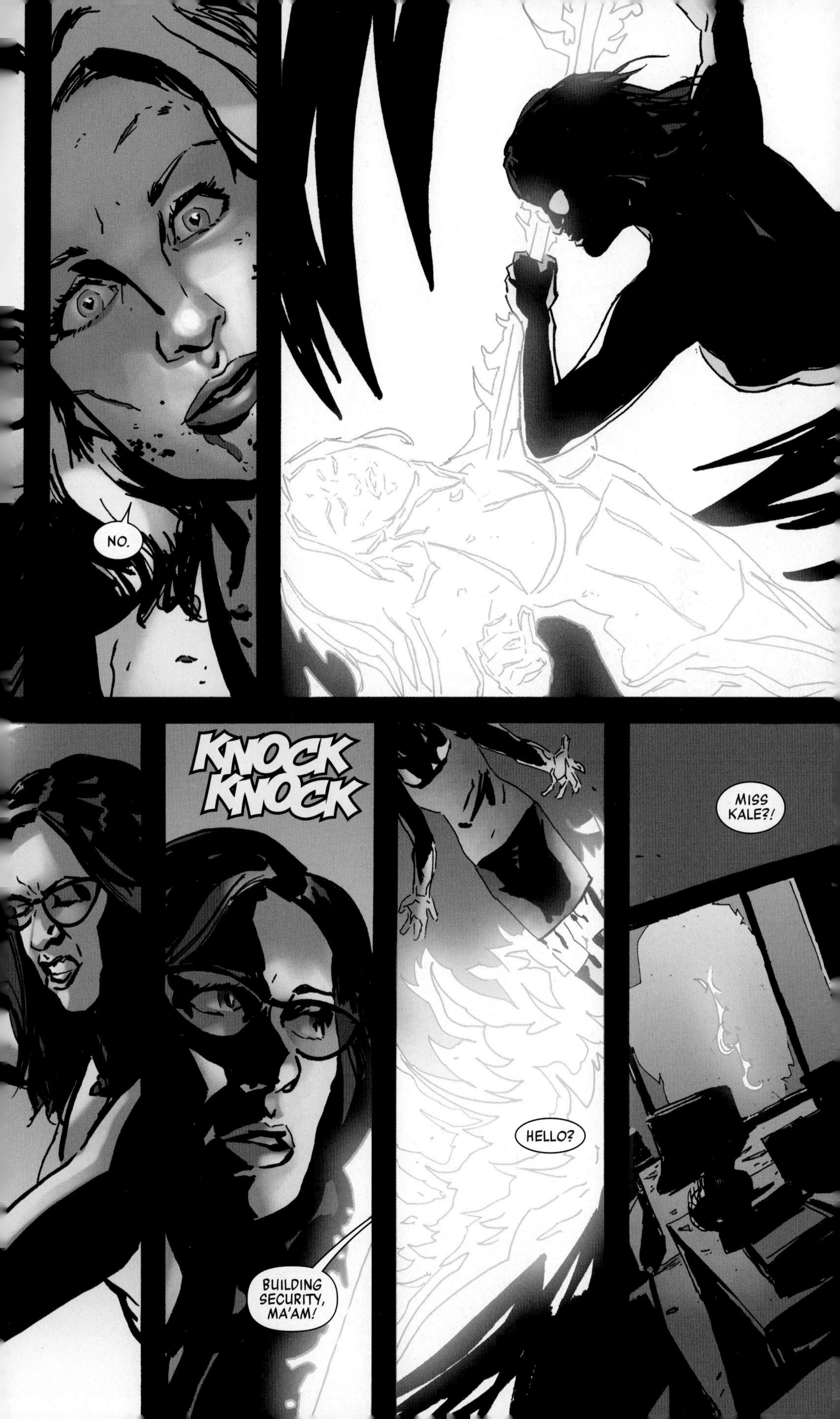
NO.
KNOCK KNOCK
BUILDING SECURITY, MA'AM!
HELLO?
MISS KALE?!

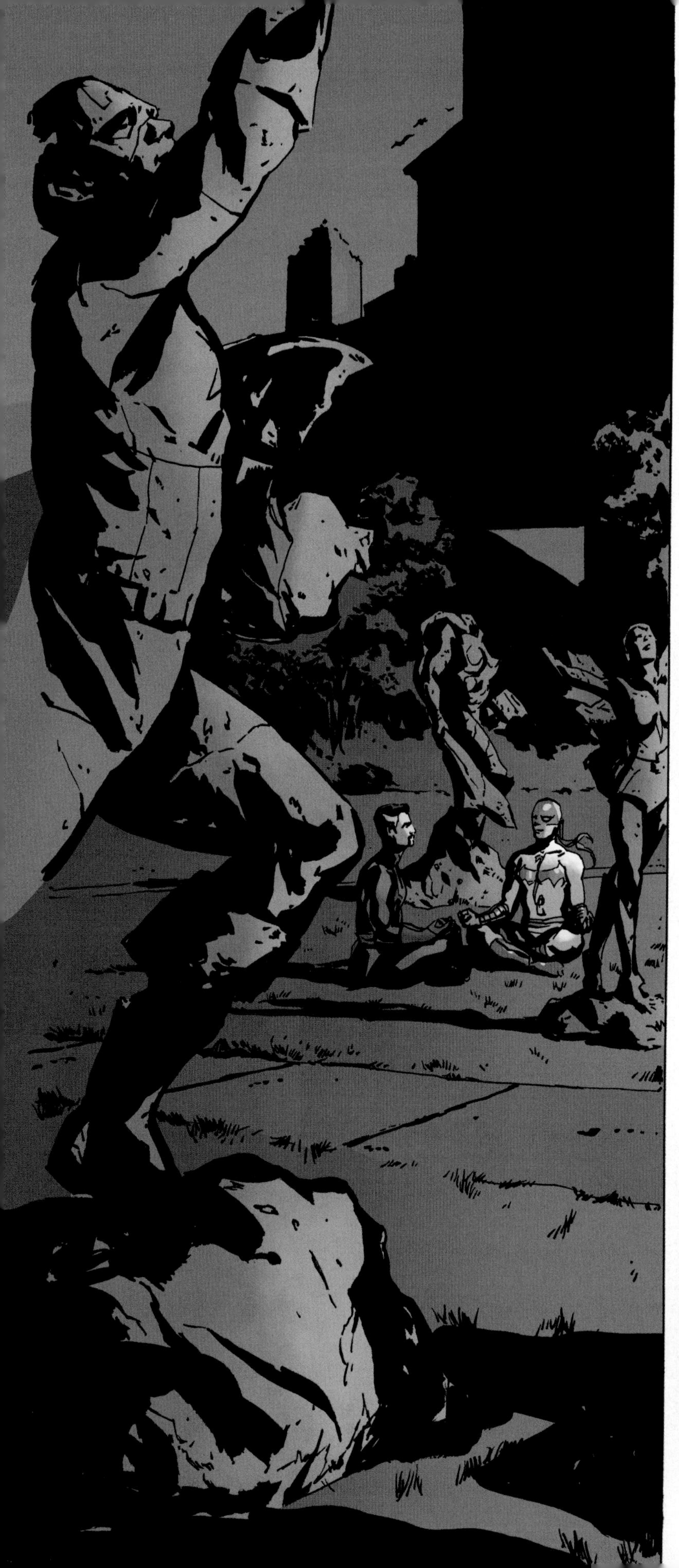

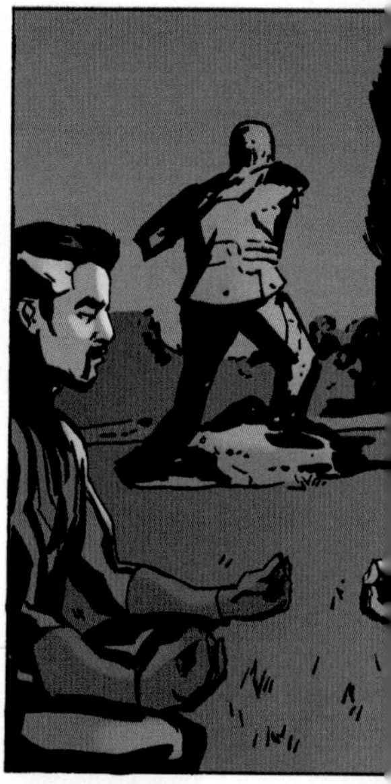

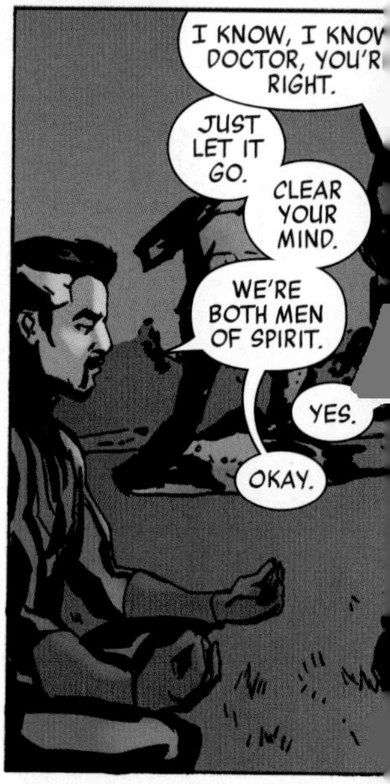
I KNOW, I KNOW
DOCTOR, YOU'R
RIGHT.
JUST LET IT GO.
CLEAR YOUR MIND.
WE'RE BOTH MEN OF SPIRIT.
YES.
OKAY.

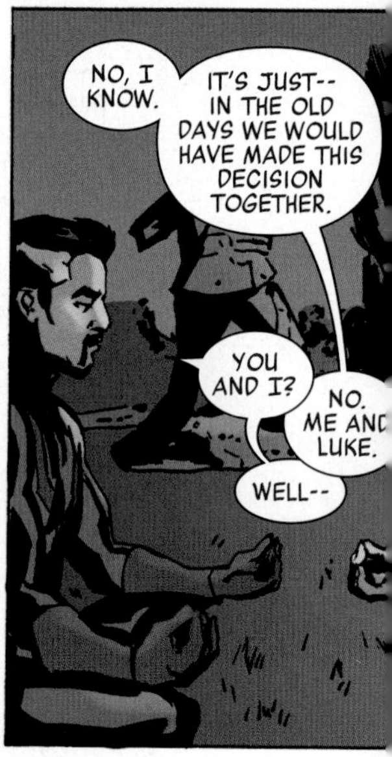
NO, I KNOW.
IT'S JUST-- IN THE OLD DAYS WE WOULD HAVE MADE THIS DECISION TOGETHER.
YOU AND I?
NO. ME AN
LUKE.
WELL--

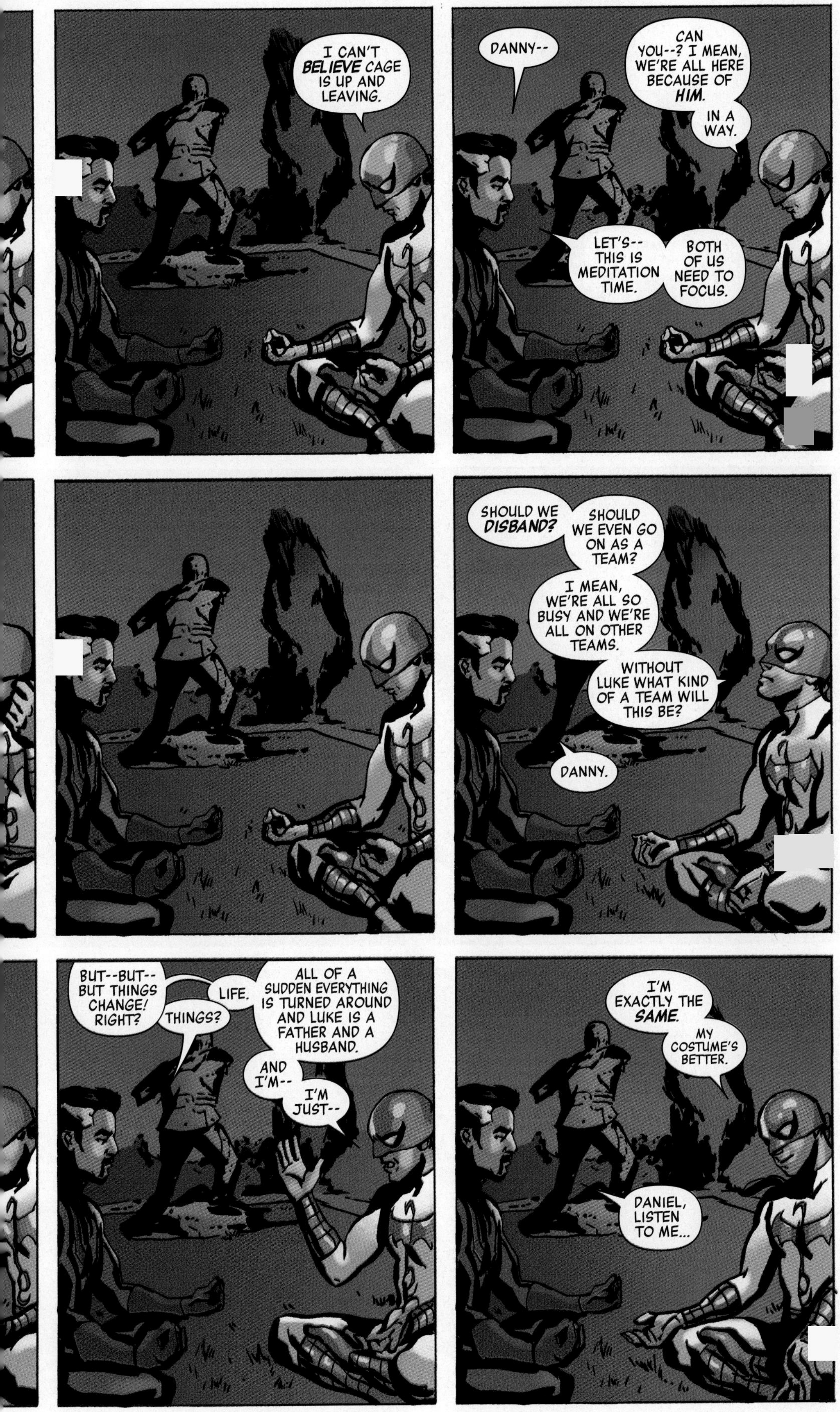
I CAN'T **BELIEVE** CAGE IS UP AND LEAVING.
DANNY--
CAN YOU--? I MEAN, WE'RE ALL HERE BECAUSE OF **HIM**.
IN A WAY.
LET'S-- THIS IS MEDITATION TIME.
BOTH OF US NEED TO FOCUS.
SHOULD WE **DISBAND?**
SHOULD WE EVEN GO ON AS A TEAM?
I MEAN, WE'RE ALL SO BUSY AND WE'RE ALL ON OTHER TEAMS.
WITHOUT LUKE WHAT KIND OF A TEAM WILL THIS BE?
DANNY.
BUT--BUT-- BUT THINGS CHANGE! RIGHT?
LIFE.
THINGS?
ALL OF A SUDDEN EVERYTHING IS TURNED AROUND AND LUKE IS A FATHER AND A HUSBAND.
AND I'M--
I'M JUST--
I'M EXACTLY THE **SAME**.
MY COSTUME'S BETTER.
DANIEL, LISTEN TO ME...

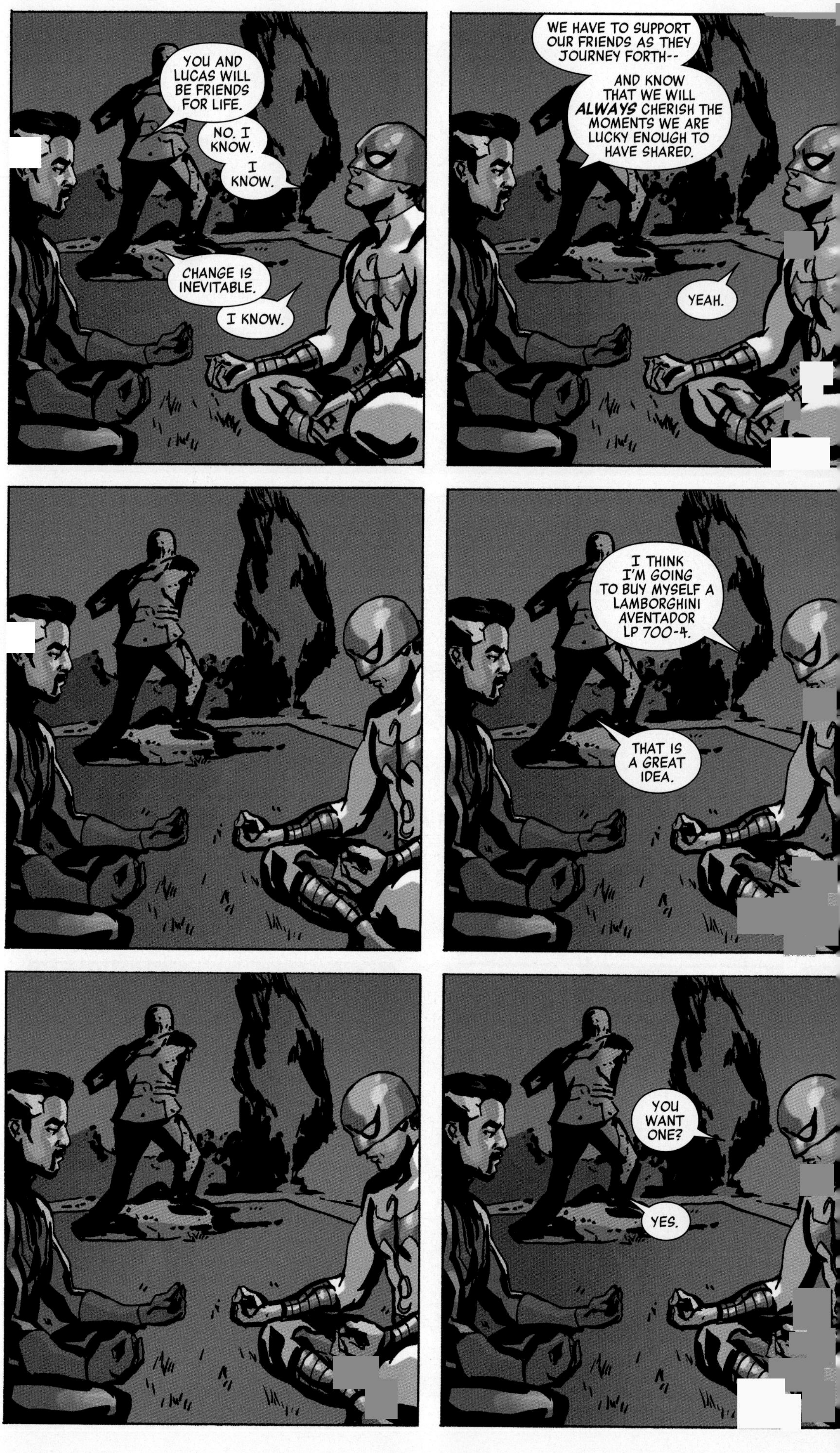
YOU AND LUCAS WILL BE FRIENDS FOR LIFE.
NO. I KNOW.
I KNOW.
CHANGE IS INEVITABLE.
I KNOW.
WE HAVE TO SUPPORT OUR FRIENDS AS THEY JOURNEY FORTH--
AND KNOW THAT WE WILL ALWAYS CHERISH THE MOMENTS WE ARE LUCKY ENOUGH TO HAVE SHARED.
YEAH.
I THINK I'M GOING TO BUY MYSELF A LAMBORGHINI AVENTADOR LP 700-4.
THAT IS A GREAT IDEA.
YOU WANT ONE?
YES.

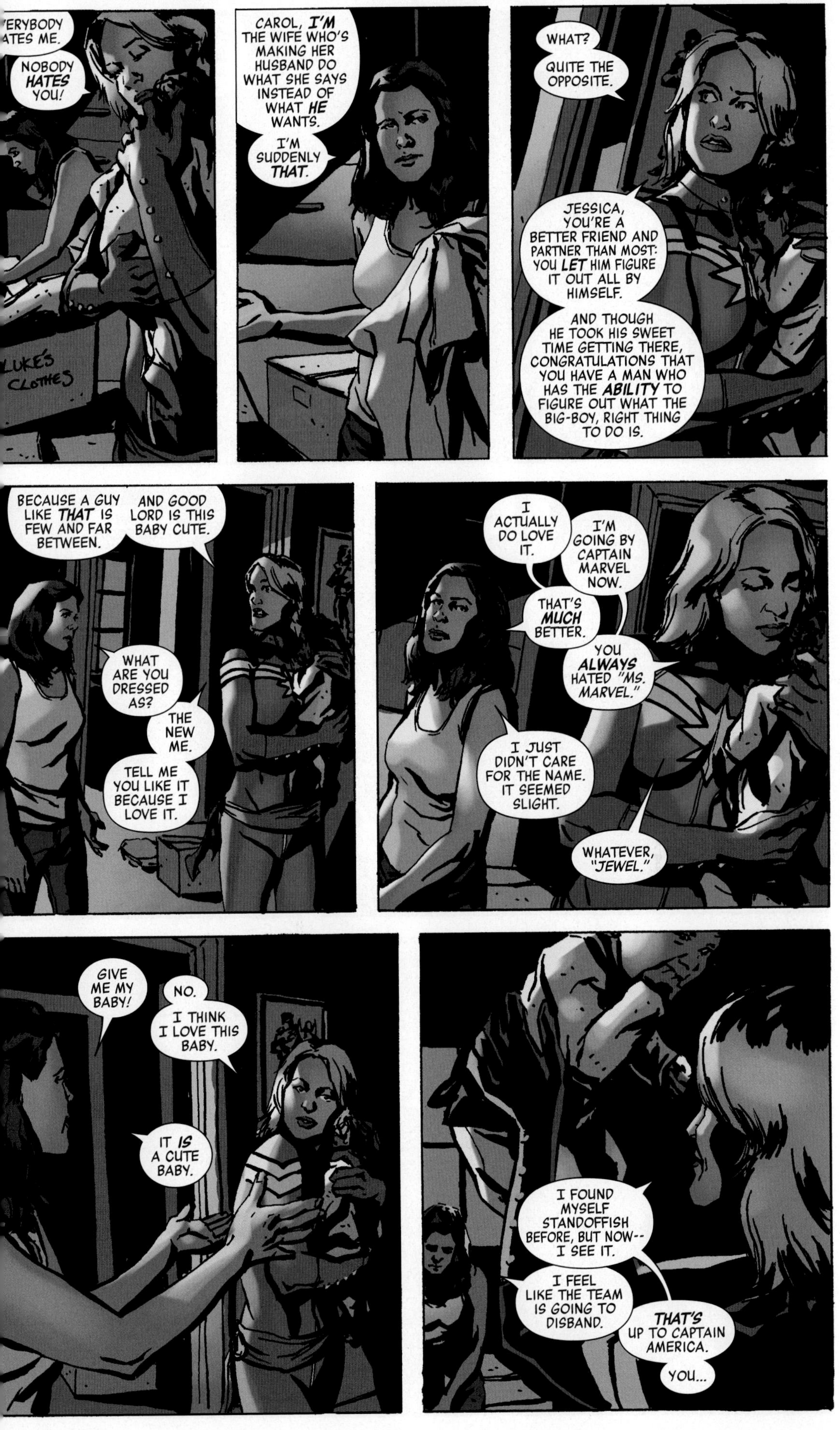

ERYBODY
ATES ME.
NOBODY HATES YOU!
CAROL, I'M THE WIFE WHO'S MAKING HER HUSBAND DO WHAT SHE SAYS INSTEAD OF WHAT HE WANTS.
I'M SUDDENLY THAT.
LUKE'S CLOTHES
WHAT?
QUITE THE OPPOSITE.
JESSICA, YOU'RE A BETTER FRIEND AND PARTNER THAN MOST: YOU LET HIM FIGURE IT OUT ALL BY HIMSELF.
AND THOUGH HE TOOK HIS SWEET TIME GETTING THERE, CONGRATULATIONS THAT YOU HAVE A MAN WHO HAS THE ABILITY TO FIGURE OUT WHAT THE BIG-BOY, RIGHT THING TO DO IS.
BECAUSE A GUY LIKE THAT IS FEW AND FAR BETWEEN.
AND GOOD LORD IS THIS BABY CUTE.
WHAT ARE YOU DRESSED AS?
THE NEW ME.
TELL ME YOU LIKE IT BECAUSE I LOVE IT.
I ACTUALLY DO LOVE IT.
I'M GOING BY CAPTAIN MARVEL NOW.
THAT'S MUCH BETTER.
YOU ALWAYS HATED "MS. MARVEL."
I JUST DIDN'T CARE FOR THE NAME. IT SEEMED SLIGHT.
WHATEVER, "JEWEL."
GIVE ME MY BABY!
NO.
I THINK I LOVE THIS BABY.
IT IS A CUTE BABY.
I FOUND MYSELF STANDOFFISH BEFORE, BUT NOW-- I SEE IT.
I FEEL LIKE THE TEAM IS GOING TO DISBAND.
THAT'S UP TO CAPTAIN AMERICA.
YOU...

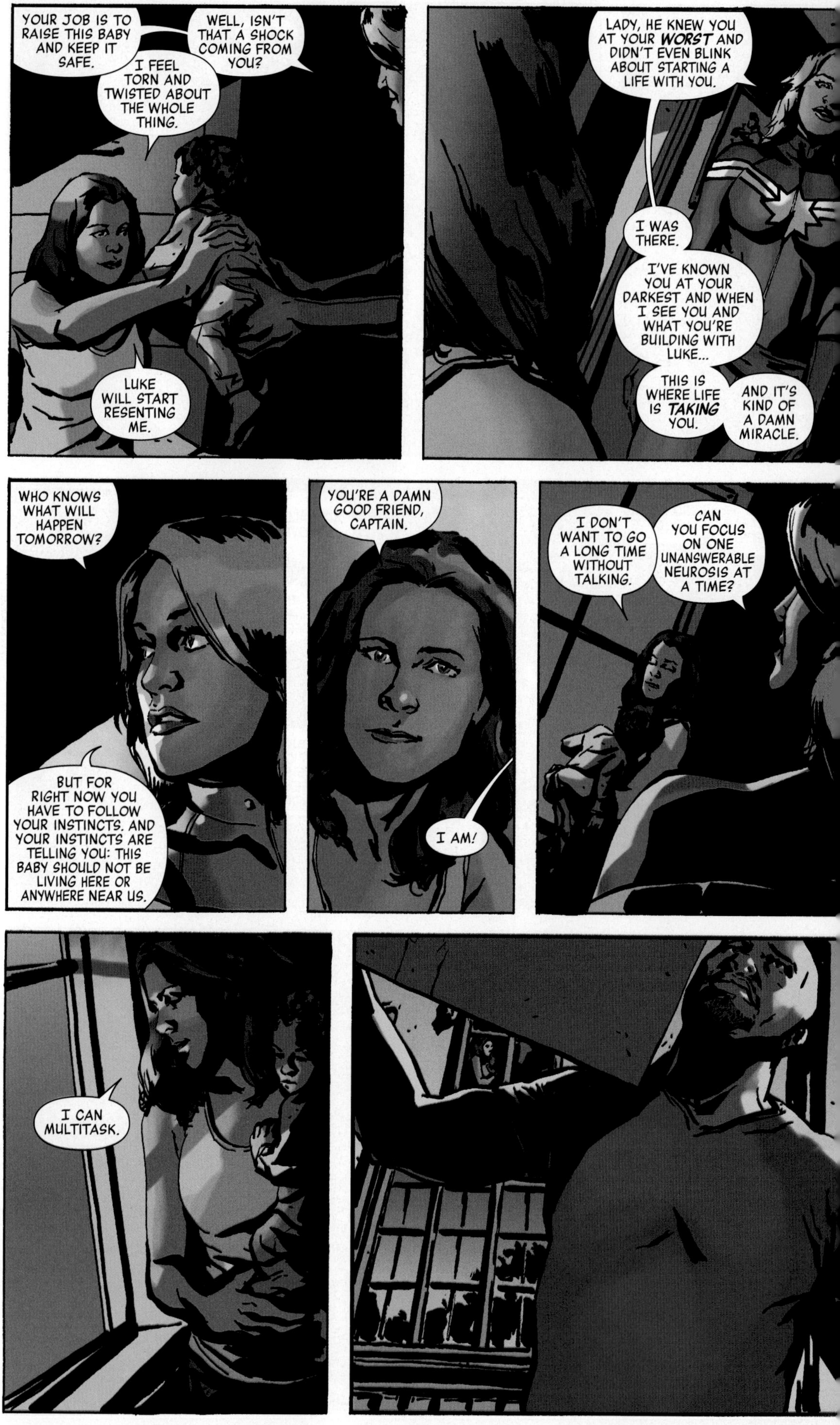
YOUR JOB IS TO RAISE THIS BABY AND KEEP IT SAFE.
WELL, ISN'T THAT A SHOCK COMING FROM YOU?
I FEEL TORN AND TWISTED ABOUT THE WHOLE THING.
LUKE WILL START RESENTING ME.
LADY, HE KNEW YOU AT YOUR WORST AND DIDN'T EVEN BLINK ABOUT STARTING A LIFE WITH YOU.
I WAS THERE.
I'VE KNOWN YOU AT YOUR DARKEST AND WHEN I SEE YOU AND WHAT YOU'RE BUILDING WITH LUKE...
THIS IS WHERE LIFE IS TAKING YOU.
AND IT'S KIND OF A DAMN MIRACLE.
WHO KNOWS WHAT WILL HAPPEN TOMORROW?
BUT FOR RIGHT NOW YOU HAVE TO FOLLOW YOUR INSTINCTS. AND YOUR INSTINCTS ARE TELLING YOU: THIS BABY SHOULD NOT BE LIVING HERE OR ANYWHERE NEAR US.
YOU'RE A DAMN GOOD FRIEND, CAPTAIN.
I AM!
I DON'T WANT TO GO A LONG TIME WITHOUT TALKING.
CAN YOU FOCUS ON ONE UNANSWERABLE NEUROSIS AT A TIME?
I CAN MULTITASK.

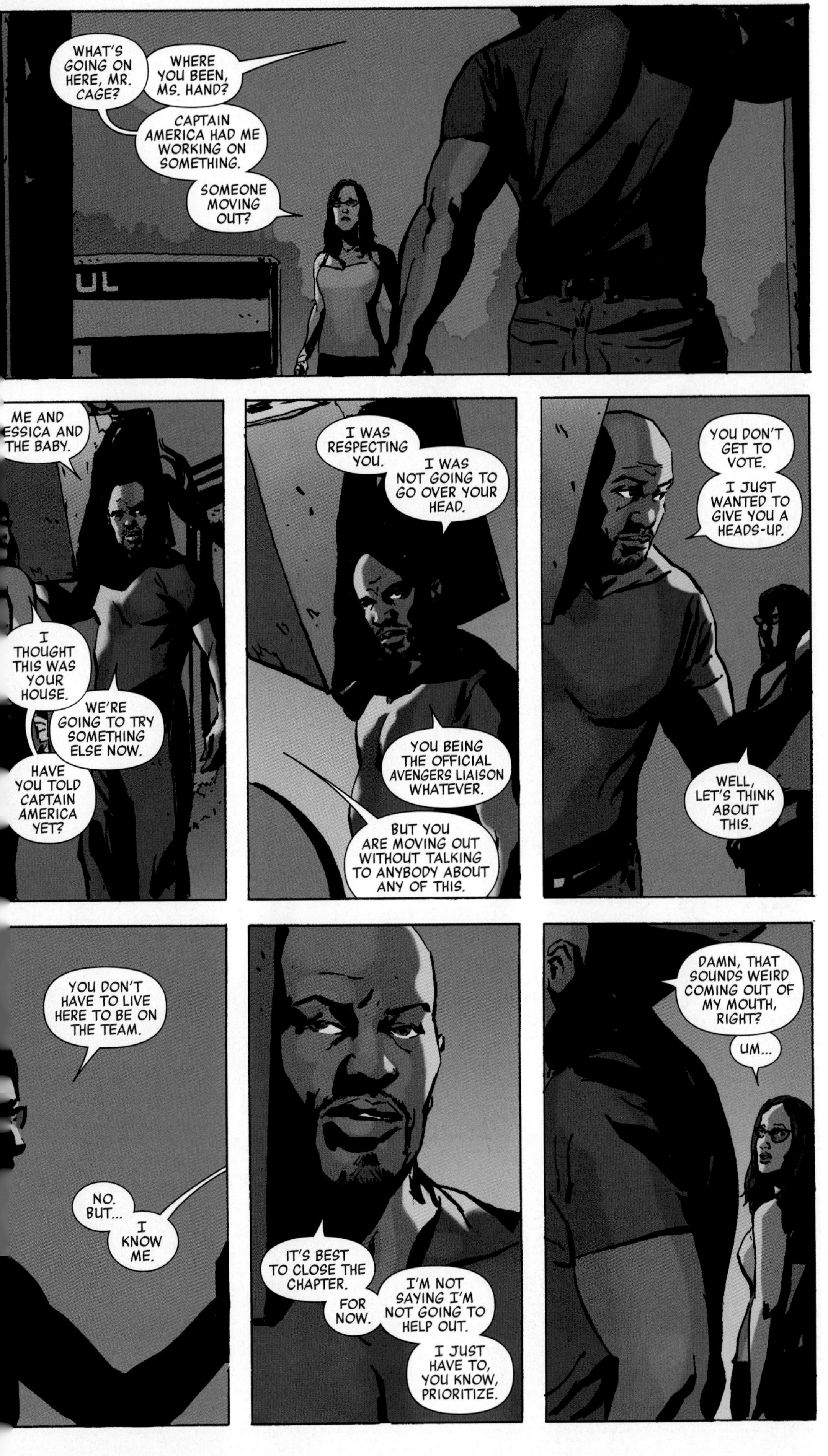
WHAT'S GOING ON HERE, MR. CAGE?
WHERE YOU BEEN, MS. HAND?
CAPTAIN AMERICA HAD ME WORKING ON SOMETHING.
SOMEONE MOVING OUT?
ME AND ESSICA AND THE BABY.
I THOUGHT THIS WAS YOUR HOUSE.
WE'RE GOING TO TRY SOMETHING ELSE NOW.
HAVE YOU TOLD CAPTAIN AMERICA YET?
I WAS RESPECTING YOU.
I WAS NOT GOING TO GO OVER YOUR HEAD.
YOU BEING THE OFFICIAL AVENGERS LIAISON WHATEVER.
BUT YOU ARE MOVING OUT WITHOUT TALKING TO ANYBODY ABOUT ANY OF THIS.
YOU DON'T GET TO VOTE.
I JUST WANTED TO GIVE YOU A HEADS-UP.
WELL, LET'S THINK ABOUT THIS.
YOU DON'T HAVE TO LIVE HERE TO BE ON THE TEAM.
NO. BUT...
I KNOW ME.
IT'S BEST TO CLOSE THE CHAPTER.
FOR NOW.
I'M NOT SAYING I'M NOT GOING TO HELP OUT.
I JUST HAVE TO, YOU KNOW, PRIORITIZE.
DAMN, THAT SOUNDS WEIRD COMING OUT OF MY MOUTH, RIGHT?
UM...

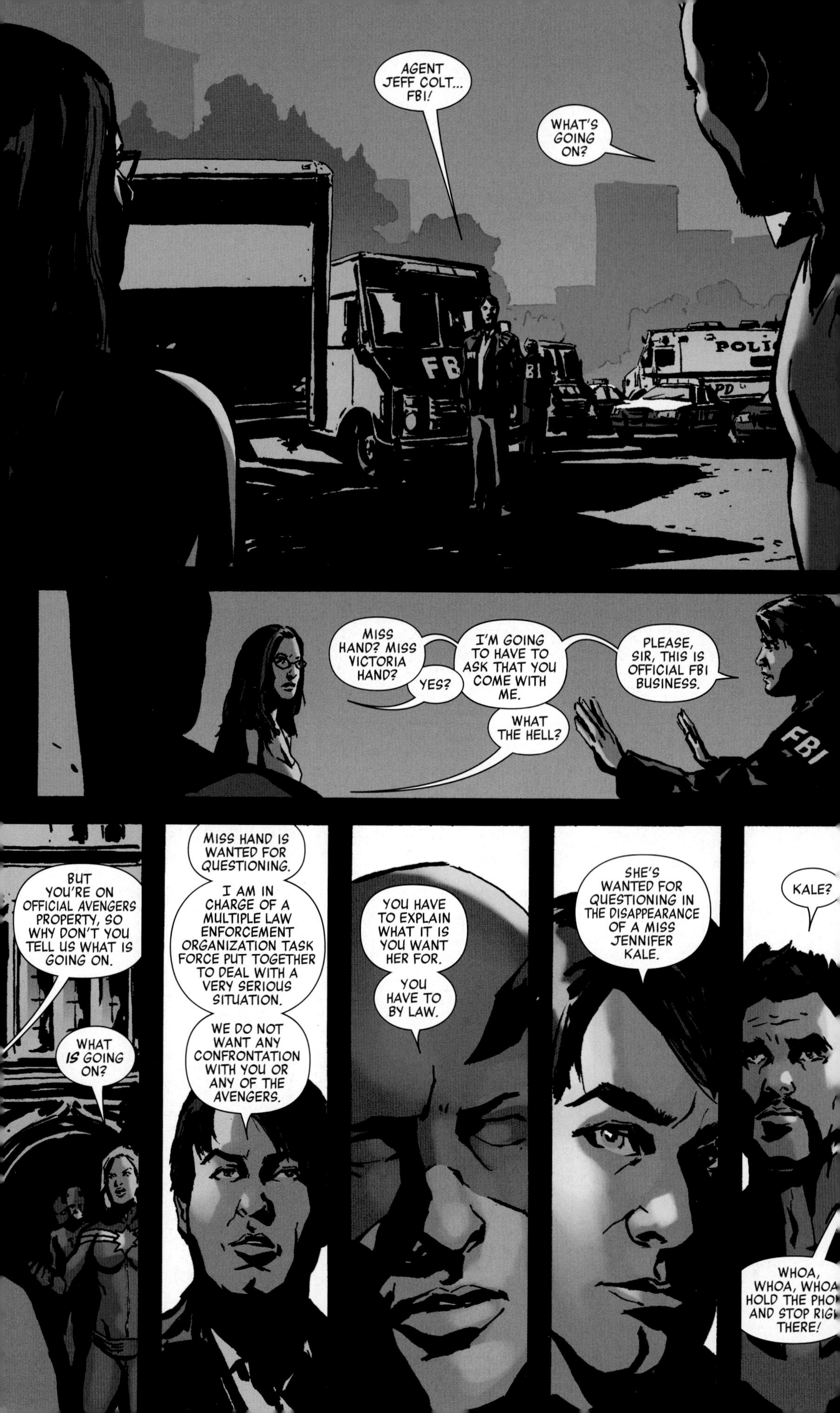
AGENT JEFF COLT... FBI!
WHAT'S GOING ON?
MISS HAND? MISS VICTORIA HAND?
YES?
I'M GOING TO HAVE TO ASK THAT YOU COME WITH ME.
PLEASE, SIR, THIS IS OFFICIAL FBI BUSINESS.
WHAT THE HELL?
BUT YOU'RE ON OFFICIAL AVENGERS PROPERTY, SO WHY DON'T YOU TELL US WHAT IS GOING ON.
WHAT *IS* GOING ON?
MISS HAND IS WANTED FOR QUESTIONING.
I AM IN CHARGE OF A MULTIPLE LAW ENFORCEMENT ORGANIZATION TASK FORCE PUT TOGETHER TO DEAL WITH A VERY SERIOUS SITUATION.
WE DO NOT WANT ANY CONFRONTATION WITH YOU OR ANY OF THE AVENGERS.
YOU HAVE TO EXPLAIN WHAT IT IS YOU WANT HER FOR.
YOU HAVE TO BY LAW.
SHE'S WANTED FOR QUESTIONING IN THE DISAPPEARANCE OF A MISS JENNIFER KALE.
KALE?
WHOA, WHOA, WHOA HOLD THE PHO AND STOP RIG THERE!

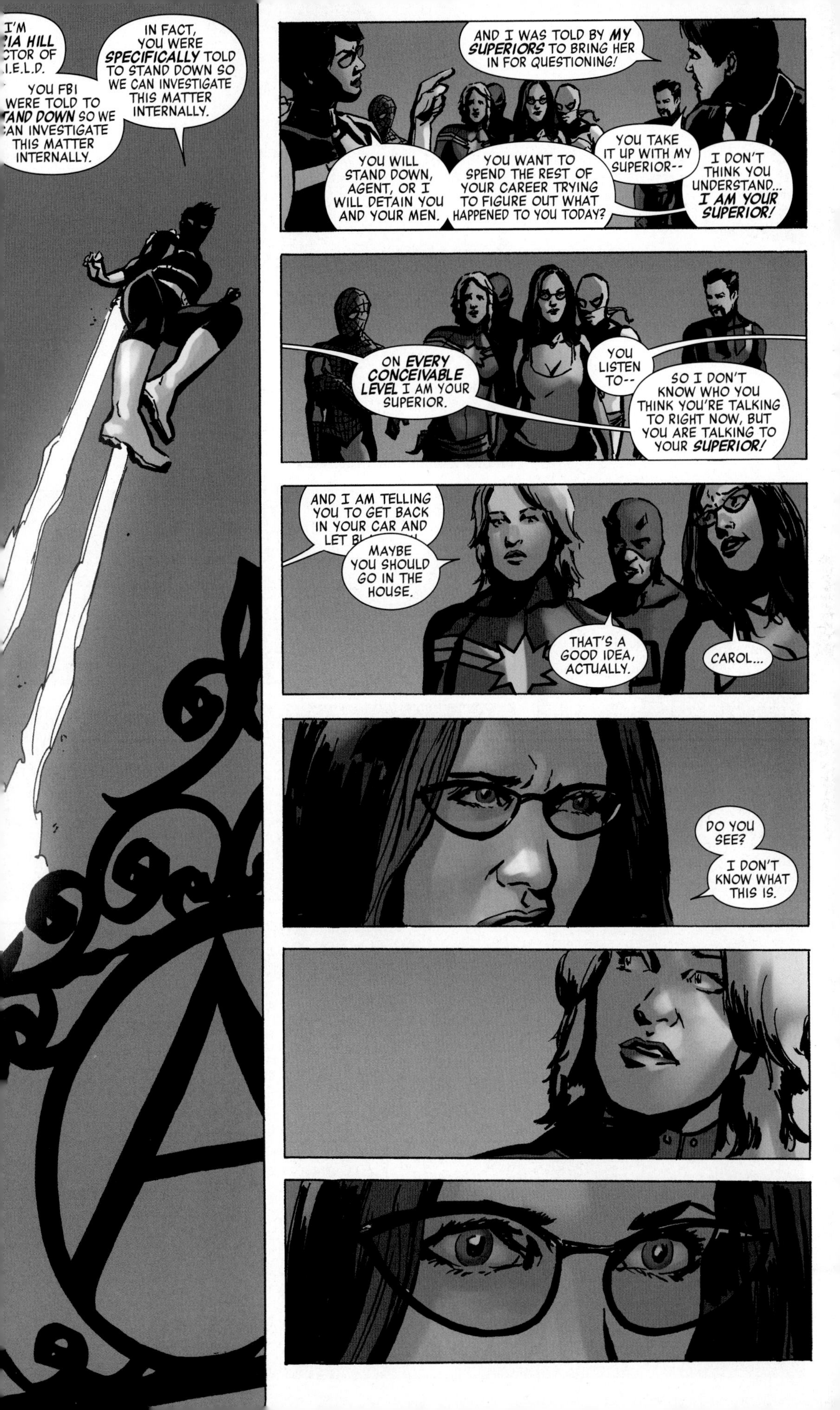

I'M
ZIA HILL
CTOR OF
.I.E.L.D.
YOU FBI WERE TOLD TO TAND DOWN SO WE AN INVESTIGATE THIS MATTER INTERNALLY.
IN FACT, YOU WERE SPECIFICALLY TOLD TO STAND DOWN SO WE CAN INVESTIGATE THIS MATTER INTERNALLY.
AND I WAS TOLD BY MY SUPERIORS TO BRING HER IN FOR QUESTIONING!
YOU WILL STAND DOWN, AGENT, OR I WILL DETAIN YOU AND YOUR MEN.
YOU WANT TO SPEND THE REST OF YOUR CAREER TRYING TO FIGURE OUT WHAT HAPPENED TO YOU TODAY?
YOU TAKE IT UP WITH MY SUPERIOR--
I DON'T THINK YOU UNDERSTAND... I AM YOUR SUPERIOR!
ON EVERY CONCEIVABLE LEVEL I AM YOUR SUPERIOR.
YOU LISTEN TO--
SO I DON'T KNOW WHO YOU THINK YOU'RE TALKING TO RIGHT NOW, BUT YOU ARE TALKING TO YOUR SUPERIOR!
AND I AM TELLING YOU TO GET BACK IN YOUR CAR AND
MAYBE YOU SHOULD GO IN THE HOUSE.
THAT'S A GOOD IDEA, ACTUALLY.
CAROL...
DO YOU SEE?
I DON'T KNOW WHAT THIS IS.

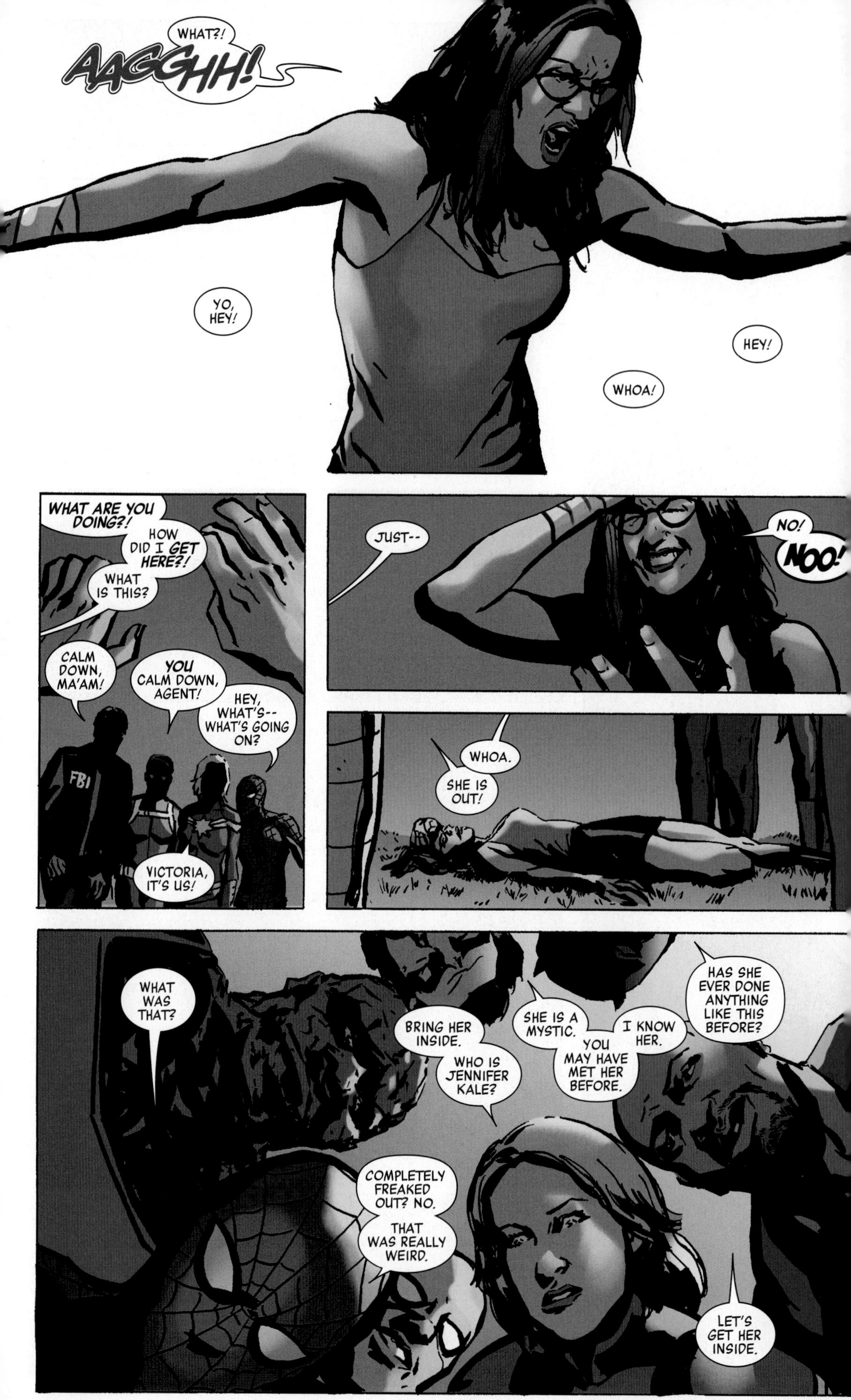
WHAT?!
AAGGHH!
YO, HEY!
HEY!
WHOA!
WHAT ARE YOU DOING?!
HOW DID I GET HERE?!
WHAT IS THIS?
CALM DOWN, MA'AM!
YOU CALM DOWN, AGENT!
HEY, WHAT'S-- WHAT'S GOING ON?
FBI
VICTORIA, IT'S US!
JUST--
NO!
NOO!
WHOA.
SHE IS OUT!
WHAT WAS THAT?
BRING HER INSIDE.
WHO IS JENNIFER KALE?
SHE IS A MYSTIC.
YOU MAY HAVE MET HER BEFORE.
I KNOW HER.
HAS SHE EVER DONE ANYTHING LIKE THIS BEFORE?
COMPLETELY FREAKED OUT? NO.
THAT WAS REALLY WEIRD.
LET'S GET HER INSIDE.

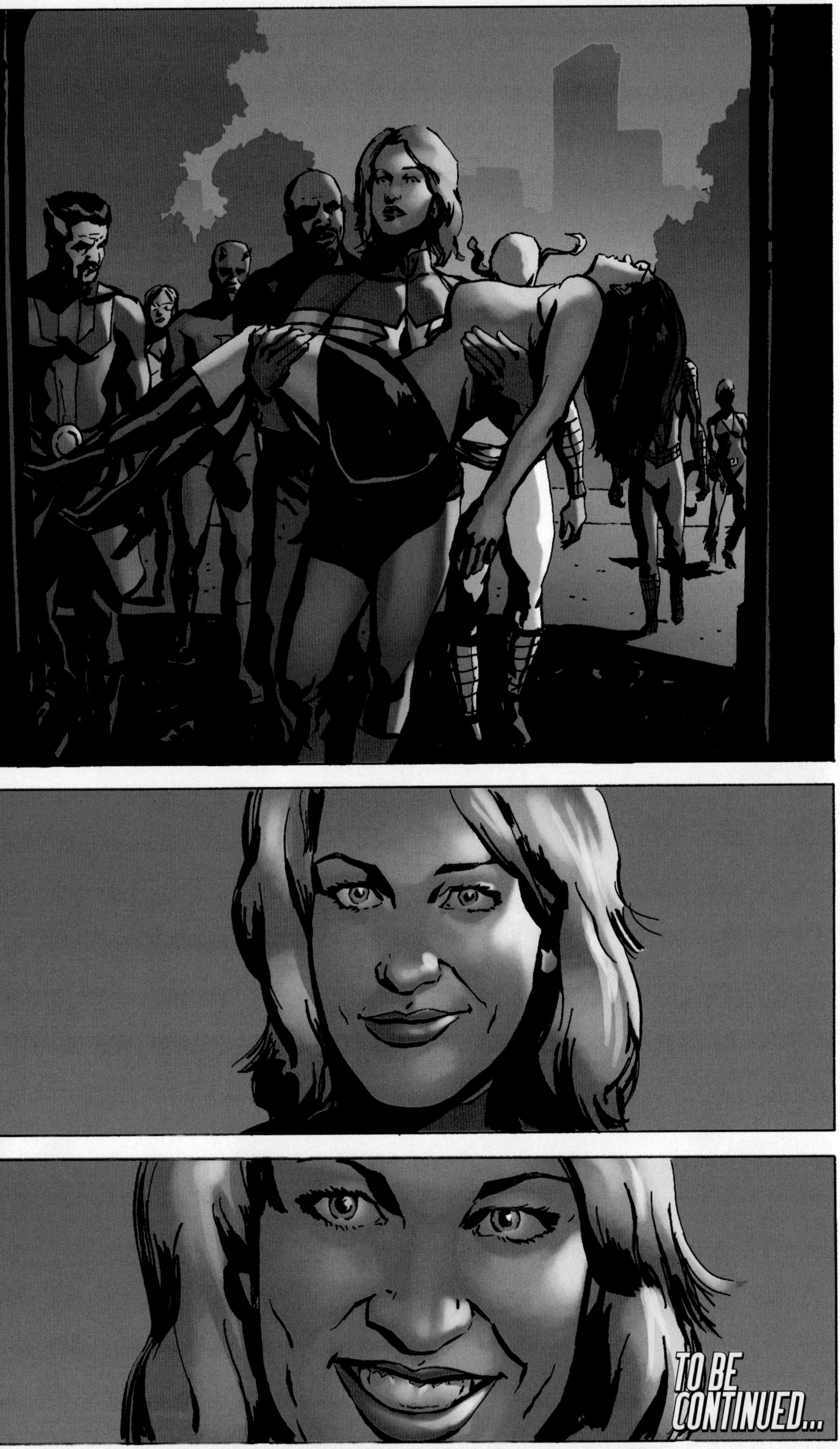
TO BE CONTINUED...

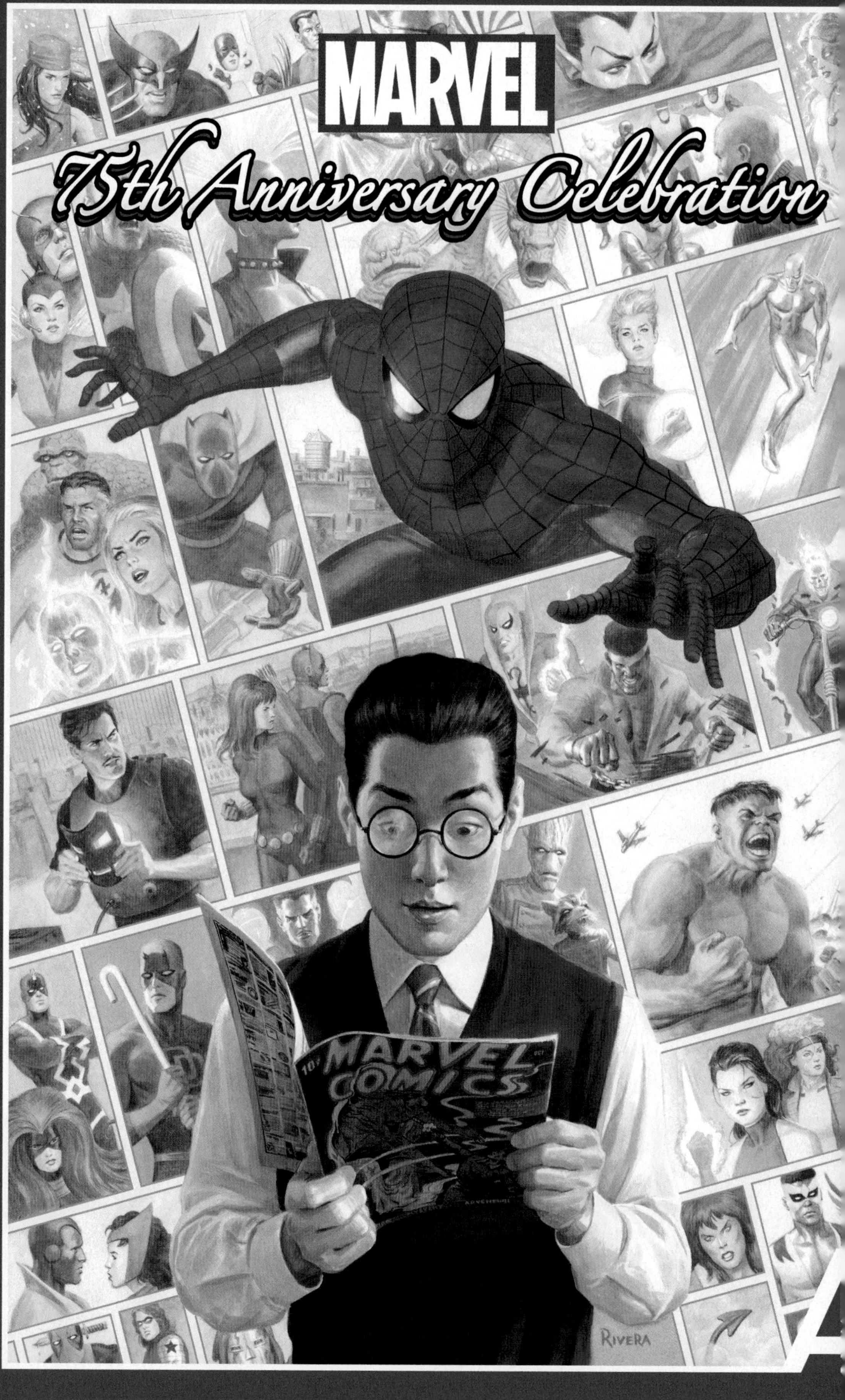
MARVEL
75th Anniversary Celebration
MARVEL COMICS
RIVERA

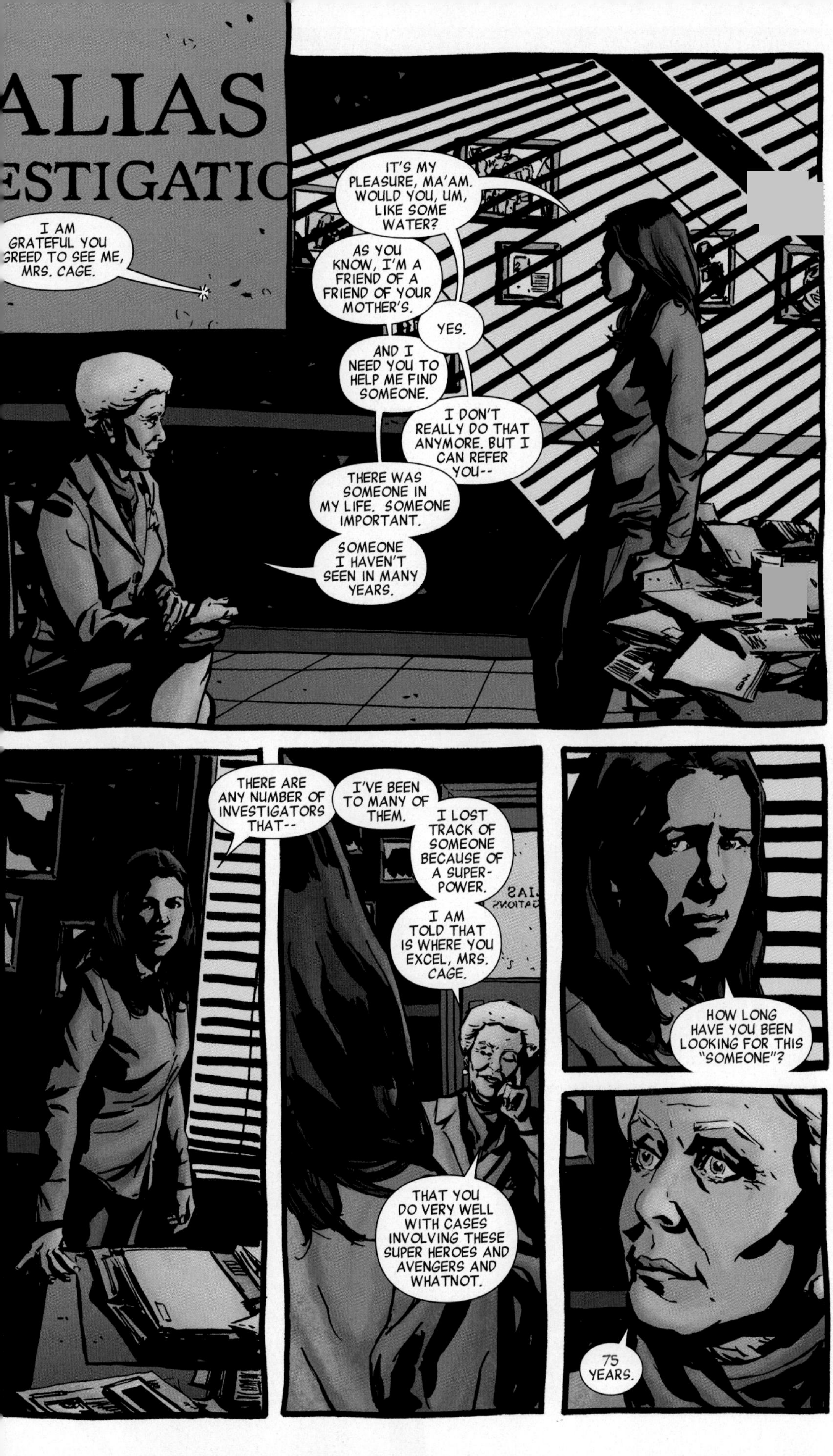
ALIAS
ESTIGATIC
I AM GRATEFUL YOU GREED TO SEE ME, MRS. CAGE.
IT'S MY PLEASURE, MA'AM. WOULD YOU, UM, LIKE SOME WATER?
AS YOU KNOW, I'M A FRIEND OF A FRIEND OF YOUR MOTHER'S.
YES.
AND I NEED YOU TO HELP ME FIND SOMEONE.
I DON'T REALLY DO THAT ANYMORE. BUT I CAN REFER YOU--
THERE WAS SOMEONE IN MY LIFE. SOMEONE IMPORTANT.
SOMEONE I HAVEN'T SEEN IN MANY YEARS.
THERE ARE ANY NUMBER OF INVESTIGATORS THAT--
I'VE BEEN TO MANY OF THEM.
I LOST TRACK OF SOMEONE BECAUSE OF A SUPER-POWER.
I AM TOLD THAT IS WHERE YOU EXCEL, MRS. CAGE.
THAT YOU DO VERY WELL WITH CASES INVOLVING THESE SUPER HEROES AND AVENGERS AND WHATNOT.
HOW LONG HAVE YOU BEEN LOOKING FOR THIS "SOMEONE"?
75 YEARS.

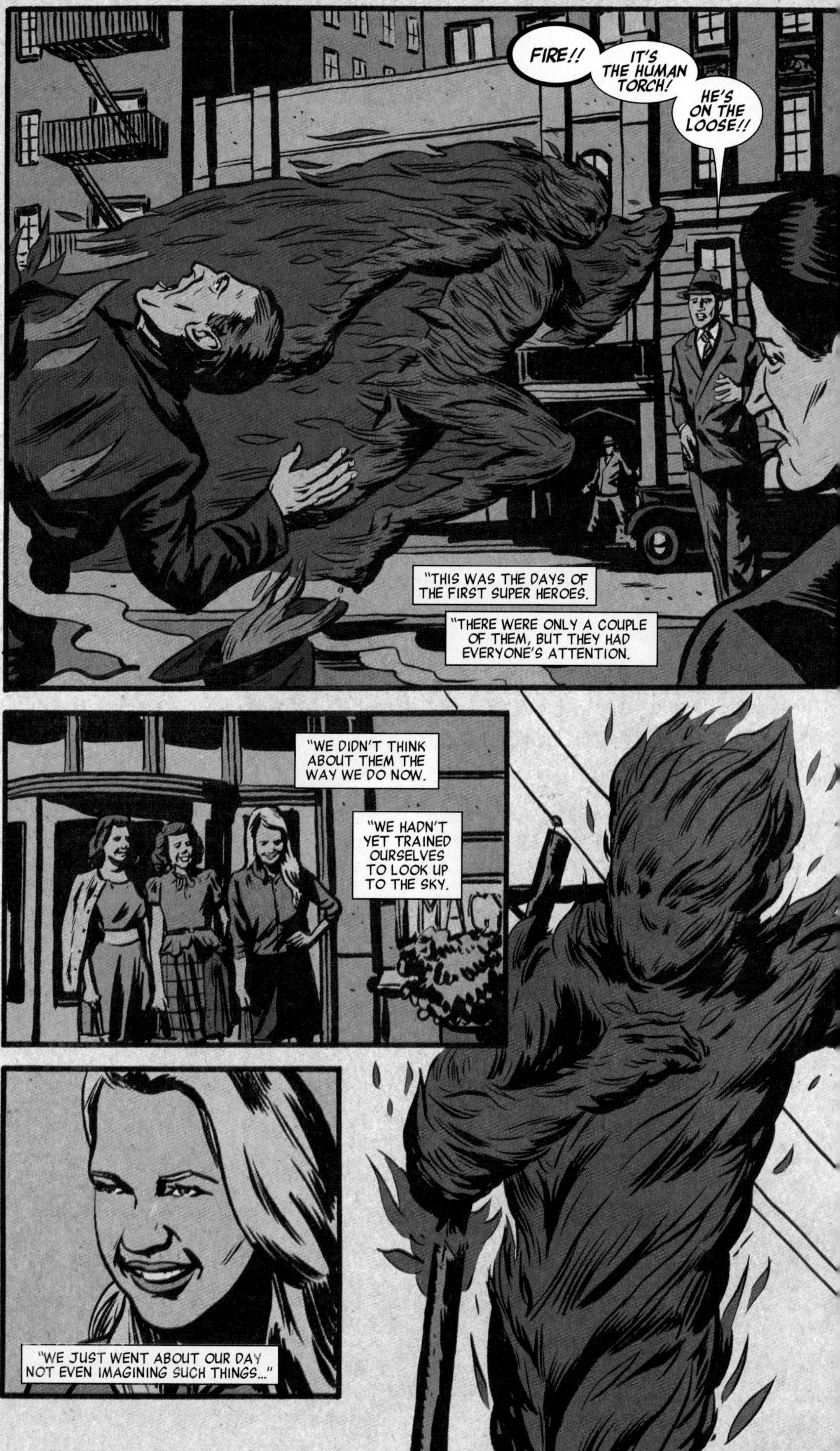
FIRE!!
IT'S THE HUMAN TORCH!
HE'S ON THE LOOSE!!
"THIS WAS THE DAYS OF THE FIRST SUPER HEROES.
"THERE WERE ONLY A COUPLE OF THEM, BUT THEY HAD EVERYONE'S ATTENTION.
"WE DIDN'T THINK ABOUT THEM THE WAY WE DO NOW.
"WE HADN'T YET TRAINED OURSELVES TO LOOK UP TO THE SKY.
"WE JUST WENT ABOUT OUR DAY NOT EVEN IMAGINING SUCH THINGS..."

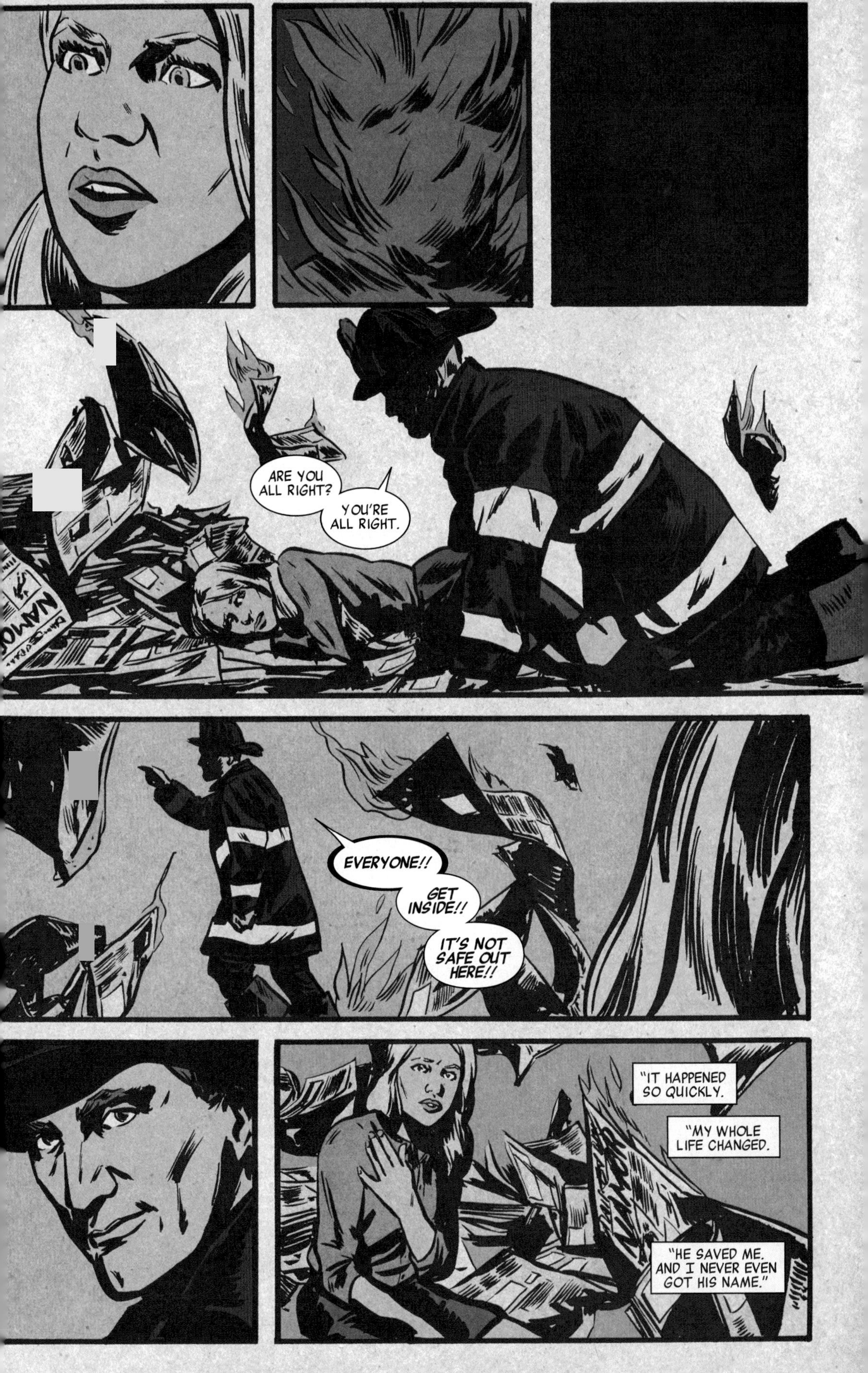
ARE YOU ALL RIGHT?
YOU'RE ALL RIGHT.
EVERYONE!!
GET INSIDE!!
IT'S NOT SAFE OUT HERE!!
"IT HAPPENED SO QUICKLY.
"MY WHOLE LIFE CHANGED.
"HE SAVED ME. AND I NEVER EVEN GOT HIS NAME."

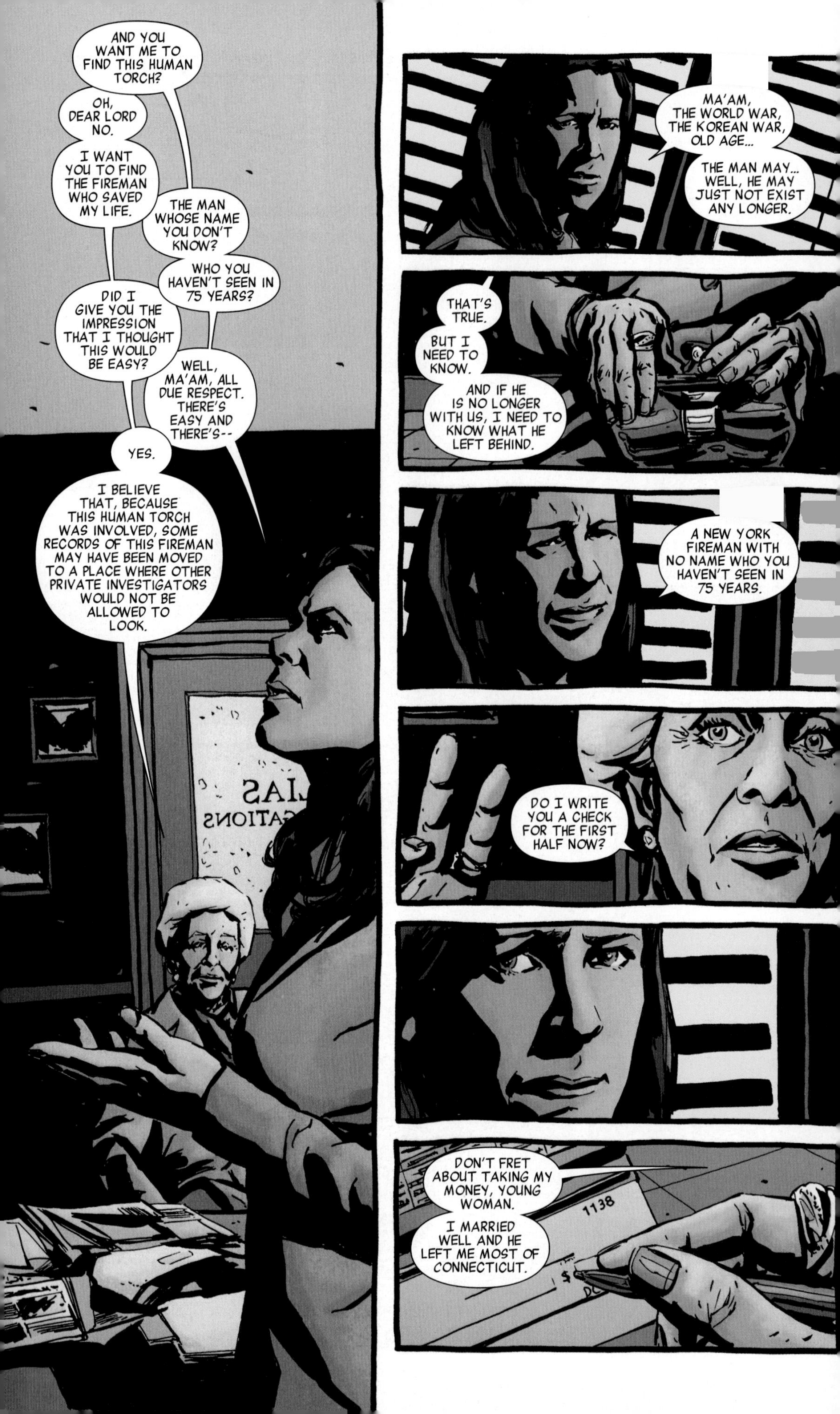
AND YOU WANT ME TO FIND THIS HUMAN TORCH?
OH, DEAR LORD NO.
I WANT YOU TO FIND THE FIREMAN WHO SAVED MY LIFE.
THE MAN WHOSE NAME YOU DON'T KNOW?
WHO YOU HAVEN'T SEEN IN 75 YEARS?
DID I GIVE YOU THE IMPRESSION THAT I THOUGHT THIS WOULD BE EASY?
WELL, MA'AM, ALL DUE RESPECT. THERE'S EASY AND THERE'S--
YES.
I BELIEVE THAT, BECAUSE THIS HUMAN TORCH WAS INVOLVED, SOME RECORDS OF THIS FIREMAN MAY HAVE BEEN MOVED TO A PLACE WHERE OTHER PRIVATE INVESTIGATORS WOULD NOT BE ALLOWED TO LOOK.
MA'AM, THE WORLD WAR, THE KOREAN WAR, OLD AGE...
THE MAN MAY... WELL, HE MAY JUST NOT EXIST ANY LONGER.
THAT'S TRUE.
BUT I NEED TO KNOW.
AND IF HE IS NO LONGER WITH US, I NEED TO KNOW WHAT HE LEFT BEHIND.
A NEW YORK FIREMAN WITH NO NAME WHO YOU HAVEN'T SEEN IN 75 YEARS.
DO I WRITE YOU A CHECK FOR THE FIRST HALF NOW?
DON'T FRET ABOUT TAKING MY MONEY, YOUNG WOMAN.
I MARRIED WELL AND HE LEFT ME MOST OF CONNECTICUT.
1138

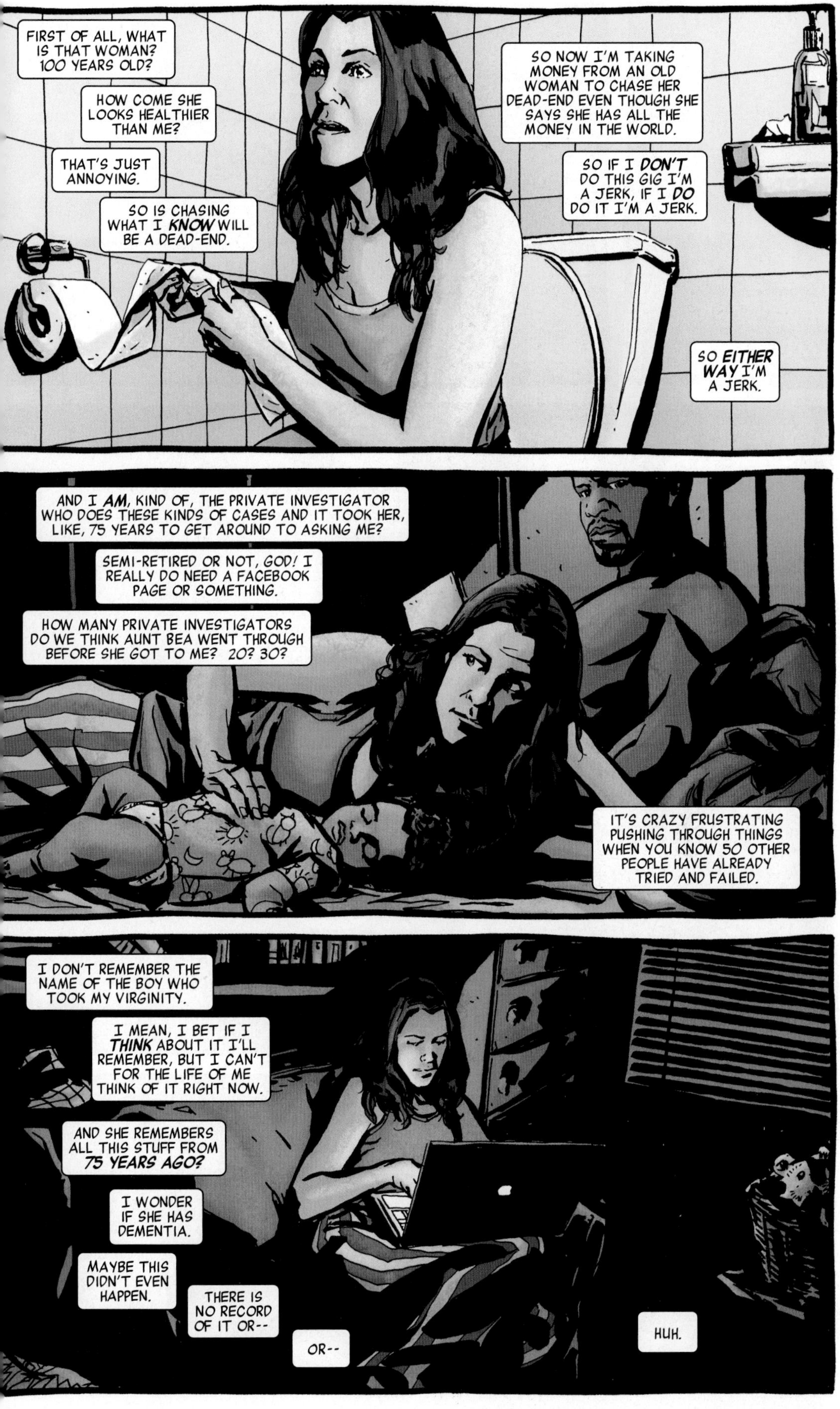
FIRST OF ALL, WHAT IS THAT WOMAN? 100 YEARS OLD?
HOW COME SHE LOOKS HEALTHIER THAN ME?
THAT'S JUST ANNOYING.
SO IS CHASING WHAT I KNOW WILL BE A DEAD-END.
SO NOW I'M TAKING MONEY FROM AN OLD WOMAN TO CHASE HER DEAD-END EVEN THOUGH SHE SAYS SHE HAS ALL THE MONEY IN THE WORLD.
SO IF I DON'T DO THIS GIG I'M A JERK, IF I DO DO IT I'M A JERK.
SO EITHER WAY I'M A JERK.
AND I AM, KIND OF, THE PRIVATE INVESTIGATOR WHO DOES THESE KINDS OF CASES AND IT TOOK HER, LIKE, 75 YEARS TO GET AROUND TO ASKING ME?
SEMI-RETIRED OR NOT, GOD! I REALLY DO NEED A FACEBOOK PAGE OR SOMETHING.
HOW MANY PRIVATE INVESTIGATORS DO WE THINK AUNT BEA WENT THROUGH BEFORE SHE GOT TO ME? 20? 30?
IT'S CRAZY FRUSTRATING PUSHING THROUGH THINGS WHEN YOU KNOW 50 OTHER PEOPLE HAVE ALREADY TRIED AND FAILED.
I DON'T REMEMBER THE NAME OF THE BOY WHO TOOK MY VIRGINITY.
I MEAN, I BET IF I THINK ABOUT IT I'LL REMEMBER, BUT I CAN'T FOR THE LIFE OF ME THINK OF IT RIGHT NOW.
AND SHE REMEMBERS ALL THIS STUFF FROM 75 YEARS AGO?
I WONDER IF SHE HAS DEMENTIA.
MAYBE THIS DIDN'T EVEN HAPPEN.
THERE IS NO RECORD OF IT OR--
OR--
HUH.

REALLY!

MISS HILL. THIS IS MY PRIVATE TIME.

I TOTALLY RELATE.

MY PRIVATE TIME TO EAT MY FAVORITE--

SO I WON'T WASTE ANY OF IT.

I AM HELPING AN OLD WOMAN FIND SOMEBODY SHE CAN'T FIND, AND I DISCOVERED THAT SOMEBODY, PROBABLY S.H.I.E.L.D., HAD A BUNCH OF OLD FILES WIPED OUT OF THE PUBLIC RECORD.

YOU DON'T SAY.

MOST PRIVATE INVESTIGATORS WOULDN'T EVEN KNOW WHAT IT LOOKS LIKE WHEN YOU DO SOMETHING LIKE THAT, BUT I REMEMBER SEEING SOMETHING LIKE THIS ONCE BEFORE.

THIS HAPPENED AROUND THE ORIGINAL HUMAN TORCH'S FIRST APPEARANCE.

WHO TOLD YOU I WAS HERE? NO ONE KNOWS I'M HERE.

SOMEONE KNOWS.

NOBODY-- UGH. THAT CAROL DANVERS. WHAT A YENTA.

I NEED TO FIND A FIREMAN.

WHO DOESN'T?

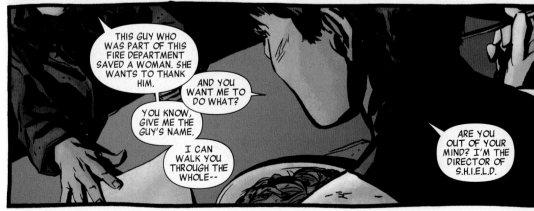

THIS GUY WHO WAS PART OF THIS FIRE DEPARTMENT SAVED A WOMAN. SHE WANTS TO THANK HIM.

AND YOU WANT ME TO DO WHAT?

YOU KNOW, GIVE ME THE GUY'S NAME.

I CAN WALK YOU THROUGH THE WHOLE--

ARE YOU OUT OF YOUR MIND? I'M THE DIRECTOR OF S.H.I.E.L.D.

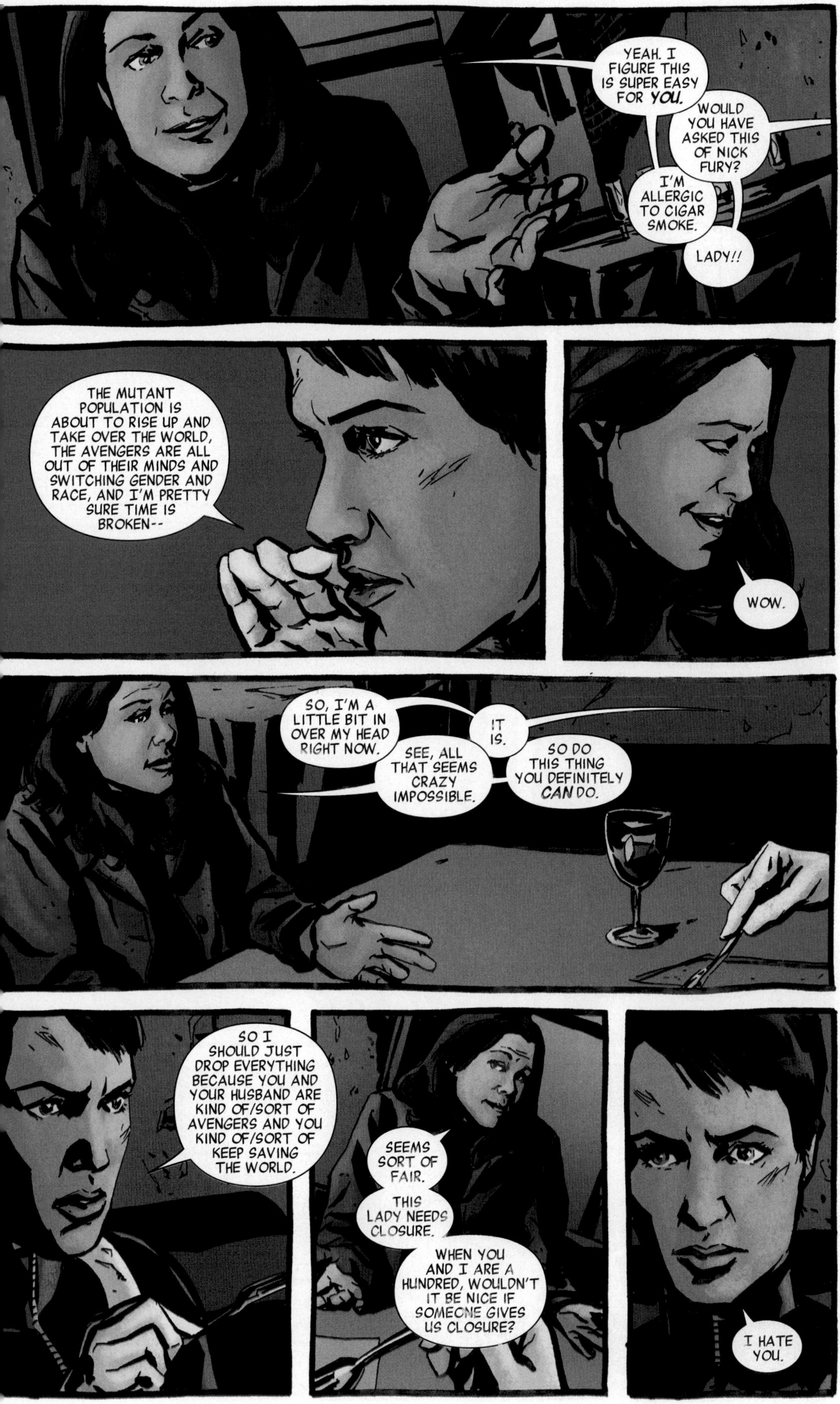

YEAH. I FIGURE THIS IS SUPER EASY FOR YOU.
WOULD YOU HAVE ASKED THIS OF NICK FURY?
I'M ALLERGIC TO CIGAR SMOKE.
LADY!!
THE MUTANT POPULATION IS ABOUT TO RISE UP AND TAKE OVER THE WORLD, THE AVENGERS ARE ALL OUT OF THEIR MINDS AND SWITCHING GENDER AND RACE, AND I'M PRETTY SURE TIME IS BROKEN--
WOW.
SO, I'M A LITTLE BIT IN OVER MY HEAD RIGHT NOW.
IT IS.
SEE, ALL THAT SEEMS CRAZY IMPOSSIBLE.
SO DO THIS THING YOU DEFINITELY CAN DO.
SO I SHOULD JUST DROP EVERYTHING BECAUSE YOU AND YOUR HUSBAND ARE KIND OF/SORT OF AVENGERS AND YOU KIND OF/SORT OF KEEP SAVING THE WORLD.
SEEMS SORT OF FAIR.
THIS LADY NEEDS CLOSURE.
WHEN YOU AND I ARE A HUNDRED, WOULDN'T IT BE NICE IF SOMEONE GIVES US CLOSURE?
I HATE YOU.

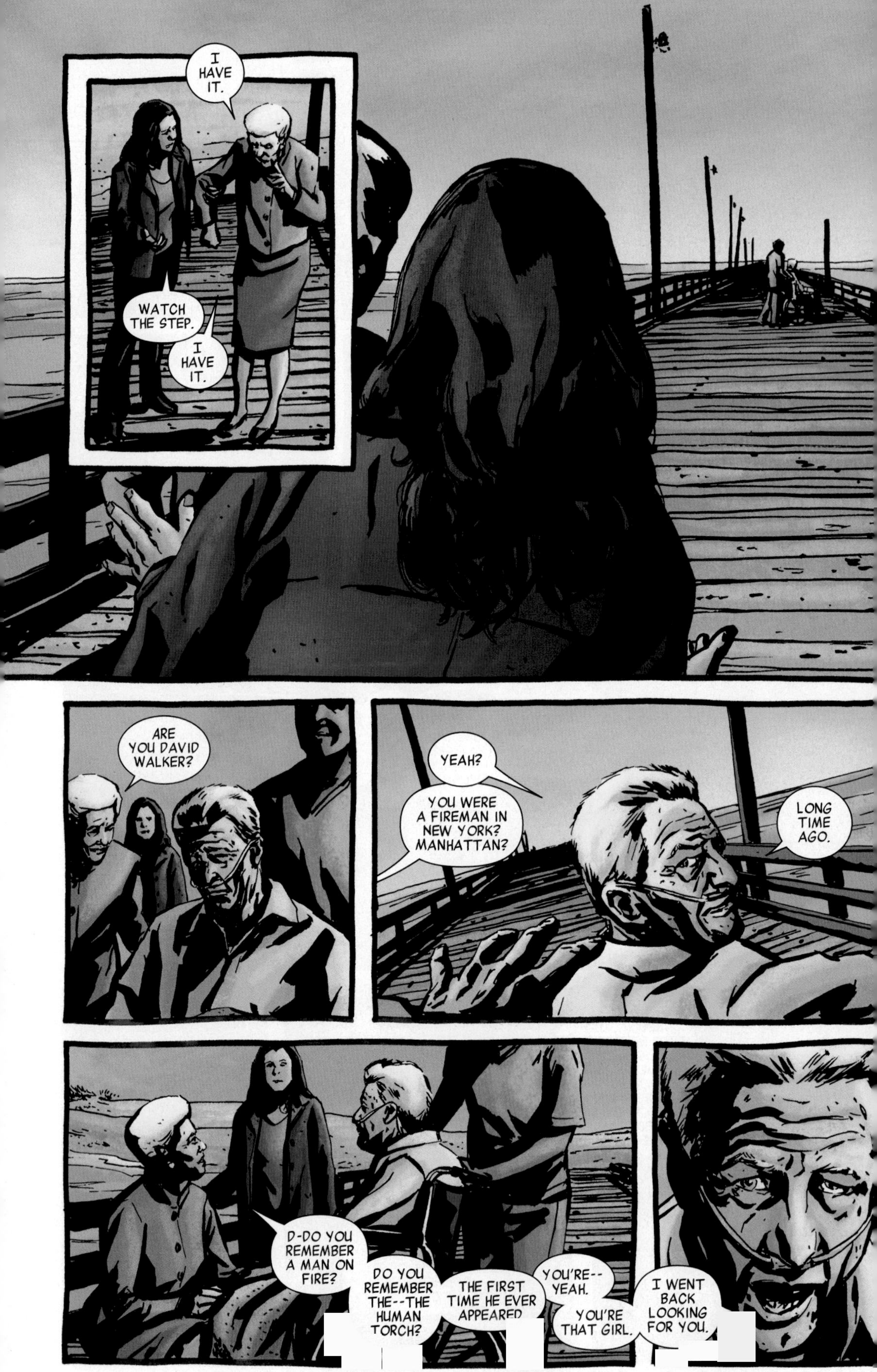

I HAVE IT.
WATCH THE STEP.
I HAVE IT.
ARE YOU DAVID WALKER?
YEAH?
YOU WERE A FIREMAN IN NEW YORK? MANHATTAN?
LONG TIME AGO.
D-DO YOU REMEMBER A MAN ON FIRE?
DO YOU REMEMBER THE--THE HUMAN TORCH?
THE FIRST TIME HE EVER APPEARED
YOU'RE-- YEAH.
YOU'RE THAT GIRL.
I WENT BACK LOOKING FOR YOU.

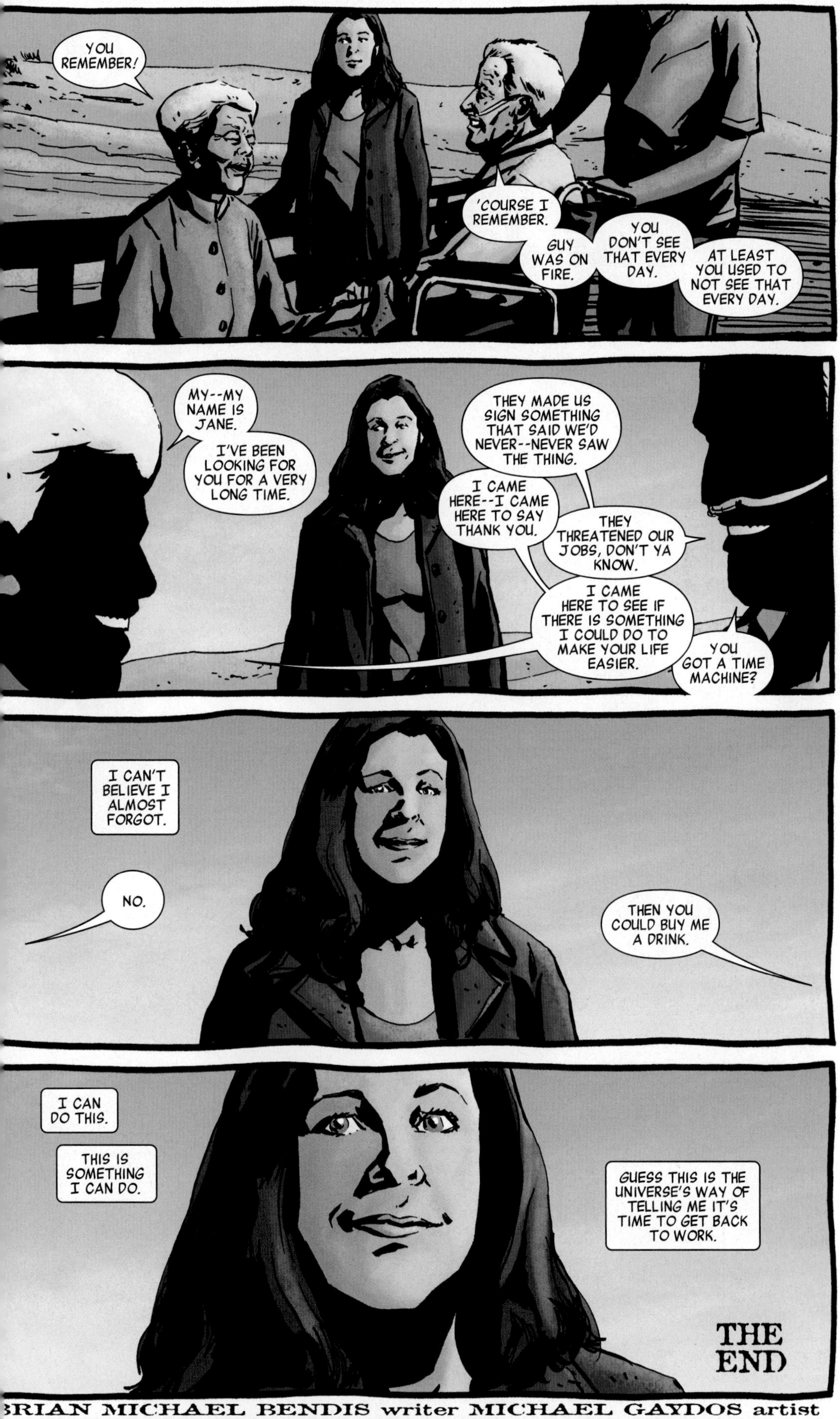
YOU REMEMBER!
'COURSE I REMEMBER.
GUY WAS ON FIRE.
YOU DON'T SEE THAT EVERY DAY.
AT LEAST YOU USED TO NOT SEE THAT EVERY DAY.
MY--MY NAME IS JANE.
I'VE BEEN LOOKING FOR YOU FOR A VERY LONG TIME.
THEY MADE US SIGN SOMETHING THAT SAID WE'D NEVER--NEVER SAW THE THING.
I CAME HERE--I CAME HERE TO SAY THANK YOU.
THEY THREATENED OUR JOBS, DON'T YA KNOW.
I CAME HERE TO SEE IF THERE IS SOMETHING I COULD DO TO MAKE YOUR LIFE EASIER.
YOU GOT A TIME MACHINE?
I CAN'T BELIEVE I ALMOST FORGOT.
NO.
THEN YOU COULD BUY ME A DRINK.
I CAN DO THIS.
THIS IS SOMETHING I CAN DO.
GUESS THIS IS THE UNIVERSE'S WAY OF TELLING ME IT'S TIME TO GET BACK TO WORK.
THE END

BRIAN MICHAEL BENDIS writer MICHAEL GAYDOS artist
MATT HOLLINGSWORTH colorist VC'S CORY PETIT letterer

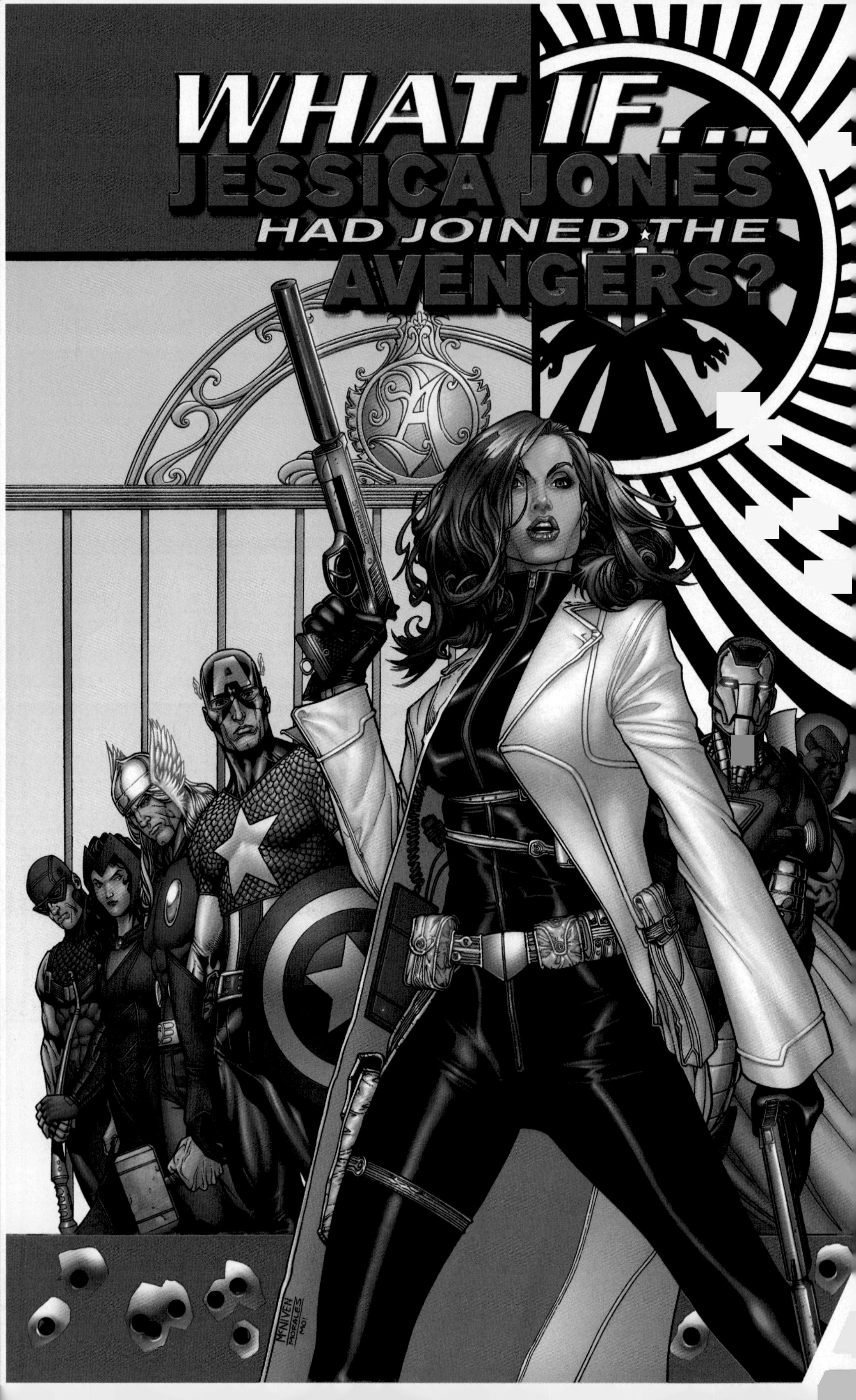
WHAT IF...
JESSICA JONES
HAD JOINED THE
AVENGERS?
McNIVEN
MORALES
MOI

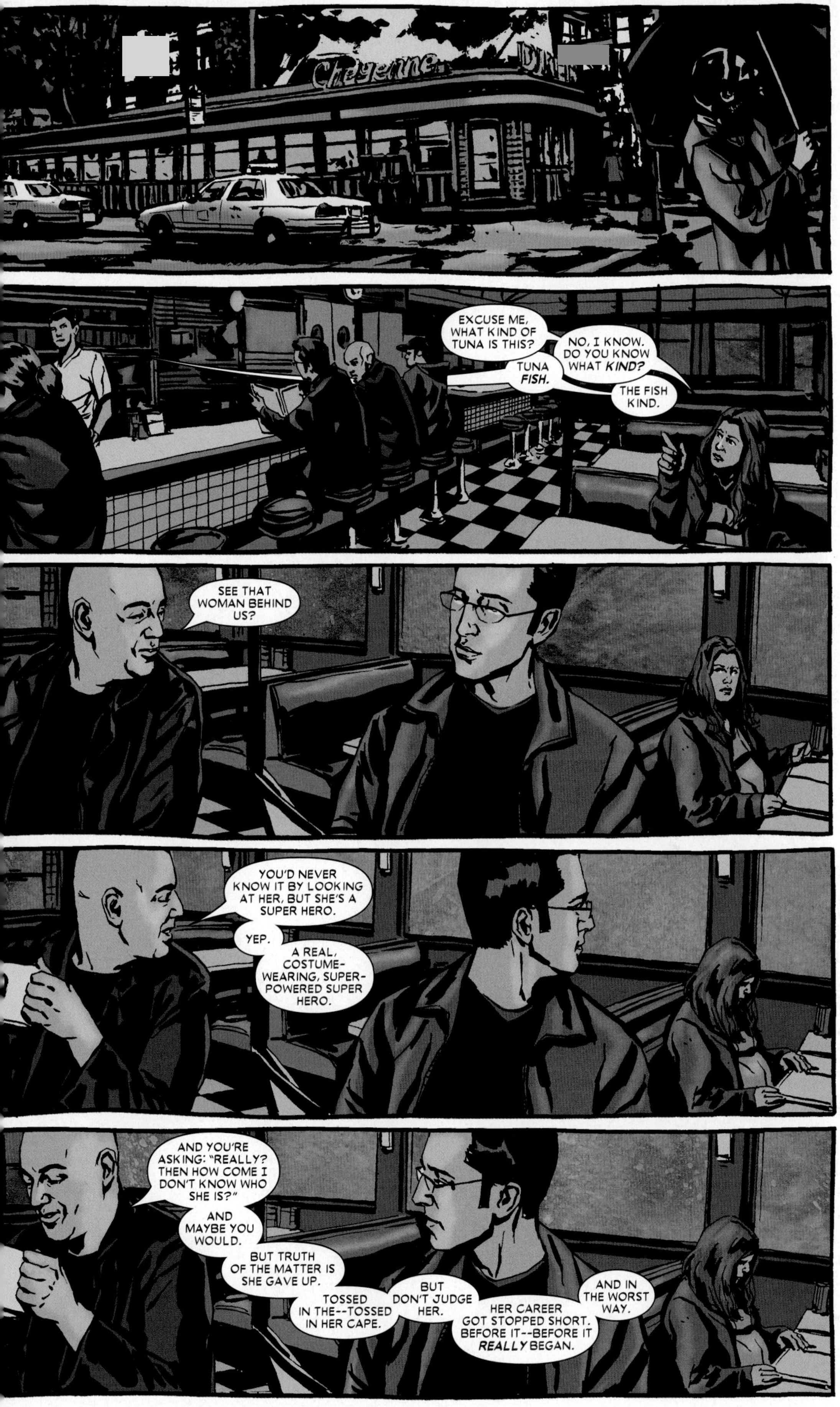
Cheyenne
EXCUSE ME, WHAT KIND OF TUNA IS THIS?
TUNA *FISH.*
NO, I KNOW. DO YOU KNOW WHAT *KIND?*
THE FISH KIND.
SEE THAT WOMAN BEHIND US?
YOU'D NEVER KNOW IT BY LOOKING AT HER, BUT SHE'S A SUPER HERO.
YEP.
A REAL, COSTUME-WEARING, SUPER-POWERED SUPER HERO.
AND YOU'RE ASKING: "REALLY? THEN HOW COME I DON'T KNOW WHO SHE IS?"
AND MAYBE YOU WOULD.
BUT TRUTH OF THE MATTER IS SHE GAVE UP.
TOSSED IN THE--TOSSED IN HER CAPE.
BUT DON'T JUDGE HER.
HER CAREER GOT STOPPED SHORT. BEFORE IT--BEFORE IT *REALLY* BEGAN.
AND IN THE WORST WAY.

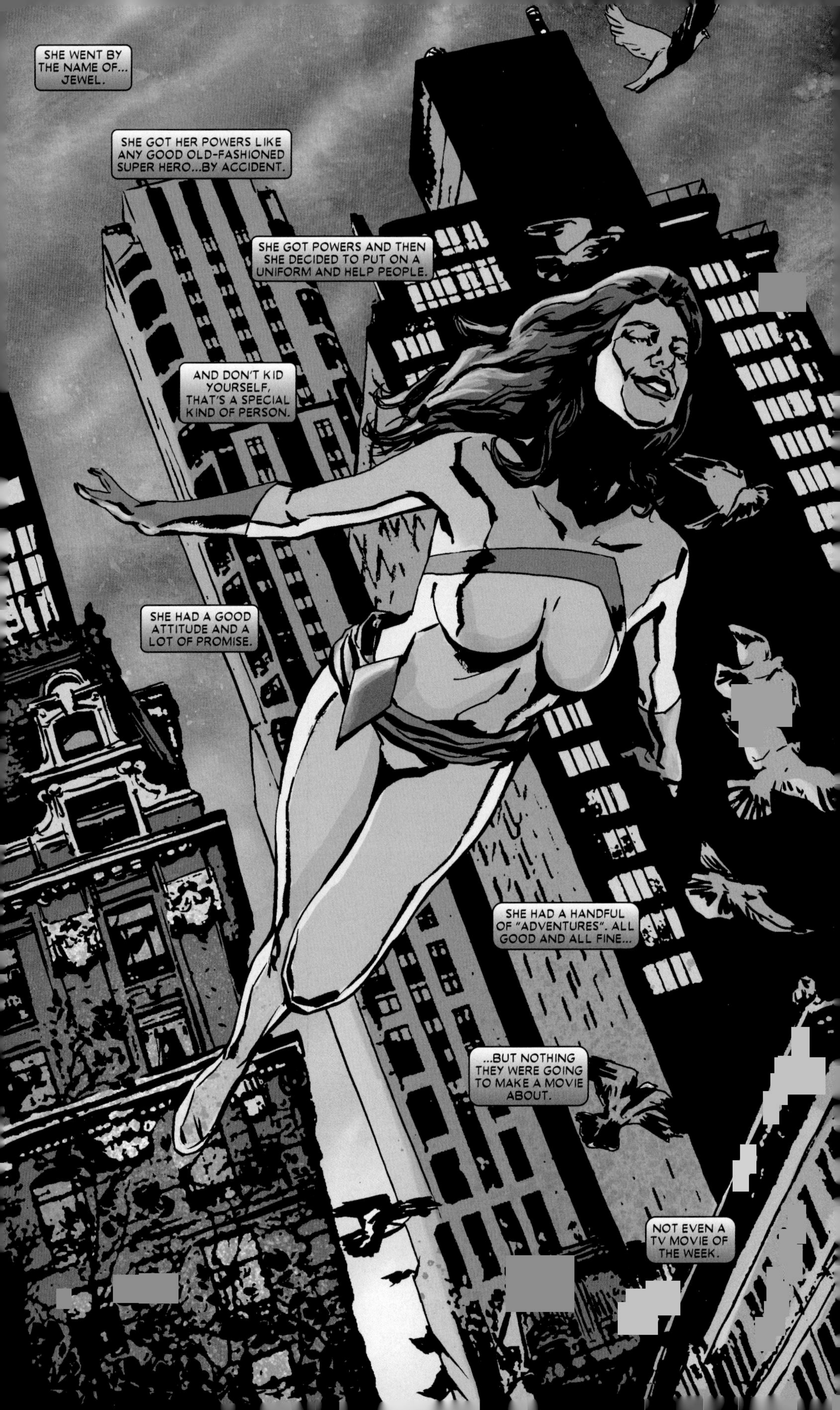
SHE WENT BY THE NAME OF... JEWEL.
SHE GOT HER POWERS LIKE ANY GOOD OLD-FASHIONED SUPER HERO...BY ACCIDENT.
SHE GOT POWERS AND THEN SHE DECIDED TO PUT ON A UNIFORM AND HELP PEOPLE.
AND DON'T KID YOURSELF, THAT'S A SPECIAL KIND OF PERSON.
SHE HAD A GOOD ATTITUDE AND A LOT OF PROMISE.
SHE HAD A HANDFUL OF "ADVENTURES". ALL GOOD AND ALL FINE...
...BUT NOTHING THEY WERE GOING TO MAKE A MOVIE ABOUT.
NOT EVEN A TV MOVIE OF THE WEEK.

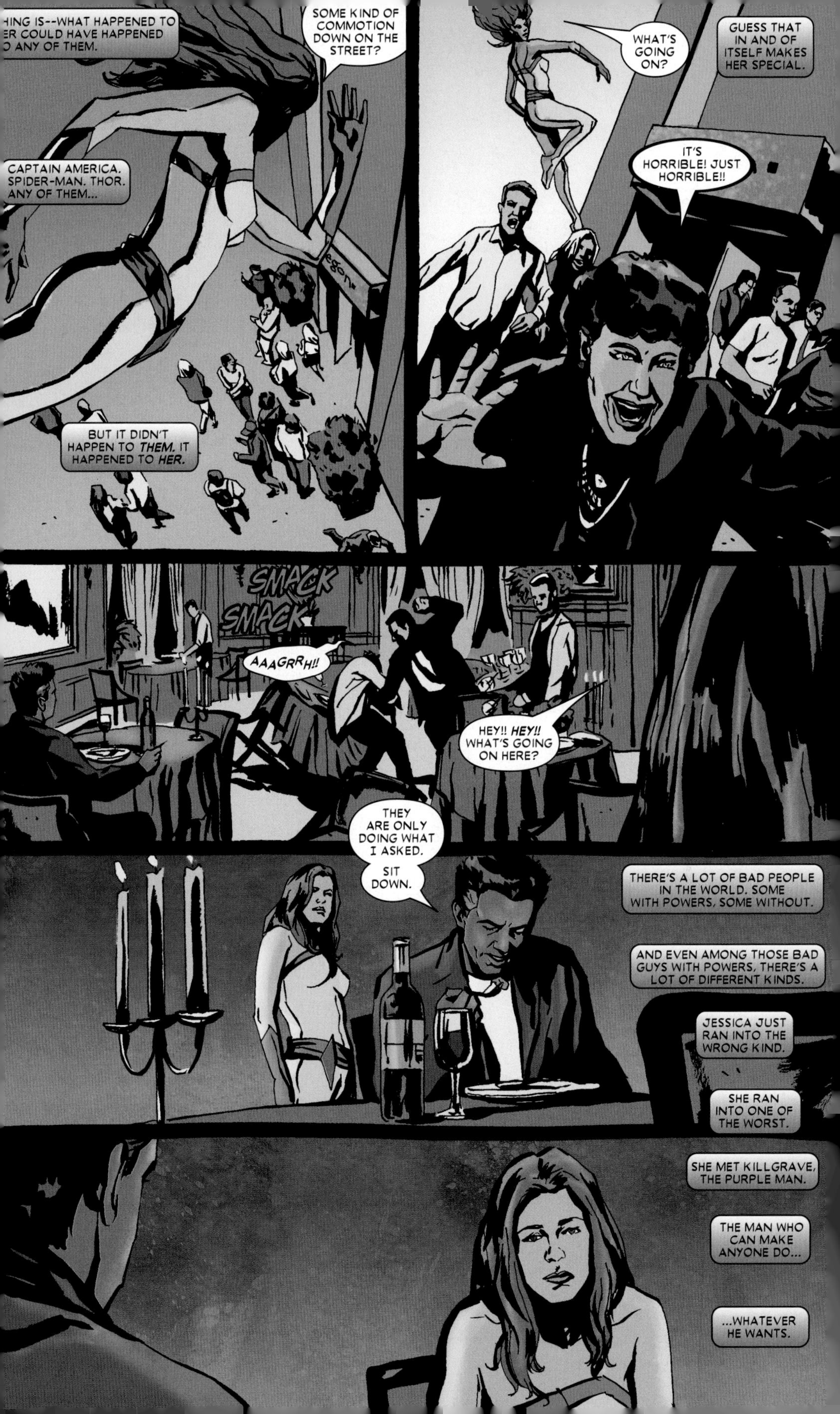

HING IS--WHAT HAPPENED TO
ER COULD HAVE HAPPENED
O ANY OF THEM.
SOME KIND OF COMMOTION DOWN ON THE STREET?
CAPTAIN AMERICA. SPIDER-MAN. THOR. ANY OF THEM...
BUT IT DIDN'T HAPPEN TO *THEM.* IT HAPPENED TO *HER.*
WHAT'S GOING ON?
GUESS THAT IN AND OF ITSELF MAKES HER SPECIAL.
IT'S HORRIBLE! JUST HORRIBLE!!
SMACK
SMACK
AAAGRRH!!
HEY!! *HEY!!* WHAT'S GOING ON HERE?
THEY ARE ONLY DOING WHAT I ASKED.
SIT DOWN.
THERE'S A LOT OF BAD PEOPLE IN THE WORLD. SOME WITH POWERS, SOME WITHOUT.
AND EVEN AMONG THOSE BAD GUYS WITH POWERS, THERE'S A LOT OF DIFFERENT KINDS.
JESSICA JUST RAN INTO THE WRONG KIND.
SHE RAN INTO ONE OF THE WORST.
SHE MET KILLGRAVE, THE PURPLE MAN.
THE MAN WHO CAN MAKE ANYONE DO...
...WHATEVER HE WANTS.

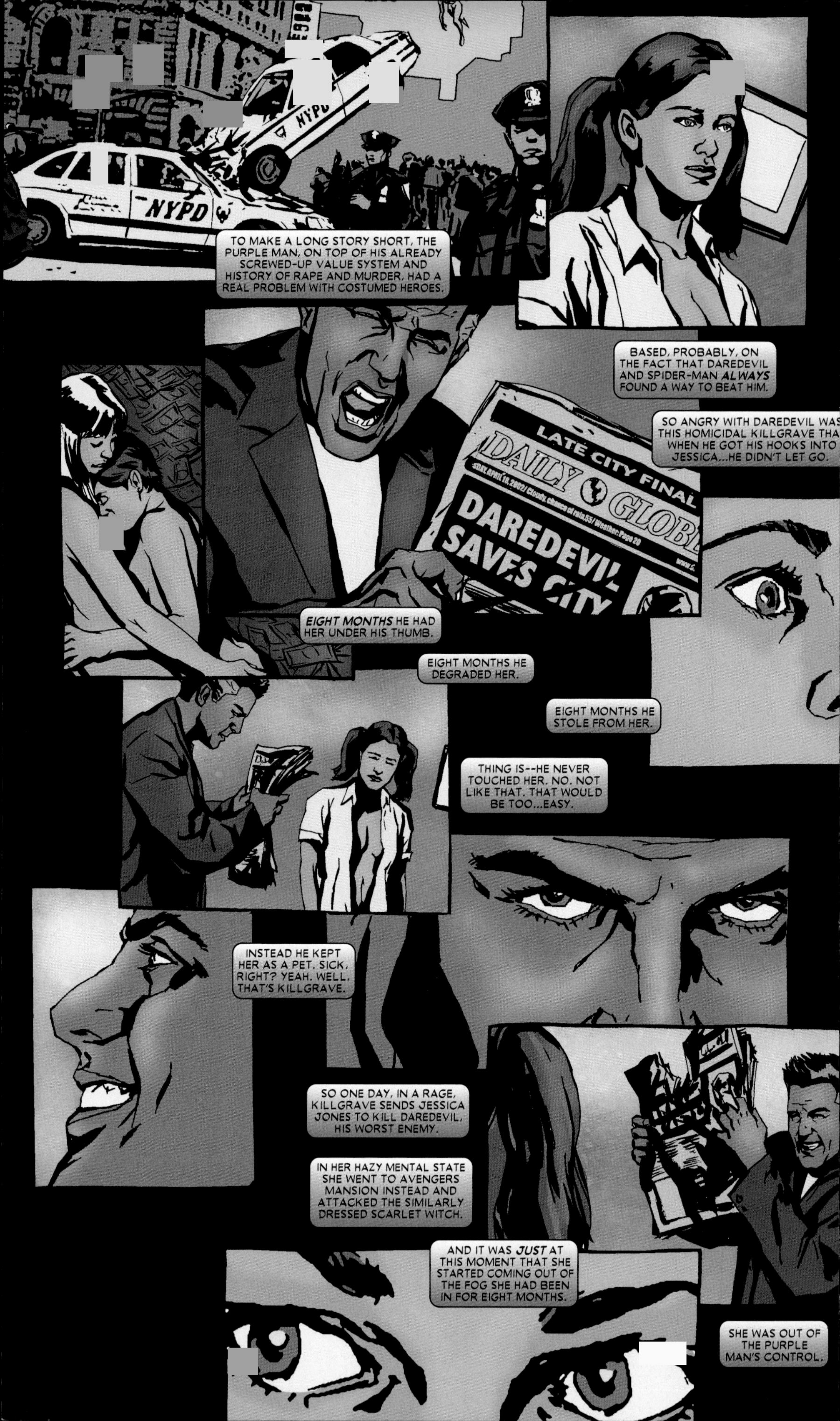

TO MAKE A LONG STORY SHORT, THE PURPLE MAN, ON TOP OF HIS ALREADY SCREWED-UP VALUE SYSTEM AND HISTORY OF RAPE AND MURDER, HAD A REAL PROBLEM WITH COSTUMED HEROES.
BASED, PROBABLY, ON THE FACT THAT DAREDEVIL AND SPIDER-MAN *ALWAYS* FOUND A WAY TO BEAT HIM.
SO ANGRY WITH DAREDEVIL WAS THIS HOMICIDAL KILLGRAVE THAT WHEN HE GOT HIS HOOKS INTO JESSICA...HE DIDN'T LET GO.
LATE CITY FINAL
DAREDEVIL SAVES CITY
EIGHT MONTHS HE HAD HER UNDER HIS THUMB.
EIGHT MONTHS HE DEGRADED HER.
EIGHT MONTHS HE STOLE FROM HER.
THING IS--HE NEVER TOUCHED HER. NO. NOT LIKE THAT. THAT WOULD BE TOO...EASY.
INSTEAD HE KEPT HER AS A PET. SICK, RIGHT? YEAH. WELL, THAT'S KILLGRAVE.
SO ONE DAY, IN A RAGE, KILLGRAVE SENDS JESSICA JONES TO KILL DAREDEVIL, HIS WORST ENEMY.
IN HER HAZY MENTAL STATE SHE WENT TO AVENGERS MANSION INSTEAD AND ATTACKED THE SIMILARLY DRESSED SCARLET WITCH.
AND IT WAS *JUST* AT THIS MOMENT THAT SHE STARTED COMING OUT OF THE FOG SHE HAD BEEN IN FOR EIGHT MONTHS.
SHE WAS OUT OF THE PURPLE MAN'S CONTROL.

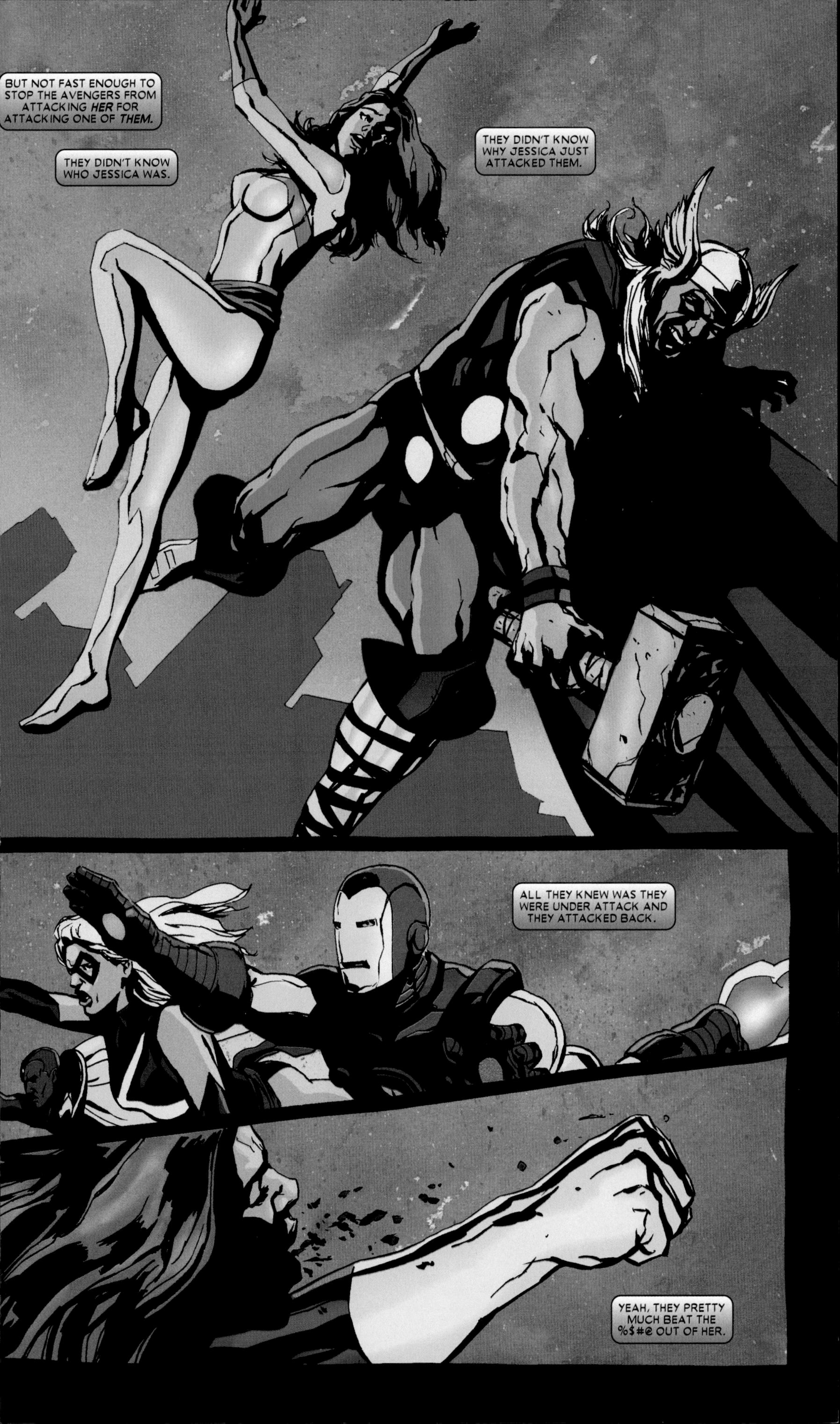
BUT NOT FAST ENOUGH TO STOP THE AVENGERS FROM ATTACKING HER FOR ATTACKING ONE OF THEM.
THEY DIDN'T KNOW WHO JESSICA WAS.
THEY DIDN'T KNOW WHY JESSICA JUST ATTACKED THEM.
ALL THEY KNEW WAS THEY WERE UNDER ATTACK AND THEY ATTACKED BACK.
YEAH, THEY PRETTY MUCH BEAT THE %$#@ OUT OF HER.

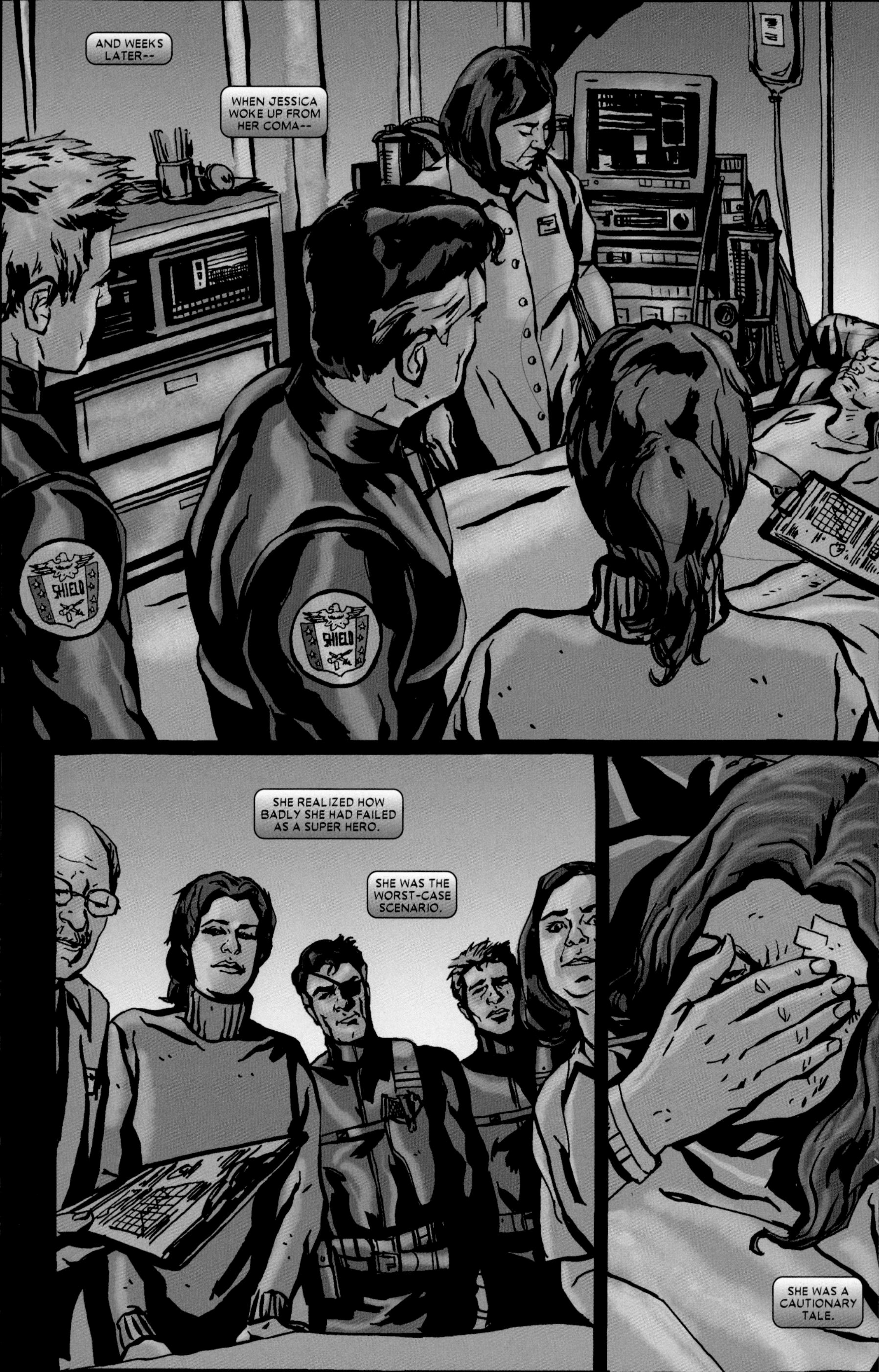
AND WEEKS LATER--
WHEN JESSICA WOKE UP FROM HER COMA--
SHIELD
SHIELD
SHE REALIZED HOW BADLY SHE HAD FAILED AS A SUPER HERO.
SHE WAS THE WORST-CASE SCENARIO.
SHE WAS A CAUTIONARY TALE.

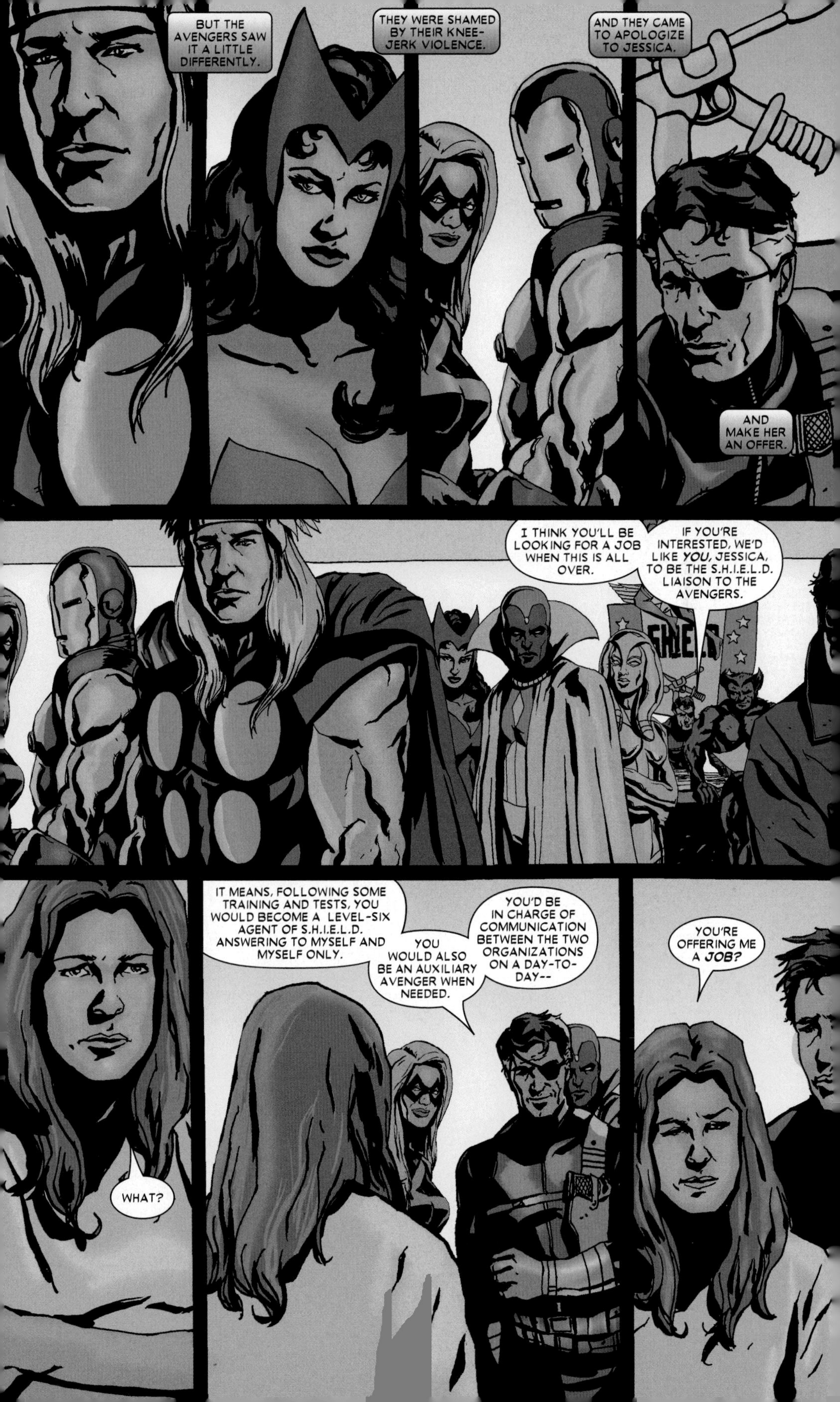

BUT THE AVENGERS SAW IT A LITTLE DIFFERENTLY.
THEY WERE SHAMED BY THEIR KNEE-JERK VIOLENCE.
AND THEY CAME TO APOLOGIZE TO JESSICA.
AND MAKE HER AN OFFER.
I THINK YOU'LL BE LOOKING FOR A JOB WHEN THIS IS ALL OVER.
IF YOU'RE INTERESTED, WE'D LIKE *YOU,* JESSICA, TO BE THE S.H.I.E.L.D. LIAISON TO THE AVENGERS.
WHAT?
IT MEANS, FOLLOWING SOME TRAINING AND TESTS, YOU WOULD BECOME A LEVEL-SIX AGENT OF S.H.I.E.L.D. ANSWERING TO MYSELF AND MYSELF ONLY.
YOU WOULD ALSO BE AN AUXILIARY AVENGER WHEN NEEDED.
YOU'D BE IN CHARGE OF COMMUNICATION BETWEEN THE TWO ORGANIZATIONS ON A DAY-TO-DAY--
YOU'RE OFFERING ME A *JOB?*

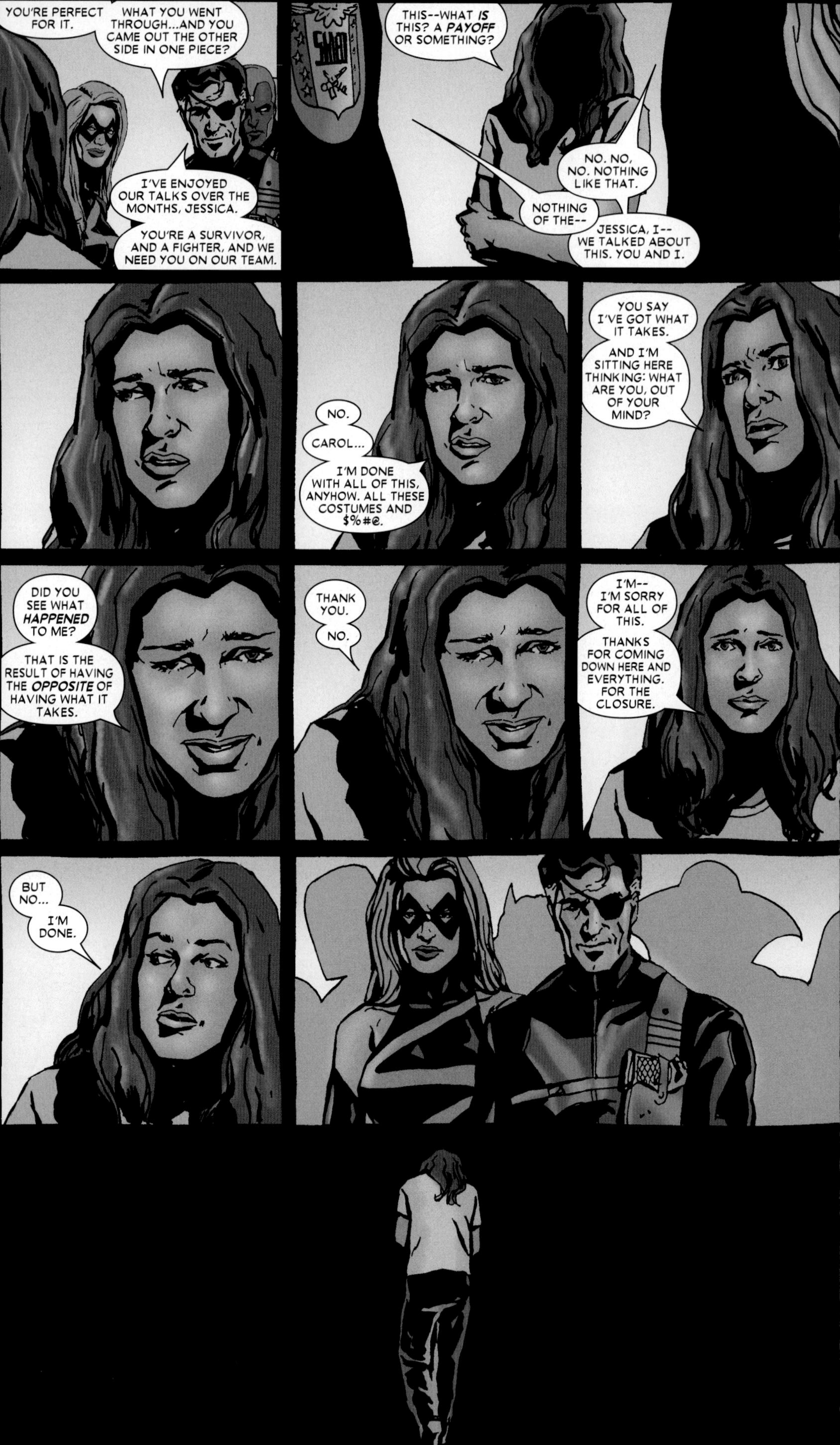

YOU'RE PERFECT FOR IT.
WHAT YOU WENT THROUGH...AND YOU CAME OUT THE OTHER SIDE IN ONE PIECE?
I'VE ENJOYED OUR TALKS OVER THE MONTHS, JESSICA.
YOU'RE A SURVIVOR, AND A FIGHTER, AND WE NEED YOU ON OUR TEAM.
THIS--WHAT *IS* THIS? A *PAYOFF* OR SOMETHING?
NO. NO, NO. NOTHING LIKE THAT.
NOTHING OF THE--
JESSICA, I-- WE TALKED ABOUT THIS. YOU AND I.
NO.
CAROL...
I'M DONE WITH ALL OF THIS, ANYHOW. ALL THESE COSTUMES AND $%#@.
YOU SAY I'VE GOT WHAT IT TAKES.
AND I'M SITTING HERE THINKING: WHAT ARE YOU, OUT OF YOUR MIND?
DID YOU SEE WHAT *HAPPENED* TO ME?
THAT IS THE RESULT OF HAVING THE *OPPOSITE* OF HAVING WHAT IT TAKES.
THANK YOU.
NO.
I'M-- I'M SORRY FOR ALL OF THIS.
THANKS FOR COMING DOWN HERE AND EVERYTHING. FOR THE CLOSURE.
BUT NO...
I'M DONE.

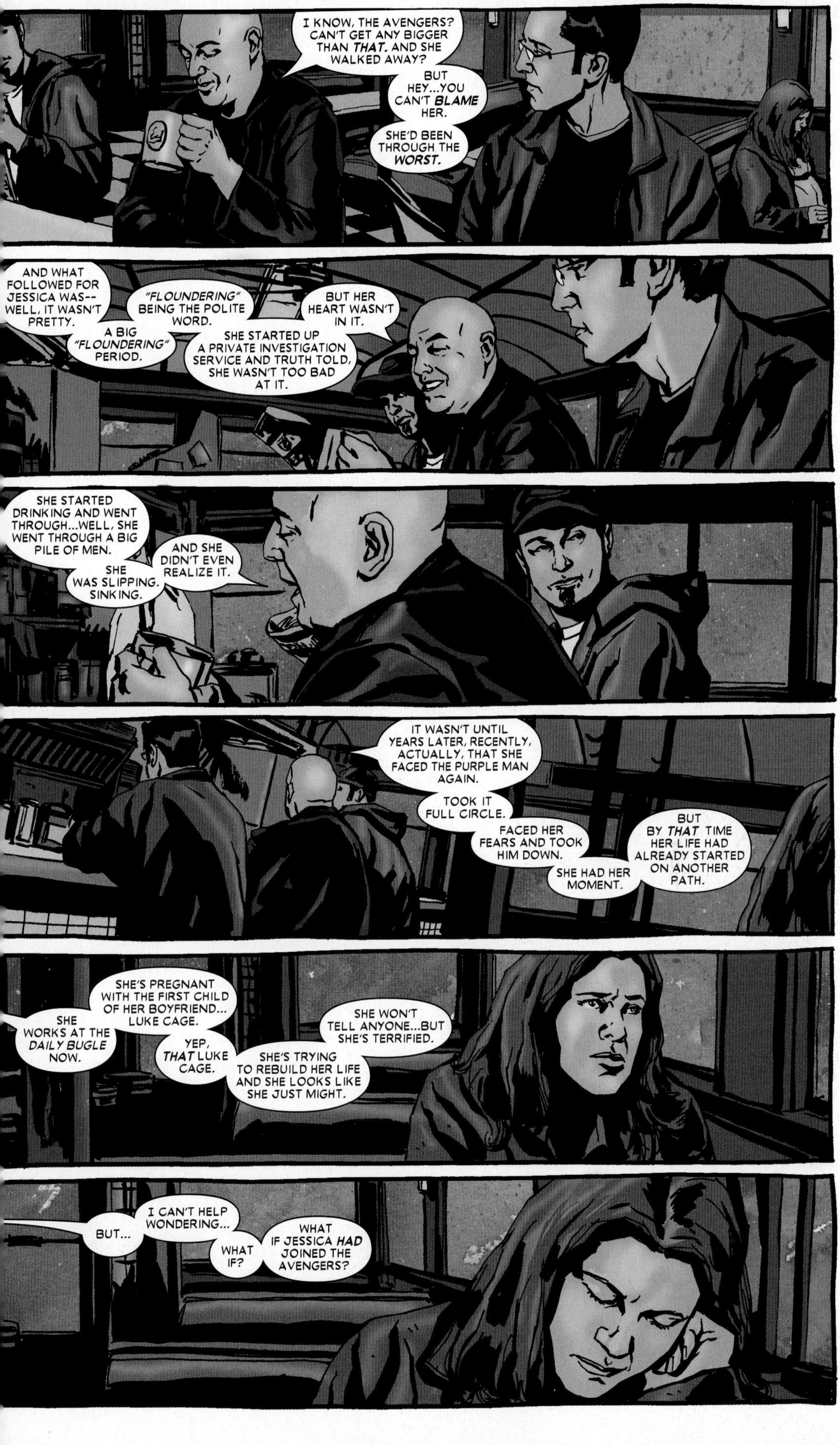
I KNOW, THE AVENGERS? CAN'T GET ANY BIGGER THAN THAT. AND SHE WALKED AWAY?
BUT HEY...YOU CAN'T BLAME HER.
SHE'D BEEN THROUGH THE WORST.
AND WHAT FOLLOWED FOR JESSICA WAS-- WELL, IT WASN'T PRETTY.
A BIG "FLOUNDERING" PERIOD.
"FLOUNDERING" BEING THE POLITE WORD.
SHE STARTED UP A PRIVATE INVESTIGATION SERVICE AND TRUTH TOLD, SHE WASN'T TOO BAD AT IT.
BUT HER HEART WASN'T IN IT.
SHE STARTED DRINKING AND WENT THROUGH...WELL, SHE WENT THROUGH A BIG PILE OF MEN.
SHE WAS SLIPPING. SINKING.
AND SHE DIDN'T EVEN REALIZE IT.
IT WASN'T UNTIL YEARS LATER, RECENTLY, ACTUALLY, THAT SHE FACED THE PURPLE MAN AGAIN.
TOOK IT FULL CIRCLE.
FACED HER FEARS AND TOOK HIM DOWN.
SHE HAD HER MOMENT.
BUT BY THAT TIME HER LIFE HAD ALREADY STARTED ON ANOTHER PATH.
SHE WORKS AT THE DAILY BUGLE NOW.
SHE'S PREGNANT WITH THE FIRST CHILD OF HER BOYFRIEND... LUKE CAGE.
YEP, THAT LUKE CAGE.
SHE'S TRYING TO REBUILD HER LIFE AND SHE LOOKS LIKE SHE JUST MIGHT.
SHE WON'T TELL ANYONE...BUT SHE'S TERRIFIED.
BUT...
I CAN'T HELP WONDERING...
WHAT IF?
WHAT IF JESSICA HAD JOINED THE AVENGERS?

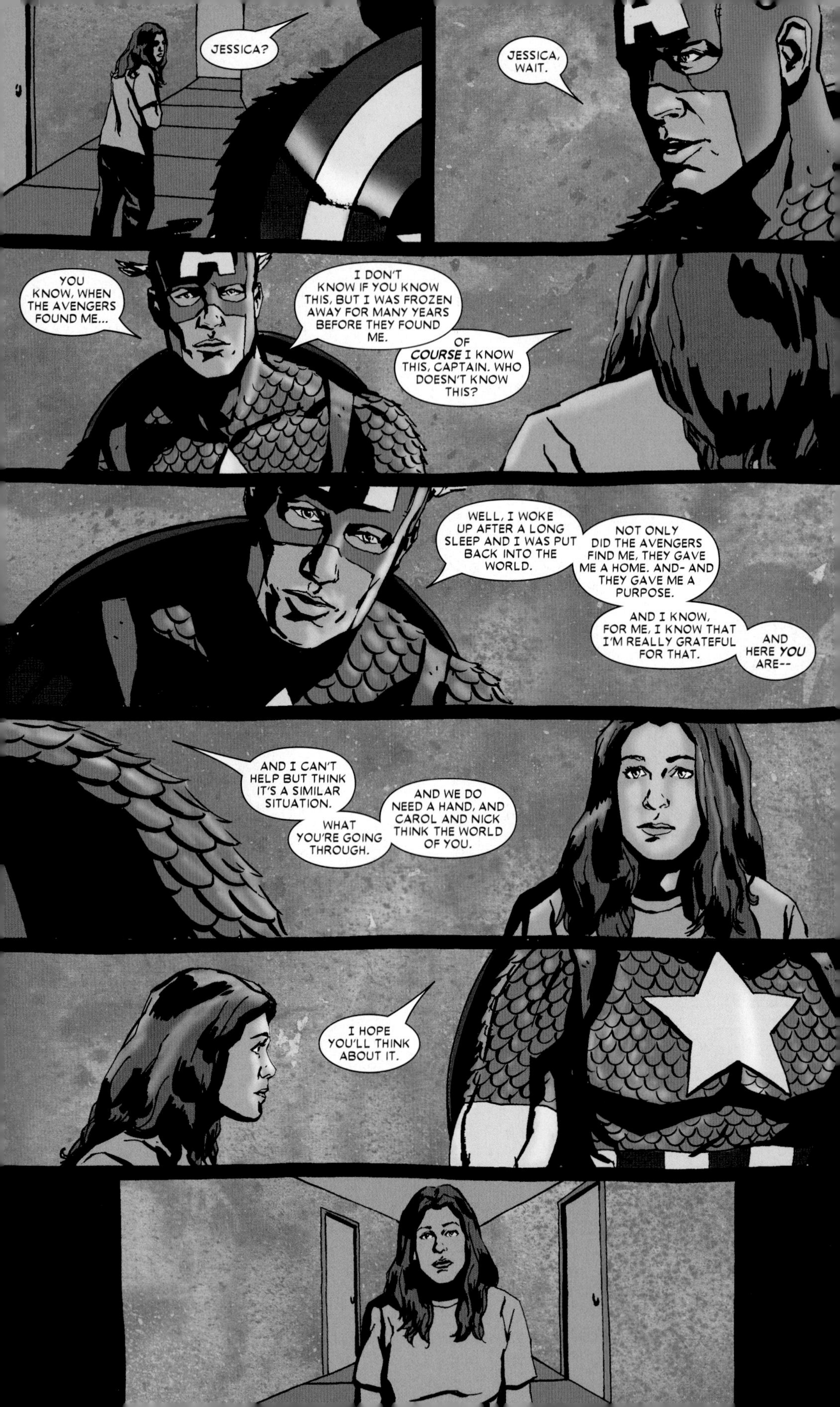
JESSICA?
JESSICA, WAIT.
YOU KNOW, WHEN THE AVENGERS FOUND ME...
I DON'T KNOW IF YOU KNOW THIS, BUT I WAS FROZEN AWAY FOR MANY YEARS BEFORE THEY FOUND ME.
OF *COURSE* I KNOW THIS, CAPTAIN. WHO DOESN'T KNOW THIS?
WELL, I WOKE UP AFTER A LONG SLEEP AND I WAS PUT BACK INTO THE WORLD.
NOT ONLY DID THE AVENGERS FIND ME, THEY GAVE ME A HOME. AND- AND THEY GAVE ME A PURPOSE.
AND I KNOW, FOR ME, I KNOW THAT I'M REALLY GRATEFUL FOR THAT.
AND HERE *YOU* ARE--
AND I CAN'T HELP BUT THINK IT'S A SIMILAR SITUATION.
WHAT YOU'RE GOING THROUGH.
AND WE DO NEED A HAND, AND CAROL AND NICK THINK THE WORLD OF YOU.
I HOPE YOU'LL THINK ABOUT IT.

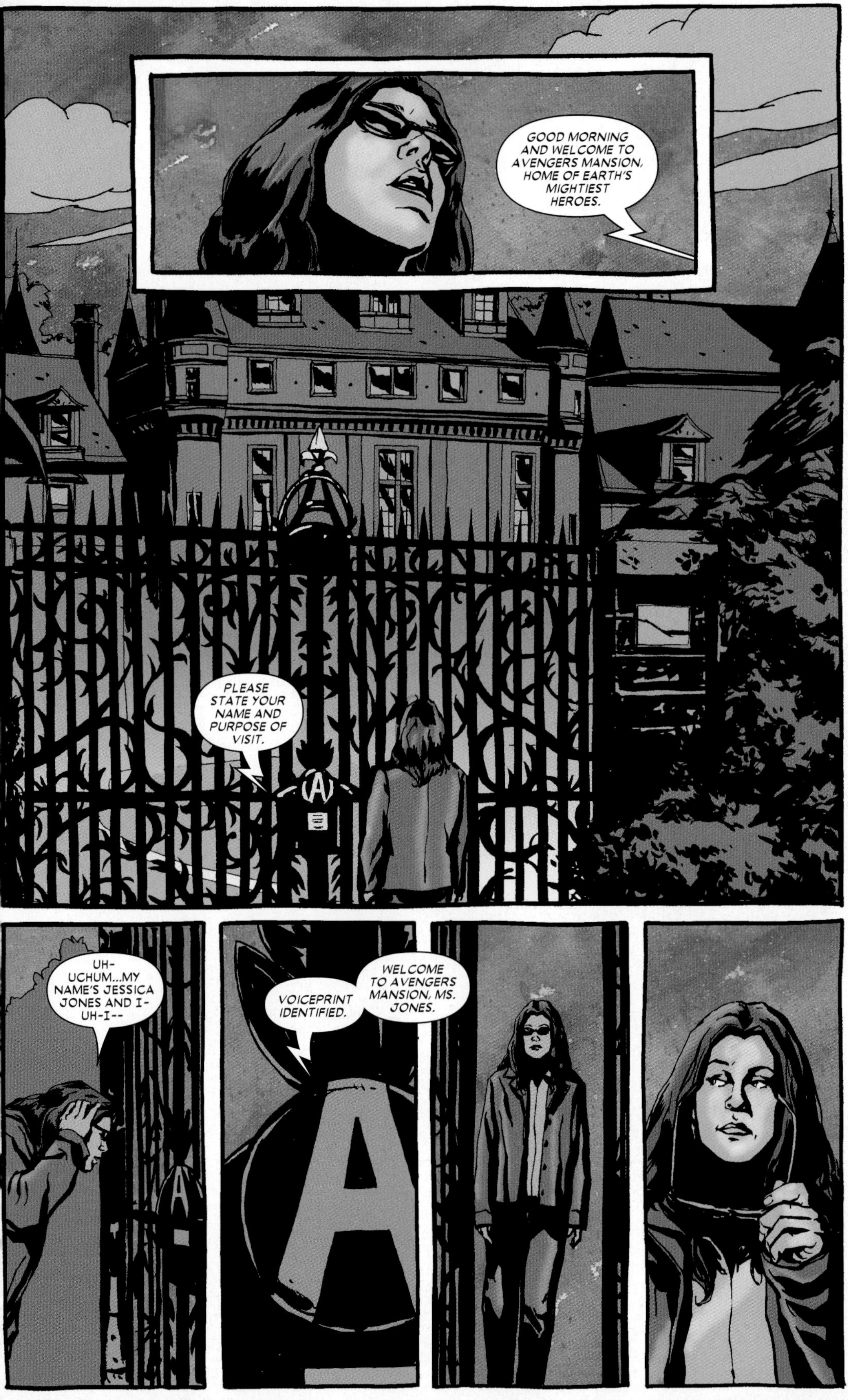
GOOD MORNING AND WELCOME TO AVENGERS MANSION, HOME OF EARTH'S MIGHTIEST HEROES.
PLEASE STATE YOUR NAME AND PURPOSE OF VISIT.
UH-UCHUM...MY NAME'S JESSICA JONES AND I-UH-I--
VOICEPRINT IDENTIFIED.
WELCOME TO AVENGERS MANSION, MS. JONES.

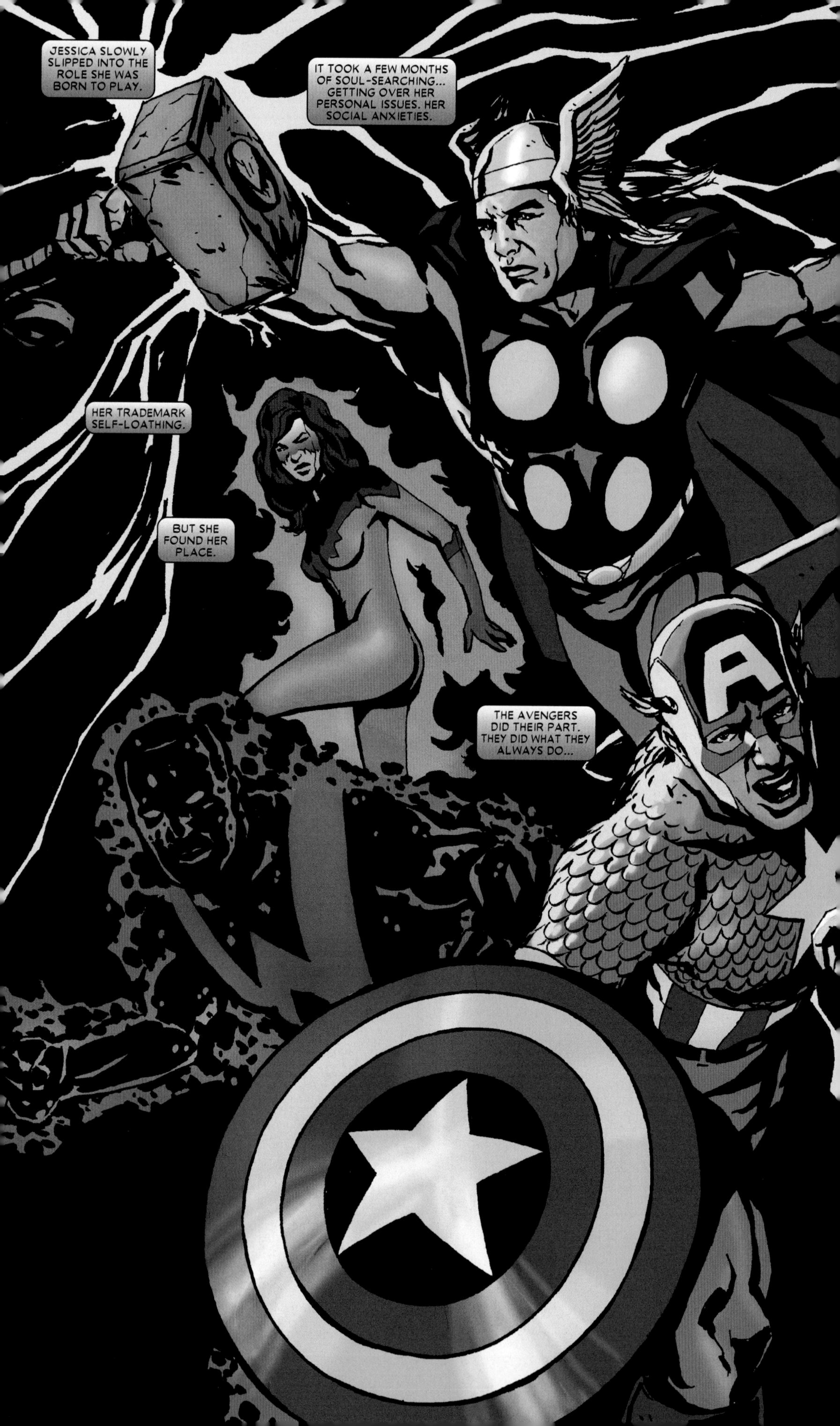
JESSICA SLOWLY SLIPPED INTO THE ROLE SHE WAS BORN TO PLAY.
IT TOOK A FEW MONTHS OF SOUL-SEARCHING... GETTING OVER HER PERSONAL ISSUES. HER SOCIAL ANXIETIES.
HER TRADEMARK SELF-LOATHING.
BUT SHE FOUND HER PLACE.
THE AVENGERS DID THEIR PART. THEY DID WHAT THEY ALWAYS DO...

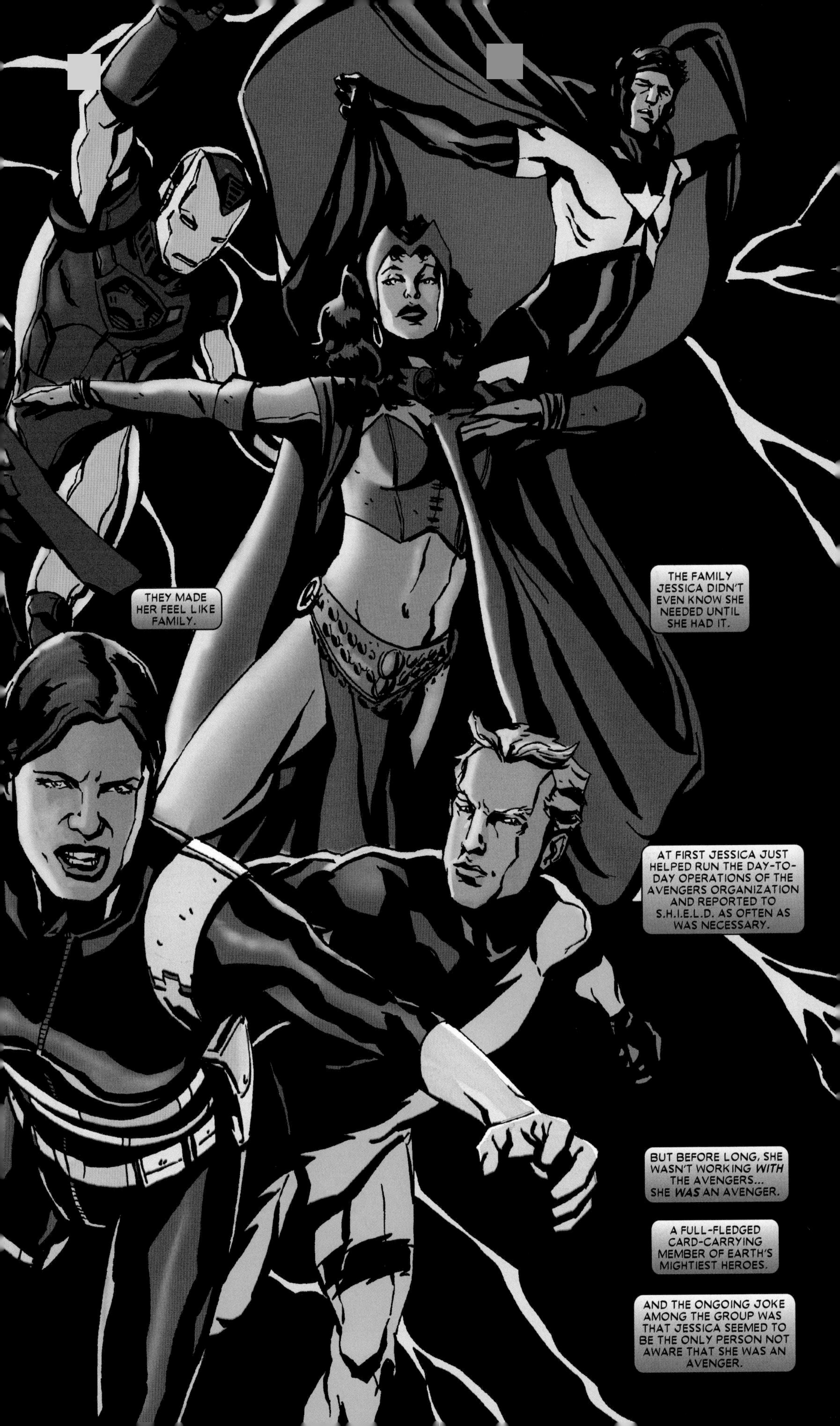
THEY MADE HER FEEL LIKE FAMILY.
THE FAMILY JESSICA DIDN'T EVEN KNOW SHE NEEDED UNTIL SHE HAD IT.
AT FIRST JESSICA JUST HELPED RUN THE DAY-TO-DAY OPERATIONS OF THE AVENGERS ORGANIZATION AND REPORTED TO S.H.I.E.L.D. AS OFTEN AS WAS NECESSARY.
BUT BEFORE LONG, SHE WASN'T WORKING *WITH* THE AVENGERS... SHE *WAS* AN AVENGER.
A FULL-FLEDGED CARD-CARRYING MEMBER OF EARTH'S MIGHTIEST HEROES.
AND THE ONGOING JOKE AMONG THE GROUP WAS THAT JESSICA SEEMED TO BE THE ONLY PERSON NOT AWARE THAT SHE WAS AN AVENGER.

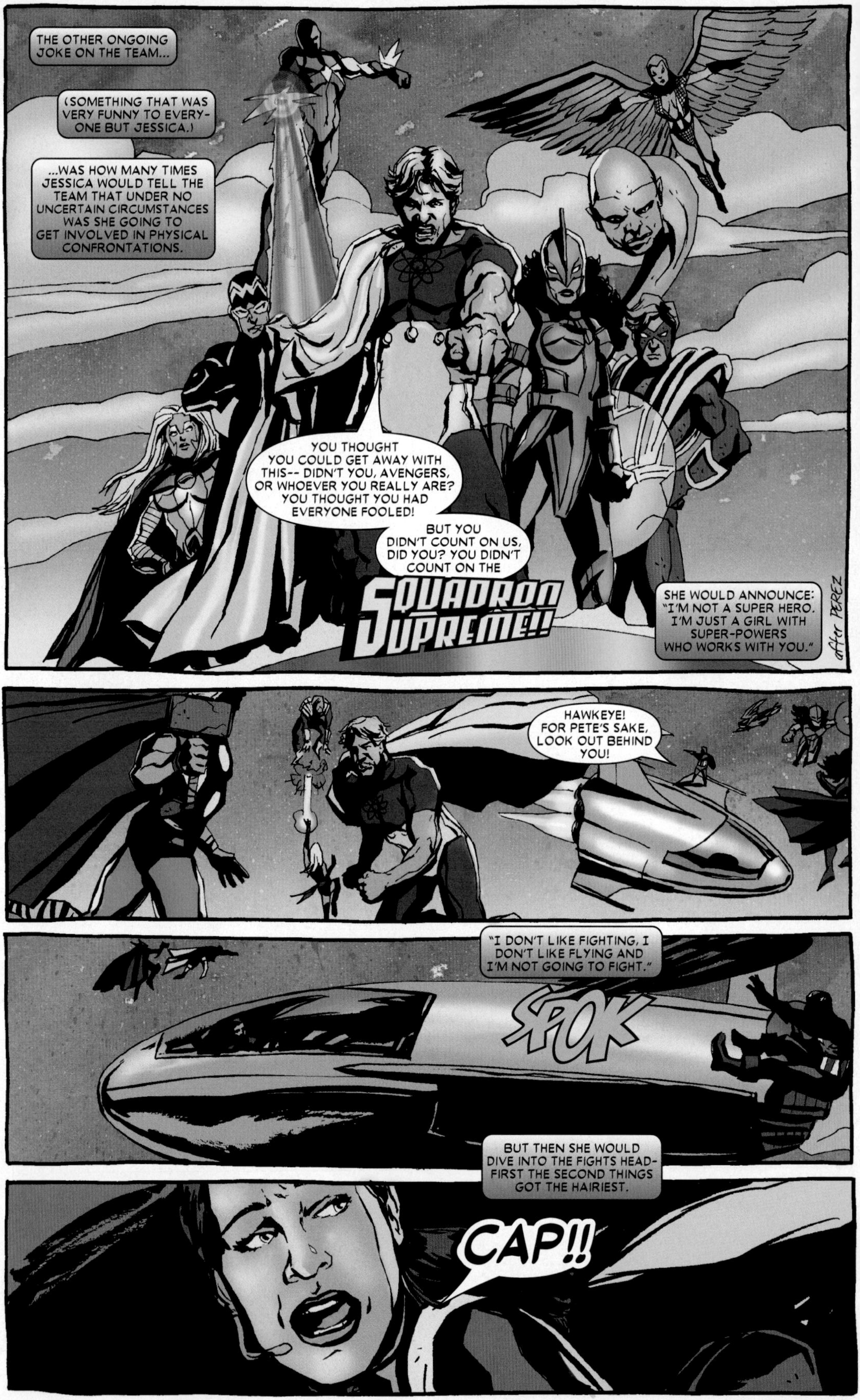
THE OTHER ONGOING JOKE ON THE TEAM...
(SOMETHING THAT WAS VERY FUNNY TO EVERY-ONE BUT JESSICA.)
...WAS HOW MANY TIMES JESSICA WOULD TELL THE TEAM THAT UNDER NO UNCERTAIN CIRCUMSTANCES WAS SHE GOING TO GET INVOLVED IN PHYSICAL CONFRONTATIONS.
YOU THOUGHT YOU COULD GET AWAY WITH THIS-- DIDN'T YOU, AVENGERS, OR WHOEVER YOU REALLY ARE? YOU THOUGHT YOU HAD EVERYONE FOOLED!
BUT YOU DIDN'T COUNT ON US, DID YOU? YOU DIDN'T COUNT ON THE
SQUADRON SUPREME!!
SHE WOULD ANNOUNCE: "I'M NOT A SUPER HERO. I'M JUST A GIRL WITH SUPER-POWERS WHO WORKS WITH YOU."
after PEREZ
HAWKEYE! FOR PETE'S SAKE, LOOK OUT BEHIND YOU!
"I DON'T LIKE FIGHTING, I DON'T LIKE FLYING AND I'M NOT GOING TO FIGHT."
SPOK
BUT THEN SHE WOULD DIVE INTO THE FIGHTS HEAD-FIRST THE SECOND THINGS GOT THE HAIRIEST.
CAP!!

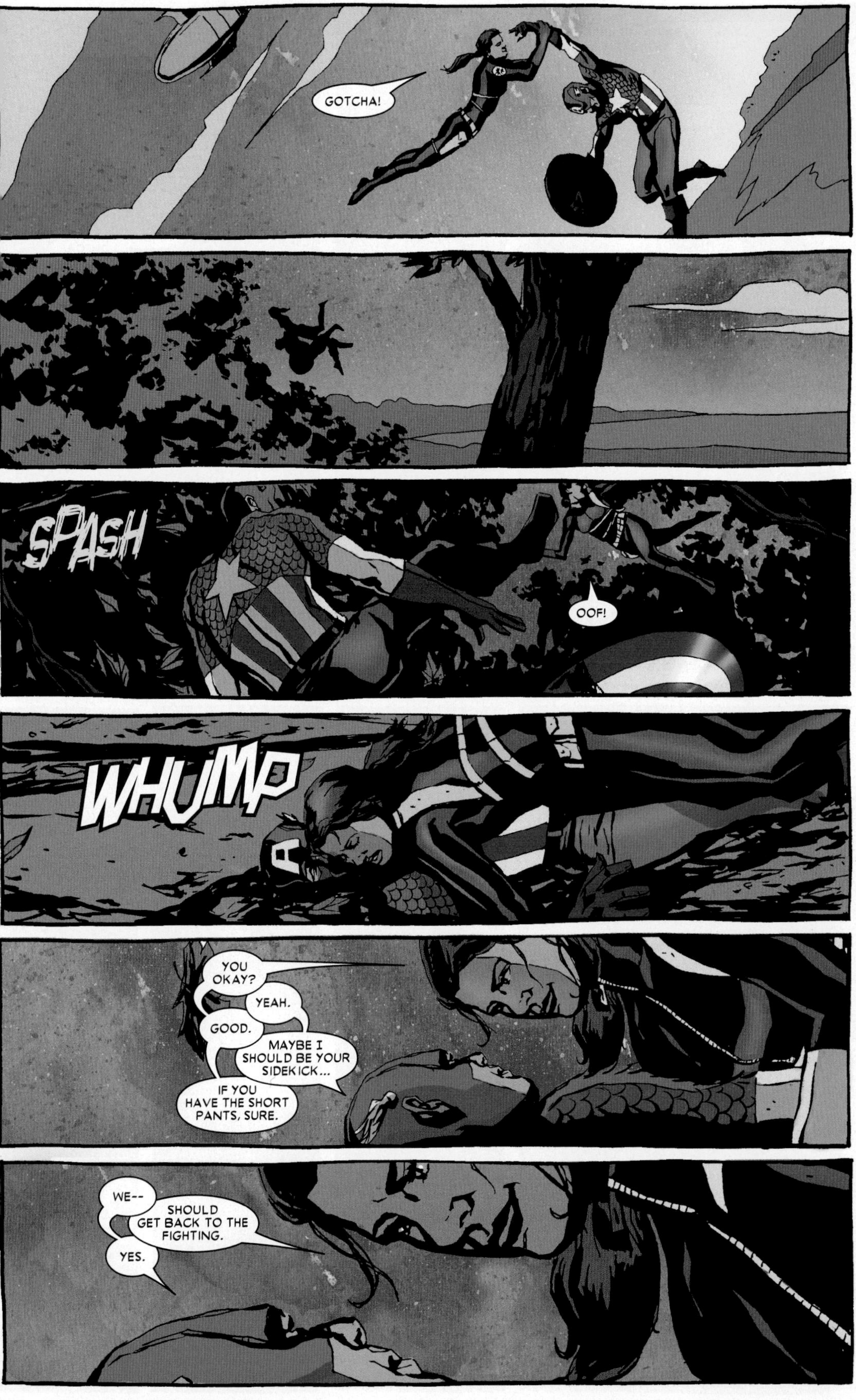
GOTCHA!
SPASH
OOF!
WHUMP
YOU OKAY?
YEAH.
GOOD.
MAYBE I SHOULD BE YOUR SIDEKICK...
IF YOU HAVE THE SHORT PANTS, SURE.
WE--
SHOULD GET BACK TO THE FIGHTING.
YES.

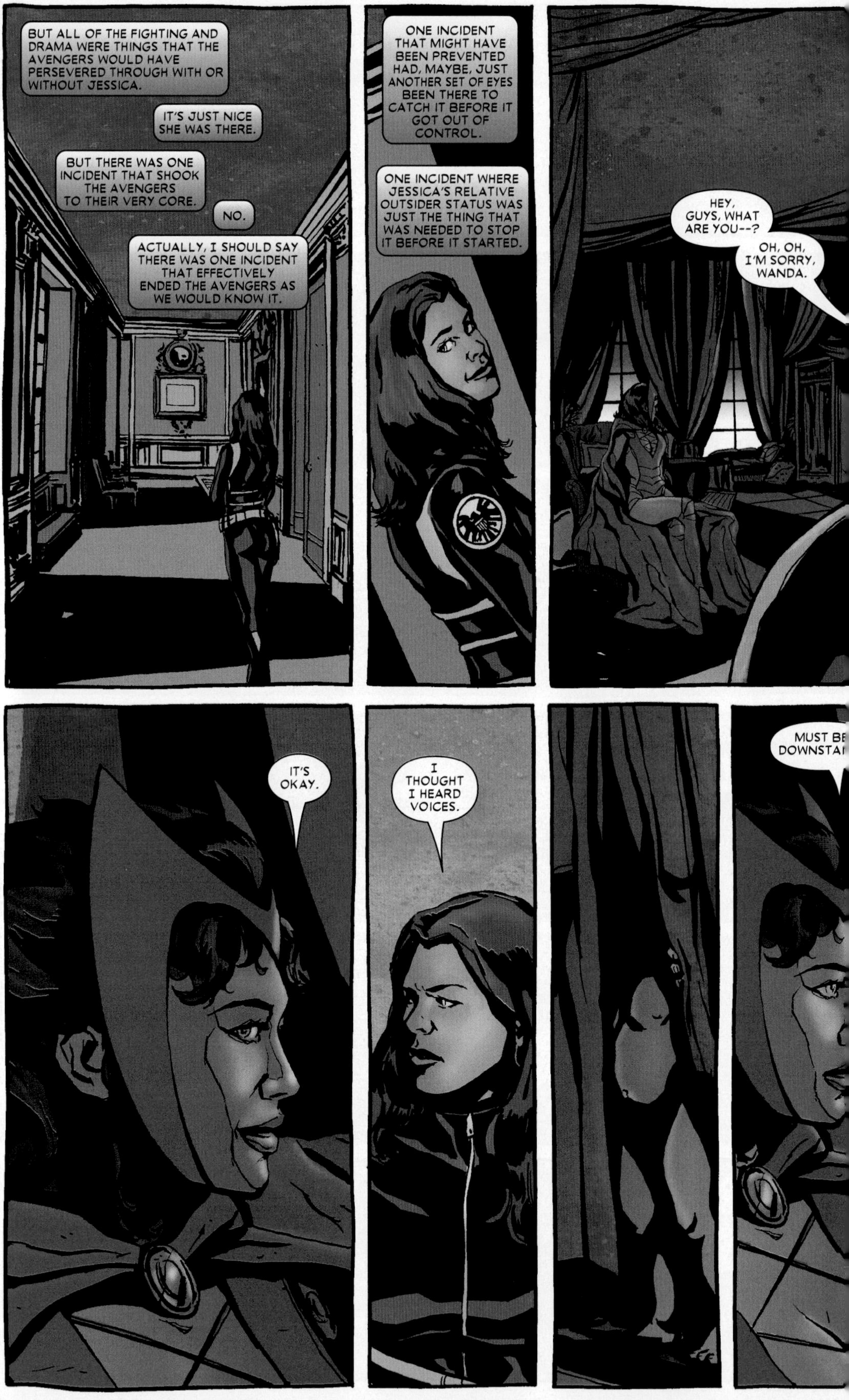
BUT ALL OF THE FIGHTING AND DRAMA WERE THINGS THAT THE AVENGERS WOULD HAVE PERSEVERED THROUGH WITH OR WITHOUT JESSICA.
IT'S JUST NICE SHE WAS THERE.
BUT THERE WAS ONE INCIDENT THAT SHOOK THE AVENGERS TO THEIR VERY CORE.
NO.
ACTUALLY, I SHOULD SAY THERE WAS ONE INCIDENT THAT EFFECTIVELY ENDED THE AVENGERS AS WE WOULD KNOW IT.
ONE INCIDENT THAT MIGHT HAVE BEEN PREVENTED HAD, MAYBE, JUST ANOTHER SET OF EYES BEEN THERE TO CATCH IT BEFORE IT GOT OUT OF CONTROL.
ONE INCIDENT WHERE JESSICA'S RELATIVE OUTSIDER STATUS WAS JUST THE THING THAT WAS NEEDED TO STOP IT BEFORE IT STARTED.
HEY, GUYS, WHAT ARE YOU--?
OH, OH, I'M SORRY, WANDA.
IT'S OKAY.
I THOUGHT I HEARD VOICES.

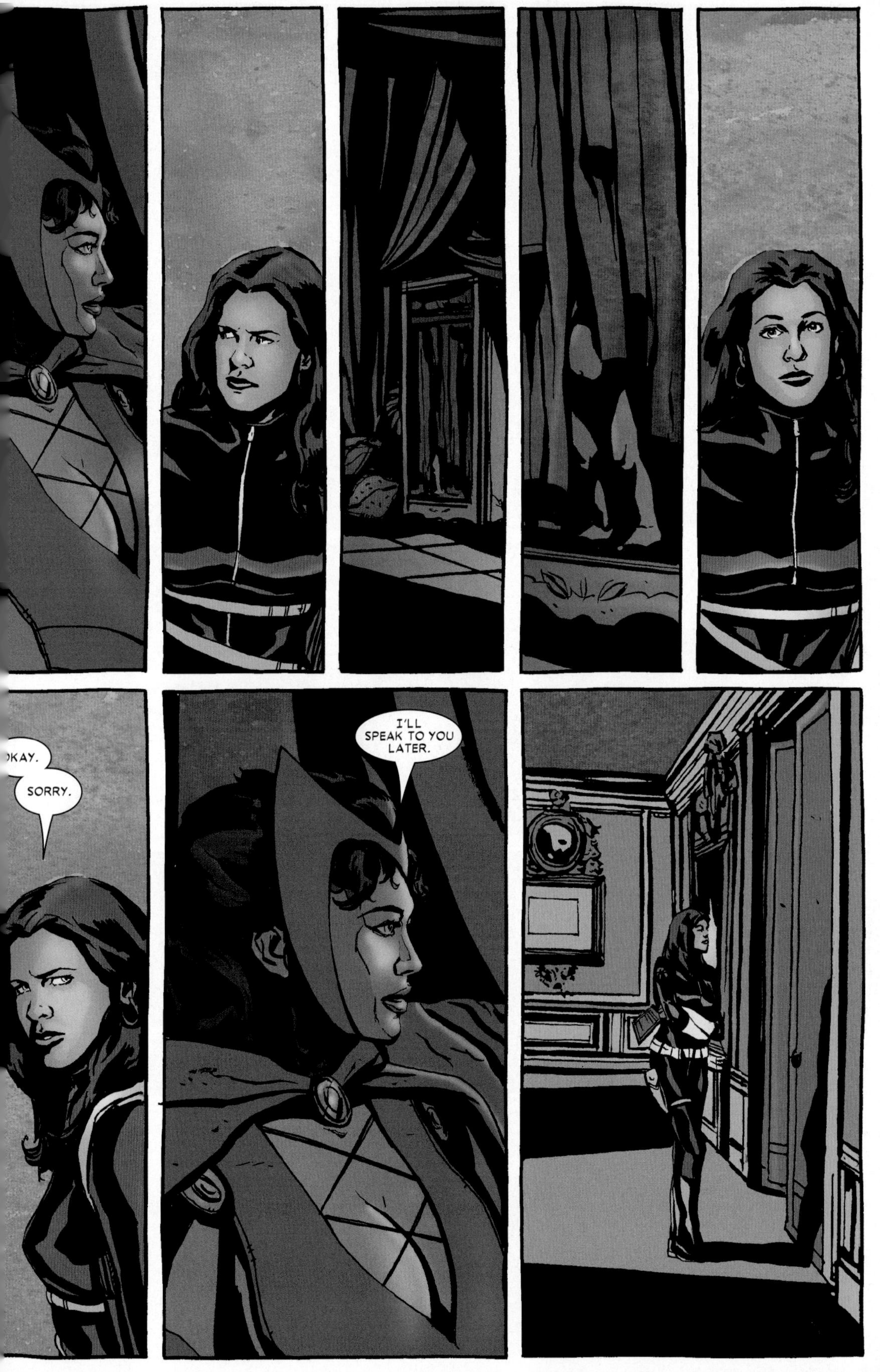

OKAY.
SORRY.
I'LL SPEAK TO YOU LATER.

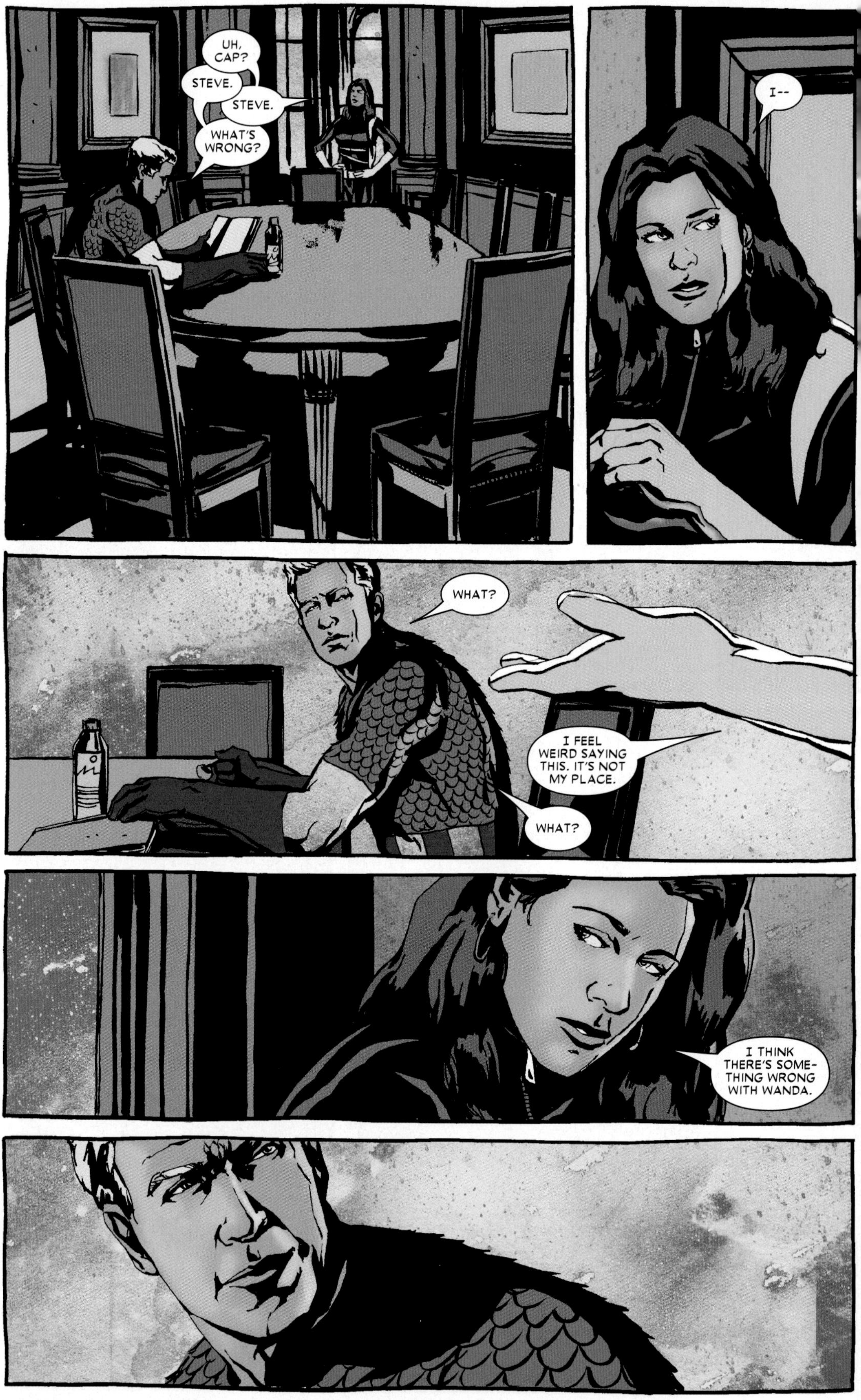
UH, CAP?
STEVE.
STEVE.
WHAT'S WRONG?
I--
WHAT?
I FEEL WEIRD SAYING THIS. IT'S NOT MY PLACE.
WHAT?
I THINK THERE'S SOME-THING WRONG WITH WANDA.

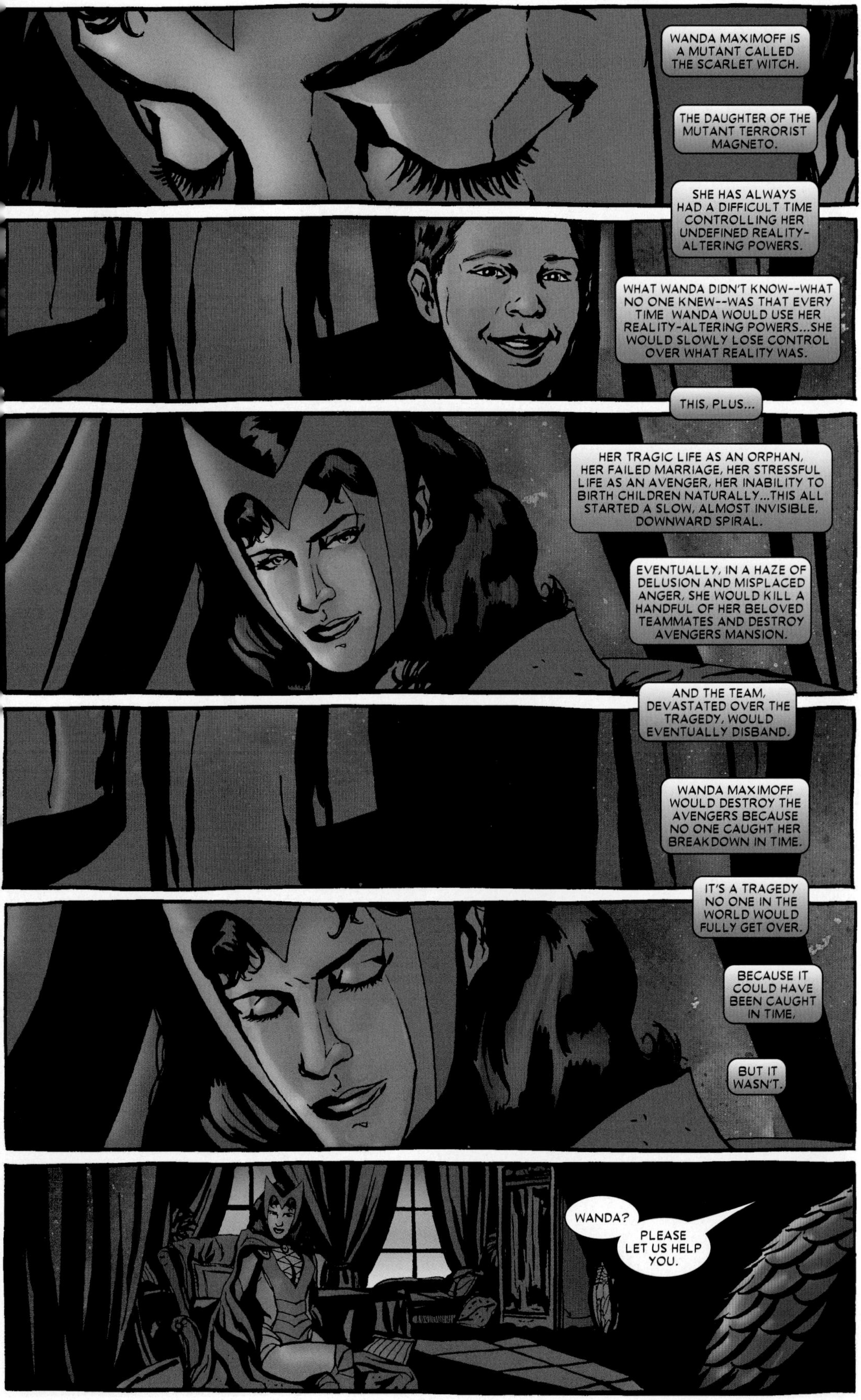
WANDA MAXIMOFF IS A MUTANT CALLED THE SCARLET WITCH.
THE DAUGHTER OF THE MUTANT TERRORIST MAGNETO.
SHE HAS ALWAYS HAD A DIFFICULT TIME CONTROLLING HER UNDEFINED REALITY-ALTERING POWERS.
WHAT WANDA DIDN'T KNOW--WHAT NO ONE KNEW--WAS THAT EVERY TIME WANDA WOULD USE HER REALITY-ALTERING POWERS...SHE WOULD SLOWLY LOSE CONTROL OVER WHAT REALITY WAS.
THIS, PLUS...
HER TRAGIC LIFE AS AN ORPHAN, HER FAILED MARRIAGE, HER STRESSFUL LIFE AS AN AVENGER, HER INABILITY TO BIRTH CHILDREN NATURALLY...THIS ALL STARTED A SLOW, ALMOST INVISIBLE, DOWNWARD SPIRAL.
EVENTUALLY, IN A HAZE OF DELUSION AND MISPLACED ANGER, SHE WOULD KILL A HANDFUL OF HER BELOVED TEAMMATES AND DESTROY AVENGERS MANSION.
AND THE TEAM, DEVASTATED OVER THE TRAGEDY, WOULD EVENTUALLY DISBAND.
WANDA MAXIMOFF WOULD DESTROY THE AVENGERS BECAUSE NO ONE CAUGHT HER BREAKDOWN IN TIME.
IT'S A TRAGEDY NO ONE IN THE WORLD WOULD FULLY GET OVER.
BECAUSE IT COULD HAVE BEEN CAUGHT IN TIME.
BUT IT WASN'T.
WANDA? PLEASE LET US HELP YOU.

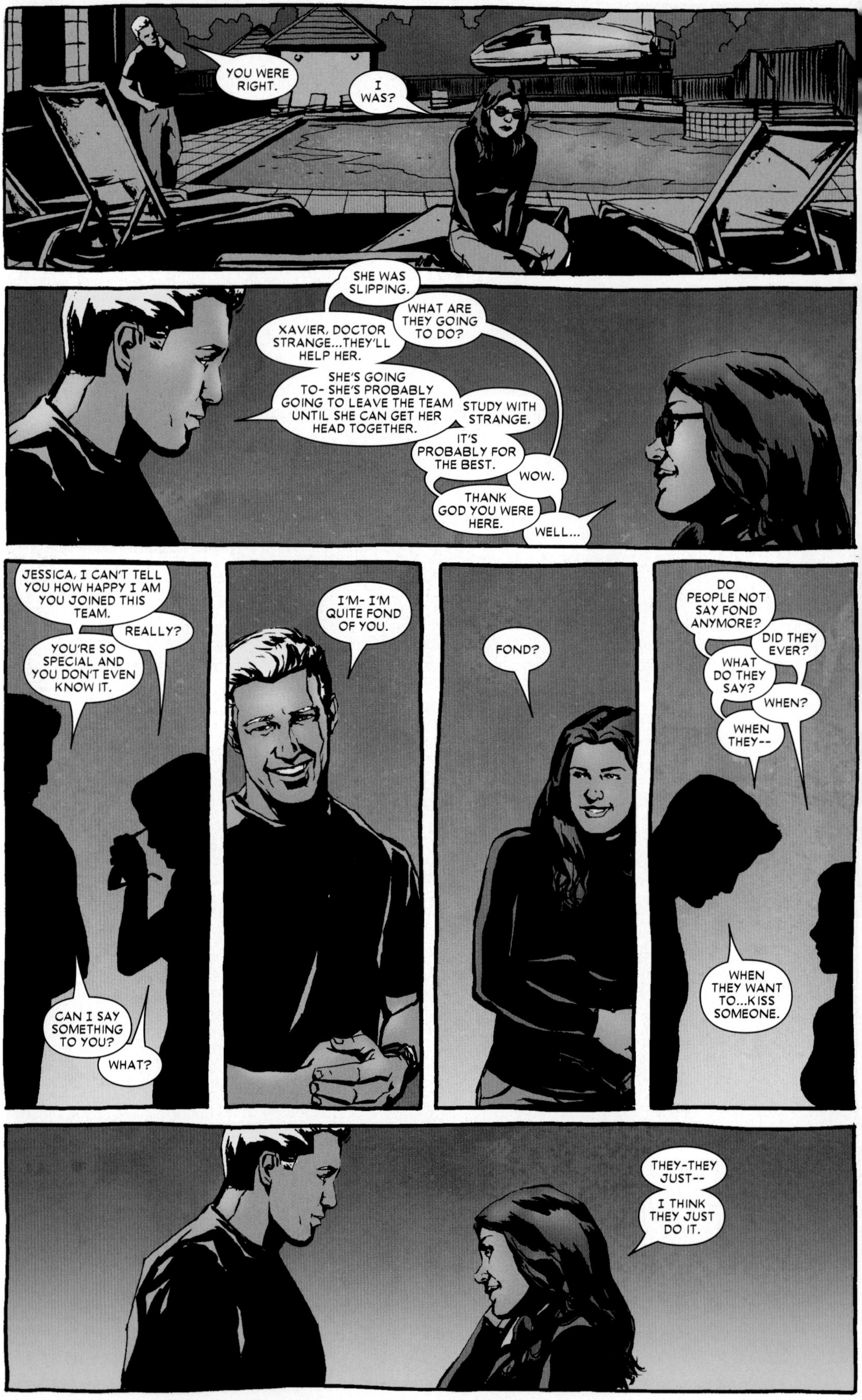
YOU WERE RIGHT.
I WAS?
SHE WAS SLIPPING.
XAVIER, DOCTOR STRANGE...THEY'LL HELP HER.
WHAT ARE THEY GOING TO DO?
SHE'S GOING TO- SHE'S PROBABLY GOING TO LEAVE THE TEAM UNTIL SHE CAN GET HER HEAD TOGETHER.
STUDY WITH STRANGE.
IT'S PROBABLY FOR THE BEST.
WOW.
THANK GOD YOU WERE HERE.
WELL...
JESSICA, I CAN'T TELL YOU HOW HAPPY I AM YOU JOINED THIS TEAM.
REALLY?
YOU'RE SO SPECIAL AND YOU DON'T EVEN KNOW IT.
CAN I SAY SOMETHING TO YOU?
WHAT?
I'M- I'M QUITE FOND OF YOU.
FOND?
DO PEOPLE NOT SAY FOND ANYMORE?
DID THEY EVER?
WHAT DO THEY SAY?
WHEN?
WHEN THEY--
WHEN THEY WANT TO...KISS SOMEONE.
THEY-THEY JUST--
I THINK THEY JUST DO IT.

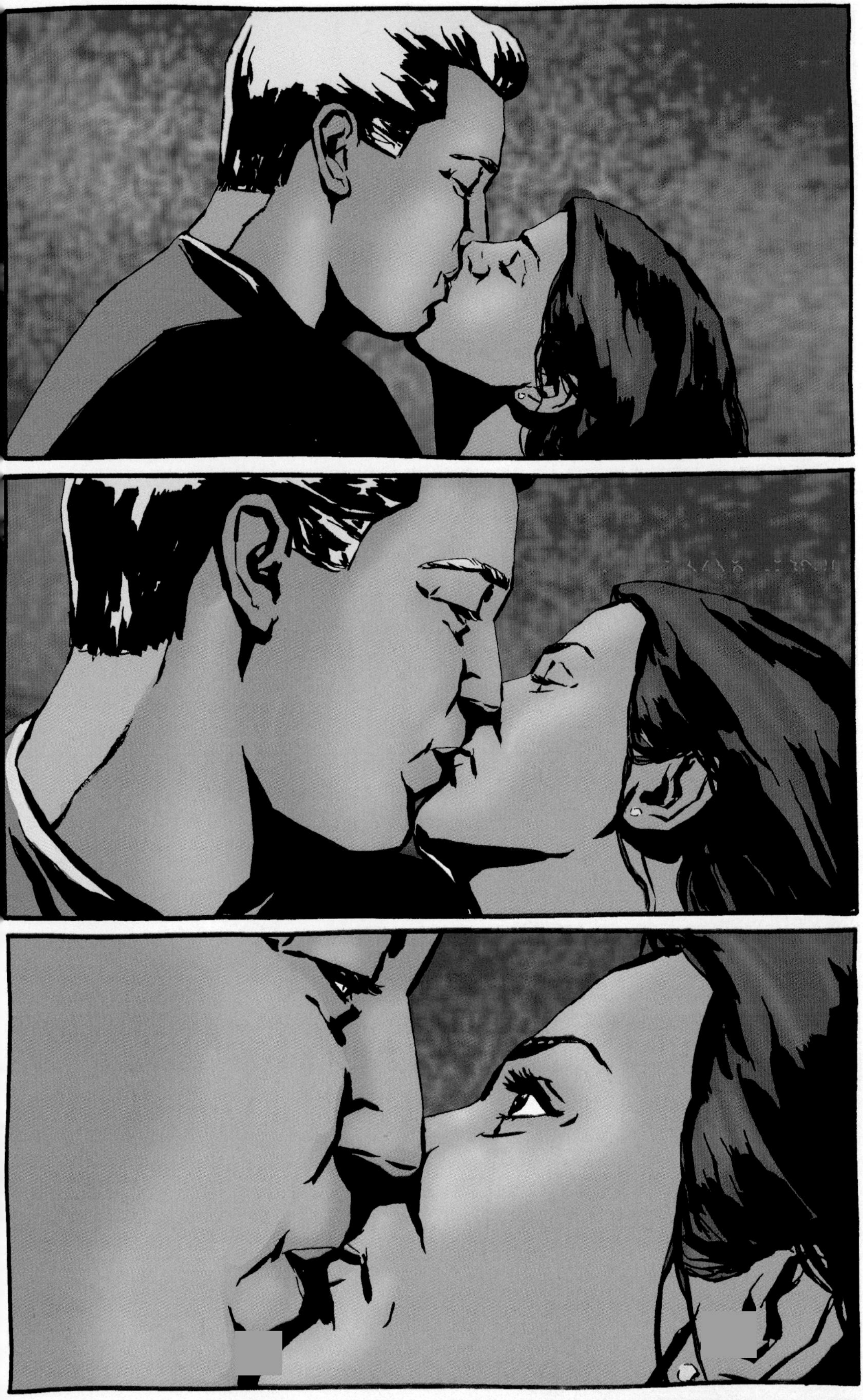

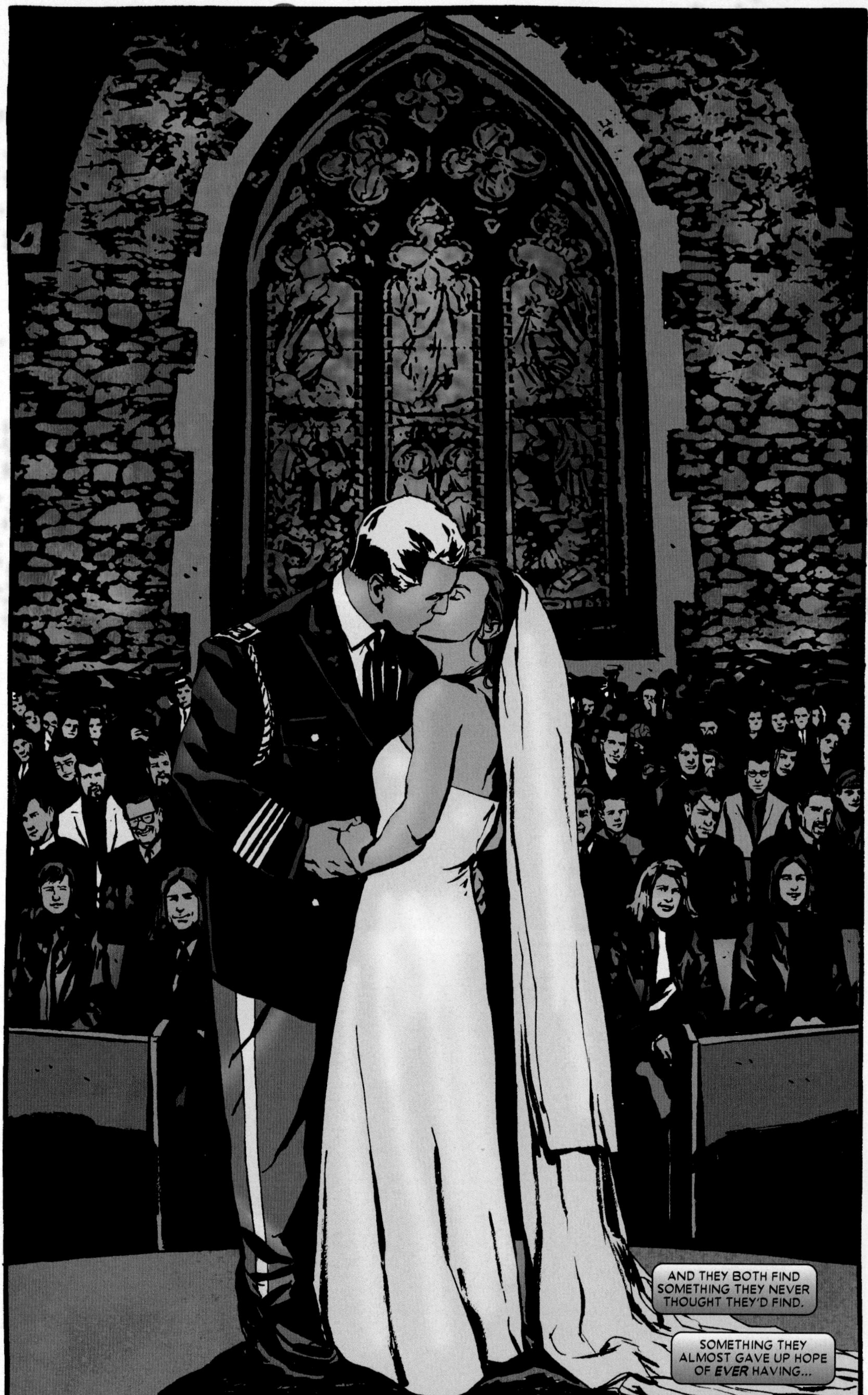
AND THEY BOTH FIND SOMETHING THEY NEVER THOUGHT THEY'D FIND.
SOMETHING THEY ALMOST GAVE UP HOPE OF *EVER* HAVING...

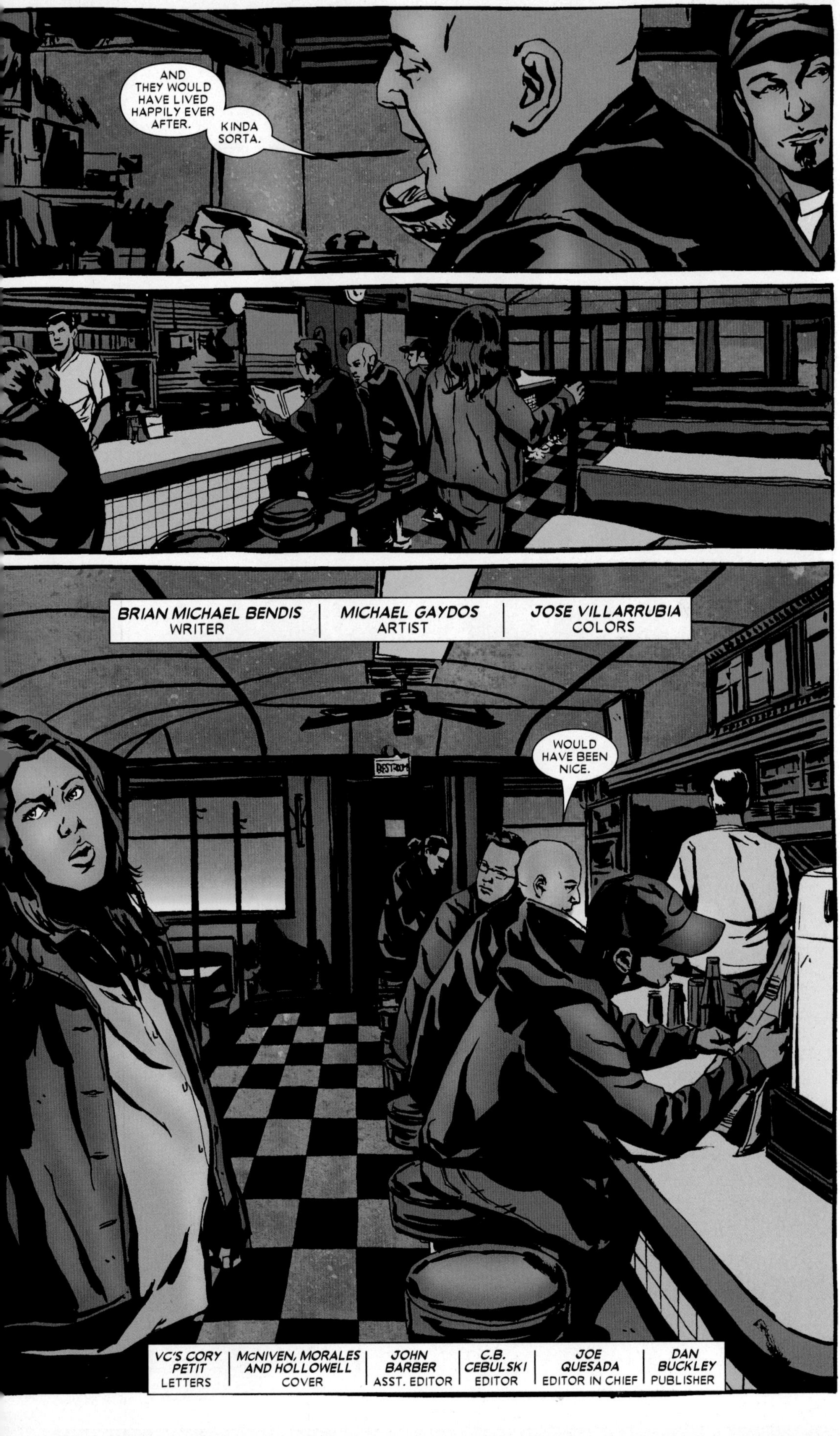
AND THEY WOULD HAVE LIVED HAPPILY EVER AFTER.
KINDA SORTA.
BRIAN MICHAEL BENDIS WRITER
MICHAEL GAYDOS ARTIST
JOSE VILLARRUBIA COLORS
RESTROOMS
WOULD HAVE BEEN NICE.
VC'S CORY PETIT LETTERS
McNIVEN, MORALES AND HOLLOWELL COVER
JOHN BARBER ASST. EDITOR
C.B. CEBULSKI EDITOR
JOE QUESADA EDITOR IN CHIEF
DAN BUCKLEY PUBLISHER

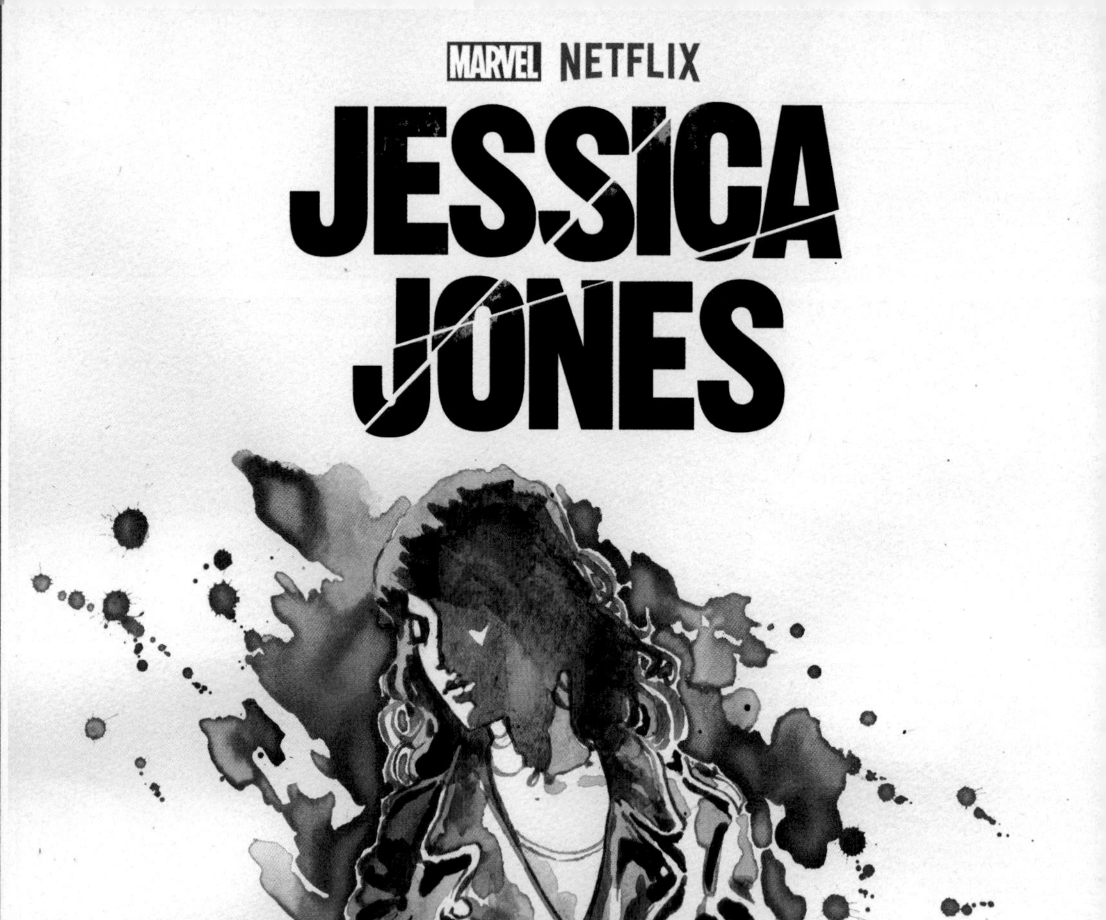
MARVEL NETFLIX
JESSICA JONES
ALSO IN THIS ISSUE
DAREDEVIL
MACK
1

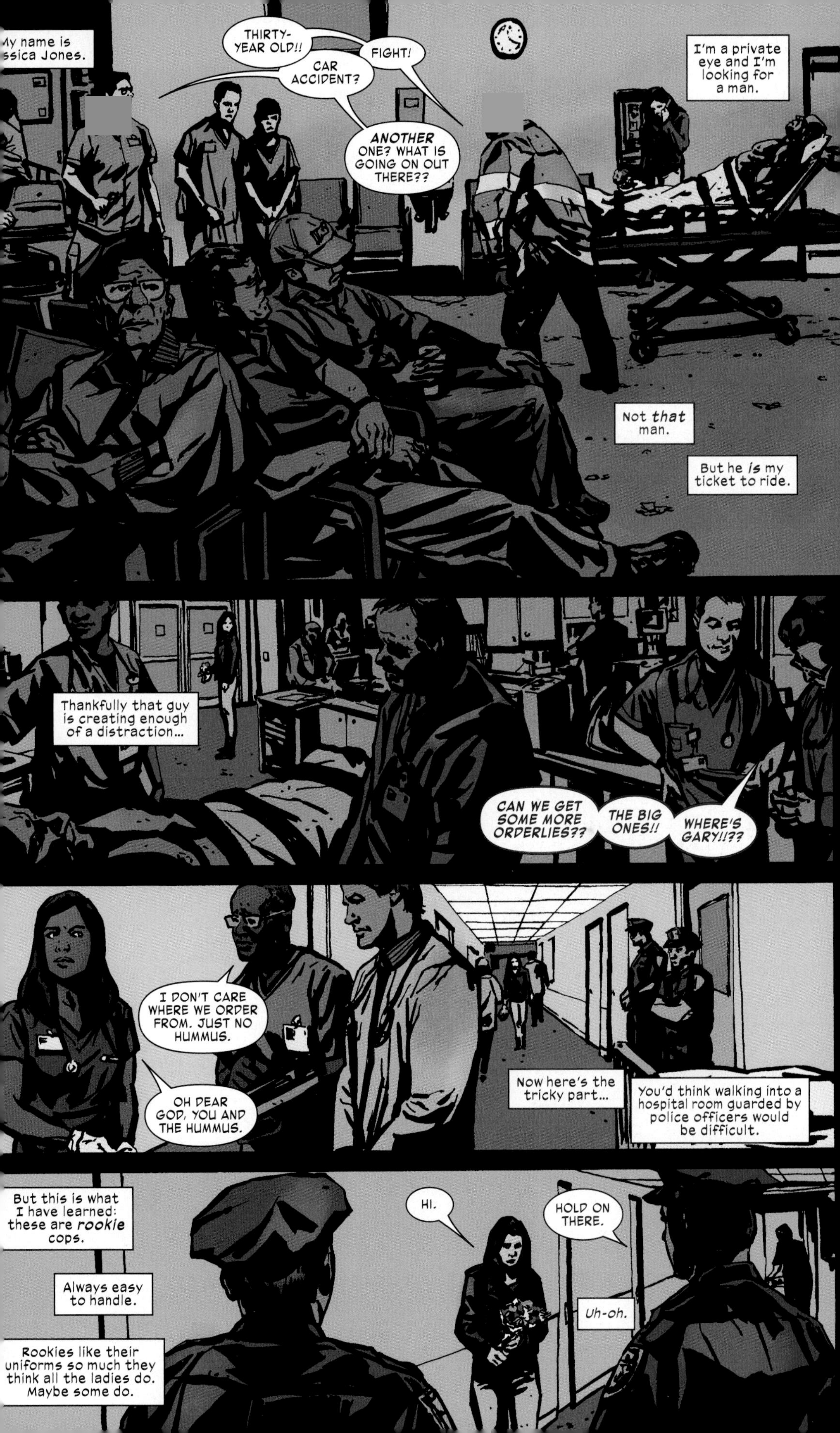

y name is
ssica Jones.
THIRTY-YEAR OLD!!
CAR ACCIDENT?
FIGHT!
ANOTHER ONE? WHAT IS GOING ON OUT THERE??
I'm a private eye and I'm looking for a man.
Not that man.
But he is my ticket to ride.
Thankfully that guy is creating enough of a distraction...
CAN WE GET SOME MORE ORDERLIES??
THE BIG ONES!!
WHERE'S GARY!!??
I DON'T CARE WHERE WE ORDER FROM. JUST NO HUMMUS.
OH DEAR GOD, YOU AND THE HUMMUS.
Now here's the tricky part...
You'd think walking into a hospital room guarded by police officers would be difficult.
But this is what I have learned: these are rookie cops.
Always easy to handle.
Rookies like their uniforms so much they think all the ladies do. Maybe some do.
HI.
HOLD ON THERE.
Uh-oh.

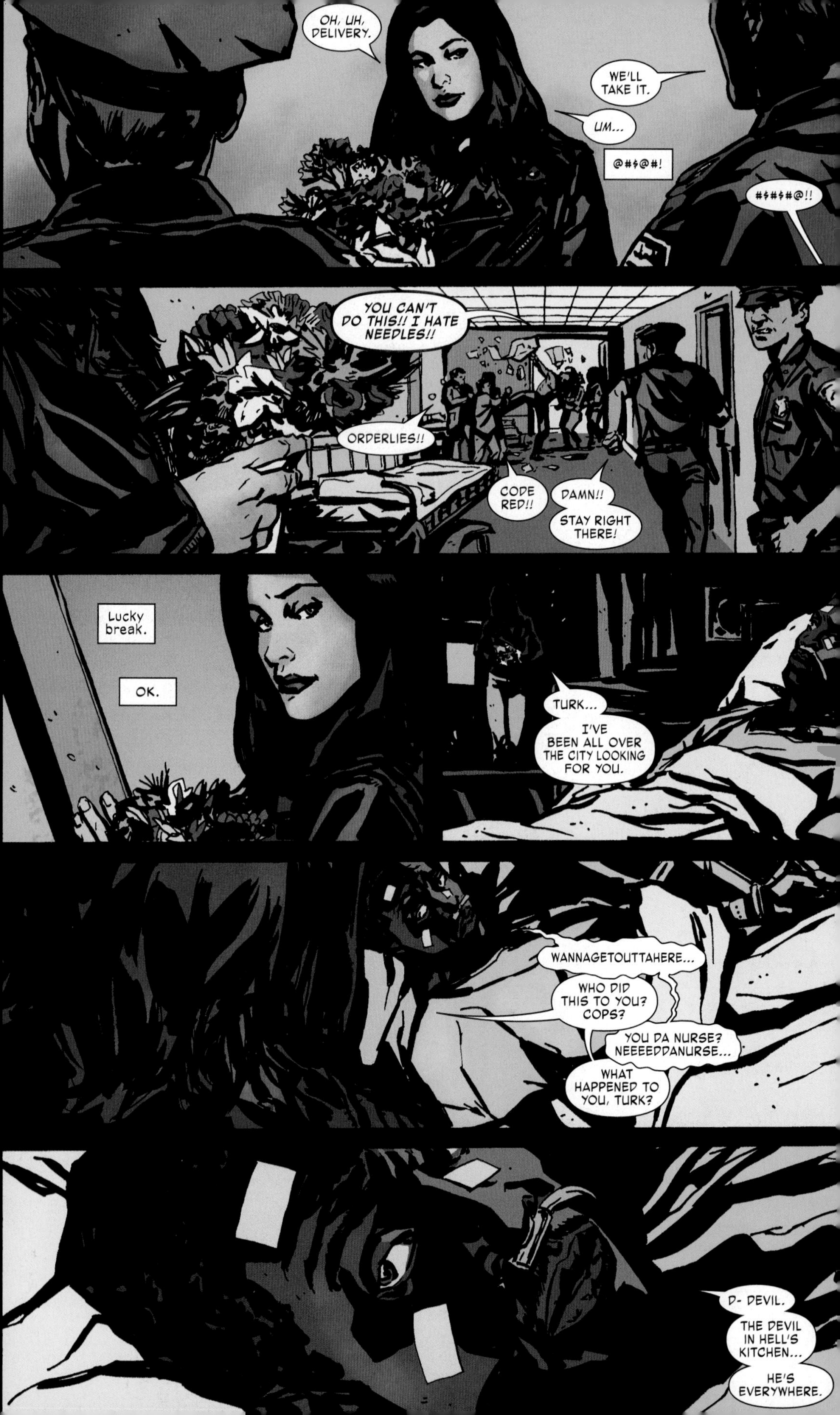

OH, UH, DELIVERY.
WE'LL TAKE IT.
UM...
@#$@#!
#$#$#@!!
YOU CAN'T DO THIS!! I HATE NEEDLES!!
ORDERLIES!!
CODE RED!!
DAMN!!
STAY RIGHT THERE!
Lucky break.
OK.
TURK...
I'VE BEEN ALL OVER THE CITY LOOKING FOR YOU.
WANNAGETOUTTAHERE...
WHO DID THIS TO YOU? COPS?
YOU DA NURSE? NEEEEDDANURSE...
WHAT HAPPENED TO YOU, TURK?
D- DEVIL.
THE DEVIL IN HELL'S KITCHEN...
HE'S EVERYWHERE.

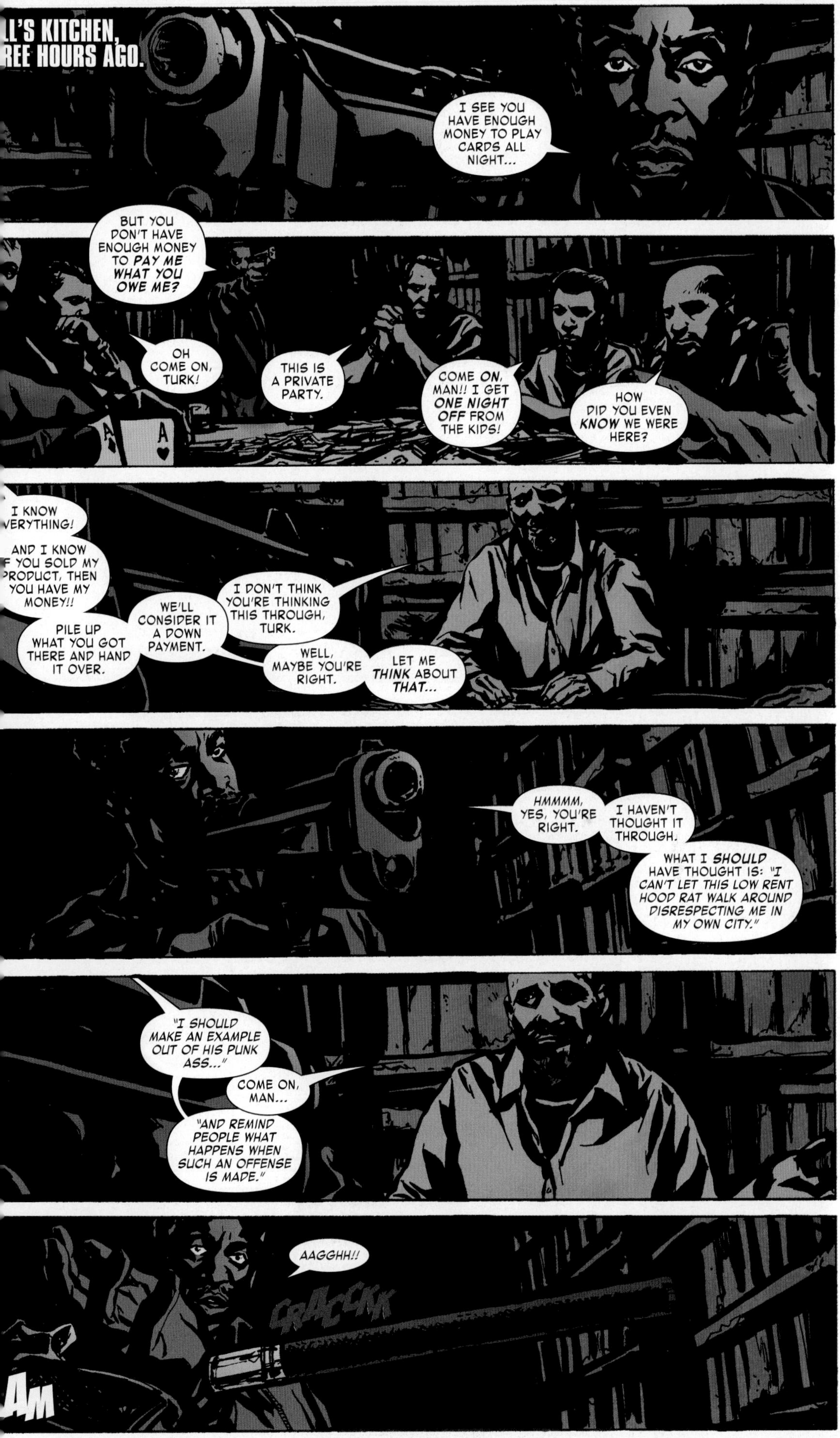
LL'S KITCHEN,
REE HOURS AGO.
I SEE YOU HAVE ENOUGH MONEY TO PLAY CARDS ALL NIGHT...
BUT YOU DON'T HAVE ENOUGH MONEY TO PAY ME WHAT YOU OWE ME?
OH COME ON, TURK!
THIS IS A PRIVATE PARTY.
COME ON, MAN!! I GET ONE NIGHT OFF FROM THE KIDS!
HOW DID YOU EVEN KNOW WE WERE HERE?
I KNOW VERYTHING!
AND I KNOW F YOU SOLD MY PRODUCT, THEN YOU HAVE MY MONEY!!
PILE UP WHAT YOU GOT THERE AND HAND IT OVER.
WE'LL CONSIDER IT A DOWN PAYMENT.
I DON'T THINK YOU'RE THINKING THIS THROUGH, TURK.
WELL, MAYBE YOU'RE RIGHT.
LET ME THINK ABOUT THAT...
HMMMM, YES, YOU'RE RIGHT.
I HAVEN'T THOUGHT IT THROUGH.
WHAT I SHOULD HAVE THOUGHT IS: "I CAN'T LET THIS LOW RENT HOOD RAT WALK AROUND DISRESPECTING ME IN MY OWN CITY."
"I SHOULD MAKE AN EXAMPLE OUT OF HIS PUNK ASS..."
COME ON, MAN...
"AND REMIND PEOPLE WHAT HAPPENS WHEN SUCH AN OFFENSE IS MADE."
AAGGHH!!
CRACCKK
AM

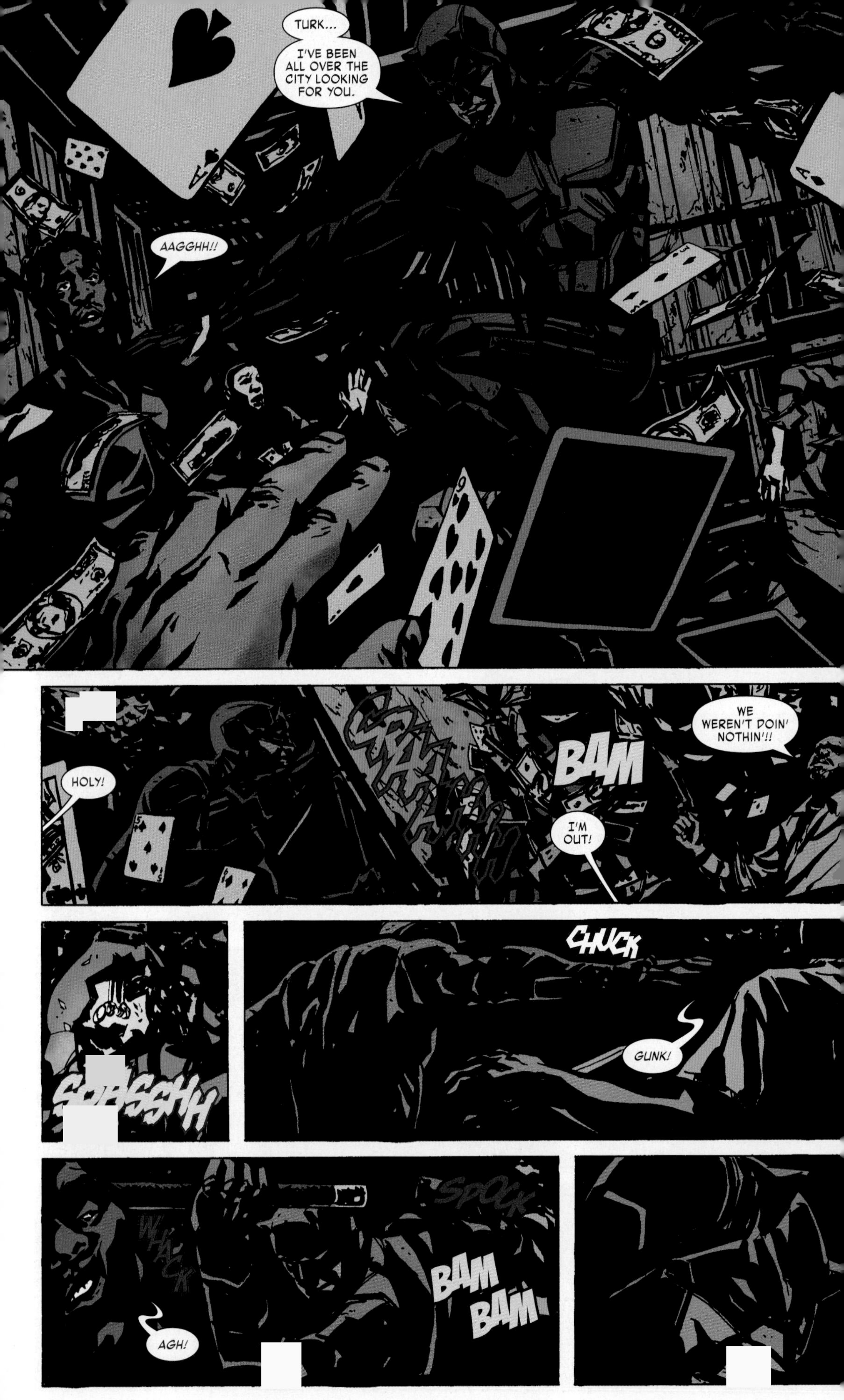
TURK...
I'VE BEEN ALL OVER THE CITY LOOKING FOR YOU.
AAGGHH!!
HOLY!
BAM
WE WEREN'T DOIN' NOTHIN'!!
I'M OUT!
CHUCK
GUNK!
WHACK
SPOCK
BAM
BAM
AGH!

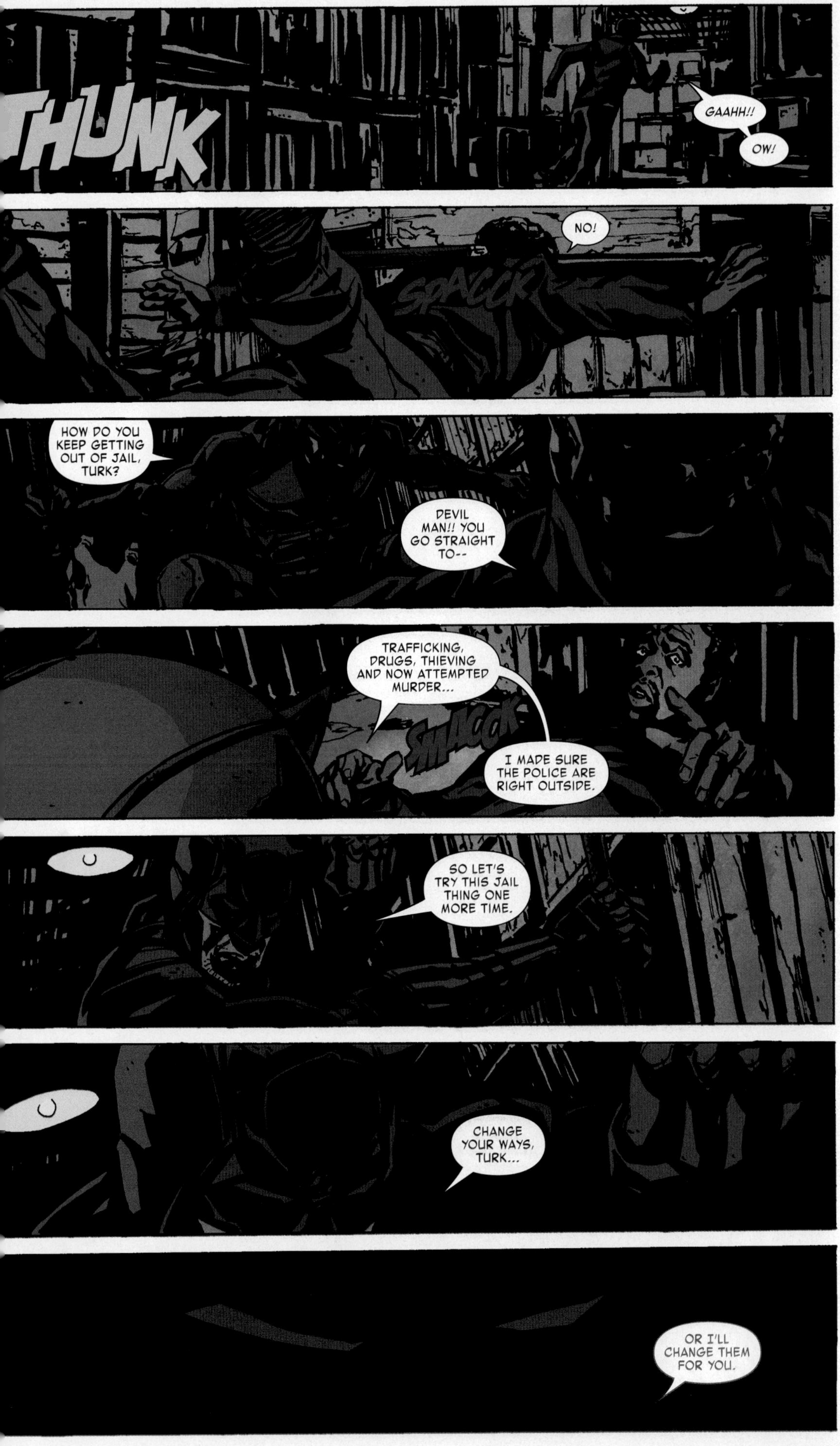
THUNK
GAAHH!!
OW!
NO!
SPACCK
HOW DO YOU KEEP GETTING OUT OF JAIL, TURK?
DEVIL MAN!! YOU GO STRAIGHT TO--
TRAFFICKING, DRUGS, THIEVING AND NOW ATTEMPTED MURDER...
SMACCK
I MADE SURE THE POLICE ARE RIGHT OUTSIDE.
SO LET'S TRY THIS JAIL THING ONE MORE TIME.
CHANGE YOUR WAYS, TURK...
OR I'LL CHANGE THEM FOR YOU.

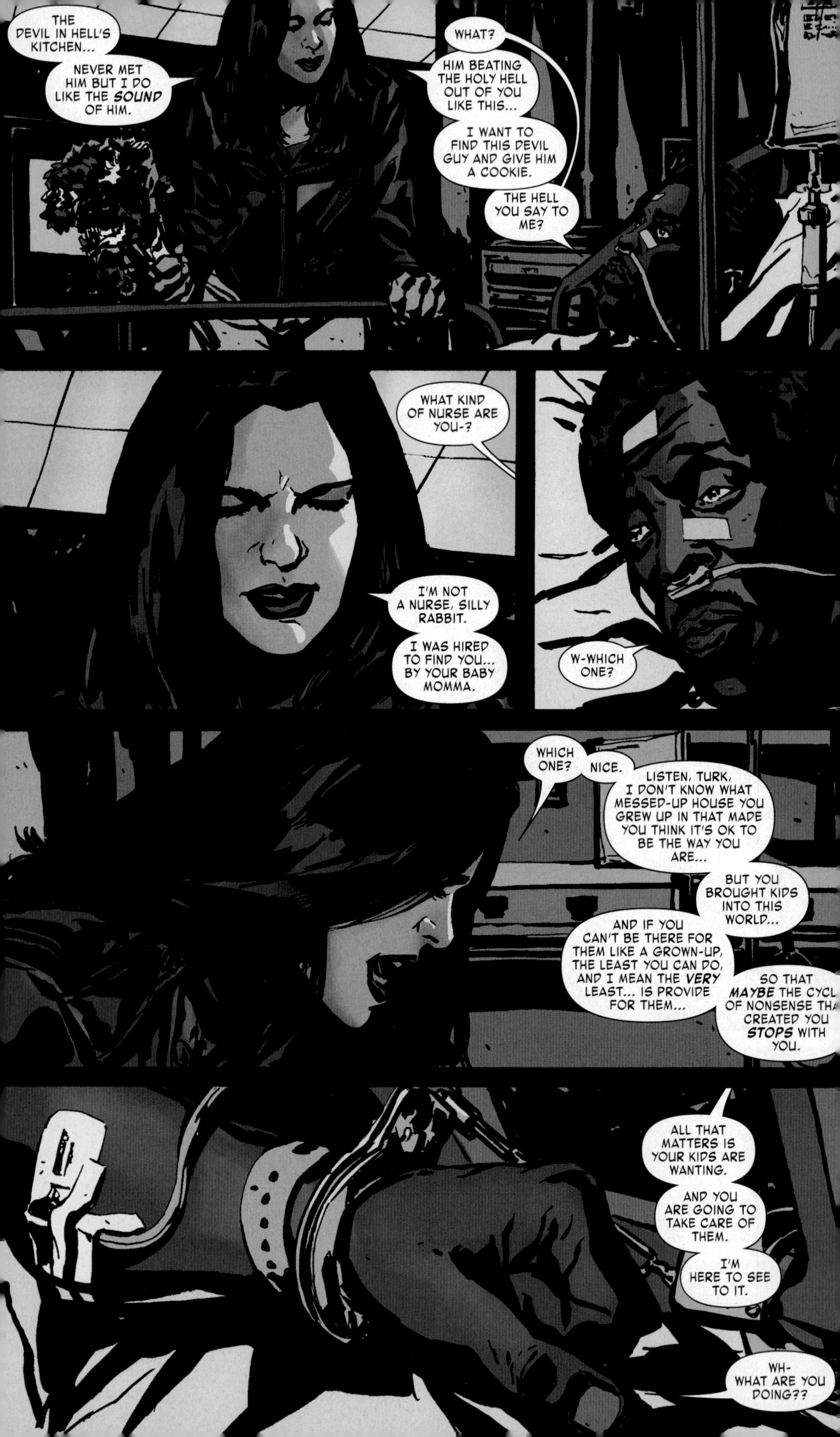
THE DEVIL IN HELL'S KITCHEN...
NEVER MET HIM BUT I DO LIKE THE SOUND OF HIM.
WHAT?
HIM BEATING THE HOLY HELL OUT OF YOU LIKE THIS...
I WANT TO FIND THIS DEVIL GUY AND GIVE HIM A COOKIE.
THE HELL YOU SAY TO ME?
WHAT KIND OF NURSE ARE YOU-?
I'M NOT A NURSE, SILLY RABBIT.
I WAS HIRED TO FIND YOU... BY YOUR BABY MOMMA.
W-WHICH ONE?
WHICH ONE?
NICE.
LISTEN, TURK, I DON'T KNOW WHAT MESSED-UP HOUSE YOU GREW UP IN THAT MADE YOU THINK IT'S OK TO BE THE WAY YOU ARE...
BUT YOU BROUGHT KIDS INTO THIS WORLD...
AND IF YOU CAN'T BE THERE FOR THEM LIKE A GROWN-UP, THE LEAST YOU CAN DO, AND I MEAN THE VERY LEAST... IS PROVIDE FOR THEM...
SO THAT MAYBE THE CYCL OF NONSENSE THA CREATED YOU STOPS WITH YOU.
ALL THAT MATTERS IS YOUR KIDS ARE WANTING.
AND YOU ARE GOING TO TAKE CARE OF THEM.
I'M HERE TO SEE TO IT.
WH- WHAT ARE YOU DOING??

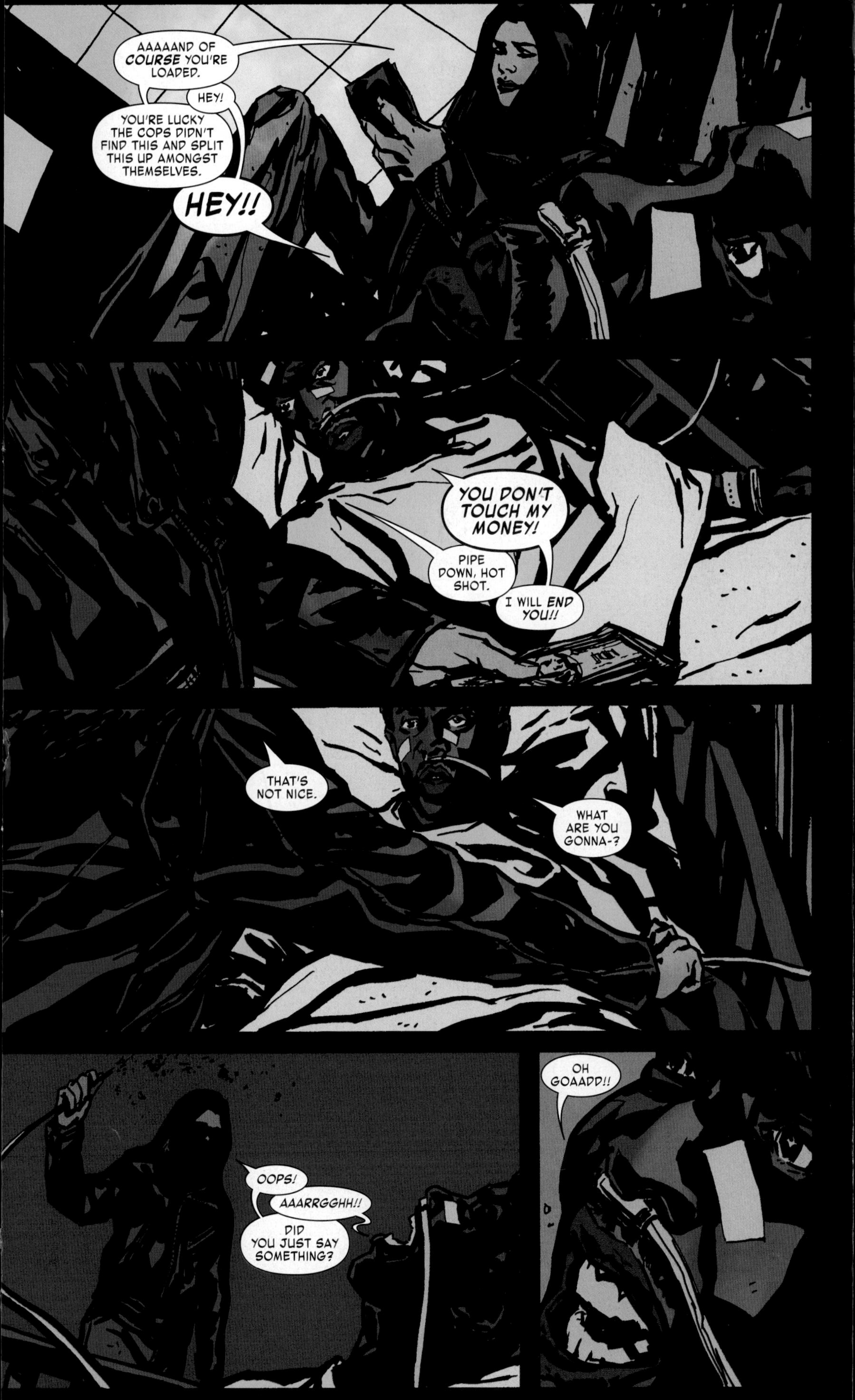
AAAAAND OF COURSE YOU'RE LOADED.
HEY!
YOU'RE LUCKY THE COPS DIDN'T FIND THIS AND SPLIT THIS UP AMONGST THEMSELVES.
HEY!!
YOU DON'T TOUCH MY MONEY!
PIPE DOWN, HOT SHOT.
I WILL END YOU!!
THAT'S NOT NICE.
WHAT ARE YOU GONNA-?
OOPS!
AAARRGGHH!!
DID YOU JUST SAY SOMETHING?
OH GOAADD!!

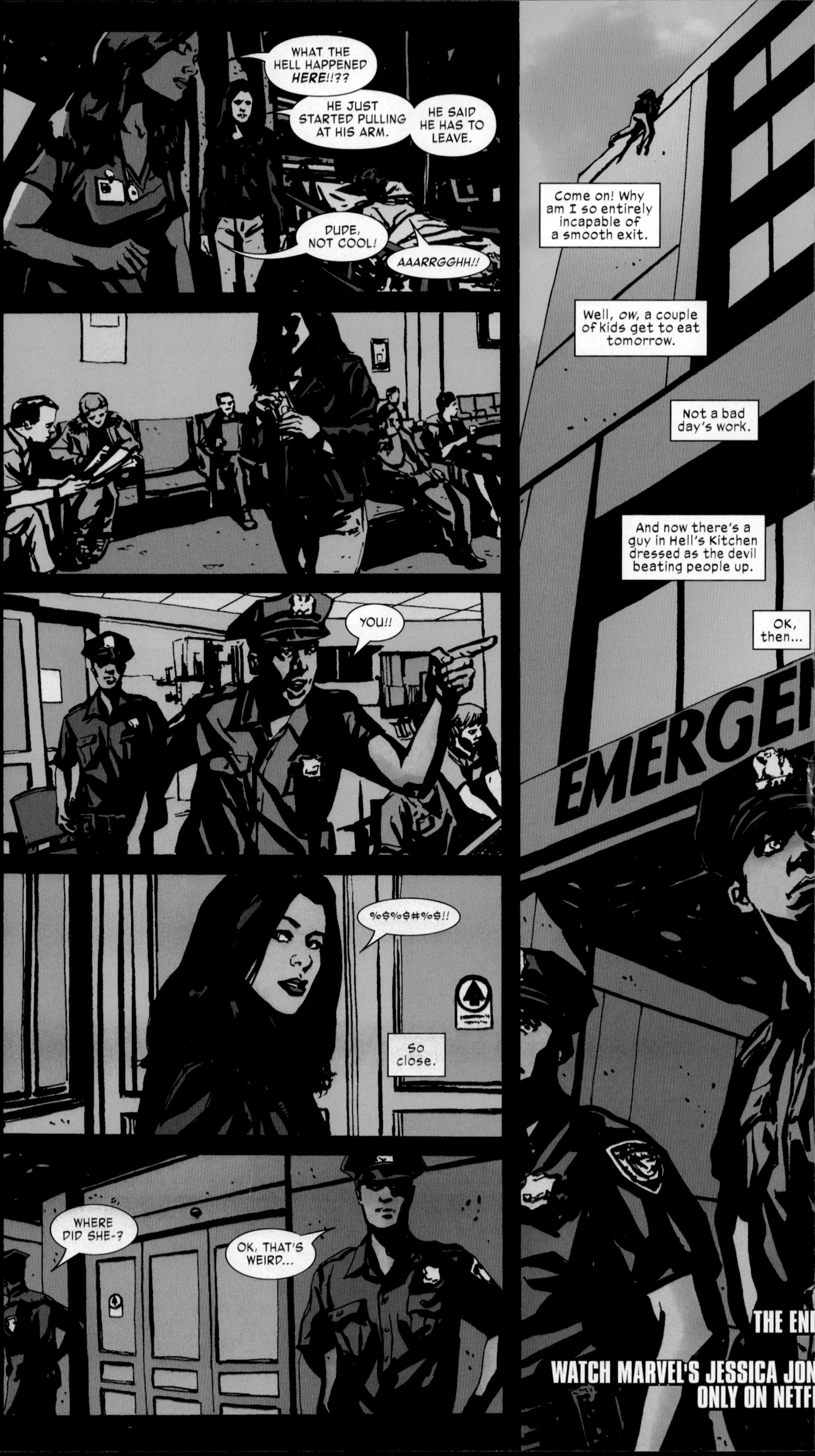
WHAT THE HELL HAPPENED *HERE*!!??
HE JUST STARTED PULLING AT HIS ARM.
HE SAID HE HAS TO LEAVE.
DUDE, NOT COOL!
AAARRGGHH!!
YOU!!
%$%$#%$!!
So close.
WHERE DID SHE-?
OK, THAT'S WEIRD...
Come on! Why am I so entirely incapable of a smooth exit.
Well, *ow*, a couple of kids get to eat tomorrow.
Not a bad day's work.
And now there's a guy in Hell's Kitchen dressed as the devil beating people up.
OK, then...
EMERGE
THE EN
WATCH MARVEL'S JESSICA JON
ONLY ON NETF

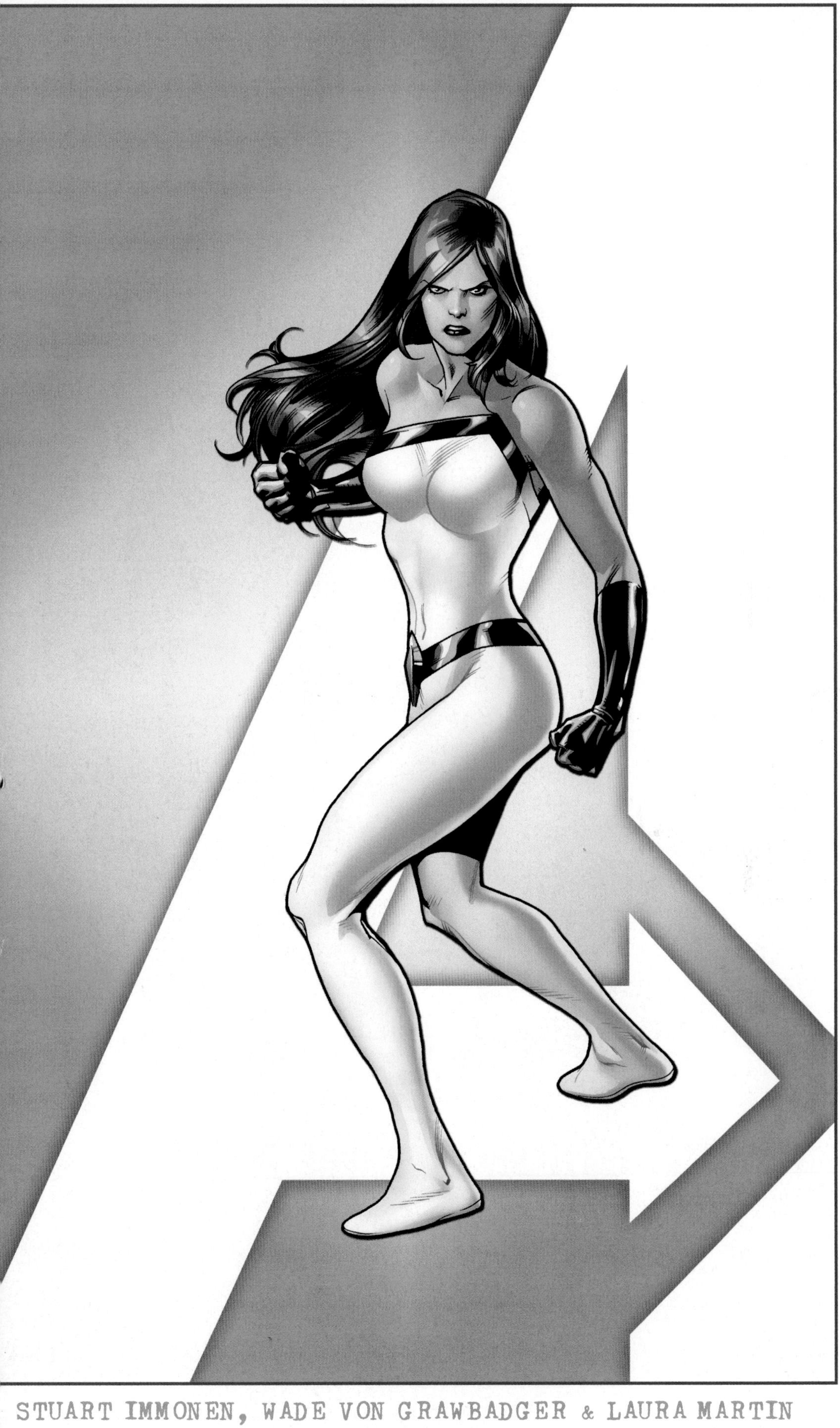

STUART IMMONEN, WADE VON GRAWBADGER & LAURA MARTIN

NEW AVENGERS (2010) #4 VARIANT

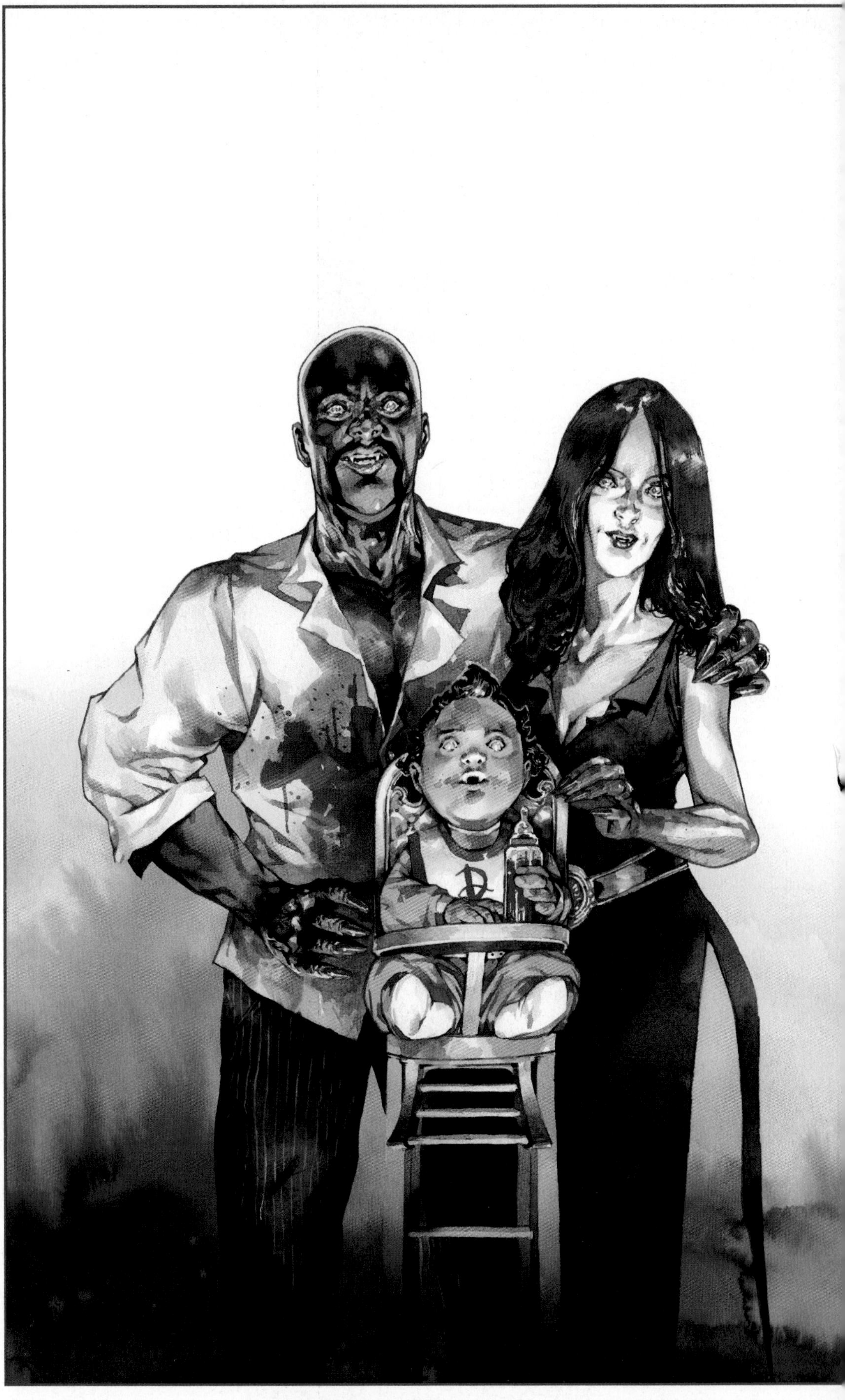

STEPHANIE PERGER

NEW AVENGERS (2010) #7 VAMPIRE VARIANT